A Corporal's Story

A Corporal's Story

Civil War Recollections of the Twelfth Massachusetts

George Kimball

Edited by
Alan D. Gaff and Donald H. Gaff

University of Oklahoma Press : Norman

Library of Congress Cataloging-in-Publication Data

Kimball, George, 1840–1916.
A corporal's story : Civil War recollections of the Twelfth Massachusetts /
George Kimball ; edited by Alan D. Gaff and Donald H. Gaff.
    pages cm
Includes bibliographical references and index.
ISBN 978-0-8061-4480-1 (hardcover : alk. paper)
1. Kimball, George, 1840–1916. 2. United States. Army. Massachusetts
Infantry Regiment, 12th (1861–1864) 3. Massachusetts—History—Civil War,
1861–1865—Personal narratives. 4. United States—History—Civil War,
1861–1865—Personal narratives. 5. Soldiers—Massachusetts—Boston—
Biography. 6. Boston (Mass.)—Biography.
I. Gaff, Alan D. II. Gaff, Donald H., 1970– III. Title. IV. Title: Civil War
recollections of the Twelfth Massachusetts.
E513.512th .K56 2014
973.7'444—dc23
                              2014002871

The manufacturer's authorized representative in the EU for product safety is Mare
Nostrum Group B.V., Mauritskade 21D, 1091 GC Amsterdam, The Netherlands,
email: gpsr@mare-nostrum.co.uk

To Jeff and Elaine

He, though dead, still liveth! Yes, and until that canvas crumbles into dust, until these walls shall decay and perish, the noble form of Webster says to us, "Preserve the Union for which I toiled and wept and prayed! Preserve the Union, and do not, do not disgrace my image, which has proclaimed it forever!"

Nathaniel B. Shurtleff, Jr.
Faneuil Hall, February 1861

Contents

Illustrations

Figures

Maps

Preface

George Kimball was a storyteller. As a veteran of the American Civil War, this was not unusual since former soldiers had been telling and retelling their adventures long before Homer wrote down the exploits of the ancient Greeks during the Trojan War. While George Kimball is certainly not in the category of Homer, he does have an exciting and interesting tale to tell of his military service. Kimball's recollections are a special kind of history. Writing from the perspective of an enlisted man, he relates only the personal and human aspects of his Civil War experience. Avoiding the pitfalls of relating events and conversations that he did not personally witness, the author has left a unique glimpse of soldiers who are today known only as statistics and names on a roster or headstone. Kimball's words breathe life into individuals who have been dead for many generations, but whose cumulative efforts live on in American history.

Born August 8, 1840, in Saco, Maine, George was the son of William and Eliza Kimball.[1] He entered the newspaper trade on the staff of the *Biddeford Journal* at the age of sixteen and four years later moved to Boston, where he worked as a printer for the *Boston Post*. He enlisted on June 25, 1861, in Company A, Twelfth Massachusetts Volunteers, and was mustered into federal service the following day. Kimball served his three-year enlistment, attaining the exalted rank of corporal, and mustered out on July 8, 1864.

---

1. The family of William and Eliza Kimball consisted of Deborah, William, George, Sarah, and Melvin. 1850 Census and 1860 Census, Maine, York County, Town of Saco, RG 29, National Archives (hereafter cited as NA).

After returning to civilian life, George found employment with the *Boston Journal* and stayed continuously with that newspaper as a printer and proofreader for forty-one years. He retired in 1908 after a two-year stint as clerk in the Massachusetts State House. George had married Martha Caroline Stevens in Boston on July 28, 1865, and the couple spent their retirement years in a home at 21 Forest Street in Lexington, Massachusetts. Kimball joined the Grand Army of the Republic in 1869, holding joint membership in John A. Andrew Post 15, of Boston, and George G. Meade Post 119, of Lexington, twice serving on the staff of the national commander-in-chief. An honorary member of the Franklin Typographical Society, he retained membership in the First Parish Church and Seaman's Friends Society, both of Boston. An original member of the Twelfth (Webster) Regiment Association, George Kimball acted as secretary of that group "during practically all of its existence" until his death from heart disease on February 10, 1916. He was survived by his widow and their two daughters, Jessie and Florence; a son, Charles, had died as a child. Kimball is buried in Munroe Cemetery in Lexington.[2]

Lieutenant Colonel Benjamin F. Cook's *History of the Twelfth Massachusetts Volunteers,* ghostwritten by James Beale[3] of Company I and published in 1882, was an uneven and disappointing treatment of one of the Civil War's most famous regiments. The following year, Kimball joined with two other Bay State veterans— George W. Powers,[4] Thirty-eighth Massachusetts, and Edward F.

2. *Boston Journal,* February 11, 1916; *Boston Herald,* February 11, 1916.

3. James Beale enlisted as a private in Co. I, Twelfth Massachusetts, on August 11, 1862. Although a latecomer to the regiment, Beale was wounded at Fredericksburg, Gettysburg, and the Wilderness before being mustered out on July 8, 1862. He wrote copiously about his regiment after the war in articles and pamphlets of limited distribution. Beale died at Berwyn, Pennsylvania, on February 17, 1897. His authorship of the regimental history is noted by celebrated collector John Page Nicholson. *Massachusetts Soldiers,* 2:55; Dornbusch, *Regimental Publications* 1, pt. 3, 56–57; *Boston Journal,* February 18, 1897; *Library of John Page Nicholson,* 163.

4. George W. Powers enlisted as a private in Co. F, Thirty-eighth Massachusetts, on August 12, 1862, and was mustered out on June 30, 1865, as a corporal. A proofreader until his death, Powers died in Dorchester, Massachusetts, on April 1, 1903. *Massachusetts Soldiers,* 4:27; *Boston Herald,* April 4, 1903.

Rollins,[5] Thirteenth Massachusetts—in a publishing venture titled *The Bivouac,* which was advertised as "An Independent Military Monthly." All three editors contributed numerous recollections of their Civil War experiences, and from 1883 through 1885 Kimball wrote both feature articles and anecdotes about his regiment for *The Bivouac.* Simultaneously with his *Bivouac* writing, he contributed a series of articles to the *Boston Journal.* In both publications, readers knew that the appearance of "G. K." was a guarantee of a rousing story.

The Bivouac folded after three years when Kimball, citing "impaired health," announced his departure. George's stories of army life had been far more interesting than those that had appeared in the Cook/Beale book, and his old comrades surely missed his talented pen. One newsman noted Kimball's reputation as "a most entertaining writer on army life" and praised "his graphic pen pictures of the humor and pathos, the calm and storm of the days of '61–'65.'"[6] Despite his declining health, Kimball continued to write stories for the Boston press and various publications. One of his Gettysburg articles appeared in *Century Magazine,*[7] and a letter was printed in the prestigious *Battles and Leaders of the Civil War* series.[8] He wrote an article titled "The Origin of the John Brown Song" for *New England Magazine.*[9] James H. Stine, historian of the First Army Corps, used Kimball's description of the Antietam battle in *History of the Army of the Potomac*[10] to best illustrate the actions of Hartsuff's brigade that day.

George Kimball certainly had an eventful story to tell. He joined the Second Battalion of Infantry, Massachusetts State Militia, in

5. Edward F. Rollins enlisted on June 1, 1861, as a corporal in Co. D, Thirteenth Massachusetts. Promoted to sergeant and first sergeant, he was commissioned second lieutenant on May 29, 1863, and first lieutenant on April 6, 1864. Rollins was mustered out as first lieutenant of Co. C on August 1, 1864. He was proprietor of a hotel when he died in Winthrop, Massachusetts, on February 6, 1898. *Massachusetts Soldiers,* 2:95; *Boston Daily Advertiser,* February 8, 1898; *Boston Journal,* February 10, 1898.

6. *Boston Journal,* November 29, 1892.

7. "Young Hero of Gettysburg," 133–34.

8. *Battles and Leaders,* 2:550–51.

9. "John Brown Song," 371–76.

10. Stine, *Army of the Potomac,* 198–201.

May 1861 and witnessed the birth of "The John Brown Song" at
Fort Warren in Boston Harbor. When that unit was not accepted
into service, he promptly enlisted in Company A, Twelfth Massachusetts Volunteers, commanded by Colonel Fletcher Webster,
son of the famous American statesman Daniel Webster. Kimball
served three years in the ranks, fighting in the battles of Cedar
Mountain, Second Bull Run, South Mountain, Antietam, Fredericksburg, Gettysburg, Wilderness, Spotsylvania, and Petersburg.
Of course, he did not emerge unscathed from such hard service.
At Fredericksburg, a rebel ball struck his leg below the knee, and
at Gettysburg another missile tore through his left groin and hip,
inflicting what was thought to be a mortal wound. But Kimball
recovered and returned to the ranks in time for General Grant's
1864 campaign, being just one of three soldiers from Company
A who left the Petersburg trenches to return home after the regiment's term of service had expired. He claimed never to have
straggled or reported for sick call during his entire enlistment,
attributing "his good health to the fact that he abstained from
the use of liquors and took care of himself." Kimball would later
receive a pension from the federal government for ten dollars per
month, effective April 20, 1874, for disabilities caused by gunshot
wounds to the right hip and leg.

George wrote his recollections for two audiences. On the one
hand, he hoped to instill a feeling of patriotism among young
readers, just as those feelings had been instilled in him by reading
of the deeds of early intrepid Americans. He relates the story of a
common soldier. There is no attempt to confuse young people by
describing the movements of divisions, corps, and armies in detail, as if the battlefield were a chessboard on which various units
moved from place to place. Beyond the regimental level, officers
are mentioned only when necessary to explain the narrative or
to recount incidents in Kimball's own experience. This is not an
officer's history, but the recollections of a humble enlisted man
who uses humor to temper the horror of Civil War combat for his
civilian readers.

On the other hand, Kimball wrote his stories for comrades in
the Grand Army of the Republic. The G.A.R. was established as
a fraternal organization in 1866, membership being limited to

George Kimball, while serving with the Twelfth Massachusetts. After original in *Boston Journal,* May 6, 1893, p. 5.

George Kimball, at the time of writing his recollections. After original in *Boston Journal,* May 6, 1893, p. 5.

Civil War veterans of the army, navy, marines, and revenue service. Over time the national organization grew to about 500,000 members, generally supported Republican politicians, and strenuously lobbied for pensions for disabled veterans. Perhaps the G.A.R.'s greatest contribution was to provide a systematic way for veterans to stay in touch with one another. Members joined local posts, generally named after prominent leaders, local heroes, or famous battles, which sent delegates to state departments, which in turn sent delegates to a national encampment.

The most popular feature of a local post's meeting was the campfire, an informal portion of the program devoted to singing wartime songs and swapping stories with friends. George Kimball's mention of campfires in his narrative refers to this exchange of wartime yarns, tall tales, and the occasional outright lie. One interesting feature of these meetings was that, over time, the repeated telling of stories began to homogenize history, wherein one veteran would listen to other accounts so often that he began to believe those stories were actually his own. Therein lies the problem of recollections—the further they are removed from events, the more unreliable they become. But this is not true of George Kimball's story. Before composing his stories, Kimball opened the packet of letters that he had written to relatives and used them as a framework, as well as to refresh his memory. Going yet one step further, George also consulted and quoted from letters written by comrades to fill in gaps and amplify his narrative. He also depended on the *Battles and Leaders of the Civil War* series, as well as the one-volume abridgment titled *Century War Book*.[11] It should be noted that with the limited perspective of a corporal, Kimball had to rely on sources such as these for army strengths and casualty figures, statistics that are now acknowledged as inaccurate by modern scholars.

Recollections and memoirs have recently fallen out of favor with Civil War historians, who now prefer to publish contemporary letters and diaries. Of course, it is always better to use sources

---

11. *Century War Book, People's Pictorial Edition* (New York, 1894), was a one-volume abridgement of the four-volume *Battles and Leaders of the Civil War* (New York, 1884).

composed as close to an event as possible while *writing* history, but the *reading* of an entire volume of personal letters or diary entries is never riveting and is generally downright boring to the general reader. This is due to the army lifestyle more than any other factor, Civil War soldiers generally having had to endure long periods of monotonous camp life between active campaigns. Recollections are more entertaining than diaries and letters because they allow the writer to go beyond mere facts and connect with the reader; they are essentially a written version of oral history.

While George Kimball gives us personal recollections of his Civil War service, that story has much in common with other soldiers from the war. Many veterans were not comfortable in relating their experiences until several decades or more had passed, so some of the best Civil War accounts are those written years after the fighting ended. Reminiscences were usually front-loaded, with more space devoted to the early months of service than to the more painful last days of military life. Over time, veterans generally became more tolerant of their former enemies as they recognized a shared experience and acknowledged that courage, fortitude, and virtue were to be found on both sides. Wartime animosity diminished with the passing of the years, perhaps best illustrated by Myrta L. Avary's use of the phrase "our friends, the enemy" to describe affairs in the aftermath of the fall of Richmond.[12]

In addition to these points, Kimball's narrative emphasizes the three stages of a Civil War volunteer's time in the service. First of all is the adventure of leaving home as a young, strong and naive soldier—"ready to do or die," in Kimball's own words. The volunteer meets new people, makes new friends, and travels to places he never imagined he would see. This stage is followed by a realization that the soldier has exchanged his old family for a new one that becomes more important to him than his blood relatives. Then members of this new family begin to die or become disabled in ever-increasing numbers, often in combat but usually as a result of camp diseases. The adventure is gone and grim reality sets in. Finally the volunteer observes that death, crippling wounds, and debilitating sickness strike seemingly at random, and he realizes

12. Avary, *Dixie after the War*, 107.

that his turn may come next. He spends his last days simply trying to stay alive long enough to go home.

While sharing many experiences with other enlisted men, George Kimball was in a distinct minority as an abolitionist in the Union army. He supported freedom for the slaves throughout his entire adult life, but Kimball was trapped in the sensibilities of the nineteenth century. Even while extolling the saintliness of John Brown in his quest to erase the stain of American slavery, Kimball could simultaneously refer to individuals by the pejorative terms of darkies, uncle, auntie, and pickaninny. In the late nineteenth century such terms were perfectly acceptable in the Boston press, even though Massachusetts had been a leader in the recruitment of black soldiers during the Civil War. Freedom for the slaves and equality for black citizens were obviously two separate issues.

We have collected George Kimball's various writings into one continuous narrative and, to enhance the story, have included two new appendixes—a Roll of Honor for the Twelfth Massachusetts and a compilation of accounts pertaining to events immediately prior to and subsequent to Colonel Fletcher Webster's death. We have standardized spelling, capitalization, verb tense—all of which varied depending on the publications where the accounts originally appeared—and corrected a few minor errors of fact. For clarity, first names of individuals are supplied. On rare occasions a few words of transition have been added, but the narrative remains Kimball's account in his own words.

We cannot overlook the significant contribution of Maureen, wife and mother, whose incomparable research skills have greatly added to the usefulness of the notes. Her mastery of obscure historical sources is amazing and has allowed us to give context to many of the individuals mentioned by the author.

Among those other individuals who have aided this project, most deserving recognition and our gratitude is Charles Rankin, associate director and editor-in-chief at the University of Oklahoma Press. We have enjoyed collaborating with Chuck, and readers should know that his enthusiasm for this book equaled our own and was essential to bringing you George Kimball's story.

George Kimball was a keen observer of human nature and this, combined with an entertaining writing style, allows us to share every aspect of his military life. He was an interesting fellow, thrust into remarkable situations, and his recollections offer a compelling glimpse of Civil War life. Solid and dependable, yet capable of great mirth, George Kimball was the kind of man you would want beside you when the bullets began to fly.

Alan D. Gaff and Donald H. Gaff

A Corporal's Story

Introduction

Boys, we are growing old. We have begun to look old—that is, the great majority of us. The bent form, the unsteady step and the silver threads of old age are fast coming. The "boys" of '61 are surely moving toward the setting sun. We have only to look about us to see indications of this. Stand at the roadside on Memorial Day, as a Grand Army of the Republic Post files past on its way to the silent resting place of the dead, and scan the faces of the men—do you not see abundant evidence of this sad fact? Yes, there is no need of argument to prove it. We are being pushed aside.

A new generation has come upon the stage of action and we are nearing the end of our long march. Take, for instance, a large assemblage of people. Do we not know that a great proportion of them were either unborn or were children when the great conflict began? But, after all, there is nothing strange in all this. It only *seems* strange. Generation has been succeeding generation ever since time began. Mankind is like an endless procession, surging on and on forever. The great workshop of Nature is continually producing new peoples. Nations rise and fall and the great drama of human history is being repeated over and over again.

I often wonder, as I look upon the young men of today, how we appear to them. Do they ever reflect concerning us? Do they sometimes place us back, in imagination, and see us as we once were? Do they ever picture to their minds the long processions of men in blue, as they marched away with steady tread, ready to do or die, at the call of our country? And if they do, do they see that we were then as young as they? And we sometimes ask whether, if placed in the same circumstances and the same exigency should arise, they would as willingly defend the flag as we did? I think they would, for if our country was worth fighting for in 1861, with all its imperfections, it certainly is now. For now are we not a free people? Do we not number fifty millions instead of forty as then and are not all the forces of civilization and enlightenment at work as they never were before, in every section over which our flag flies? How many years will it be before these glorious forces will transform every state of the Union into communities as cultured and prosperous as any of which the most pronounced optimist ever dreamed?

Many who have given thought and study to the personnel of the Union armies have expressed astonishment at finding that so large a number were mere youths. One would naturally suppose that such gigantic battles, such long and weary marches, such heroic endurance as was continually displayed by the armies of the Rebellion period, would necessarily be undertaken by men of mature age, or supposedly strong physical nature and development, and when we look into the matter and find that thousands of the best and bravest were mere striplings, we stand aghast. Do you not remember the "ponies" on the left of the company line? "Knapsack, where are you going with that man?" "We'll show you by-and-by!" came the proud retort.

In the regiment in which I had the honor to serve, there were 369 soldiers under twenty-one years of age and probably every regiment in the army could show as large or a larger proportion of young men.

But we are young no longer. Many of us, it is true, are yet seemingly strong and full of manly vigor, but the hardships of the great campaigns through which we passed in those eventful years have surely left their withering mark upon the hidden fountains of life within us and, in a few years at most, the tottering steps of old age will come. But though the body may grow old, the heart and spirit will be ever young and at many hearthstones, in years to come, the scene described by Oliver Goldsmith in "The Deserted Village" will be repeated, where

> The broken soldier, kindly bade to stay,
> Sate by his fire, and talked the night away;

Wept o'er his wounds, or tales of sorrow done,
Shouldered his crutch and shewed how fields were won.[1]

Yes, boys, we are growing old; but as years creep on apace, let us draw taut the cord of fraternity that binds us together; and, as in battle days, when a comrade falls out, stricken down by disease and death, let us close up on the colors and present an unbroken front till every comrade of the Grand Army grasps the hands extended to him from the "other shore."

1. Goldsmith, *Deserted Village*, 9.

CHAPTER 1

War

It is popularly supposed that our great Civil War was occasioned by the triumph, in the autumn of 1860, of the principles represented by Abraham Lincoln, but there are authorities who think it was inevitable from the moment that government by the common people was established in Massachusetts in virtual opposition to the plutocracy of Virginia. Others think that it had its origin in the landing of the first cargo of African slaves upon our shores; in the early and continued agitation of the slavery question and particularly in those heated discussions which preceded the adoption of the Missouri Compromise in 1820; in South Carolina's attempted nullification during Jackson's administration; in the subsequent encroachments of the slave power; in the passage of the Rendition Bill at the behest of the Southern oligarchy; in the emphatic assertion of the Northern sentiment in the great campaign of 1856; in the troubles in Kansas and Nebraska; in the John Brown raid at Harpers Ferry. But with me, individually, it certainly did begin in the fall of 1860 and the place where it began was Bowdoin Square, Boston. It was precipitated by a brick thrown by a ruffian while I was trying to listen to a speech by Anson Burlingame[1] in the open air.

I was not only enough by a twelve-month to vote, but being nearly six feet tall, and fairly well proportioned, I was desirable

---

1. A native of New York, Anson Burlingame graduated from Harvard in 1846 and commenced a law practice in Boston. A noted orator, he served in Congress from 1855 to 1861, but was defeated in the election of 1860 and appointed minister to China in 1861. Burlingame died on February 23, 1870. *Dictionary of American Biography*, 3:289–90.

timber for a Wide Awake.[2] So I joined. The first parade of the company to which I became attached was to the locality named. Burlingame was particularly aggressive that night and was hissed and jeered by a crowd of roughs in Chardon Street. My company happened to be opposite the head of that thoroughfare and consequently we had to bear the brunt of the battle. As an offset, we inaugurated a counter demonstration, more friendly to the Republican cause. This so riled the disturbers that they finally threw missiles as well as epithets and one of the former, as well as many of the latter, landed on my ear. After breaking the pole that supported my torch upon the head of one of the nearest and noisiest of the blackguards, I started for home with blood actually in my eye.

I was ready to have war declared at once. That brick was to me as much a *casus belli* as was the firing upon Fort Sumter and from that moment I was ready to identify myself with any organization which should have for its object the emphatic assertion of Northern sentiment.

All that winter the political caldron boiled as it never boiled before. My associates among the Wide Awakes were ready to a man to enlist the moment they should be called upon. In fact, it is safe to say that ninety-nine per cent of the men who aided as torch bearers in the election of Lincoln in the fall of 1860 were ready in the spring of 1861 to march forth as soldiers to uphold him in his efforts to sustain the Union. Many companies even maintained their organizations until the crisis came.

The grand uprising of the North, in the winter and spring of 1861, excited the wonder of the civilized world. A degree of enthusiasm prevailed throughout the Loyal States that was truly phenomenal. It surprised even the philosophers themselves. No one had ever before dreamed that the proverbially cold-blooded Northerner could be stirred to such depths. Prayer meetings were turned into war meetings; stores were changed into recruiting stations; workshops became rallying places for men who had no

2. Young supporters of Abraham Lincoln in the 1860 presidential election formed political groups known as Wide Awakes. These local organizations were characterized by torch-lit nighttime marches and enthusiastic support throughout the northern states. Grinspan, "Young Men for War," 357.

heart for anything except solicitude for the safety of the Government and for free institutions; while at every tea table and around every fireside naught was discussed in the closing days of President James Buchanan's administration save the question that was uppermost in every mind: What will the new president do?

The 4th of March came and the inauguration of President Lincoln was peacefully accomplished. A feeling of partial relief now set in, but the enthusiasm increased and men everywhere became more and more determined to resist the conspirators should they indulge in an open revolt. The inaugural address of the incoming chief announced a policy and that announcement gave no uncertain sound. Its tones rang out clear and loud in every town and village in the land, for men everywhere were ready and waiting for the word. The president would stand by the Union and the Constitution.

While the people of the North waited for the word to spring to arms, the Southern plot went on. The secessionists of the South accepted the inaugural as a virtual declaration of war. Soon after its delivery, the Congress of the Confederate States passed their Army Bill and began to organize for resistance to constituted authority. On the 12th of March the Confederate Commissioners addressed a note to Secretary of State William Seward[3] containing the impudent proposition that the disaffected states be allowed to peacefully secede. On the 18th, by a general order, the supply of fuel, water and provisions was cut off from the armed vessels in Pensacola harbor.

At Savannah, Georgia, on the 21st, Alexander H. Stephens[4] announced the principles upon which the Confederacy was founded.

3. A graduate of Union College in 1820, Seward pursued a law career until he was elected governor of New York. Elected to the United States Senate in 1848, he became the embodiment of the antislavery movement and coined the phrase "an irrepressible conflict." Outmaneuvered by Lincoln in the Republican convention, Seward served as secretary of state during the war and in 1867 would negotiate the purchase of Alaska from Russia. He died in Auburn, New York, on October 10, 1872. *Dictionary of American Biography*, 16:615–20.

4. A graduate of the University of Georgia, Stephens was a lawyer and state politician prior to his election to Congress in 1843. While representing his state, Stephens argued that the Southern economic system was the best available for "the Negro race." He retired from Congress and resumed his law practice until elected vice president of the Confederacy on February 9, 1861. An outspoken

He said: "Its foundations are laid, its corner stone rests, upon the great truth that the negro is not equal to the white man; that slavery, subordination to the superior race, is his natural and normal condition. This, our new government, is the first in the history of the world based upon this great physical, philosophical and moral truth." This announcement stirred still deeper the moral sensibilities of the people of the free states of the North. Men began to think that the days of Nero and Caligula had come again.

Then came the acts that brought the agitations of the hour to an actual issue—the firing upon the *Star of the West* and the attack upon Fort Sumter. The world knows the rest of the story by heart; how the outraged sentiment of the loyal masses could brook no further parleying and delay; how that never did British blood nor Celtic ire leap quicker to resent an outrage than did the farmers and mechanics of the North to defend the flag. On the 15th of April, the day after the surrender of Major Robert Anderson,[5] came the proclamation of President Lincoln calling for 75,000 militia to execute the laws.

The die having thus been cast and the gauntlet thrown down, nothing now remained but an appeal to the sword and we all know how the young men of the Loyal States rushed *en masse* to the recruiting stations. No sooner had the organized militia regiments left for the protection of the capital than new regiments of untried but determined soldiers were forming everywhere. It would have been as easy to have raised an army of a million men as to have filled the small requisitions that followed.

Having outlined the great uprising and hinted at some of the causes that brought it about, let us consider briefly the motive that actuated the young volunteers of 1861. We shall find, at the same

---

proponent of the South following the war, Stephens eventually served again in Congress, was elected governor of Georgia, and died in Atlanta on March 4, 1883. *Dictionary of American Biography*, 17:569–75.

5. A graduate of West Point in 1825, Anderson served in the Blackhawk War, against the Seminoles in Florida, and in Mexico, where he won two brevets. Promoted to major of the First United States Artillery on October 5, 1857, he commanded the garrison at Fort Sumter at Charleston, South Carolina. Rewarded with a promotion to brigadier general on May 15, 1861, his ill health led to desk duties and his retirement on October 27, 1863. General Anderson died in Nice, France, on October 26, 1871. Warner, *Generals in Blue*, 7–8; Heitman, *Historical Register*, 2:164.

time, that the same influences controlled the thousands who, later in the war, stung by reverses to our arms, rallied to the defense of the Union. There has been much discussion since the close of the great conflict as to the actual cause which impelled the young volunteer to leave his home and enter upon the hard and hazardous life of the soldier. Various reasons have been assigned by the veterans themselves; they who should know most about it. It is a common thing to hear men say "Oh, I suppose it was excitement as much as anything that took me into it." Is this true? I say no.

Every young man considered well the step he was taking when he signed his name to the roll of volunteers. Excitement might draw him to war meetings; it might influence him to join the crowds in the streets; it might attract him to the flag-raising in the public square; but it would hardly cause him to offer his life in the defense of his country. Men stop to consider such a grave step as that. Excitement gives place then to a deeper feeling. Excitement at best is but the effervescence of human feeling, only the froth that bubbles up from the surface.

Even if we were to admit that excitement did have some influence in thickly-settled communities, how about the farmer's boy, away from all these great popular demonstrations, alone with his cattle and his plow? Did excitement cause him to drop the goad and the hoe and hasten to where men were forming for the march? And despite the father's plea and the mother's tears? How many thousands of noble young fellows there were who went simply because they could not help it, even though she who was dearer than everybody and everything else, except duty and country, pleaded and begged and turned broken-hearted as they disappeared one after another down the lane! To these no great tumult appealed, no strains of martial music spoke. Nothing moved them but the deep, strong prompting of conscience, the conviction that it was their duty to go.

Was it love of adventure that drew the volunteer into the conflict? Was his mind fired by the romance and fascination of military life? Was he dazzled by anything he had read of the wild charge and the gorgeous pageant of moving battalions? I think not to any great extent. The American people are not a military people. We had had no war within the recollection of the young men of 1861, of any consequence, except the Mexican War, and of that we then knew but little, for that was a war of conquest and there was little in it to excite or move us.

For my own part, I confess that what I had read of the struggles of the early settlers of New England, the sacrifices of the Fathers in the Revolution, the bravery displayed in the War of 1812, had some influence in helping me to come to a decision as to what was my own duty. But this was not the grand moving force itself; it was only the lever that helped to raise me to the higher plane. The motive was deeper and stronger than desire for adventure and was inspired by something grander than the glamour of romance.

Was it a desire to travel over hitherto unknown parts of our country that influenced us to enlist? That may have had weight with some, but if so it was only a secondary consideration and bore but little relation to the real underlying motive itself. If the volunteer entered the service with the expectation of getting much enjoyment out of the privilege, he soon discovered his mistake and the "opportunity for travel" thereafter became a byword and a joke.

Was it the hope of winning personal renown or the expectation of promotion to high command, with its consequent advantages in after life, that drew the volunteer from his home to the tented field? To those belonging to wealthy and influential families this undoubtedly had more weight than any other consideration I have named, except what has been discovered between the lines; but to the great mass of men, to the average volunteer, to the son of the poor man—he who won his bread by the sweat of his brow—it was a contingency scarcely thought of. What chance was there for a farmer's boy or a plain mechanic, no matter how much genius or heroism there might be lying dormant and unseen in his nature, to obtain high places, when applicants were numbered by thousands with plenty of wealth and home influence to back them? The great masses of the army, and the bravest and best, too, were those who had hitherto led uneventful lives and were among the world's poor—the toiling millions of our farms and workshops.

Though we have no half-fed peasantry in this country, like those of Europe, we have nevertheless a grand constituency of noble men, the very bone and sinew of our land, on whom the safety of our institutions depends, and to them be the chief honor, rather than to any *coterie* of dainty children of idleness and ease, for the great results of our Civil War, a contest grander in itself and its outcome than any war of modern times. While there were many from the ranks of the wealthy and cultured who won laurels and did great deeds, the masses who formed that solid front before the foes of the Union were made up almost wholly of the plain men of the time.

Now what was the motive that moved them to leave their workshops and their farms, even though those dear to them saw no way of living without their aid? It can all be summed up in one word: *patriotism*. They loved their country because it was worthy of their love. They had read and studied its history. They had been impressed with the sacrifices made by the Fathers of the Republic for the common weal. They had read of the heroes of Lexington and Bunker Hill. They felt it their duty to take up arms in defense of the Union. They enlisted naturally and because they could not help it.

Red, white and blue were everywhere in the North the favorite colors and, upon all the fashionable promenades, elegantly dressed ladies and gentlemen illustrated their loyalty by appearing with knots of tri-colored ribbon and rosettes of varied hues *in lieu* of the customary boutonnieres. Indeed, one not so adorned was often looked upon with something like suspicion. Badges of various shapes, designs and sizes were also freely worn, all being emblematic either of sympathy with the Lincoln Administration or of devotion to the cause of the Union.

But to me the most curious expressions of loyal feeling were seen in the almost universal adornment of stationery, the market at times becoming almost flooded with the truck. Amateur poets appeared to vie with each other in their efforts to give voice to their patriotic feeling in their own and often unique way and the corners of envelopes and writing paper bore ample evidence of the loyalty of the Muses. Portraits of gallant soldiers and distinguished statesmen adorned many of these, but the scenes and portraits displayed were often more suggestive of hatred of treason than of regard for artistic merit. Many of these pictures were ludicrous in the extreme, some quite pathetic.

The favorite personage for caricature, of course, was Jefferson Davis[6] and the "arch conspirator" was depicted in every phase of his supposed career, now thrusting his guilty hands into the archives or arsenals of the nation, then chasing after runaway contrabands and finally dangling at full length from the gallows.

Before me lies a package of nearly one hundred of these famous relics of the war. The collection forms an interesting study of one of the prominent features of the great contest and speaks loudly of the loyalty of the masses. It may also be said with some truth, as a friend at my elbow suggests, that they also illustrate the ingenuity of the Yankee and show his propensity to take advantage of every favorable opportunity to turn an honest dollar. Be that as it may, every dealer had the goods for sale and nearly everybody bought them.

On the evening of the 19th of April, 1861, being intensely excited by the news of the cowardly attack upon the Sixth Massachusetts Regiment in the streets of Baltimore, I went to the armory of what was then called the Second Battalion of Infantry ("Tigers") at Boylston Hall in Boston. There I joined Company B.[7] The battalion, whose motto was "Death or an Honorable Life," comprised three companies, commanded by Major Ralph Newton.[8] Night and day was heard the tramp of feet and the clatter of arms as

6. A student at Transylvania University when he received a nomination to West Point, Davis graduated from the military academy in 1824. He resigned as a first lieutenant in the First Dragoons on June 30, 1845. He became a planter in Mississippi until he served as colonel of the First Mississippi Rifles during the Mexican-American War. Appointed to the United States Senate in 1847, he served four years as secretary of war and reentered the Senate. Elected president of the Confederacy in 1861, Davis was jailed for two years after the war, and his broken health led to his death in New Orleans on December 6, 1889. *Dictionary of American Biography*, 5:123–30.

7. Company B of the Second Battalion of Militia was organized at Boylston Hall on March 28, 1861, and Charles O. Rogers was elected captain. *Boston Herald*, March 29, 1861.

8. Ralph W. Newton was a wealthy Boston commission merchant who had been active in the city militia as captain of Co. A, Second Battalion, until his elevation to command of the battalion as major on April 17, 1861. On February 22, 1860, his friends had presented him a gold medal, valued at $125. This medal, in the shape of a Maltese cross, bore the image of a tiger holding in its jaws a scroll that bore the company motto. Major Newton held no active field command during the war and later moved to New York City, where he died on May 26, 1869.

the embryo soldiers learned their lessons. My captain was the late proprietor and publisher of the *Boston Journal,* Charles O. Rogers,[9] and a more generous, patriotic man it was never my good fortune to meet. He was a superb soldier, too, and had he found it possible to forsake the engrossing cares of his great newspaper for the tented field, he would doubtless have won a place among the foremost heroes of the age.

One day, soon after joining the "Tigers," I met my brother, then employed as a compositor in the office of the *Boston Post.*[10] He was three years older than I and took a manlier view of life and its affairs than I did, for I was boyish in many ways. We walked to the Common. I noticed that he was more serious than usual that day and, as we seated ourselves beneath one of the spreading elms of that historic inclosure, he said:

"George, do you know what all this excitement means? It means that we are going to have a great war. It will be no child's play. It will be the duty of every man who loves his country to go. I have carefully considered the question, have concluded that it is my duty to enlist and, as you are the youngest and as father and mother cannot spare us both, I want you to remain at home and look after them. I have already enlisted. I joined a company this morning and we are going to be attached to Fletcher Webster's regiment."

It was a long time before I could summon the courage to tell him what I had done and what were my intentions, but when I did he seized my hand and, with tears streaming from his eyes, cried: "We'll do our duty together. God's hand is in this affair. If we love

Boston Daily Advertiser, February 24, 1860; *Boston Traveler,* April 18, 1861; *New York Herald,* May 27, 1869.

9. A native of Worcester, Charles O. Rogers entered the newspaper trade with his father and brother, becoming sole proprietor of the *Boston Journal* in 1855 following their deaths. He was a delegate to the Chicago Convention that nominated Abraham Lincoln in 1860. Long a member of various militia units, Rogers was universally called "Major," although asthma kept him from wartime service in the field. He had amassed a fortune estimated at $1.5 million at the time of his death in Boston on April 15, 1869. *Boston Journal,* April 17, 1869; April 15, 1893.

10. William L. Kimball enlisted as a private in Co. A, Twelfth Massachusetts, on April 20, 1861. Appointed corporal after Second Bull Run, he was wounded at Antietam and Gettysburg. Appointed sergeant on March 1, 1864, Kimball was mustered out July 8, 1864, and died in Milwaukee, Wisconsin, on September 19, 1868. *Massachusetts Soldiers,* 2:8; *Boston Herald,* September 30, 1868.

our home it is our duty to defend it. If we do our duty, God will in some way provide for those we leave behind." I mention this incident not because it was exceptional. It was having its counterpart all over our broad land. Yes, in the South, too, for the brave boys down there were striving to do their duty as they understood it. It is all history now.

Many strange scenes were witnessed in churches. The Mariners' Church (Congregational), at the foot of Summer Street, which I attended, was patriotic to the core. Reverend Elijah Kellogg,[11] who since the war has won fame as a writer of boys' stories, was the pastor. He was very popular with young men and an eloquent speaker. His Sunday evening prayer meetings were largely attended. Hundreds of young people came from other churches, particularly from Park Street. He was so prophetic, outlining so accurately what afterward proved to be the extent and course of the Secession movement, that many of us have since thought him to have been inspired. One Sunday evening, soon after I became a "Tiger," he spoke feelingly of the impending crisis. The place was crowded. On this particular evening, the prayers, the songs of praise and the exhortations were especially earnest and seemed to be pervaded by the thought that God would hold not only individuals but communities together by His all-pervading love. Indeed, love was the theme of all the speakers and the belief was frequently expressed that the Prince of Peace would yet rule the hearts of men North and South.

The meeting closed in the usual form and then one of the strangest anomalies I ever witnessed took place. When he had finished, he asked Charles F. Browne,[12] who had joined Company F

11. Elijah Kellogg was a graduate of Bowdoin College and Andover Seminary. He was a minister at Harpswell, Maine, from 1844 to 1855, when he became chaplain of the Boston Seaman's Friends Society. Following the war, Kellogg began to write fiction stories for young boys and eventually authored more than two dozen titles. He returned to his ministry at Harpswell, where he died on March 17, 1901. *Boston Journal*, March 18, 1901.

12. Browne enlisted on May 24, 1861, as a corporal in Co. F, First Massachusetts, and was wounded at Fredericksburg, Chancellorsville, and Gettysburg. He was discharged on October 19, 1863, to accept an appointment as captain in the Thirty-seventh United States Colored Troops, where he served until August 31, 1867. Browne died on October 5, 1868, at Fort Macon, North Carolina. *Massachusetts Soldiers*, 1:35; 7:292; *Boston Post*, October 12, 1868.

of Colonel Robert Cowdin's[13] Regiment (the First), a young man named Mitchell,[14] whose first name and whose regiment I have forgotten, and me, to step to the desk. Then, amid a scene such as is rarely witnessed in a sacred edifice, he talked to us personally, while the great audience showed its sympathy by applause and tears. Addressing us and the audience by turns, he denounced in emphatic terms the insurrection of the South and made as good a war speech as I ever heard. He then announced that the young men standing before them had enlisted to fight this cursed Rebellion and presented each of us with a Colt revolver and a package of cartridges. We responded in turn and all joined with spirit in singing "My country 'tis of thee." It seemed strange to lay so much stress upon love and peace and then not only advocate war, but present weapons with which to take human life—and in a prayer meeting too! But the war feeling ran high at that time and pervaded all classes.

We were momentarily expecting to be ordered upon active duty by Governor John A. Andrew.[15] The Third, Fourth, Fifth, Sixth, and Eighth Regiments went to the front and orders came for the

13. Cowdin first joined the state militia in 1830 and by wartime had risen to the rank of colonel of the First Regiment. Commissioned colonel of the First Massachusetts on May 22, 1861, and brigadier general on September 26, 1862, Cowdin served until Congress refused to approve this promotion and his generalship lapsed on March 4, 1862. Cowdin had five bullets pass through his uniform at Second Bull Run, but escaped injury although one of his sons would be killed at Cold Harbor in 1864. He returned to his civilian career in the lumber industry, served in some local and state political posts, and died in Boston on July 9, 1874. Warner, *Generals in Blue*, 96–97; Heitman, *Historical Register*, 1:231; *Massachusetts Soldiers*, 1:2; *Boston Journal*, July 9, 1874.

14. Mitchell cannot be positively identified.

15. John Andrew graduated from Bowdoin College in 1837 and moved to Boston, where he followed the profession of law and served in the state legislature for two years. Returning from the 1860 Republican Chicago Convention, Andrew proclaimed, "I would trust my country's cause in Abraham Lincoln's care as its Chief Magistrate, while the wind blows and the water runs." Following his election as governor that fall, Andrew proclaimed his devotion to Lincoln and the Union in General Order No. 4, dated January 16, 1861, in which he ordered the Sixth and Eighth Regiments of Militia to be ready to march at a moment's notice to defend Washington, D.C. A prominent antislavery spokesman, Governor Andrew took the lead in the recruiting of black soldiers to fill the Fifty-fourth and Fifty-fifth Massachusetts Regiments. Andrew retired after serving five years as governor and died on October 30, 1867. *Boston Journal*, October 31, 1867; *Boston Post*, October 31, 1867.

Fourth Battalion ("New England Guards"), commanded by Major Thomas G. Stevenson,[16] afterward Colonel of the Twenty-fourth Massachusetts and a Brigadier General who fell at Spotsylvania at the head of a division, to garrison Fort Independence and for the Second Battalion ("Tigers") to proceed to Fort Warren. Both organizations had been stationed at Boylston Hall.

Some delay occurred, but on the 29th of April the "Tigers" were let loose, 250 strong, and, headed by Patrick Gilmore's Band,[17] we marched to the wharf where we took a steamer for the fort. All along the route we were cheered to the echo and we were very proud to be looked upon as defenders of Old Glory. Here is a roster of the officers:

Major, Ralph W. Newton; Adjutant, T. Bigelow Lawrence;[18]

16. Stevenson was employed by the Boston and Lowell Railroad when Fort Sumter was fired upon. A sergeant in Boston's New England Guards, he received permission to recruit a new militia company and was soon elevated to command the entire battalion. He spent the summer training troops until Governor Andrew commissioned him colonel of the Twenty-fourth Massachusetts on August 31, 1861. Stevenson's regiment took part in the New Bern expedition in 1862, and he was appointed brigadier general on December 26, 1862. After commanding a brigade in operations around Charleston Harbor in 1863, General Stevenson joined General Grant's Overland Campaign in 1864 and was killed in action at Spotsylvania on May 10, 1864. *Presentation of a Bronze Relief*, 33–51; *Massachusetts Soldiers*, 2:776; 6:774.

17. Born on Christmas Day, 1829, Patrick S. Gilmore taught music in Ireland before arriving in Boston at the age of nineteen. He led a series of bands in the Boston area and became known as one of the best E-flat cornet players in the entire country. He enlisted as leader of the Twenty-fourth Massachusetts band on September 16, 1861, and served until regimental bands were mustered out on August 30, 1862. He is most famous for composing the lyrics to "When Johnny Comes Marching Home" in 1863. After the war he specialized in organizing grand jubilees that employed thousands of musicians and singers. Gilmore died in St. Louis on September 24, 1892. *Boston Journal*, June 16, 1869; September 26, 1892; *Massachusetts Soldiers*, 2:277.

18. Bigelow graduated from Harvard in 1846 and from 1850 to 1855 served on the staff of the U.S. Embassy in London. He became active in militia affairs but declined the office of major of the Second Battalion of Militia despite being unanimously elected to the post. He received a staff appointment in 1861, but deafness kept him out of Federal service. He was selected first lieutenant of the Ancient and Honorable Artillery Company in 1862 but relinquished his post in July to accept an appointment as consul general in Florence, Italy. He died March 21, 1869, while in Washington, D.C., on diplomatic business. Lawrence, *T. Bigelow Lawrence*, 12–13; *Boston Evening Transcript*, June 4, 1860; *Boston Post*, June 5, 1862; *Springfield (Mass.) Republican*, July 9, 1862.

Quartermaster, J. Franklin Bates;[19] Surgeon, Allston W. Whitney;[20] Assistant Surgeon, Edward A. Whiston;[21] Sergeant Major, Robert C. Nichols;[22] Quartermaster Sergeant, Israel M. Rice.[23]

19. John Franklin Bates was a fixture in the Massachusetts militia during the 1850s as captain of the Woburn Phalanx, whose members presented him with a pair of epaulets, a sword, and a sash. He later served on the staff of the Massachusetts governor. He was appointed first lieutenant in the Ninety-ninth New York on August 21, 1861 and served as adjutant until promoted to captain of Co. H on January 17, 1862. Bates was promoted to major on August 23, 1862, and was mustered out July 2, 1864. He was employed by the Comptroller of the Currency when he died in Washington, D.C., on May 2, 1884. *Boston Herald,* June 23, 1858; *Boston Evening Transcript,* March 15, 1855; *Washington (D. C.) Critic-Record,* May 3, 1884; *Massachusetts Soldiers,* 6:652.

20. Whitney was a physician with a large practice in Framingham when he was commissioned surgeon of the Thirteenth Massachusetts on July 16, 1861. He received the appointment of medical director of the Second Division, First Army Corps, in January 1863, but he was captured during the Battle of Chancellorsville and kept at Libby Prison until his release in December 1863. Whitney was mustered out on August 1, 1864, and in 1867 was brevetted lieutenant colonel effective March 13, 1865. Doctor Whitney died November 12, 1881, in Newton, Massachusetts. *Massachusetts Soldiers,* 2:71; *Boston Recorder,* January 29, 1863; *Boston Liberator,* December 11, 1863; *Boston Traveler,* May 3, 1867; *Boston Herald,* November 12, 1881.

21. Whiston graduated from Harvard Medical School and began the practice of medicine at Framingham. He received a commission as assistant surgeon of the Sixteenth Massachusetts on August 5, 1861, and served until promoted to surgeon of the First Massachusetts on March 3, 1863. Whiston was mustered out May 28, 1864, and resumed a civilian practice but gave it up for a business career. He died in Springfield, Massachusetts, on February 3, 1909. *Massachusetts Soldiers,* 1:2; 2:215; *Springfield Republican,* February 24, 1909.

22. When the Second Battalion of Militia returned to Boston in May, Nichols remained in Fort Warren as acting adjutant of the Twelfth Massachusetts, as well as brigade major for all troops stationed at that post. The following month, the Webster Committee presented him with an elegant French sword, belt, sash, and set of epaulets in appreciation of his efforts for the regiment. He rejoined the Second Battalion and served as adjutant until his elevation to major in August 1862. Nichols was commissioned major of the Forty-third Massachusetts but was forced to resign because of an affliction of his eyes that effectually ended his military career. He died in the Insane Asylum in Worcester, Massachusetts, on August 16, 1894. *Boston Post,* May 27 and June 10, 1861; *Boston Evening Transcript,* August 8, 1862; *Boston Daily Advertiser,* October 15, 1862; *Boston Traveler,* October 21, 186; *Boston Journal,* August 17, 1894; *Boston Herald,* August 19, 1894.

23. Rice sold boots and shoes made from his patented "anatomical lasts" in Boston, but he used his business skills on behalf of the Second Battalion. He acted as treasurer for the unit and was responsible for the delivery of mail and newspapers to the men while they were at Fort Warren. Rice died in New York

Company A—Captain, John C. Whiton;[24] First Lieutenant, Daniel G. Handy;[25] Second Lieutenant, Joshua M. Cushing;[26] Third Lieutenant, John M. Pierce;[27] Fourth Lieutenant, James C. Laughton.[28]

City on March 26, 1890. *Boston Traveler,* February 11, 1858; *Boston Evening Transcript,* March 21, 1861; May 6, 1861; *Boston Journal,* March 29, 1890.

24. John Whiton was an organizer for the Boston Light Infantry, serving on the executive committee and planning public balls and drills. He was commissioned lieutenant colonel of the Forty-third Massachusetts on October 13, 1862, and served until discharged to become lieutenant colonel of the Fifty-eighth Massachusetts on July 30, 1863. Whiton commanded the regiment after its organization until being mustered out on July 26, 1865. He died in Dorchester, Massachusetts, on January 2, 1905. *Boston Herald,* February 17, 1858; January 3, 1905; *Boston Evening Transcript,* January 10, 1859; *Massachusetts Soldiers,* 4:231; 5:2.

25. Daniel Handy was appointed captain of Co. C, Twelfth Massachusetts, on June 26, 1861, was promoted to major on November 30, 1862, and resigned on July 22, 1863. He was commissioned captain of Co. B, Seventh Massachusetts Militia, a successor of the Second Battalion, on November 4, 1864; was elevated to lieutenant colonel on August 21, 1865; and advanced to colonel the following November. He was discharged from the regiment on January 12, 1869, and left for New York City, where he lived until July 6, 1880. *Massachusetts Soldiers,* 2:19; *Boston Journal,* July 8, 1880.

26. A member of the Tigers since 1855, Cushing rose steadily through the ranks to the position of battalion adjutant in 1861; he was the first officer of the guard at Fort Warren. Although he remained active in the Tiger organization until 1889, he never again served in the field. He became a member of the Ancient and Honorable Artillery Company in 1864 and died in Duxbury, Massachusetts, on February 2, 1909. Roberts, *Ancient and Honorable Artillery Company,* 3:390–91; *Boston Herald,* February 2, 1909.

27. John M. Pierce was the proprietor of a Boston shop that sold white goods, lace, hosiery, and embroidery at 255 Washington Street. He never served during the war, although he did, along with other merchants, periodically close his store to support the enlistment of others. Pierce disappears from Boston records after the war. *Boston Traveler,* October 16, 1860; August 11, 1862.

28. James Laughton was the exclusive dealer for Fleming's Golden Ale when he was not drilling with the Boston Light Infantry. His only tangible contribution to the war effort in 1861 seems to have resulted from a trip to Washington on which he acquired a rebel flag from the infamous Marshall House in Alexandria, Virginia, site of the murder of Colonel Elmer Ellsworth. In August 1862 he attempted to fill a company for the Forty-third Massachusetts but did not sign up enough recruits to receive a commission. He remained active in the Boston Light Infantry Veteran Corps well into the 1890s and died on August 19, 1908, in Boston. *Boston Evening Transcript,* September 13, 1859; July 8, 1861; August 18, 1862; *Boston Journal,* February 9, 1893; Return of a Death—1908, City of Boston, Massachusetts Vital Records (hereafter cited as MVR).

Company B—Captain, Charles O. Rogers; First Lieutenant, Andrew G. Smith;[29] Second Lieutenant, Charles H. Allen;[30] Third Lieutenant, Edward G. Quincy.[31]

Company C—Captain, George D. Wells;[32] First Lieutenant, Robert B. Brown;[33] Second Lieutenant, James H. Hart;[34] Third Lieutenant, Samuel Hichborn;[35] Fourth Lieutenant, John L. Swift.[36]

29. Andrew Smith had spent several years in the Boston Light Guard prior to the Civil War, occasionally commanding the company as a lieutenant. He retained his membership throughout his lifetime and in 1867 was accepted into the Ancient and Honorable Artillery Company. Smith died in Boston on February 19, 1878. *Boston Herald*, February 15, 1858; *Boston Traveler*, June 30, 1859; *Boston Daily Advertiser*, February 21, 1878; Roberts, *Ancient and Honorable Artillery Company*, 4:39.

30. Charles H. Allen's membership certificate in the Boston Light Infantry bore the date of May 1855, and by June 1858 he had attained the rank of lieutenant. He commanded Co. C of the Second Battalion in May 1862 and continued on the company rolls. He joined the Ancient and Honorable Artillery Company in 1861. A merchant and popular alderman, Allen died in Boston on March 31, 1907. Roberts, *Ancient and Honorable*, 3:361; *Report of the Adjutant General*, 16; Rand, *One of a Thousand*, 12; *Boston Journal*, October 20, 1873; April 1, 1907.

31. Quincy was elected third lieutenant of the company on March 28, 1861. He received a captain's commission in Co. B, Forty-third Massachusetts, on September 18, 1862, and was mustered out on July 30, 1863. Captain Quincy died in Brooklyn, New York, on December 22, 1898. *Boston Evening Transcript*, March 29, 1861; *Massachusetts Soldiers*, 4:235; Pratt, *Forty-third Regiment*, 7.

32. Captain Wells received his office on April 27, 1861, when Co. C, Second Battalion, was organized. He was commissioned lieutenant colonel of the First Massachusetts on May 22, 1861, and served until promoted to colonel of the Thirty-fourth Massachusetts on July 11, 1862. Colonel Wells was wounded at New Market and killed in action at Cedar Creek on October 13, 1864. He was posthumously brevetted brigadier general effective as of October 12, 1864. *Boston Herald*, April 29, 1861; *Massachusetts Soldiers*, 1:2; 3:590.

33. Robert B. Brown joined the Boston Light Infantry in 1855. Brown was commissioned captain of Co. E, Thirtieth Massachusetts, on February 20, 1862, and served until discharged on January 18, 1865. He died in Boston on March 9, 1881. *Massachusetts Soldiers*, 3:358; *Boston Herald*, March 12, 1881.

34. Hart was commissioned captain of Co. E, Ninety-ninth New York, on August 21, 1861. He was wounded at South Quay Bridge, Virginia, on May 1, 1863, and was killed in action June 16, 1863, near Franklin, Virginia. *Boston Daily Advertiser*, June 22, 1863; *Massachusetts Soldiers*, 6:675.

35. Samuel Hichborn joined the Boston Light Infantry in 1855 and was associated with the organization until his death in Boston on August 16, 1907. He joined the Ancient and Honorable Artillery Company in May 1863. *Boston Journal*, August 17, 1907; Roberts, *Ancient and Honorable*, 3:381.

36. Lieutenant Swift was appointed to a position at the Boston Custom House in June 1861 but resigned and enlisted as a private in Co. K, Thirty-fifth

Major Daniel G. Handy.
Courtesy of the U.S.
Army Heritage and
Education Center

A jollier, lighter-hearted set of fellows I never saw. Song and jest were constant, with never a murmur or complaint. It was more like setting out for a grand frolic than for the serious business of guarding Government property. Most of us thought, too, that we were to be summoned to Washington as soon as the authorities there could be prevailed upon to accept our services. Just then, however, there appeared to be too much hesitation—it seemed

---

Massachusetts, on August 1, 1862. Appointed sergeant, he was en route to the Antietam battlefield when he was offered a commission as captain of Co. C, Third Massachusetts Cavalry. Captain Swift served in the Department of the Gulf until his resignation on June 1, 1864, when he was appointed adjutant general of Louisiana. He died in Boston on February 19, 1895. *Boston Herald*, February 20, 1895; *Worcester (Mass.) Daily Spy*, February 20, 1895; *Massachusetts Soldiers*, 3:707; 6:349.

so to us, our ardor was so great. Perhaps the military authorities at the front thought there would not be Rebellion enough to go round if all came who wanted to come.

There were serious men, however, among us. Captain George D. Wells was a Judge of the Police Court of Boston and judges are always supposed to be serious men. He was afterward Lieutenant Colonel of the First Massachusetts, finally Colonel of the Thirty-fourth and was killed at Cedar Creek.

General John L. Swift, then a Lieutenant, was known the country over as a campaign speaker.

Daniel G. Handy was afterward a Major in the Twelfth Massachusetts.

Captain John C. Whiton, afterward Lieutenant Colonel of the Forty-third ("Tiger") Regiment and Colonel of the Fifty-eighth, is now Superintendent of city institutions at Deer Island.

Frank H. Underwood,[37] *litterateur,* and Consul at Glasgow under the Cleveland administration, was at that time Clerk of the Superior Criminal Court of Suffolk County.

Sheriff John M. Clark[38] was a private soldier in the battalion.

Edward B. Blasland,[39] afterward Major in the Thirty-third Massachusetts, now in the City Collector's Office, was a prominent "Tiger."

37. A founder of *Atlantic Magazine* in 1857, Francis Underwood apparently dropped out of the Second Battalion and turned his attention to editorial work at the magazine. He pursued a successful writing career after the war and served as U.S. consul at Glasgow, Scotland, during the first Grover Cleveland administration. Returning home from this post, Underwood found that he was treated like a "genial old fogey" and lamented, "I was more than 65 years old, and that was enough for them. In the places where I was known they wanted smart, young men; they had no use for a veteran." Appointed to the same post during Cleveland's second administration, Underwood vowed never to return to Boston; he died in Glasgow on August 4, 1894, and is buried there. *Boston Herald,* August 20, 1894; Underwood, *Underwood Families of America,* 1:184–87.

38. Clark assumed the position of sheriff of Suffolk County in 1855 and held that job continuously until 1883. He served as chairman of the Ward 5 committee responsible for securing volunteers and was a representative from Massachusetts at the dedication of the National Cemetery at Gettysburg. He died in Boston on June 22, 1902. *Boston Herald,* June 23, 1902; *Springfield Republican,* June 24, 1902.

39. Blasland had enlisted in the Boston Light Infantry in 1858 and was a sergeant in 1861. He received a commission as captain of Co. H, Thirty-third Massachusetts, on June 2, 1862, and was wounded at Wauhatchie, Tennessee, on

Erastus L. Clark,[40] who distinguished himself as a Captain in the Twelfth Massachusetts and was severely wounded at Gettysburg, was a corporal in the battalion.

Louis N. Tucker[41] was an Orderly Sergeant. He was afterward Captain and Brevet Major in the Eighteenth Massachusetts.

Fred R. Shattuck[42] was a corporal in Company B. He afterward served as a Lieutenant in the Twelfth Massachusetts and, as Captain in the Signal Corps, originated and first sent the famous message, "All quiet on the Potomac."

John Brown,[43] a jolly Scotchman, with whom, or, rather, in connection with whom, the "John Brown Song" originated, was a private in Company B.

October 29, 1863. Promoted to major on November 3, 1864, he was brevetted lieutenant colonel effective March 13, 1865. Blasland captured the battle flag of the Twenty-sixth Tennessee at Bentonville, North Carolina. After the war he joined the Ancient and Honorable Artillery Company and died on January 29, 1893, in South Boston. *Boston Journal,* January 30, 1893; *Massachusetts Soldiers,* 4:201; Roberts, *Ancient and Honorable,* 4:201.

40. Captain Erastus L. Clark enlisted as first sergeant in Co. E, Twelfth Massachusetts, on June 11, 1861. He received commissions as second lieutenant on December 9, 1861, and captain on September 9, 1862. Wounded at Fredericksburg and Gettysburg, he was discharged on February 3, 1864, while commanding Co. A. Captain Clark joined the Sixth Regiment, Veteran Reserve Corps, and served until mustered out on June 25, 1867. Shortly after, Captain Clark was killed in a duel fought with pocket knives wherein Clark and Jacob Garrett hacked each other to death in Catahoula Parish, Louisiana. *Massachusetts Soldiers,* 2:30; 7:147; *Boston Journal,* July 30, 1867.

41. Regarded as one of the best drill masters in Boston when the war started, Tucker was commissioned captain of Co. A, Eighteenth Massachusetts, on August 20, 1861. Wounded at Fredericksburg and the Wilderness, Captain Tucker was mustered out September 3, 1864, and brevetted major effective March 13, 1865. He remained active in the Tiger organization until his death at Dorchester, Massachusetts, on March 18, 1902. Cook, *History of Norfolk County,* 1:340; *Massachusetts Soldiers,* 2:356; *Boston Herald,* March 13, 1898.

42. Shattuck was commissioned first lieutenant of Co. B, Twelfth Massachusetts, on June 26, 1861, and detached to the Signal Corps on August 16, 1861. While stationed at Darnestown, Maryland, Lieutenants Shattuck and W. W. Rowley, Twenty-eighth New York, composed the phrase "All quiet on the Potomac." After additional signal service in Kentucky, Shattuck resigned July 6, 1862. He died on February 13, 1917, in Lowell, Massachusetts. *Massachusetts Soldiers,* 2:16; Brown, *Signal Corps,* 228–29, 861, 867; Frederick R. Shattuck Pension Records, RG 15, NA.

43. Brown enlisted in Co. A, Twelfth Massachusetts, on July 8, 1861, and accidentally drowned in the Rappahannock River near Front Royal, Virginia, on June 6, 1862. *Massachusetts Soldiers,* 2:5.

Then there were George C. Blanchard,[44] Benjamin F. Talbot,[45] Caleb E. Niebuhr,[46] Gurdon S. Brown,[47] Charles E. B. Edgerly,[48]

44. Blanchard had a wife and two small children, so he elected to remain at home and work as a bookkeeper during the war. A veteran of Patrick Gilmore's Band, George eventually moved to New York City, where he died on January 21, 1896. 1860 Census, Massachusetts, Middlesex County, Town of Malden, RG 29, NA; *New York Tribune*, January 22, 1896.

45. Benjamin Talbot began recruiting his own company on April 22, 1861, but was unsuccessful in this endeavor. He was commissioned first lieutenant in Co. A, Thirty-third Massachusetts, on June 1, 1862, and promoted to captain, commissary of subsistence, on November 7, 1862. Talbot was brevetted major effective July 10, 1865, and was mustered out July 15, 1865. Following the war Major Talbot joined the Ancient and Honorable Artillery Company. He committed suicide in Boston on April 16, 1891. *Boston Daily Advertiser*, April 23, 1861; *Massachusetts Soldiers*, 3:543; 6:774; Roberts, *Ancient and Honorable*, 4:40; *Boston Journal*, April 17, 1891.

46. Niebuhr joined the Boston Light Infantry in 1856 and served as orderly sergeant from April 22, 1861. He remained in Boston as a member until February 26, 1862, when he was commissioned in what would become Co. A, First Battalion, Massachusetts Heavy Artillery. Promoted to captain on November 3, 1862, he was mustered out June 29, 1865, as captain of Co. B. Captain Niebuhr served as company commander in the Seventh Regiment of Militia from 1865 to 1867, in which year he joined the Ancient and Honorable Artillery Company. He remained active in militia affairs until his death in Boston on July 14, 1914. Roberts, *Ancient and Honorable*, 4:33; *Massachusetts Soldiers*, 6:88; *Boston Evening Transcript*, January 3, 1862; *Boston Herald*, July 15, 1914.

47. Gurdon S. Brown received his commission as first lieutenant of Co. A, Thirtieth Massachusetts, on February 20, 1862, and served until his resignation on July 12, 1865, as first lieutenant of Co. E. He returned to Boston and immediately joined the Seventh (Tiger) Regiment of Militia as a company commander. Brown died on November 11, 1889, in Cambridge, Massachusetts. *Massachusetts Soldiers*, 3:336; *Boston Traveler*, August 14, 1865; Deaths Registered in the Town of Cambridge for the Year 1889, Massachusetts Vital Records.

48. Edgerly enlisted in Co. E, Twelfth Massachusetts, on June 26, 1861, and served as a sergeant until his discharge for disability on November 11, 1862. He regained his health and was commissioned second lieutenant of Co. I, Eighty-fourth United States Colored Troops, on December 18, 1863. He was again discharged for disability on July 28, 1864, while assigned to Co. D. Edgerly rejoined the Boston Light Infantry and rose to command its successor, the Seventh Regiment of Militia, as its colonel, before dying in New Market, New Hampshire, on October 14, 1896. *Massachusetts Soldiers*, 2:31; 7:296; *Worcester Daily Spy*, October 18, 1892; *Boston Daily Advertiser*, October 17, 1896.

Newton J. Pernette,[49] James H. Jenkins,[50] Oliver N. Eldredge,[51] and Henry J. Hallgreen,[52] all well-known Bostonians.

We found Fort Warren in a very sorry state and had to almost dig our way into it, but, after hard work made room enough in an old building which then stood in the centre of the parade ground for quarters for the night, regular garrison duty began.

49. Newton J. Pernette (also known as J. Newton Pernette) enlisted in Co. E, Twelfth Massachusetts, on June 26, 1861, as a corporal. He was reported as missing at Second Bull Run but returned and was mustered out July 8, 1864, as a sergeant. Pernette died November 23, 1893, in the State Insane Hospital at Augusta, Maine. *Massachusetts Soldiers*, 2:33; *Report of Town of Madison*, 7; Maine Death Records 1617–1922, Maine State Archives.

50. James H. Jenkins enlisted as a sergeant in Co. A, Twelfth Massachusetts, on July 18, 1861. He was discharged to accept a promotion as second lieutenant of Co. B, Twenty-first Wisconsin, on August 7, 1862. Promoted to adjutant on February 1, 1863, Jenkins was captured at Chickamauga and resigned on March 24, 1865, after being exchanged. He died in Oshkosh, Wisconsin, on October 18, 1922. *Massachusetts Soldiers*, 2:7; 6:752; *Roster of Wisconsin Volunteers*, 2:164; James H. Jenkins Pension Records, RG 15, NA.

51. Oliver Eldredge enlisted in Co. A, Twelfth Massachusetts, on June 25, 1861, as first sergeant. He was mustered out July 8, 1864, as a private. He died in Cambridge, Massachusetts, on August 5, 1871. Although the Massachusetts adjutant general lists his last name as "Eldridge" and his pension index card states it as "Elbridge," all other records, including the 1860 Census, 1860 *Boston Directory*, and 1860 *Cambridge Directory*, list him as "Oliver N. Eldredge." The National Park Service Civil War Soldiers database gives "Eldredge" as an alternate spelling. *Massachusetts Soldiers*, 2:6; *Boston Post*, August 10, 1871.

52. Henry J. Hallgreen first put on the bearskin shako of the Boston Light Infantry in 1854 and remained a steadfast member of the organization throughout his lifetime. He was commissioned captain of Co. A, Forty-third Massachusetts, on October 14, 1862, and was mustered out July 30, 1863. Hallgreen died at Malden, Massachusetts, on October 10, 1927. *Boston Herald*, February 23, 1917; *Massachusetts Soldiers*, 4:231; Henry J. Hallgreen Pension Records, RG 15, NA.

CHAPTER 2

Fort Warren

In time of peace, garrison duty is doubtless very dull music, but with a great war opening and events transpiring which excited their enthusiasm to the highest pitch, the 250 men of the Second Battalion of Infantry found life at Fort Warren exceedingly pleasant. The fort was comparatively new and had never before been occupied by troops. Piles of rubbish of every kind encumbered not only the spacious parade ground, but every casemate and every nook and corner was filled with it. So we set to work with a will to put our house in order and had manual labor galore. It was interesting to see professional men, merchants, clerks and others, as busy as bees with shovel and wheelbarrow and broom, while song and jest and heartiest laughter rose continually as an accompaniment.

The men were a merry-hearted set of fellows and, while tugging with pick, shovel, and wheelbarrow, an occupation which differed somewhat from yardstick-handling and the other light employments to which they had been accustomed, sang lustily the popular songs of the day. Our evenings were chiefly spent in singing and, as there were many good singers among us, we derived much pleasure and entertainment from this source. We sang all the popular songs of the day and many favorite hymns.

It was out of these conditions that the famous "John Brown Song" sprang and, if the "Tigers" had done nothing else to help the cause of the Union, this song alone would have been sufficient to entitle them to gratitude, for it is impossible to overestimate the effect it had all through the war as an inspirational force upon the armies in the field. It was pre-eminently *the* song of the war and was sung in camp and on the march with a heartiness and dash that I never saw equaled in the case of any other. It even invaded England after performing its mission in this country and was almost as popular there as it had been here. Richard Grant White,[1] in 1866, said that the song had "a certain rhythm, or *lilt,* which seizes upon the memory and bewitches without always pleasing the ear" and that "the alternate jig and swing of the air caused it to stick in the uneducated ear as burrs stick to a blackberry girl."

We had a soldier in the battalion named John Brown. We were ready to seize upon everything that promised fun and so guyed Brown unmercifully because of his name. He would be greeted by, "Hi, Hi there, John Brown! You are doing mighty little in freeing the slaves; you seem to be doing nothing at all to free 'em. Oh, no! He's not the real John! The original John Brown and the only, is dead—dead. John, you sure are not the old hero of Harpers Ferry; his body is decaying in his North Elba grave." He was a jolly Scotchman and entered heartily into the nonsense.

There were many good singers among us, Brown himself being one. Then there were Newton J. Pernette, James H. Jenkins, Charles E. B. Edgerly, James E. Greenleaf,[2] Gurdon S. Brown,

1. Regarded as "a man of letters," Richard Grant White also had the reputation, prior to his death in 1885, of being a "humorless snob"—according to the introduction to White's *Poetry Lyrical, Narrative, and Satirical of the Civil War* (vii). On page 66 he makes this disparaging remark about the John Brown song: "The origin of this senseless farrago . . . is, I believe, quite unknown. But sung to a degraded and jiggish form of a grand and simple old air, it was a great favorite in the early part of the war. It was heard everywhere in the streets; regiments marched to it, and the air had its place in the programme of every barrel-organ grinder." *Dictionary of American Biography*, 20:113–14.

2. James Greenleaf was a purveyor of high-quality Kentucky bourbon whiskey, a valuable addition to the roster of any militia group. When not selling liquor or drilling with the Second Battalion, he spent Sundays playing a church organ in Charlestown, Massachusetts. He briefly moved his business operation to New York City but by August 1865 was back leading a company in the Seventh Regiment of Militia. He died on March 7, 1900, in Charlestown. *Springfield Republican*, July 7, 1860; *Boston Directory* (1861), 194; Coffin, *Marching to Victory*, 21; *Boston Herald*, January 16, 1865; *Boston Traveler*, August 14, 1865; *Boston Herald*, March 8, 1900.

Louis N. Tucker, Caleb E. Niebuhr, Henry J. Hallgreen, Brooks[3] and many others that I do not now recall.

I belonged to the Boston Young Men's Christian Association before my enlistment and boarded with L. Perkins Rowland,[4] the librarian. Rowland one day brought down fifty copies of *The Melodeon*, a collection of hymns compiled by the late Reverend J. W. Dadmun.[5] I distributed these. One of the hymns in the book, then very popular, was "Say Brothers, Will You Meet Us." The first verse was as follows.

> Say, brothers, will you meet us,
> Say, brothers, will you meet us,
> Say, brothers, will you meet us,
> On Canaan's happy shore.
>
> CHORUS
>
> Glory, glory, hallelujah,
> Glory, glory, hallelujah,
> Glory, glory, hallelujah,
> For ever, evermore.

We sang this hymn a great deal, both while at work cleaning up rubbish and during the long evenings in barracks. As I have said, we often guyed our Scotch comrade on account of his suggestive name and some of the wags finally hit upon the idea of making parodies in his honor upon the above hymn, thinking, probably, that

3. Brooks cannot be positively identified.

4. Levi Perkins Rowland, Jr., oversaw the YMCA's library in Tremont Temple, which social organization had been formed in 1851. During the war he collected stores for the United States Christian Commission, corresponded with soldiers and sailors, and worked actively for the Bible Society of Massachusetts. *Boston Directory* (1861), 385; *Boston Directory* (1862), 539; *United States Christian Commission*, 31–38; Butterfield, *Delegate's Story*, n.p.; *Annual Report of the Bible Society*, 51–52; *Boston Herald*, November 5, 1932.

5. Reverend John W. Dadmun's *The Melodeon* was published by J. P. Magee in Boston in 1860. Riding the wave of patriotic fervor, Dadmun, a Methodist clergyman, later produced a volume titled *Army and Navy Melodies* that by the spring of 1862 was already in its tenth edition. He died in Boston on August 6, 1890. *Salem (Mass.) Register*, May 8, 1862; *Boston Journal*, August 7, 1890.

this might "rattle" him, but it didn't—he took it good-naturedly, as he did everything else, and even helped us along.

I cannot say whether any of the several verses of doggerel rhyme used at the fort eventually became parts of the song as sung by the army beyond "John Brown's body lies moldering in the grave," "He's gone to be a soldier in the army of the Lord" and "We'll hang Jeff Davis to a sour apple tree," but am certain that these three did. We had to quicken the music of the hymn a bit to make it conform to our doggerel rhymes, but the grand old chorus was unchanged. I have no copy now of *The Melodeon*, but have *The Revivalist*, a collection of hymns arranged and published by Joseph Hillman of Troy, New York, in 1872, and this contains "Say, Brothers, Will You Meet Us."[6]

It may seem odd that such prominence should be given to the statement that the old martyr had "joined the silent majority" and that his body was "moldering in the grave," but this came from frequent emphatic denials, playfully made, that our Scotch laddie was actually with us. We would say, "Why, you're dead," "Your body is moldering in the grave," etc., and from this kind of nonsense finally sprang the beginning of the song. Then it grew.

There was a germ of inspiration in the idea that John Brown "had gone to be a soldier in the army of the Lord," and this, with the glorious chorus, together with the fact that the music was just right for a marching air, made it immensely popular. Major Newton and others thought that it would be better to commemorate the services of some distinguished soldier and "Ellsworth's body" was tried, but it would not go.[7]

Greenleaf was organist of a church in Charlestown and he naturally had much to do with the early arrangement of the notes of the song. Mr. C. S. Hall, an acquaintance of Mr. Greenleaf, often

6. Joseph Hillman's *The Revivalist* originally appeared in 1868.

7. Colonel E. E. Ellsworth, a personal friend of Lincoln and commander of the New York Fire Zouaves, was killed on May 24, 1861, while tearing down a rebel flag at the Marshall House in Alexandria, Virginia. While still captain of the Chicago Zouaves, Ellsworth's company had visited Boston and used the Second Battalion's armory as a base before putting on an impressive public drill exhibition in the city on July 23, 1860. *Boston Herald*, July 23, 1860; *Boston Post*, May 30, 1861.

visited the fort and, becoming interested in the song, he took hold with his friend to see what could be done with it.[8] Mr. C. B. Marsh[9] also helped and the result was the composition of additional lines and the issue of the production as a penny ballad, on common printing paper, surrounded by a pretentious border. It bore this imprint: "Published at 256 Main street, Charlestown, Mass."

Later, Mr. Hall issued a more elaborate copy, giving both words and music, and headed it with a cut of the national bird. It bore the words, "Origin, Fort Warren" and "Music arranged by C. B. Marsh." At the bottom was the imprint, as before, and a statement that it had been "Entered according to act of Congress in the year 1861, by C. S. Hall, in the Clerk's office of the District Court of Massachusetts." I have ascertained by inquiry of the Librarian of Congress that the date of this copyright was July 16, 1861.

When the song was growing fast, the Twelfth Massachusetts Regiment, raised by Fletcher Webster,[10] son of the illustrious

8. C. Sprague Hall gave Greenleaf credit for selecting the tune for the John Brown song, then explained how he came to compose the lyrics: "Let it be understood that several young men, residents of Charlestown, who were glee singers, suggested to me that the wants of the public required a song to be started under the title of the John Brown song, at the same time assuring me that it would be hailed with delight everywhere. In reply to their request that I should compose such a song, I told them that I was incompetent to conform to their wishes, but would consult with Mr. H. Partridge, of whom I had bought songs, to hire some poet to get it up, but as he declined, the singers alluded to insisted that I should do my best, and the result is before the world." *Our War Songs*, 8.

9. The sheet music alluded to by the author contains the notation, "Music arranged by C. B. Marsh." The John Brown song, often referred to simply as "Glory Hallelujah," was seemingly pirated by every person with a facile pen and a desire to cash in on its popularity. By the end of July the firm of Russell and Patee published the song "in a cheap form." About the same time Oliver Ditson came out with new lyrics substituting "Ellsworth" for "John Brown." In August several new versions appeared, including "The Patriot Song" and "Song of the Massachusetts Thirteenth." Perhaps the most bizarre arrangement came in September when the celebrated Peak Family gave a performance "with splendid effect upon the bells." *Salem Register*, July 29, 1861; *Boston Traveler*, July 29, 1861; *Salem (Mass.) Observer*, August 24, 1861; *Boston Evening Transcript*, September 12, 1861.

10. A graduate of the Harvard class of 1833, Daniel Fletcher Webster, commonly referred to as Fletcher Webster to avoid confusion with his more famous father, attained modest success as a lawyer but gave up his career to act as secretary when Daniel Webster was appointed secretary of state in 1841. From 1843 to 1845 he served as secretary of legation in China. From 1850 until the outbreak of war in 1861 Fletcher served as surveyor of the Port of Boston. Following the

Colonel Fletcher
Webster. Courtesy of the
U.S. Army Heritage and
Education Center

statesman Daniel Webster,[11] came to the fort and it took the men
of that organization by storm, as indeed it did every body of soldiers that ran up against it. Pernette, Edgerly, Brown, Jenkins and
I finally joined the Twelfth. My four comrades formed a quartet,

---

death of his father in 1852, Fletcher began editing the famous statesman's correspondence, an effort that produced the two-volume *Private Correspondence of
Daniel Webster* in 1857. Webster announced in the Boston press on April 20, 1861,
his intention to raise a regiment. *Harvard Memorial Biographies*, 21–30; *Boston Evening Transcript*, April 20, 1861.

11. A native of New Hampshire, Daniel Webster (1782–1852) was recognized
in the nineteenth century as one of America's greatest statesmen. A graduate
of Dartmouth College, he served as a congressman, senator, and presidential
candidate, in addition to being secretary of state for Presidents William Henry
Harrison and John Tyler. During nearly forty years of public service, Webster was
an eloquent orator on behalf of the American Union and the industrial interests
of the Northeast. *Dictionary of American Biography*, 19:585–92.

Brown singing second tenor, and they frequently made melody in the camp of our regiment, to the delight of the soldiers, and often enlivened brigade and division headquarters by their serenades. The Eleventh Massachusetts came to the fort and later the Fourteenth (afterwards First Heavy Artillery) Massachusetts and the song became popular with both these organizations. Everybody knows how later it spread throughout the army.

I have given the origin of this famous song somewhat in detail because there has been so much needless discussion about it. The men of the Second Battalion merely claim that, and in this they are supported by thousands of Bostonians and others who know whereof they speak, the *words* of the song and its *idea* had their origin among them in April and May, 1861, in the old wooden barracks in Fort Warren.

A neat illustration of the fact that all men are brothers was given when Colonel Webster's regiment came to the fort. Some of the companies had been quartered in Faneuil Hall and, when orders came to proceed to Fort Warren, all the stray companies were summoned to the "Cradle of Liberty" to prepare for the start. A captain, with neither discretion nor propriety, advised the men to prepare themselves for a cold reception at Fort Warren, saying that the stronghold was garrisoned by "kid-gloved soldiers." "A little bird" or some other messenger brought the tidings down. Think you the men of the battalion indulged in a towering rage? They did not. We simply laughed, for we knew that the captain was laboring under a misapprehension.

Our officers suggested that we show them by a hearty reception that all men engaged in the suppression of the Rebellion occupied the same broad platform—that we were all Americans. So, when the steamer bringing the regiment came, we began to cheer as soon as they could hear us and kept it up until they landed. Then we escorted them to their quarters and, while they were wondering what we were up to, we stacked arms and broke ranks and, returning to the wharf on the run, seized mattresses and every bit of camp equipage we could lay hands upon and started back, screaming with delight, as though the labor afforded us infinite pleasure. What little false impression the captain's remark had created vanished into thin air and the captain himself took it all back with tears in his eyes. After that the men of the two organizations were fast friends. When the Eleventh came, we repeated the performance for fear that they, too, might think we were "stuck up."

Gilmore's and the Boston Brigade bands, which alternately visited the fort on Sundays, had learned to play the "John Brown Song" so Sunday, May 12th, was a great day. Reverend George H. Hepworth[12] of the Church of the Unity, chaplain of the battalion, preached an eloquent war sermon, after which we had a grand flag-raising. Judge George D. Wells made a speech. Miss Louisa B. Rogers[13] raised the flag amid the cheers of the men, and we sang:

> Emblem of liberty,
> Float thou o'er earth and sea;
>   By thee we stand.
> Stay thou our enemies,
> God of the earth and sky;
> Under this flag we'll die,
>   God bless our land.

to the tune of "America." Then Miss Rogers was made "Daughter of the Battalion." At a dress parade that night all the troops were combined and, when Gilmore's Band, which played for us on this occasion, started up the long line from the left, they astonished and delighted everybody by playing "John Brown." This was the first time the piece was performed publicly by a military band.

---

12. A graduate of Harvard Divinity School, Hepworth founded the Church of the Unity and became so popular that his congregation soon numbered 1,500. Reverend Hepworth expressed his feelings on the outbreak of war in this manner: "From the very first I desired to go to war. I felt that no man has any right to look about him for an excuse to stay at home." Commissioned chaplain of the Forty-seventh Massachusetts on November 6, 1862, Hepworth accepted a discharge on February 11, 1863, to take an appointment as first lieutenant in the Seventy-sixth United States Colored Troops. He resigned on July 17, 1863, and returned home to write an account of his military service in Louisiana. He died in New York City on June 7, 1902. *Boston Journal,* June 9, 1902; *Massachusetts Soldiers,* 4:389; 7:300; Hepworth, *Whip, Hoe and Sword,* 9.

13. Louisa B. Rogers was the eight-year-old daughter of Captain Charles O. Rogers. 1860 Census, Massachusetts, Suffolk County, Boston, RG 29, NA.

Brigadier General Ebenezer W. Pierce[14] took command of the fort on May 15th and, ten days after, the battalion, finding that the Government would not accept their services as an organization, returned to the city. The Eleventh and Twelfth regiments got square with us by toting our luggage to the steamer and Companies D and E of the Twelfth, under Captains Nathaniel Shurtleff and Edward Saltmarsh[15] respectively, accompanied us to the Hub. Marching up State Street, headed by Gilmore's superb organization, the men sang the now famous song, which created great popular enthusiasm.

It now looked as if I must hustle if I intended to get at the enemy before he surrendered, so I ran about looking for a favorable opportunity to enlist. I finally ended up in the camp of the First Regiment in Cambridge and spent several days there, but that organization was full. Finally Senator Henry Wilson[16] advised Secretary of War Simon Cameron[17] to send for Colonel Webster's

14. Ebenezer Pierce had served in the militias of New York and Massachusetts since 1843, becoming a brigadier general in the latter state on November 7, 1855. He acted as a volunteer aide on the staff of General Benjamin Butler during the spring of 1861 and commanded the Union forces in the first battle of the war at Big Bethel, Virginia, on June 10. Pierce was commissioned colonel of the Twenty-ninth Massachusetts on December 13, 1861, lost his right arm at White Oak Swamp, and resigned on November 8, 1864. He died at Assonet, Massachusetts, on August 14, 1902. *History of Freetown*, 103–105; *Massachusetts Soldiers*, 3:277.

15. Edward C. Saltmarsh organized his company on April 27, 1861, and was commissioned captain on June 26 when it joined the Twelfth Massachusetts as Co. E. He resigned on May 1, 1862, but on June 14, 1862, received a commission as second lieutenant in the United States Marine Corps. Promoted to first lieutenant on April 12, 1864, Saltmarsh served at that rank until his resignation on July 1, 1871. He died on January 4, 1899, in the Soldiers Home in Chelsea, Massachusetts. *Boston Evening Transcript*, April 29, 1861; *Massachusetts Soldiers*, 2:34; 8:889; *Boston Herald*, January 5, 1899.

16. Born Jeremiah J. Colbath, he legally changed his name to Henry Wilson and before the age of thirty began a political career that culminated in his elevation to the United States Senate in 1855. A general in the state militia, this Massachusetts senator took the lead in recruiting the Twenty-second Massachusetts and received an appointment as its colonel on September 2, 1861. Although he resigned on October 8, the unit was thereafter known as "The Henry Wilson Regiment." Wilson was elected vice president of the United States in the election of 1872 and died in the Capitol Building on November 22, 1875. *Dictionary of American Biography*, 20:322–25; *Massachusetts Soldiers*, 2:649, 651.

17. Cameron, a senator from Pennsylvania, sought the Republican presidential nomination in 1860. His supporters assured the nomination of Abraham

regiment and, hearing that recruits were wanted, I returned to the fort and joined Company A.

Fletcher Webster, the organizer and first colonel of the Twelfth Massachusetts Infantry, was a true type of the Northern volunteer —cultured, brave and patriotic. Although, like thousands of his companions, he was without previous experience in actual war, he inherited much of that military instinct which makes true soldiers from even the crudest material when great public exigencies arise. The family had not only given to the country one of the greatest statesmen of his time, but it had produced men who successfully defended their native land in the field as well as in the forum. Captain Ebenezer Webster,[18] the grandfather of Fletcher, was a frontier ranger in the Seven Years' War that preceded the Revolutionary struggle and, at the battle of Bennington, commanded a regiment in the patriot army. The colonel's only brother, Major Edward Webster,[19] died in the service of his country in the war with Mexico.

Fletcher Webster was a genial, warm-hearted man and was greatly beloved by all who knew him. He was the favorite companion of his distinguished father and it is said that the great Defender of the Constitution was always glad to be seated at the family fireside with his gifted and witty son or to be accompanied by him upon those little fishing and hunting excursions in which both took so much delight.

Lincoln by switching their support in return for Cameron receiving a cabinet post. After appointing him secretary of war, Lincoln quickly found that his business and political experience did not translate well into military affairs and replaced him. He died at Maytown, Pennsylvania, on June 26, 1889. *Dictionary of American Biography*, 3:437–39.

18. Ebenezer Webster participated in the capture of Ticonderoga and Crown Point. He received a grant of land at Salisbury, New Hampshire, and during the Revolutionary War served as a captain at Bennington and Saratoga. A militia officer and judge in later life, the father of Daniel Webster died at Salisbury on April 22, 1806. *Salem Register*, October 25, 1849.

19. A graduate of Dartmouth College and a lawyer, in 1843 Edward Webster acted as secretary to the commission charged with establishing the boundary between the United States and Canada. He raised a company of volunteers in the Mexican-American War and was elevated to major of the Massachusetts Regiment. Major Webster died at San Angel, Mexico, on January 25, 1848. Curtis, *Life of Daniel Webster*, 2:318–20.

The colonel was a dear lover of books, well read, of generous views and graceful in expressing them. His letters were models of sweetness, without a suspicion of affectation or carelessness. Many of his father's famous state papers during the Harrison and Tyler administrations were from his pen. Whatever he touched was golden. In social life there was a fascination in his conversation none could resist. His heart was deep as a summer sky and, even in the darker hour when he saw no light, there were always bright, clear words for others, stars of the first magnitude. There was a knightly grandeur about his contempt for anything mean and a lavish way of serving friends that would have left him poor as Belisarius, though he had every year the treasures of Rome. But this very openness of heart led him to trust everyone. If the world had been like him in kindness, he would have been the glory of his race.

Fletcher Webster's conversations charmed many a group about the campfire after a weary march. Often as his spirits rose, he would quote half pages of Milton or Homer, of Butler or Cicero, until at length his father's presence came back and the orations, which were to him perfect words, ended every conversation. No one who heard him then will forget the richness of his selections, as flash after flash of eloquence fell from his lips—his eyes lighted, his gestures graceful and powerful, his whole person thrilled with feeling. When he had reached the fullness of thought, whether he discoursed on jurisprudence or metaphysics or theology, he invariably added, "So my father said."

When civil war was openly threatened in the spring of 1861, Fletcher Webster was Surveyor of the Port of Boston. He was a Democrat in politics and on the inauguration of President Lincoln immediately tendered his resignation. When the call for volunteers came, he was among the very first to respond. A few days after the famous meeting in State Street, at which the organization of the Webster Regiment began, he was met by a personal friend who said, "Fletcher, they tell me you are going into the army." "Yes," replied he, "when a man's house is burned down over his head he must needs turn soldier."

It has often been asserted that there was some prejudice against Webster at the State House in those early days of the war on account of his political affiliations. Just how much truth there is in the story will probably never be known, but if at that time there was any distrust, either of his ability or of his patriotism, on the part of any official of the State Government, it was entirely misplaced. A truer or braver soldier than Fletcher Webster never marched under the pale banner of the old Bay State.

His regiment was the first three years regiment organized, armed and equipped in Massachusetts. But Webster was somewhat crowded from the front rank and from the precedence which rightfully belonged to him in the pressure and hurry then prevailing at the office of the Adjutant General and his regiment failed of proper recognition at first, finally being designated as the Twelfth. In getting away to the front he was equally unfortunate, for long after his men had become efficient in drill and discipline they were retained at Fort Warren. It was not until after the first battle of Bull Run, when the Government was willing to accept everything that was offered, that the Webster Regiment was sent forward. Six other Massachusetts three years regiments got away before it.

The question is often asked, "Did Colonel Fletcher Webster exhibit any of that remarkable talent for public speaking so characteristic of his distinguished father?" In reply it may be said that while he never rose to such heights of eloquence, such grandeur and power in his public utterances, he was nevertheless a good speaker. His sentences were clear, concise and well worded and his stage presence was pleasing. He produced a favorable impression whenever he appeared upon the platform. In 1846 he delivered the Fourth of July oration before the City Government of Boston. The effort was one that would have been creditable to many of the leading orators of the day.

On the 17th of June, 1861, while his regiment was at Fort Warren, he attended a flag-raising on Bunker Hill by invitation of Governor Andrew. His speech upon the occasion was brief, but it contained much that is suggestive of ability as a speaker. His closing words, delivered in a natural and easy manner that completely captivated his hearers, were as follows:

"My father made the oration when the corner-stone of this monument was laid and again when it was completed. I well remember the preliminary meetings of the committee selected to decide upon its size, character, design and site. I remember the appearance of most of them, as their meetings were frequently held at my father's house. As a boy I was present at the laying of the corner-stone of this great obelisk, under whose shadow we now are. Lafayette laid the stone with appropriate and imposing Masonic ceremonies. The vast procession, impatient at unavoidable delay, broke the line of march, and in a tumultuous crowd rushed toward the orator's platform. I was saved from being trampled under foot by the strong arm of Mr. George Sullivan, who lifted me on his shoulders, shouting, 'Don't kill the orator's son!' Bearing me through the crowd, he placed me on the staging, at my father's feet. I felt somewhat embarrassed at that notice, as I do now at this unforeseen notice by His Excellency, but I had no occasion to make an acknowledgement of it.

"I also witnessed the ceremonies at the monument's completion. Many distinguished persons from all parts of our country were present, some of whom, I regret to say, would hardly like now to renew that visit or recall that scene. A few days after this I left the country and sailed for China, and, while light and eyesight lasted, I watched its lofty summit as it faded from view. I now stand again at its base and renew the vows once more on its national altar— not for the first time made—of devotion to my country, its Constitution and Union. From this spot I take my departure, like the mariner beginning his voyage, and wherever my eyes close, they will turn hitherward toward this north; and, in whatever event, grateful will be the reflection that this monument still stands— still is gilded by the earliest beams of the rising sun and that still departing day lingers and plays upon its summit."

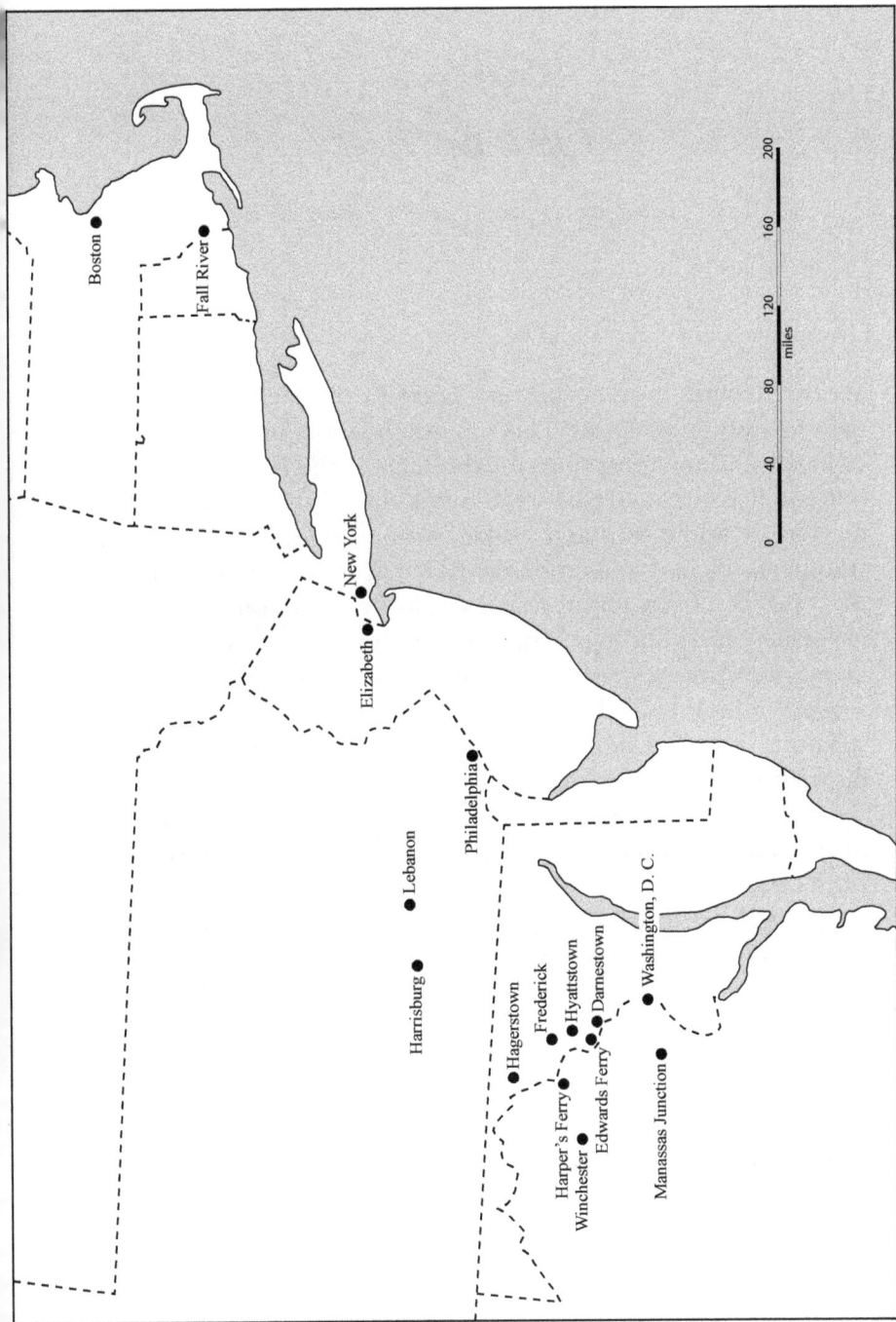

Theater of Operations, 1861.

Boston
Fall River
New York
Elizabeth
Philadelphia
Lebanon
Harrisburg
Hagerstown
Frederick
Hyattstown
Darnestown
Harper's Ferry
Winchester
Edwards Ferry
Washington, D. C.
Manassas Junction

0   40   80   120   160   200
miles

CHAPTER 3

Off to the Front

My first feeling on entering the ranks of the Webster Regiment was one of homesickness. This was not in consequence of any lack of warmth in my reception, for the men of the company, already quite well acquainted with each other, did all they could to make me feel at home. But as I looked around me and saw so many strange faces and remembered how happy I had been among the "Tigers," I was afraid that I could never become contented in my new surroundings. This feeling disappeared, however, as if by magic, when, a week or two later, I had discarded my "Tiger" toggery, which had all along rendered me uncomfortably conspicuous, and had donned that great obliterator of all personal distinctions, the matchless old army blue.

I can say deliberately that the proudest and most solemn day of my life was Wednesday, June 26, 1861. On this day we were sworn in. As the men stood with heads uncovered and right arms extended toward heaven, a weighty responsibility descended upon them, and a Voice said to every heart: "Be faithful, be fearless, be true; you are now your country's defenders." All heard it—I certainly did—and it knit us together in ties that were indissoluble.

The Fourth of July was celebrated with great éclat. The fort was full of visitors. The Eleventh had left for Camp Cameron, but the Fourteenth (afterward First Massachusetts Heavy Artillery) had arrived and the military display was imposing. Then there were exercises of a patriotic nature, with music, and at noon we had a sumptuous dinner provided by the city of Boston. Caterer Joshua B. Smith,[1] who fed the men of the Webster Regiment all

1. In addition to being the foremost caterer in Boston, Smith, although never a slave himself, fervently backed the antislavery movement and the recruitment

40

OFF TO THE FRONT   41

the time they were at the fort, did the honors. He was probably the most famous caterer of his day and generation, a former slave and a friend of Governor Andrew and Senator Charles Sumner.[2] The reader may rest assured that no one went hungry under his care. But on the Fourth, aided by the city, he outdid even himself. In addition to a long list of good things, each company had a whole roasted pig. Whether any insinuations were intended or not, it is certain that this was the only incident of a swinish nature that happened during our stay at Fort Warren.

The men of the Twelfth Regiment were probably the best cared for set of fellows that left the Bay State for the war, thanks to the Webster Committee, a body of leading Bostonians, friends of the colonel and Harvard classmates, Class of '33, organized for this special purpose. This committee contributed $14,000 at once for the equipment of the regiment and later became responsible for $70,000 more, which the Government of our great country afterward refused to make good and which was finally paid by a patriotic Bostonian and member of the committee, who has always insisted that the matter should not be made public. What wonder that Massachusetts led all other states of the Union in the splendid condition of the troops she sent to the field, when such men stood at her back? The active members of this famous committee were William Dehon,[3]

---

of black soldiers during the war. He was well regarded among Boston society, at one time worked for the family of Robert Gould Shaw, and was widely known as "Charles Sumner's Friend." When he died in Cambridge on July 5, 1879, Smith was still pursuing a claim in the Massachusetts legislature for his expenses in feeding Fletcher Webster's regiment in 1861. *Boston Journal*, February 14, 1879; *Boston Daily Advertiser*, July 7, 1879.

2. A graduate of Harvard, Charles Sumner pursued a law career prior to commencing a political career in 1846. A famed orator, he entered the Senate in 1851 and is famously remembered as the victim of a vicious personal attack while at his seat in the Senate Chamber by Representative Preston Brooks of South Carolina. An antislavery Republican, he died in Washington, D.C., on May 11, 1874. One Boston editor proclaimed him a pillar of "moral Heroism." *Dictionary of American Biography*, 18:208–14; *Boston Journal*, March 12, 1874.

3. Dehon received his Harvard degree in 1834, a year after his classmates, and began a highly successful law career. Although never personally interested in running for office, he idolized Daniel Webster so it was only natural that he should act as head of the executive committee. A colleague said of his efforts: "He generally did all that man can do for the organization and success of the

Peter Butler,[4] Henry L. Hallett,[5] George Eaton[6] and Rufus B. Bradford.[7] During the whole three years the Twelfth was in service they maintained their organization and many were their kindnesses to the boys in the field and to those home upon furloughs.

The poor fellows of the Fourteenth, I am sorry to say, did not fare as well as we did. One day, while walking about the interior of the fort, I was attracted by loud noises to a casemate occupied by a company of the Fourteenth. This commotion drew a party of our fellows over to their quarters, where a crowd had formed around a huge camp kettle filled with "bean porridge hot." They were all laughing. A soldier whose real name was Stevens,[8] but whom the boys called "Bungy," had partially stripped and was perched on a barrel beside the kettle of bean soup. An officer came in and,

---

regiment. The amount of his pecuniary contributions, first and last, to it, I cannot state; but if time is money, I think he gave more than any other, almost more than all others." In addition to financial support, Dehon sent a son off to serve in the Webster Regiment. Dehon died in Boston on May 20, 1875. W. Higginson, *Class of 1833 of Harvard*, 66–71.

4. Despite Kimball's assertion, Peter Butler was not a graduate of the Harvard class of 1833. He built his fortune as a merchant and businessman, supplying many of the emigrants who moved to what was then called "The Great West" in the 1850s. He later invested in a number of New England railroads, and his business acumen led to him serving on the financial subcommittee in 1861. He died in Boston on July 1, 1894. *Boston Daily Advertiser*, April 23, 1861; July 2, 1894.

5. Like Peter Butler, Henry L. Hallett was not a classmate of Fletcher Webster, but he did graduate from Harvard in the class of 1847. After joining the law profession, he served as a deputy district attorney until appointed United States commissioner in 1858, a position he held continually until his death in Dorchester, Massachusetts, on December 15, 1892. *Boston Journal*, December 16, 1892.

6. George Eaton was a classmate of Fletcher Webster and taught at the Boston Latin School when the war broke out. He served as the secretary of the executive committee that oversaw the operations of the one-hundred-member main committee and visited the regiment in the field as well. In September 1861 he brought back to Boston more than $8,000 that soldiers of the Webster Regiment had sent home to their families. Eaton died in Grantville, Massachusetts, on May 7, 1877. *Boston Daily Advertiser*, April 23, 1861; *Boston Evening Transcript*, October 1, 1861; W. Higginson, *Class of 1833 of Harvard*, 78–80.

7. Rufus Bradford joined the Ancient and Honorable Artillery Company in 1858 and continued in the ranks until 1875. He was a wine and liquor merchant and former member of the common council and board of alderman when he joined the Webster Committee. He died at Cottage City, Massachusetts, on July 26, 1890. Roberts, *Ancient and Honorable*, 3:299–300; *Boston Directory* (1861), 59; *Boston Journal*, July 29, 1890.

8. Stevens cannot be positively identified.

seizing him by the shoulder, demanded, "What in the world are you going to do?" "I'm going to dive," said "Bungy" quietly, "to see if I can find a bean!"

Before the men acquired sufficient skill in cooking to make palatable soups from the huge neck pieces and shins of beef that were issued to them, they were sometimes boiled whole when too tough to be cooked as steak. A chunk thus prepared was one day brought into the quarters of a company of the Fourteenth and the soldiers discovered that the meat was tainted. Much indignation and excitement ensued, which, however, soon took a good-natured turn. Someone finally suggested that the meat ought to be buried and a little later the men "fell in" in front of their casemate, where they were joined by large numbers from other companies. Officers stood about but did not interfere. A fife and drum were secured, the mimic corpse was suitably prepared and placed upon an improvised bier and when all was ready it was borne reverently through open ranks to the head of the column, the soldiers removing their caps in due form. Then the cortege proceeded with all the solemnity of a real funeral to a burial place which had been selected outside the fort, the meat was interred and I venture the opinion that, if a spectator had not been acquainted with the facts, he would not have known but what a genuine funeral was taking place.

Colonel Webster was very proud of his "boys," as he always called them and they in turn were very fond of their great-hearted colonel. Between commander and men as great a degree of confidence and personal intimacy always existed as was compatible with the requirements of the service. He was at all times extremely solicitous for the comfort and well-being of those who had placed themselves in his charge. In those early days of the war men were apt to be careless as to the laws of health. Much suffering came, also, from inexperience in cooking. Webster was familiar with these vital matters. He sought diligently to impart needed instructions. His presence in the company cookhouse was almost of daily occurrence, while his visits to the regimental hospital were frequent when there were sick ones there. In this way he won his way into every soldier's heart. They would even tell him of their personal joys and sorrows, while he listened with an interest that could not have been much keener had each and all of them been his own children. At night the sentinels about the camp often saw him gliding noiselessly from one sleeping form to another to replace the blankets that had been thrown off in sleep.

Captain Nathaniel B. Shurtleff, Jr.,[9] of Company D of the Twelfth, the first man to offer himself to Colonel Webster when the enlistment of the regiment began, was a graduate of the Boston Latin School. On the 11th of July the pupils of both the Boys' and Girls' Latin Schools came down in a body. They brought $400, which they wished to have expended for flannels, stockings, etc., for the men; a purse of $75 for Captain Shurtleff; and a handsome company emblem, in the form of an old Roman standard, surmounted by an eagle and bearing a medallion head of Daniel Webster. This incident showed that the school boys and girls of 1861 were not far behind their elders in devotion to the men in blue. One of the most pathetic incidents of the war is furnished by the fact that Captain Shurtleff, the first man in the regiment to enlist, was also the first to fall in battle, being killed at Cedar Mountain on the 9th of August, 1862. His portrait now adorns the hall of the Boys' Latin School, where also the Roman standard may be seen.

About this time I came up to the city on furlough, desiring to bid my friends good-by, and was waltzing up Summer Street with my friend Reverend Elijah Kellogg, while it rained in torrents, each of us having an umbrella. I had not thought of it before, but was soon sharply reminded by a crowd of urchins that this was not

9. Many of Nathaniel B. Shurtleff, Jr.'s, ancestors had arrived in Massachusetts on board the first three ships to carry the Pilgrims to America. Preparing for entry to Harvard at the Boston Latin School, he graduated from college in 1859. While enrolled at Harvard, Shurtleff renounced his Protestant upbringing and converted to the Roman Catholic faith, enrolling in a Jesuit institution at Frederick, Maryland. Failing health forced him to forsake the order; instead he joined a law office in Boston, where he studied under the eminent attorney William Brigham. A former member of the Independent Company of Cadets, Shurtleff used his militia and social connections to raise a company for the Twelfth Massachusetts in just three days. Commissioned captain on June 26, 1861, he served for a short period as judge advocate of General Banks's division in 1862. Captain Shurtleff was killed at Cedar Mountain on August 9, 1862. Palmer, *Necrology of Alumni of Harvard*, 513–17; *Massachusetts Soldiers*, 2:28.

"good form" in one who had become a bluecoat, they shouting, "Ha, ha! ha! ha! Soldier with an umbrella!" I folded mine and walked on, with the realizing sense that if I were to win the respect of the little ones I must make up my mind to rough it.

From noon to dewy eve and from candlelight to taps at Fort Warren was one continued round of jollity which would require a volume. Discipline was not forgotten, neither was drill, but Colonel Webster loved his boys and his boys loved him and the happier they were the better the good man liked it. One favorite amusement was to "take off" the lieutenant colonel. We had a fellow in Company A, named John J. Townley,[10] who could do it "to a T." This wag would muster the whole regiment with mock dignity and, armed with broomsticks and strips of wood, the men would fall in and go through the ceremony of dress parade, our pseudo-commander imitating the lieutenant colonel's voice and manner to a nicety. Meanwhile there was no more amused spectator than the officer satirized.

Our lieutenant colonel[11] was somewhat noted for pomposity. He had also a powerful voice and was distinguished for corpulence—especially in the abdominal region. All that saved him from the suspicion of having served his city in an aldermanic capacity was the fact that he never had any city to serve, being an inhabitant of a small town; and it is doubtful whether such a municipality would have been able to get along and pay junketing bills had he been a member of its upper board.

10. John J. Townley enlisted in Co. A, Twelfth Massachusetts, on April 20, 1861. After being taken prisoner at Second Bull Run, he was paroled and then deserted on February 28, 1863. *Massachusetts Soldiers*, 2:10.

11. Timothy M. Bryan, Jr., graduated from West Point in 1855 and was assigned to the Tenth United States Infantry as a second lieutenant on August 25, 1855. He resigned January 1, 1857, and was in Newton, Massachusetts, when the war commenced. Bryan was promptly named to the committees formed in that community to acquire uniforms and arms for their volunteers. Men with military training were in great demand, so Bryan accepted the post of lieutenant colonel of the Twelfth Massachusetts, receiving his commission on June 26, 1861. He resigned on October 7, 1862, but was commissioned colonel of the Eighteenth Pennsylvania Cavalry on December 24, 1862. Colonel Bryan received a disability discharge on December 24, 1864, and died at Vincentown, New Jersey, on April 8, 1881. Heitman, *Historical Register*, 1:257; Smith, *History of Newton*, 597–98; *Massachusetts Soldiers*, 2:3, 6:749; *Trenton (N.J.) State Gazette*, April 13, 1881.

Lieutenant Colonel
Timothy M. Bryan.
Courtesy of the U.S.
Army Heritage and
Education Center

However, notwithstanding his immense proportions, Lieutenant Colonel Timothy M. Bryan was a good drillmaster. He was also a very strict disciplinarian. It was reported that before joining with us in an endeavor to crush the Rebellion, he had been an officer in the Regular Army and that his somewhat hasty abandonment of that promising career was brought about by him having fought a duel with a brother officer which resulted in the demise of his rash opponent. When hearing this story, however, I could never quite believe it, as it never seemed wholly possible that there could be, in the Regular Army or anywhere else, so poor a marksman as his opponent must have been.

The 18th of July was a great day. It marked the presentation of a flag to the regiment on Boston Common by the ladies of Boston. We landed at Commercial Wharf, where the Second Battalion was found drawn up in line with Gilmore's Band. Preceded by the battalion, the route was through Commercial, State, Washington,

Bandmaster William J.
Martland. Courtesy of
the U.S. Army Heritage
and Education Center

School and Beacon Streets to the Common. It was, doubtless, a magnificent display, for both the battalion and regiment were at that time splendidly drilled. Indeed, it has been said that the troops moved on this occasion with the precision of a machine. The regiment had an excellent band then, William J. Martland's of Brockton.[12] As we entered State Street, Gilmore, knowing what

12. William J. Martland was leader of the North Bridgewater Band when he enlisted as bandmaster of the Twelfth Massachusetts on July 10, 1861, joined by eleven of the eighteen members. He was mustered out May 8, 1862. This wholesale muster out of the band apparently resulted from a "feeling that they had been discourteously and unjustly treated by Lieut. Col. Timothy M. Bryan" and "had their discharge brought about by their own influence." Martland enlisted a second time on November 30, 1863, as a private in Co. B, Fifty-sixth Massachusetts. Appointed principal musician on August 1, 1864, Martland was mustered out July 12, 1865. In 1885, after thirty years as bandleader, he gave up his baton, although the Martland Band name lived on long after his death at Brockton on June 6, 1906. *Massachusetts Soldiers,* 2:4; 4:772; *Boston Journal,* February 24, 1885; *Boston Herald,* June 9, 1906; *Springfield Republican,* June 10, 1906.

he was about, struck up the "John Brown Song." Martland followed suit. Then the 1,200 men of the two organizations sang the ennobling air with a spirit never excelled in this goodly city and all who had the good fortune to see and to hear them were wild with delight.

When we reached the Common, the battalion returned to the State House and, receiving Governor Andrew and staff, members of the State Government and officers of the Independent Corps of Cadets, they escorted them to the parade ground. Then we had a grand review, passing His Excellency three times, in common, quick and double-quick time. After these maneuvers we came into line, officers and color guard advanced to the front and the Honorable Edward Everett,[13] the distinguished orator, in behalf of the ladies of Boston, made one of his great speeches, presenting to Colonel Webster and the regiment a beautiful flag, which the survivors still have and still cherish. A part of Mr. Everett's speech is now in one of the school readers—*Franklin's Fifth*.[14]

Colonel Webster's reply, worthy of the son of Daniel Webster, was apt and well delivered and, in view of his death a little more than a year later at the second battle of Bull Run and of the death of so many of his associates in that and other battles of the war, the closing sentences will be seen to have a pathetic interest. The speech was reported in the newspapers of the day as follows:

"In the name and on behalf of the Twelfth Regiment of Infantry of Massachusetts, I accept from your hands, sir, this beautiful standard. I accept it with no feelings of thoughtless exultation, but regard it as a very sacred trust, bringing with it grave responsibilities and duties. We are here under arms, not for the sake of display, nor attracted by the glitter and pomp of military life. Like thousands of others, we have left our occupations and our homes and

13. A politician and orator of national reputation, Everett was a graduate of Harvard, where he served at various times as professor, overseer, and president. Terms as congressman and senator led to his nomination as vice president in 1860 on the Constitutional Union ticket. Everett died in Boston on January 15, 1865. He is today best remembered for giving the long-winded classical oration prior to Lincoln delivering his memorable address at Gettysburg. *Dictionary of American Biography*, 6:223–26.

14. Extracts of Everett's address can be found in Hillard, *Franklin Fifth Reader*, 289–92.

those who make home dear to us, for the purpose of defending, maintaining and upholding those institutions of civil government which have protected and made profitable those occupations and safe those homes and we do not propose to return with this work unaccomplished. The plainest dictates of duty to God, to our ancestry and to our children call us to this task. We are well aware of the difficulties and dangers in our path; but, trusting in Heaven and the justice of our cause, we are prepared to encounter them. When next, sir, you shall see this banner, it may offer a strong contrast to its present radiant appearance. You may see its brilliancy gone, its gay colors dimmed with smoke and its silken folds battered by shot, but it shall never bear a stain of dishonor. Some of us will bring it back, and it shall hang in our halls when

> Danger's troubled night is o'er,
> And the star of peace returns.

We offer to you and to those friends who through you have intrusted us with the keeping of this standard, our warm and heartfelt thanks for this mark of their kindness and confidence."

Then we did justice to an abundance of edibles which the city of Boston had placed under the trees of the Beacon Street Mall for us and the ladies honored us with their presence and attentions. It was, taken altogether, a grand occasion and we returned to the fort more determined than ever to behave ourselves.

It may be interesting to add that when the Webster mansion at Marshfield burned in 1878, this flag was in the library. The colonel's son, Ashburton,[15] after all had left the burning building and while flames were leaping from nearly every window, suddenly thought of it and, crying out, "My father's flag!" he leaped into

---

15. The Webster mansion, three stories and thirty-eight rooms, burned down on February 14, 1878. Although many Webster mementos had been removed long before, the main losses included books, artwork, and the family silver. Ashburton Webster, the last direct descendant of the famous statesman, died January 22, 1879, of "laryngeal consumption, brought on by a cold which he caught from exposure and over-exertion at the burning of the Webster mansion." *Lowell (Mass.) Daily Citizen and News*, February 15, 1878; *New York Herald*, January 23, 1879.

the window and brought it out, burning his hands in doing so. It was the only thing saved from the flames.

July 23d we got away. We were escorted to the landing by the Fourteenth Regiment and on reaching the city found our old friends, the "Tigers," drawn up in line to receive us. I suppose we must have been an imposing body of men, writers at the time said we were. Our faces were bronzed, the white havelocks which we wore making this more apparent. Then an element of picturesqueness was added by the red linings of our overcoats, which were neatly rolled and strapped upon the tops of our knapsacks. We numbered 1,040. Mounted upon a magnificent black horse, the gift of his college classmates, Colonel Webster marched us through the streets of Boston on the way to the battlefield.

Let the reader fancy, if he can, our beloved city threatened by some great danger—something which menaces its very existence, which calls its people into the streets, beseeching God and man to save them. Then imagine a great body of resolute men come forth who are willing, aye, more than willing, to peril life and limb in the brave attempt. Put wives and mothers and dear ones into the scene, clinging to these gallant defenders with all the strength of human love. Add a great popular acclaim, with shouts and cheers that rend the air. Have the multitude so block the way that progress is almost impossible. If you can form such a mental picture, you can get some idea of what was witnessed all along the line of march on that memorable day, for it will be remembered that this was only two days after the disaster at Bull Run and the air was full of rumors of troops fleeing, broken and disheartened, from the foe. It was the beginning of a second uprising of the North, when the remainder of those first 300,000 volunteers were hurrying to the capital, now threatened again.

In State Street, and again in Tremont Street, opposite the Common, the grand old chorus of the "John Brown Song" floated high above the tremendous popular acclaim. It gave hope and courage to the desponding and called out all that is grand, noble, uplifting and God-given in the human soul. I never witnessed anything like it before. I had never even dreamed that enthusiasm could reach such a pitch. At the Old Colony Station there was a perfect jam of humanity, and it was difficult for the men to reach the cars, but finally, after the last good-bys were said (actually the last to many of them), the long train of twenty-one cars, drawn by two engines, moved out and the dear old city of Boston was left behind.

All along the route to Fall River bonfires blazed from every commanding point. Crowds were at every station and cheers and "God bless you, boys!" were heard on every hand. On the Bay State, or the Fall River Steamboat Line, which carried the regiment to New York, the scenes were interesting. I remember one thing which, it has always seemed to me, showed the stuff that those heroes were made of. It was long after the men became quiet and supposedly asleep, with the monotonous swish, swish, swish of the water as a lullaby—a noise that is so annoying to many nervous travelers at sea. I had almost entered the "Land of Nod," when all at once, in stentorian tones, someone cried out, "Hark and hear the birds sing!" A fellow with a disposition like that could not fail of being a good soldier.

We landed at East Fourteenth Street, New York City, at 10 A.M. on the 24th. Here we were met by a large delegation of Massachusetts men, headed by the band of the New York Seventh Regiment. The march down Broadway to the Park Barracks was an ovation resembling that in Boston, only that the scenes of personal leave-taking were missing. We again sang the "John Brown Song." They had never heard it before and the people were at first startled as the inspiring air rose with such tremendous volume. Then they listened spellbound and finally broke out in deafening cheers.

Our route was via Elizabeth and Harrisburg to Baltimore. Fruit trees were in full bloom and the country looked beautiful—beautiful enough to fight for. At Lebanon, Pennsylvania we had to wait an hour or more on account of a break in one of the engines. It was high noon on July 25th. The journey from Boston had been a perfect ovation, but somewhat tiresome, crowded together as we were, and we naturally hailed with great pleasure this opportunity to stretch our legs. Springing from the cars, the men scampered in every direction like children let loose from the restraints of school. The news of our coming flashed from house to house and people flocked to the station, many of them bringing the dinners from their tables that they had prepared for their own families. Long lines of noble-looking women occupied the plank walks on either side of the train, slicing and buttering bread with the regularity of machinery. Fair ones brought the platters from their dinner tables, loaded with steaming roasts intended for family meals, and carved and passed them to the soldiers, as freely as they would have done to members of their own family circles had our hungry pack not arrived. We ate till we could eat no more.

I never saw such hospitality to strangers before or a more generous people. Officers made speeches, the band played patriotic airs and soldiers and people mingled in absolute freedom and unrestraint. It was afterward said, though I do not assert this as a positive fact, that many a soldier boy and bonnie lass exchanged addresses and breathed vows that in due time ripened into something more enduring than chance acquaintance. The last scene that met my eye as our train moved away was that of a beautiful woman, who said she had a son at the front, standing upon the depot platform with a basket of eggs and crying as if her heart would break because no one would take them as a gift. We could not take them—we were overloaded already with what the people had given us—but we gave her a "God bless you" and a parting cheer that doubtless sent her home thoughtful and happy.

Just this side of Baltimore we loaded our muskets and ammunition was distributed, but we had no occasion to use it. We were bound for Washington, but orders reached Colonel Webster here to proceed to Harpers Ferry. We finally reached the little straggling village called Sandy Hook, opposite the scene of so many stirring episodes, on the morning of the 27th, and went into camp a mile eastward in beautiful Pleasant Valley. The boys, weary after their long ride, alighted from the cars of the Baltimore and Ohio Railroad after a four days' journey from Boston and they settled down for rest and sleep and dreams of those they had left behind, while the lovely Potomac River flowed peacefully on, unconscious of the part she was henceforth to play in the now opening drama.

CHAPTER 4

Into Maryland

A hundred days had come and gone since the organization of the regiment was begun, but we were at last at the front. The authorities had finally become convinced that the services of the whole first 300,000 volunteers are needed, but it took the great disaster at Manassas to accomplish it. Regiments now poured in from every part of the loyal North and the firm step and ringing cheers of the advancing legions gave promise of final victory.

A few days after our tents were pitched in Pleasant Valley, on the Maryland side of the Potomac, opposite Harpers Ferry, a familiar figure appeared in camp. It was none other than General Nathaniel Banks,[1] who had been assigned to the command of the Department of the Upper Potomac. We were so pleased that a distinguished son of our own state should have been selected to lead us that we named our camp "Camp Banks" in his honor.

General Banks had a somewhat remarkable history. Of humble parentage, he had been obliged, at an early age when most boys are enjoying school privileges, to work in a cotton mill. The days were long, the toil almost incessant and very exhaustive and the

---

1. Starting from humble beginnings, Nathaniel P. Banks made a mark on the local and state level. Having filled the offices of local editor, legislator, congressman, Speaker of the House of Representatives, and finally governor of Massachusetts, Banks was president of the Illinois Central Railroad when war broke out. Although he indicated a willingness to act as quartermaster general, political considerations led to his appointment as major general of volunteers on May 16, 1861. Following a lackluster career as a field commander, he resigned on January 28, 1864, and, after being reelected to Congress several times, died in Waltham, Massachusetts, on September 1, 1894. *New York Herald*, May 31, 1861; *Boston Journal*, September 1, 1894; *Boston Herald*, September 2, 1894.

surroundings sufficiently depressive to well nigh stifle every ambitious tendency. But the young hero had within him that divine spirit of unrest that would not allow him to become content with a life of unambitious toil in a land where life's highest prizes are within the reach of even the humblest. Accordingly we find him poring over his books long after his associates had retired and snatching from the busy hours of the day every unoccupied moment, that he might fit himself for duties higher than those of an every-day laborer. The world not many years afterward heard of the "Bobbin Boy" as the governor of Massachusetts. It was the knowledge of these facts, as much as anything else, that so endeared him to his soldiers, for they, too, were mostly from the humbler walks of life and could therefore appreciate the difficulties he had overcome in rising to the position he then occupied.

The Second Massachusetts had been in this department, under General Robert Patterson,[2] several weeks and had been up the Shenandoah Valley as far as Winchester, Virginia. On the 3d of August, the Thirteenth Massachusetts came. The latter marched from Hagerstown, Maryland, some twenty miles away, and two companies of the Twelfth went down the road to meet them. The sons of the old Bay State began to feel quite at home in their new surroundings.

The scenery around Harpers Ferry, as everyone knows, is grand. Mountains rise like huge pillars of blue and verdant valleys nestle cozily among them. The beautiful Potomac winds in and out as though it were playing hide and seek with the rest of nature and, where it bursts through the mountains of the Blue Ridge a little above the ferry, the view is awe-inspiring. Verily, the Devine Architect has accomplished a masterstroke at this point equal to any to be seen upon our continent. One is lost in wonder as he gazes

2. A veteran of the War of 1812 and Mexican-American War, Patterson was appointed major general of the Pennsylvania militia on April 15, 1861. He was assigned to organize a militia army and instructed to defend the upper Potomac. Unjustly censured for his part in the Bull Run campaign, Patterson was mustered out July 27, 1861, and, despite repeated applications for further command, he spent the remainder of the war attending to his investments. When he died in Philadelphia on August 7, 1881, Robert Patterson's estate was estimated to be worth as much as $3 million. Heitman, *Historical Register*, 1:775; *New York Herald*, August 8, 1881; *Philadelphia Inquirer*, August 8, 1881; *Irish American Weekly*, August 20, 1881.

upon the river's rugged pathway and marvels that so suggestive a scene should be marred by roar of cannon and clash of arms.

Great curiosity was immediately excited by what appeared to be a signal tower on the summit of Maryland Heights. Officers viewed it through their field glasses, while the men gossiped and wondered. Before we had been a week in Pleasant Valley it was whispered about that Lieutenant George W. Orne[3] had volunteered to climb the mountain in the night, with a small body of men, and ascertain its nature. Volunteers were plenty, as in that early period of the war the men were anxious for anything that promised excitement and adventure. It was my good fortune to be among the "daring spirits" and after taps we set out on our perilous journey with muskets loaded and capped, forty rounds in our cartridge boxes and three days' rations in our haversacks. Instructions were given not to speak above a whisper. If we became separated in the ascent, the lieutenant was to whistle in imitation of a whippoorwill and we were to close in on him. The night was intensely dark and the underbrush uncomfortably dense. We toiled upward, through tangled underbrush and over jagged rocks, occasionally softly whistling to each other and keeping our line and our distances as perfectly as the nature of the ground would allow. Many were our falls and scratches, but we did not mind them, for we knew there was "plenty of room on top" and that glory awaited us there. We were continually upon the *qui vive* and never afterward, in all our three years of service, through many of the greatest campaigns and battles of the war, did we keep ourselves more constantly prepared to encounter the enemy.

Toward daylight we neared the mysterious tower, surrounded it and waited. In the gray dawn we closed in upon it. No rattle of musketry greeted us and no groans of wounded and dying—only the loud laughter of the whole party as we discovered that after all our hard climbing we had been "sold." It was a signal tower, sure enough, but there were no evidences of bloodthirsty foes—on the contrary, only friends.

3. Commissioned second lieutenant of Co. A, Twelfth Massachusetts, on June 26, 1861, Orne was wounded at Antietam and died October 6, 1862, in a hospital in Frederick, Maryland. *Massachusetts Soldiers*, 2:9; *Boston Traveler*, October 7, 1862.

Lieutenant George W.
Orne. Courtesy of the
U.S. Army Heritage and
Education Center

While others started in various directions to explore the locality, I climbed to the top of the observatory and enjoyed one of
the grandest views that my eyes ever feasted upon—sufficient to
make me forget for the moment all the toil and bruises of the
ascent. Harpers Ferry, with its burned bridge and ruined Government workshops, looked black and forbidding, but the Valley of
the Shenandoah, dotted by clumps of trees and threaded by the
beautiful stream from which it takes its name, lay before us in spar-
kling grandeur, walled in by mountains. Everywhere mountains
—Bolivar and Loudoun Heights—and cultivated farms and beautiful stretches of water glittered like diamonds in the morning
sun. Hill and dale, field and forest, at just the right distance from
each other, with here and there a glimpse of the Shenandoah,
shining like a silver thread in the green carpet of nature, formed a
picture more beautiful than the wildest dream of the artist. Below

Harpers Ferry, and for a mile above, the Potomac is wild and tur-
bulent, flowing over a jumble of rocks. It was so beautiful I could
scarcely realize that it was real and only wondered how it could
ever enter into the hearts of men to wage cruel war upon each
other in such a place.

On the western side of Maryland Heights the rise is gradual and
a good road reaches the summit from that direction. Farmhouses
appear here and there and a little way off stands a small schoolhouse. As I wake from my reverie in the observatory my comrades
are returning from their tour of inspection. They bring the information that the observatory was built by the Third Wisconsin
Regiment; that John Brown[4] and his men encamped upon this
beautiful spot before they made their raid upon Harpers Ferry
in October, 1859; that they frequently visited the farmhouses in
the vicinity to purchase necessary supplies; and that in the little
schoolhouse down the road they held their meetings and discussed their plans for freeing the slaves of Virginia. "This is where
the war really began," said our lieutenant and we started down-
ward chanting "Glory, Glory, Hallelujah."

A new revelation began to dawn on us. Were we Brown's suc-
cessors? Was the war upon which we had entered a continuation
of old Osawatomie's mad endeavor to strike the fetters from four
millions of bondmen? The thought was a stupendous one and,
while the majority of our party would not have it so, declaring that
the war was solely to restore the Union, to me, realizing the fact
that Virginia had arisen as one man to defend her peculiar institution and considering the effect Brown's raid had had upon the
sentiment of the entire South, it was plain that there would never
be any lasting peace until slavery was uprooted. From that time
forward my motive was "liberty *and* Union" and my only wonder
afterward was that the Emancipation Proclamation was so long

4. Boston being a hotbed of antislavery sentiment, the local press contained
extensive coverage of John Brown's attack on the Harpers Ferry Arsenal and his
subsequent execution on December 2, 1859, for treason against the Commonwealth of Virginia. This sentiment was best captured by a quotation in the *Boston
Liberator* that prophesied the coming war: "We may be done with John Brown,
but he has not done with us. He has summoned this nation to judgment." He
was often called "Osawatomie Brown," a reference to his questionable actions in
Kansas in 1856. *Boston Liberator*, December 30, 1859.

delayed. Imperceptibly almost, though surely, the soul of the old martyr was "marching on."

An incident in which comedy and pathos were strangely intermingled happened soon after this. A man was ordered to be drummed out. Inquiry revealed the fact that the man had accompanied us to the front, without having been sworn in, under a specified understanding with our officers that he was to be detailed for a certain kind of duty and that the officers had failed to perform their part of the contract. The man was therefore supposed to be insubordinate and unworthy to associate with men of honor. He must therefore be cast out and set adrift, hundreds of miles from home, without money and without friends, simply that the petty rule of a *coterie* of would-be martinets might be established, for neither the real good of the service nor the fate of the Republic would have been sacrificed if the officers had kept their agreement with the man.

At the appointed hour I followed the crowd to the guardhouse to witness the ceremony. The man was ordered out. His buttons were stripped off and a procession was formed in the usual way, with two men at shoulder arms, then the culprit, and after him two more men at charge bayonets. On ahead were drummer and fifer. The whole was under command of a sergeant. When all was ready, the order "Forward, march!" was given. The fifer now began to offend the air with a doleful tune, called the "Rogue's March" in military parlance, but known to us as "Poor Old Robinson Crusoe" and to the Britishers in our ranks as "Tight Little Island," and the drummer set up his monotonous clatter. Slowly this odd procession moved around the camp several times and the crowd increased rapidly. Before they had proceeded far, the path upon which they were marching became walled in on both sides by lines of human faces, most of them glowing with perfect satisfaction at each look of chagrin or pain on the countenance of the poor victim, while yells of wild delight were going up from hundreds of throats.

The poor fellow looked troubled at first, but after a while, seemingly in utter scorn of those who were deriding him, he gained courage, and now ensued a scene that beggars description. As the weird music proceeded, the prisoner began to beat time, apparently with his entire body, hands and arms, feet and legs, head and face, all gesticulating in the wildest fashion. As louder grew the shouts of the spectators, more demonstrative became the culprit, until it seemed as if he had reached the very limit of human possibilities in the direction in which he was aiming; he strove to give himself up with a perfect abandon to what he evidently considered showing contempt for his persecutors. Thus the strange scene went on, the disorder and noise each moment increasing, both on the part of the spectators and prisoner. It was a great exhibition of nerve.

I forgot, for the time, my feeling of pity for the poor fellow, becoming charmed with his heroism, and cheered and shouted with the rest as he went from one company street to another. By-and-by the tour of the camp was completed and the procession filed out into the road. Then began the bestowal of gifts and for half an hour after the guard had left him the man was kept busy in picking up pieces of money and other tokens of regard. It seemed evident, from the strong hold the man had obtained upon the sympathies of his late companions, that more seeds of insubordination and contempt for military authority had been sown in that brief hour than could have been scattered by a hundred drum-outs. I afterward learned that the man enlisted in another regiment and was ever afterward a brave and faithful soldier, becoming a captain before the close of the war.

Ours was the first regiment to arrive in the department clad in regulation blue and consequently we soon acquired the title of "blue breeches." Up to that time, strangely enough, gray had been in fashion, relieved occasionally by other gaudy colors, in which red figured conspicuously. Consequently we were quite noticeable for a while. The raw troops of 1861 were just a little independent and saucy, not always showing proper respect for colonels, generals and other necessary appendages of an army. When the Webster Regiment arrived at Harpers Ferry it was assigned to the brigade commanded by General John Abercrombie,[5] a genius "born to

5. John J. Abercrombie was a native of Tennessee and had graduated from West Point in 1822. He served in the Mexican-American War as major of the Fifth United States Infantry and was colonel of the Seventh United States Infantry when the Civil war started. Boasting almost forty years of military service and two

command" and one who had been reared in the atmosphere of West Point and the Regular Army. So he was greatly shocked by our nonchalance and obvious contempt of military nonsense, afterwards called discipline. But we didn't care. We were bound to see the country, anyway. Had not the recruiting officer of the Regulars posted his bills in the vicinity of our homes time and again promising opportunities for "study, travel and promotion"?

The enemy was not uncomfortably near and, save a little necessary restraint, we at once began to take things free and easy. It is true that a guard was posted about the camp, but of what account was a guard so early in the war, when all around outside the country looked so inviting and beautiful? Besides, we were opposite Harpers Ferry! So we roamed wherever we pleased and in time the country became well reconnoitered for miles in every direction. One day some officer, who had the necessary courage, sought General Abercrombie's opinion of the Webster Regiment. The "old man" replied that we were "too damned independent." Pressed for further explanation, he added: "You can't go anywhere outside the lines within ten miles but what one of those damned blue breeches comes swaggering along and asks me for a match or chew of tobacco."

Of course, being Yankees, we went everywhere soldiers were allowed to go and investigated methods of farming and phases of Southern life. We found the land of the Calverts rather behind the times, but as a rule the people treated us kindly and I do not think they had much to complain of in our behavior, except that we talked a good deal with the darkies and were extremely fond of hoecakes. One thing, however, I own, we did criticize unmercifully and that was their architecture. Why should they live in such ugly structures, with huge chimneys built out of doors, was something we could never understand. I remember passing one day on the march a modern-looking house, built of brick, with green

---

brevets for combat service, Abercrombie was elevated to brigadier general on August 31, 1861. His Regular Army ways did not sit well with his Massachusetts volunteers, one of whom commented in mid-April 1862: "Our respect for him had descended to the point of calling him 'Old Crummy.'" He was mustered out of the volunteer service on June 24, 1864, and retired from the U.S. Army on June 12, 1865. Abercrombie died January 3, 1877, at Roslyn, Long Island. Warner, *Generals in Blue*, 3; Heitman, *Historical Register*, 1:150; Davis, *Three Years in the Army*, 52; *New York Tribune*, January 6, 1877; *Philadelphia Inquirer*, January 8, 1877.

blinds. It was set back from the road and resembled in many ways a New England homestead. The regiment halted involuntarily and stared at it. Colonel Webster said: "I'll bet that fellow came from Massachusetts." Someone went to the door to inquire and, sure enough, found that the building was originally built by a son of the old Bay State who was then living in the West. We gave three rousing cheers and passed on.

Our ponderous lieutenant colonel often added to our stock of camp fun, as well as increased our misery by his curious freaks while in command and his odd method of enforcing order. I remember one notable instance of this in which the whole regiment was convulsed with laughter, although, of course, for the time obliged to suppress it. They were at dress parade. The adjutant had given the usual orders—"To the rear, open order, etc."—and the men were standing like statues, while the band was marching down the line, playing a waltz which for beauty and superb rendering I have never heard excelled at any military display. It was a beautiful scene, just at sunset on a perfect autumn day, with all Nature hushed in silence save the twittering of the birds and the murmuring of the brook in the forest back of camp. I happened to be on guard just behind the regimental line and was watching the impressive scene. All went well until the band had neared the left of the regiment, when our lieutenant colonel, who happened that night to be in command, standing with folded arms in front of the colors, fancied he saw a slight wavering or uneasiness in one of the companies. Perhaps they were scratching themselves, but I do not remember. His exalted ideas of military propriety, however, could not tolerate such a flagrant breach of discipline and, straightening himself up to his full height, he cried in a voice but slightly removed from the majestic crash of thunder or the roar of a battery of artillery in a battle, "What in hell are you wiggling about so for in Company A? Have you got wurrums?"

For some trivial offense, a soldier from Company G was put into the regimental guardhouse, where offenders were degraded and punished by being forced to perform police duty and other menial work. He was honored one morning by being placed in command of the squad that was to sweep the company streets. As they were to march by regimental headquarters, he resolved to show Colonel Webster and his associates with what alacrity and fidelity they were about to enter upon their duties. So just before reaching the colonel's tent he halted his squad and called them to attention. He cautioned them to remember that they were soldiers, told them to brace up as they were about to pass in review, gave the order, "Right shoulder, shift!" and then, in a loud voice, "Forward, march!"

As the imposing procession neared the colonel's quarters, the command was given, "Shoulder arms!" at which all the brooms were brought down with the regularity of clockwork. By this time it had become noised about that something unusual was going on and men ran from all directions to see the fun. The field and staff officers of the regiment stood in front of their tents and quite a number of staff officers and others from brigade and division headquarters happened to be present. Just as all were wondering what was coming next, the commander of the broom brigade brought matters to a climax by crying out at the top of his voice, "Double slow, march!" This last order, amid screams of laughter, was strictly obeyed.

In our company we had a good-natured Irishman, who had acquired the nickname of "Dublin,"[6] from his so often telling the boys of that being the place where he was born. One day, just before company drill, he for some reason wished to be excused and appealed to the captain, without offering any very good reason for not wishing to turn out, and was refused. He fell in with the rest of us and upon the captain's taking command, after it had been formed by the orderly sergeant, the first order given was: "Right face, without doubling—forward, march!" The captain was surprised and the rest of us amused to see him "streaking it" for his tent. His commanding officer hailed him as follows: "Say, Pat, where are you going?" "Sure, captain," came the quick-witted response, "I thought you had excused me, as you said, 'Right face, without Dublin.'" "Dublin" was excused from that drill.

Jeremiah Dyer,[7] of Company D, was very thin. He was also very narrow-shouldered and not being tall could not be considered in any way of imposing appearance. He never felt that touch of

6. Dublin cannot be further identified.
7. Dyer enlisted as a private in Co. D, Twelfth Massachusetts, on June 26, 1861. Despite his thin stature, he was wounded at Second Bull Run and left the service on a disability discharge on February 5, 1863. *Massachusetts Soldiers*, 2:25.

pardonable pride that came to fortunate men who were singled out from their fellows for guard duty in front of headquarters because of their soldierly bearing. Yet Jere was a pretty good soldier, nevertheless. He did his duty better than many others and at all times, particularly just before pay day, was able to pass muster.

Jere got along well enough in the rear rank, having plenty of room there, but when the company line was being formed and the men were being counted off in two ranks—"one, two"—"one, two"—he almost invariably managed some way to become number one. This, when the sergeant gave the order "In two ranks form company," brought Jere into the front rank. Then his rear rank man had no end of trouble. It was fun, though, for bystanders to watch proceedings in Company D when Jere was in the front rank. Those behind him, when the men were marching company front, wavered like tall grass in a cyclone. They usually stood it for a while and struggled to maintain the required thirteen inches from breast to back, treading now and then upon the heels of their file leaders and stumbling along as though they had too much "commissary," but in the end Company D's short-legged lieutenant, whom the boys called "Bobby," was compelled to take cognizance of the state of affairs. Then the company had to be halted and Jere had to be told to change places with his rear rank man. After that all went well in Company D, save the fun that the incident occasioned; but this, although not military, was harmless and did not interfere with the carrying out of every requirement of Hardee.

It went on this way for some time and Jere was the butt of his comrades, having to stand numberless gibes and jokes without an opportunity to fire back. But it is a long road, indeed, that has no turn and Jere's turn came at last. One day Company D stood in line upon the old battlefield of Bull Run, trying to resist the onslaught of General James Longstreet's legions and bullets were flying about like hailstones. The little lieutenant was flitting from right to left of the company, directing the fire of his men and urging them up to their bloody work, when his eyes fell upon Jere, standing a few paces to the rear, but pegging away as fast as he could load and discharge his piece. Thinking it a case requiring his attention, "Bobby" patted Jere familiarly upon the shoulder and said, ""Stand right up there in front, Jere, so that you can see where to fire." Jere obeyed cheerfully, but as he did so replied in his clear, shrill voice, loud enough to be heard by all who were near him, "On drill and dress parade, it's get into the rear rank, Jere, but the front rank is good enough for poor Jere now, isn't it lieutenant?"

We found the Chesapeake and Ohio Canal, which lies beside the river, an excellent place for bathing. Many found their way to the Virginia shore in one way and another and came back with startling stories about the near proximity of Stonewall Jackson.[8] Indeed, so excited did the pickets sometimes become that false alarms were raised and we would be routed out only to stand in line an hour or so and then be dismissed. Jackson was all of ten miles away and probably had no idea of troubling us just then. Rattlesnakes were nearer, however, and more plentiful than rebels. One fine specimen was killed in camp measuring three feet nine inches and having six rattles.

Our picket line was upon the towpath of the Chesapeake and Ohio Canal, only a few feet from the river's bank. My company was on picket one day and, after being relieved from guard, the captain sent me back to camp upon an errand. I walked down the towpath to the lock, upon which we usually crossed to the other side, and when I got there I noticed a well-dressed citizen on the other side, evidently getting ready to attempt the perilous passage. It was perilous, too, as we were obliged to walk upon a single stick of timber only a foot or so wide. I crossed to his side of the muddy water, but when only a few yards away from the river I was startled by cries for help and quickly returned to the lock. As I arrived, two men were pulling the unlucky citizen out of the water, into which he had fallen from the narrow pathway, his fine raiment and shiny silk hat not looking so smooth as when I left him a moment before. I afterward learned that the unfortunate man was Governor William Sprague of Rhode Island.[9] When pulled out, he was the

8. Thomas J. Jackson graduated from West Point in 1846, received two brevets for meritorious service in the Mexican-American War, and resigned in 1852. Given the nickname of "Stonewall" for his conduct as a rebel general at Manassas, Jackson became the bugaboo for Union forces on the Upper Potomac and in the Shenandoah Valley over the following year. After achieving the rank of lieutenant general, he was mortally wounded at Chancellorsville and died on May 10, 1863. Warner, *Generals in Gray*, 151–52; Heitman, *Historical Register*, 1:568.

9. William Sprague was governor of Rhode Island at the outbreak of war and enthusiastically supported the Union as his family cotton mills made a fortune

most demoralized governor I ever saw. We all had a good laugh, the governor joining heartily.

The military student need not search history for accounts of the battle of Hyattstown—he will not find it even mentioned. It is now given for the first time—as an "exclusive." The brigade reached the "field" soon after daylight on the 19th of August, 1861. The "enemy" was unaware of our intentions or approach; indeed, we did not even know ourselves what great things we were about to accomplish. An alert cavalryman had come thundering down the road to brigade headquarters with the startling announcement that he had seen a rebel enter a house in the outskirts of the town and he had reason to believe that "the woods were full of them." Bugles were blown, drums rattled and staff officers galloped in all directions with orders. Regiments fell into line, cartridge boxes were filled and all the customary preparations made for a bloody encounter. A heavy skirmish line advanced upon the astonished inhabitants of the town and, surrounding the house pointed out by the brave trooper, captured the "rebel." He was brought to General Abercrombie's headquarters, where he was immediately recognized as the servant of Captain Shurtleff of the Twelfth. He had been prowling about the country for eggs for the captain's breakfast. He was still wearing the gray uniform which the regiment had worn in Fort Warren and this had caused all the trouble, but after that the man wore blue.

In due time we found ourselves at Darnestown, a place consisting of half a dozen rude cabins, at the mouth of a small stream called Muddy Branch. We stopped here some time and while here the first death occurred in the regiment. It was that of Rufus A. Peck[10] of Stoughton, killed accidentally while slaughtering beef.

---

in supplying its armies. A thorough patriot, Sprague served briefly as an aide at Bull Run and declined a commission as brigadier general to spend the war years as governor and senator. One Rhode Island newspaper said that "he devotes his money, gives his time, uses his office, offers his whole of life to the service of his country, sharing the toil and danger of the common soldier, while contributing the power of a thousand soldiers by his untiring activity, his unwearied exertions." He died in Paris on September 11, 1915. *Dictionary of American Biography*, 17:475–76; *Springfield Republican*, September 14, 1861.

10. Rufus Peck enlisted in Co. I, Twelfth Massachusetts, on June 26, 1861, and was accidentally killed near Darnestown, Maryland, on September 23, 1861, leaving a wife and two children in Stoughton. One of Peck's comrades explained the

The funeral was peculiarly sad and it made a deep impression upon us, being the first we had witnessed.

We got to Edwards Ferry, or vicinity, too late to participate in the battle of Ball's Bluff, but not too late to listen to the story of that ill-fated movement from the lips of the men of the Fifteenth and Twentieth Massachusetts. Our boys were not favorably impressed with the generalship there displayed and it must be confessed that we began to look forward to future campaigns with diminished confidence in our leaders. The men were brave enough and they deserved to be better handled.

I remember witnessing the death of one poor fellow—a type of those who so bravely faced that murderous fire on the river's bank—in a cabin not far from the ferry and the scene made a lasting impression upon me. I think he was one of Colonel Edward Baker's[11] men, but do not know for certain. He was young, apparently not over sixteen or eighteen, with a face as fair and delicate as a girl's. A little knot of comrades surrounded the cot upon which he was lying and they were doing all that comrades could do to cheer his last moments. The little fellow did not complain —he was even "willing to die for the flag," as he expressed it. He spoke of his father and mother, but always with the request that those about him would tell them that he had tried to do his duty. This thought of duty seemed uppermost in his mind and he would appeal occasionally to a rough-bearded soldier by his side to substantiate his claim. "I did not leave till the order came, did I,

accident: "While assisting to slaughter, some distance from camp, the beam from which the beeve was hung, fell, striking him on the head, after which he lived only two hours and a half." Another soldier described his hasty burial: "Having no coffin, we knocked some boards from an old barn and made a box and buried him with military honors." They took up a collection and sent $200 to his widow, a typical gesture for early deaths but one that would quickly be abandoned as casualties began to mount. *Massachusetts Soldiers*, 2:59; *Lowell Daily Citizen and News*, October 22, 1861.

11. A sitting senator from Oregon and a Mexican-American War veteran, Edward Baker was commissioned colonel of the Seventy-first Pennsylvania on June 22, 1861. A promotion to major general had been offered but not yet accepted when he was killed at Balls Bluff, Virginia, on October 21, 1861. One Bay State newspaper called Baker's death "one of the greatest calamities that has befallen the nation since the beginning of this dreadful war." Heitman, *Historical Register*, 1:183; *Salem Observer*, October 26, 1861.

Sergeant?" he would ask and assurances that he did not, touch-
ingly given, would cause his face to brighten with a smile. He had
been shot while in the water and his comrades had got him over
somehow. As the light of life faded from his face and his sweet
spirit fled upward, our eyes filled with tears and I thought how
proud that poor mother would be of her brave little son when she
heard of his heroism.

CHAPTER 5

Army Housekeeping

I am sometimes asked how men lived in the army—how they were sheltered, what they ate, how they cooked their food, etc. These questions, of course, are from young persons and from older people who were not in the army during the war.

The systems that were employed to feed and shelter troops may be divided into three—that in vogue in the various States before the regiments proceeded to the front; that which pervaded in the early part of the war, in the days of Sibley and A tents, when company cooks were allowed; and that which, after the spring of 1862 compelled every man to become his own cook and housekeeper.

In Massachusetts, as well as other States, when men were enlisting for three years and were forming themselves into companies and regiments, they were placed in camps for organization, equipment and drill. While in these camps they were fed principally by caterers employed and paid by the State governments and were sheltered by either A tents or barracks. These latter were constructed of rough boards, to be sure, but they were comfortable and sufficiently tight to exclude wind and rain. Both tents and barracks were provided, in most cases, with floors and straw was furnished in abundance for bedding. The buildings were generally of uniform size, those for enlisted men accommodating companies of one hundred each.

When the call was sounded for breakfast, dinner and supper the men assembled in one rank and marched to the cookhouse by companies for rations. Some companies, however, provided themselves with tables and other accessories for successful and orderly housekeeping. In such cases rations were not distributed

68

individually, but the men gathered about common boards and enjoyed something like domestic felicity. There was very little grumbling, as the food was usually well-cooked and abundant, though plain, of course. It consisted of meat, bread, vegetables, rice, beans, etc. and coffee and tea were regularly served. Fresh beef was oftenest used in soups and those were palatable and nourishing. Each man was provided with a tin plate, dipper, spoon, knife and fork. To meet the expense attending this housing, feeding and equipping of volunteers in the various States, the General Government allowed a specific amount, but a great deal was done for the comfort of the men by the State authorities which was not authorized by the limit the Government had established.

In the early part of the war or until the spring of 1862, the army was provided with tents, chiefly of the A or Sibley variety. Each of these accommodated from fifteen to twenty men, consequently each company had five. They were pitched in straight rows by companies, the spaces between the rows being called company streets. The tents at the heads of the rows were occupied by the non-commissioned officers. The occupants of each tent constituted what was called a mess and these little military families were called first mess, second mess, etc., from the "non-coms" down. Opposite the heads of the companies, running lengthwise of the camp, were the tents of the captains and lieutenants and back of these were those of the field and staff. At the entrance of the camp were tents for the guard and sutler and, at convenient and appropriate points, were located those for the band, hospital, teamsters, etc.

A regimental camp usually covered three or four acres and was very pretty and picturesque, particularly in the evening, when thousands of lights gleamed beneath the white canvas houses and singing and laughter over joke or story fell pleasantly upon the ear. Then there were the campfires in the open air and the little groups of jolly fellows that surrounded each one of them and the band in front of the colonel's quarters discoursing the sweetest of music. No wonder that pleasant memories of these fascinating scenes still linger in the mind of the veteran and that attempts are so often made to commemorate them in the modern Grand Army campfire.

At the foot of each company street was the cookhouse. This comprised usually a fly or shanty to cover the cooking utensils and supplies, a pole suspended between two crotched sticks upon which was hung the camp kettles and, underneath them, when a meal was being prepared, a blazing fire. These camp kettles were of sheet iron, of the capacity of about four gallons, and in them were boiled coffee, soup, rice, beans, salt beef, etc. Back of the cook's shanty—at any rate in New England regiments, whose men were particularly ingenious—was the greatest wonder of the camp, the company oven. These useful contrivances were constructed above ground of flat stones, plastered inside and out with clay, and were about three feet high. They looked much like big turtles. In them were baked bread, light and delicious, and beans that delighted and would still delight Bostonians. Beef, too, was roasted in them in great shape.

Many things were issued that were not actually needed or desired in camp or rather that were not required in such superabundance. Among these the most prominent article was salt pork. Often a barrel of this would be accumulated for which we could find no suitable use. So an arrangement was effected by which we could dispose of it and of other superfluities, for money, and in this way were created company funds, out of which were purchased many things necessary in the preparation of dainties. It would have astonished our wives and mothers could they have broken in upon us during meal hours, when these choice and unusual dishes were served. Men belonging to regiments from the Middle and Western States doubtless learned many useful lessons in the culinary art from the cute Yankees of the East, for they often visited their camps, looked on with interest and sometimes were allowed to even sample the goodies. But these extra dishes were somewhat dependent upon an extended occupation of one camping ground and a move was sure to result in a sad interruption. Still, we always had enough good to eat, while this system of supply lasted.

Officers were allowed money *in lieu* of supplies and they therefore purchased their rations from the Brigade Commissary. They were also allowed servants, of course, and in camp fared much better than the enlisted men. The monthly allowances of officers in the infantry regiments were as follows: colonel, six rations, computed at $54, and two servants; lieutenant colonel, five rations, $45, and two servants; major, four rations, $36, and two servants; captain, four rations, $36, and one servant; and first and second lieutenants the same as captains. Staff officers had the allowances of officers of their ranks, with the addition of horses, and their monthly pay was $10 more.

It may be of interest, in this connection, to know of what a soldier's daily ration consisted. In the Regular Army—and Volunteers were upon the same standing—it was as follows: 12 ounces of pork or bacon, or 1 pound 4 ounces of fresh or salt beef; 1 pound 2 ounces of bread or flour, or 12 ounces of hard bread or 1 pound 4 ounces of corn meal; .64 of a gill of beans; 1.06 of an ounce of rice or 1.05 of an ounce of desiccated vegetables; 1.06 of an ounce of coffee, or .24 of an ounce of tea; 2.04 ounces of sugar; .32 of a gill of vinegar; .16 of an ounce of sperm candles; .64 of an ounce of soap; .16 of a gill of salt; 1 ounce of mixed vegetables.

Early in the war Congress increased the ration as follows: 22 ounces of bread or flour or 1 pound of hard bread, instead of what had been previously allowed; fresh beef was to be issued as often as the commanding officer of a regiment or detachment required it, *in lieu* of salt meat; beans and rice in the same proportion as previously provided and 1 pound of potatoes per man at least three times a week, if practicable; when these articles could not be issued in these proportions, an equivalent in value was to be issued in some other proper food; and a ration of tea was to be substituted for a ration of coffee upon the requisition of the proper officer.

I feel, in passing, that it is my duty to raise my hat to that monstrosity called salt beef, which so often marred our happiness in those days. No one ever felt able to adequately describe it, so I will not attempt that, but will simply caution the reader to not for one moment suppose that it bore the remotest resemblance to the corned beef of the present day. It was as tough, sometimes, as India rubber, and, barring the saltpeter, was nearly as tasteless. It used to be said that it was found among the stores left over from the War of 1812 and it certainly was salt enough to have been in brine that length of time. We used to vary the monotony of laborious mastication by giving it high-sounding titles, such as "salt junk," "salt horse" and so on.

Early in December, 1861, my regiment reached Frederick, Maryland and encamped about one mile north of the town. The weather had become too cold for comfort out-of-doors and the roads were too bad for campaigning, so the general told us we might make ourselves comfortable. The site selected for occupation was the southern slope of a hill, near a turnpike, at the foot of which a small stream of pure water ran. As this cantonment (it was too grand to be called a camp) was in many ways a model one, the best we had during our whole three years and the finest I saw in the whole army, I will describe it somewhat in detail. Younger readers, especially, will be interested in knowing what measures Yankees were able to devise under such circumstances to make themselves comfortable. We called our camp "Camp Hicks," in honor of the loyal governor of Maryland.[1]

The "houses" for officers and men numbered about one hundred. They were constructed of logs mainly, though timber was used for doors, floors and bunks. We had some time before begun the accumulation of company funds by selling pork and other unused supplies and these funds had reached quite respectable proportions. This money came in quite handy now, as there were many things we were obliged to pay cash for.

There were so many workers it took only a few days to build our miniature city. Men went into the woods with teams and trees were felled, the logs were cut into proper lengths and drawn out. These were split and trimmed, notched at the ends and used for the four walls of our cabins, leaving open spaces for doors and chimneys. The logs were chestnut, which splits easily and straight, and as we placed them with the smooth faces inside, interiors were as nice as one could wish. The height of the walls was about six feet. We built bunks on two sides similar to steamer bunks, laid floors, hung doors and erected chimneys with strips of wood. Then we plastered the chinks in the walls on the outside and our chimneys

---

1. Thomas H. Hicks had been elected governor of Maryland in 1857 and retained a tenuous hold on the state during the secession crisis and first days of the war. When his term expired, he was appointed senator and died in Washington, D.C., on February 13, 1865. *Dictionary of American Biography*, 9:8–9.

Camp of "The Webster Regiment"
12 Mass. Vol.
Cantonment Hicks – 1st Brigade – Gen. Banks Division,
near Frederick Md.
Col. Fletcher Webster Com.

Cantonment Hicks, near Frederick, Maryland. Courtesy of the
U.S. Army Heritage and Education Center

and fireplaces inside and out, with sticky clay, which the sun and
our roaring fires soon dried. Ridgepoles were then raised and
over them and at the ends we stretched heavy canvas. Most of the
structures were made pitch roof and six answered for a company.

Our company funds provided us with materials needed for
cooking which the Government did not furnish and, when our
cooks were not too lazy or too indifferent, we had many dainties.
In my company, the man who early chose the cookhouse as a place
in which to serve his country was a somewhat notable example of
incapacity. He was busily engaged one day in preparing dinner,
when Colonel Webster came along on one of his periodic rounds.
"Well, my man," said he, "what are you going to give the boys
today?" "Boiled rice," replied the cook. "Ah," observed the colonel, "rice is good. I see you have got it on now. How long do you
boil rice?" "Well," replied the man, "that's been on now an hour
and a half. I guess 'twill be done by dinner time." "Yes, I should
say there will be very little danger of its being rare," replied the

colonel. Thereupon the amateur cook received a lecture upon the art of cooking rice and the time required.

We had many ways of making the hours pass pleasantly: games of many kinds, indoors and out, books and newspapers (the boys were never too stingy to lend each other), songs and stories. Visitors, civil and military, were quite often entertained, among the latter being officers and men from the Second Massachusetts. The Thirteenth Massachusetts boys were too far away to come to see us. Many ladies came, too. In fact, we were rarely without their refining influences, as many officers had their wives with them from time to time.

The colonel was extremely fond of music and our long evenings in camp were frequently enlivened by airs from the leading operas and from the lighter works of Strauss. These were rendered in a superb manner by the members of the band, who, having abundant opportunity for practice, became very proficient in their line. Among so large a body of men it was an easy matter to select many good voices and thus singing of no mean quality was had in abundance. As a consequence, concerts were given that would have done credit to many of the leading musical troupes of the day. In all of these, Webster was a moving spirit.

Just before our arrival at Camp Hicks we were presented with 1,000 blankets by that generous friend of Massachusetts soldiers, Mrs. Harrison Gray Otis.[2] Then Chaplain Edward L. Clark[3] brought

2. A widow for more than twenty years, Mrs. Otis took over the management of Evans House, which the Boston City Council had established "for the reception of donations of material, garments, &c., for Boston Military." Nothing was turned down, often with unintended consequences. Who would have thought that a donation of blankets would cause a controversy? Colonel Webster said of them: "They had all, evidently, been somewhat used, and as I saw them taken one by one from the cases, I thought how many kind hearts had beat beneath them; how many little infants had nestled safe in their mothers' arms under them, quite unconscious of the storms raging without." Speaking of this same shipment of blankets, an enlisted man voiced a different observation: "Most of them were moth-eaten and rotten, however, a fact unknown to the generous donors, and the next morning were found in shreds." Mrs. Otis died in Boston on January 21, 1873. *Boston Evening Transcript,* April 30, 1861; *Frank Leslie's Illustrated Newspaper,* January 18, 1862; Cook, *History of the Twelfth Massachusetts,* 33; *Boston Journal,* January 22, 1873.

3. A graduate of Brown University, Clark spent a year touring Egypt and the Holy Land before entering Andover Theological Seminary. He was commissioned

out a large invoice of gloves, mittens (with forefinger and thumb) and stockings, donated by the ladies of Kennebunk, Maine, in which town the chaplain had many friends. The pair of mittens which warmed my hands (which happened to come from Exeter, New Hampshire) were ornamented at the wrists with the names "Jennie" and "Mary" and I modestly confess that although the owners of those names remained *incognito,* the thought of their generosity and their little joke often gave me comfort during the long, cold hours of guard and picket duty. It was one occasion in my life when the receipt of "the mitten" did not "cut me up" a bit.

Speaking of Chaplain Clark, I am admonished that he deserves more than a passing notice. When the war broke out he was a young student at Andover. He immediately organized a company, composed entirely of students. They adopted the Zouave uniform and tactics and became very proficient in drill. For some reason the company did not enter upon active service and the young captain finally sought service in the Twelfth. Colonel Webster offered him the chaplaincy. He accepted, but in order to meet the army requirements had to be ordained. So a service was arranged for this purpose at the Old South Church and in the presence of a great audience the necessary ceremony was performed. He was a good and efficient chaplain the year he remained with us and won the respect and esteem of the boys. The camp afforded many religious privileges. Prayer meetings were frequent and Captain Shurtleff, who was a devout Catholic, looked after the spiritual wants of the men of that faith.

While the Twelfth Regiment was at Camp Hicks, the officers had much trouble in keeping the boys inside of the camp guard. They would run the guard or plan some way to steal out and at last orders were read on dress parade that no soldier would be allowed past the guard or outside the lines without a pass from headquarters. The guard, on being relieved, instructed the guard relieving

---

chaplain of the Twelfth Massachusetts on June 26, 1861, and resigned on June 26, 1862. His ordination occurred at the Old South Church on August 18, 1861, and one paper reported: "The Old South was crammed from pit to dome, people standing in the aisles and on the outside at the doors and windows." Reverend Clark died February 5, 1910, in Boston. Kingman, *History of North Bridgewater,* 45; *Massachusetts Soldiers,* 2:3; *Boston Evening Transcript,* August 19, 1861; *New York Times,* February 6, 1910; *Barre (Mass.) Gazette,* August 23, 1861.

of the very strict orders that no soldier was allowed to cross his beat without a pass. Our camp not having good grounds for a drill and dress parade, we had to go outside of the camp to a high, level field and, of course, in going and returning, had to pass the beat of the guard. The night after the reading of this order the companies were called for dress parade and formed as usual, beyond the line of guards. But the regimental band was not in its proper place. The adjutant, much puzzled, waited for them to arrive, but they did not come, except for Amasa Glover[4] with his big brass instrument and it looked very much as if we were to enjoy a bass solo upon Glover's horn. After the adjutant had lost all patience, he gave the order, "Attention, battalion! To the rear, open order, march!" and we had dress parade as best we could without music. The military reader can imagine what such a performance as dress parade would be minus the music.

After returning to camp, the lieutenant colonel sent his orderly with a message for Bandmaster Martland to report at once to headquarters. Arriving there, he was asked why his band was not in its place at dress parade. The genial bandmaster naively said that the orders were not to go out of camp without a pass and the band, not having this necessary slip of paper, stayed inside, excepting the aforesaid Glover. The lieutenant colonel, somewhat in anger, said, "Consider yourself under arrest. Stay in your quarters, and tell your band, excepting Glover, to report at the guardhouse immediately." The musicians passed a sleepless night, for it was too lively in the guardhouse for them to sleep; and the next morning the prisoners were called out, as was the custom each

4. Amasa S. Glover enlisted as a musician in the Twelfth Massachusetts on July 10, 1861, and was mustered out of service on May 8, 1862. He enlisted again in Co. H, Thirty-third Massachusetts, as a private on August 1, 1862, and was mustered out of that company on June 11, 1865. A manufacturer of shoes before the war, Glover had an opportunity to show his skill in 1863 after the Battle of Chickamauga. When the supply of shoes gave out in General William T. Sherman's command, he asked for Glover's help, admitting all the raw materials he could offer was a supply of untanned hides. The general and the private quickly hatched a plan. Glover cut out shoe patterns, Sherman detailed hundreds of men for the work, and by next day they had produced enough shoes to supply the deficiency. Glover died at Brockton, Massachusetts, on July 5, 1897. *Massachusetts Soldiers*, 2:4; 3:573; *Biographical Review of Plymouth County*, 138–39; *Boston Journal*, July 6, 1897.

day, to police the camp, and with the others were the members of the band.

The writer happened to be in charge of the guard that day and it was his duty to take the party out. As he did so he said to himself, "What would the good people of North Bridgewater say if they should see these blowers of brass instruments and beaters of sheepskin sweeping the grounds about the guardhouse. Oh! what a fall was that, my countrymen!" There was one member of the band with a broom (by the way, these brooms were made of birch twigs tied to a stick, such as we now see used in stables) who did not move from his tracks for the whole hour he was on duty. He did not keep his broom moving all the time by any means, but when he did see fit to work, it was always upon the same spot. It amused me to watch him, but he looked as sober as a deacon. I think the band was not kept in the guardhouse long, but the first evening after their release, they were called up to headquarters to play, as was the custom on pleasant nights after the duties of the day were over. The first piece they played that evening was the very appropriate air, "Buy a Broom." The men loudly applauded and, although the affair ended thus pleasantly, Bandmaster Martland and his musicians never thereafter failed to be on parade, even though it was held outside of camp. They had learned that it was not always best to obey orders too strictly.

We had many things to laugh at, but the funniest thing I remember was a Pennsylvania regiment encamped beside us. It had become utterly demoralized, officers and men, and "didn't care a penny whether school kept or not." There were not a hundred muskets in the crowd that would go off. Their attempts at drill and parade were simply burlesque and they knew it, too, and would laugh as loudly as we did. The "organization" had to be disorganized finally, but the change was so slight it was hardly perceptible. The men often addressed their officers by their first names and all customary evidences of military discipline and etiquette were conspicuous by their absence. I remember being on guard one night beside their camp. The "Pennsyltuckian" who occasionally shuffled back and forth opposite my beat had a "shooting iron" that might have come over in the *Mayflower*. Once in a while he would manifest his impatience to be relieved by shouting loudly,

"Send 'round that third relief!" Pretty soon the Grand Rounds came along. He then drawled out, in a disgusted way, "Who comes there?" The answer came back in a kind of drawl, "Grand Rounds." Then the sentinel, without suggesting that the party had better halt, remarked quietly, "Look out there, Major, you'll break your damned neck over that stump."

While encamped at Frederick the Twelfth Regiment had an accession to its roll of commissioned officers in the person of a young second lieutenant named Arthur Dehon.[5] He was boyish looking in the extreme, of slender build and slightly below the average in height for a man of his years, while his face was pallid and almost beardless. Although twenty-one years of age, he appeared at least four years younger. Inquiry disclosed that he was the son of William Dehon, prominent Boston lawyer and intimate friend of Colonel Webster.

When sixteen years of age, he went to Harvard, entering the class of 1861, but in his junior year Dehon's slender constitution gave way under the weight of hard study and he was obliged to leave. In February, 1861, in the belief that a sea voyage would be beneficial, he sailed for San Francisco in a merchant ship. His dream of recovered health and strength, the bright anticipation of his friends and his own hopes for a successful future had all to be abandoned, for he felt that the country had need of his services. At the earnest solicitation of his friends he waited a while, but when the terrible Battle of Ball's Bluff came, with the heroic death of Colonel Edward Baker, he could wait no longer. The men of the Webster Regiment soon found that the young lieutenant, concerning whom their first impressions had been so unfavorable, was a man of rare worth and all began to love him.

On the evening of January 24, 1862, our band gave a concert, vocal and instrumental, in Junior Hall, Frederick, and many of the officers and men attended. It was a grand affair and the hall was

5. Arthur H. Dehon was commissioned second lieutenant of Co. F, Twelfth Massachusetts, on January 18, 1862, and promoted to first lieutenant on May 13, 1862. He acted as regimental adjutant during the 1862 campaigns in Virginia and Maryland. Transferred to the staff of General George G. Meade after Antietam, Dehon was killed December 13, 1862, at Fredericksburg. General George Hartsuff said that "a more gallant little fellow never bestrode a horse." *Massachusetts Soldiers*, 2:36; *Boston Evening Transcript*, December 22, 1862.

Lieutenant Arthur H.
Dehon. Courtesy of the
U.S. Army Heritage and
Education Center

filled. Airs and overtures from the leading operas were given and
the five Packard brothers sang several selections, including "Lake
of the Dismal Swamp," "Scatter the Gems of the Beautiful," "The
Ocean Queen" from the "Enchantress" and "The Husband Who
Uses Tobacco." One of the singers, Mr. Frederick C. Packard,[6] has
since the "late unpleasantness" made a reputation almost world-
wide as the leading tenor of the Carl Rosa Opera Troupe.

Washington's Birthday was celebrated by a grand review of all
the troops in the vicinity and the people of the town were delighted. As a special mark of respect for the man who could not
tell a lie, we drew upon our company funds for white gloves, which,

6. Packard enlisted in Co. F, Twelfth Massachusetts, on June 25, 1861, was
transferred to Co. D on November 18, 1861, and was discharged for disability
on October 17, 1862. After an international career, Packard died forgotten in an
insane asylum. *Massachusetts Soldiers*, 2:39; "Beggar Student," 371–76.

after the show was over, served more useful purposes as receptacles for coffee and sugar and salt and as wipers for musket barrels. In the evening we had a crowd of darkies in camp, ranging all the way from "uncle" and "auntie" down to the "pickaninny" of tender years, who would hover about in large numbers and listen to the music with wide-open mouths. These pickaninnies would dance their "breakdowns" to the lively strains of the music, while the older darkies and hundreds of soldiers looked on with the greatest delight. We made them dance upon a temporary stage in front of the colonel's "palace" until they were tired. Martland furnished the music and occasionally while playing lively airs suited to their odd gyrations, he had his musicians suddenly strike up such pieces as "Greenville" and "Old Hundred," when the efforts of the dancers to keep time were painful to witness. Loud shouts of laughter ended the performance as the little darkies struggled vainly to fit their step to the unsuitable music.

One of the best known men in the regiment was Julius Rabardy of Company K.[7] He was a Frenchman of distinguished family and reached this country just in time to become one of us. He had a glorious voice and in camp often aroused great enthusiasm by his excellent rendering of the "Marseillaise" in his native tongue. Rabardy parted with a leg at Antietam.

There were plenty of schemes for "raising the wind." Some engaged in peddling, while others established tonsorial establishments and laundries. Many, however, refused to encourage home industry and thought their "linen" would be more carefully handled by contrabands. They therefore sent their washing out.

A party from our regiment visited Frederick one evening to attend a dance. The men wore paper collars for the nonce, in order that they might appear as presentable as possible, and upon their return to camp threw them away, they being soiled and unfit for

7. Julius F. Rabardy enlisted in Co. K, Twelfth Massachusetts, on June 26, 1861, lost a leg at Antietam, and was discharged for disability on March 10, 1863. Proud of his French heritage, Rabardy was remembered as the amputee who "kept the whole tent full of wounded men cheerful and bright with his own cheerfulness, singing the Marseillaise and other patriot songs." He died in Manchester, Massachusetts, on March 19, 1926. *Massachusetts Soldiers*, 2:66; Brockett, *Woman's Work*, 451; Julius F. Rabardy Pension Records, RG 15, NA.

further service. One of the members of my company was quite a dude. He was a great wag, too, and, to let him tell it, a great favorite with the young ladies of Frederick. The scamp collected these articles of discarded neckwear and gravely handed them over to a darky washerwoman to be cleansed. The old lady, it is supposed, never had seen such specimens of Yankee ingenuity as paper collars and she calmly placed them in her bundle. The next day our wag received a visit from the washerwoman's "ole man," who reported that an attempt had been made to wash two of the collars, returned the debris, heartbroken and tearful, and offered to pay for the damage. His "ole ooman" had been as "kurful" as she could be, but—"oh, oh, oh." Then the wag went into a towering passion and raved and swore at a frightful rate. "What kind of soap did she use?" he demanded. "Bar, timidly replied the old man. "I told her to use nothing but Castile soap for those collars," the wag said sternly. "Now take them back and try again."

The next day the man came again. His story was even more lugubrious than before. Instead of the ragged remnants of what had once been two paper collars, he brought *all* the debris and magnanimously disclaimed any intention of charging for the wash. "But," said he, as he turned sorrowfully to go away, "I don't see how on airth your Yankee women wash them 'air things. My ole woman did her best, but she couldn't make any kind of show at it. She thinks they must be made of powful rotten stuff."

Shrewd Marylanders soon caught on to a few Yankee tricks and "New England Pies" and "New England one thing and another" appeared as signs over many stores. The keepers of these establishments sent commercial travelers to the camps. One came to us one day with "custard" pies. A sergeant in my company was extremely fond of this particular commodity, which he said his mother could make in delicious perfection, so he eagerly bought one and proceeded as eagerly to eat it, not stopping for plate or knife and fork. The first bite convinced him that something was wrong, the second that it was not custard at all, but potato and, with a grunt of disgust, he threw it at the astonished vendor, landing it square on his face, soft side on. The last seen of the pie merchant he was running toward the brook and howling with rage.

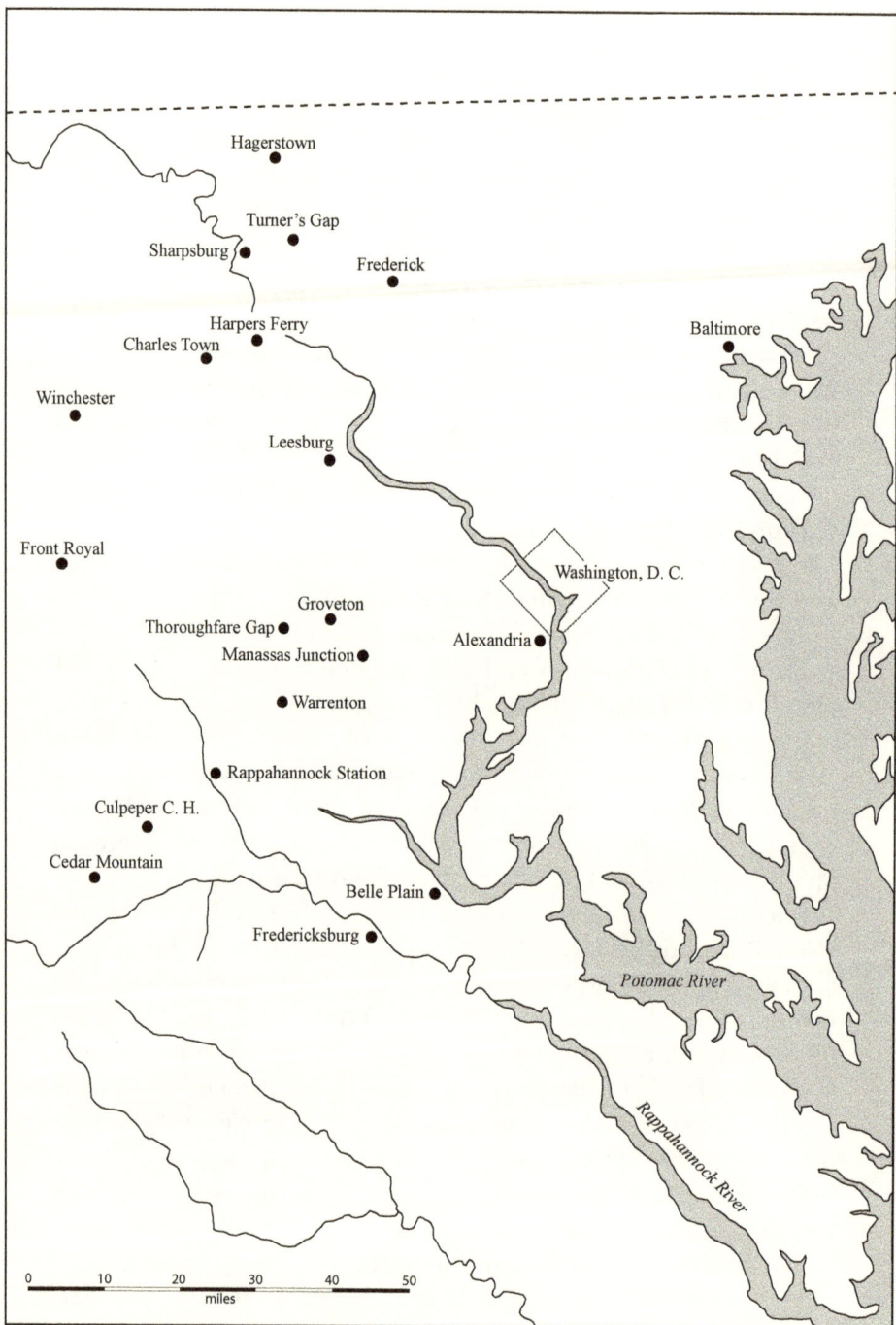

Theater of Operations, 1862.

CHAPTER 6

Active Campaigning

All things terrestrial—even good things—have an end and toward the end of February we began preparations for a move. General Ulysses S. Grant[1] had captured Forts Henry and Donelson, General Ambrose Burnside[2] was making things lively in North Carolina and if we wanted to "get there" before the fun was all over we must "stir our stumps." So we sold our earthly possessions at Camp Hicks, gave one long, lingering look at the comfortable dwellings in which we had passed so many happy hours and, with the band playing "Old Virginia Shore," marched away. At Frederick we took a train and, while the sun was sinking behind the mountains of the Blue Ridge on the 27th of February, we crossed the Potomac at Harpers Ferry on a pontoon bridge. Our first night on "sacred

1. A West Point graduate, Grant was a Mexican-American War veteran who had recruited the Twenty-first Illinois; he was quickly elevated to brigadier general. His campaign in western Tennessee led to the surrender of Fort Henry, on the Tennessee River, on February 6, 1862, and Fort Donelson, on the Cumberland River, ten days later. This was the first significant Union victory of the war. Grant would eventually rise to command all Union armies engaged in the war and win election as president for two terms. He died in Wilton, New York, on July 23, 1885. Warner, *Generals in Blue*, 183–86; Heitman, *Historical Register*, 1:470.

2. Burnside had graduated from West Point in 1847 but resigned his commission to enter the business world. Commissioned colonel of the First Rhode Island, he was soon elevated to brigadier general and in early 1862 led an expedition to North Carolina. He occupied Roanoke Island on February 8 and New Bern on March 14, giving the Union two badly needed victories as bookends to Forts Henry and Donelson. Burnside would hang around after being sacked as commander of the Army of the Potomac following the Fredericksburg debacle until he resigned on April 15, 1865. Burnside served several terms as governor of Rhode Island and died in Bristol on September 13, 1881. Warner, *Generals in Blue*, 57–58; Heitman, *Historical Register*, 1:266.

soil" was passed in an old flour mill, a mile or so from the historic village of Harpers Ferry and a more uncomfortable night than that it has not often been my lot to experience. We found the town almost a mass of ruins, but the old engine house on the arsenal grounds, where Brown and his men made their principal fight, was still standing. Those of us who had a passion for relics gathered an abundant supply.

We then moved on and passed through Charles Town with our bands playing, our colors gaily flying and the men lustily singing the grand old "John Brown Song." Down to the outbreak of the Rebellion, Charles Town exhibited to a marked degree the characteristics of nearly all Southern towns in slavery days—slow growth, a lack of energy and enterprise and ambition for little except social distinction and great, although imaginary, importance of individuals. The world at large knew but little of the town until October, 1859, when it sprang into notoriety at a single bound as the place where John Brown of Osawatomie was carried a prisoner and where the old hero was tried, convicted and hanged. The name of the town became thus linked with an immortal idea and all the world has since known that Charles Town is where a willing martyr to the cause of human liberty yielded up his life upon the gallows and thereby inaugurated a new and glorious era in the history of his country.

All through the war for the Union the armies of both sides alternately swept through the town and many desperate fights occurred either within its limits or in its immediate vicinity. On the morning of the 1st of March, 1862, Banks's division entered Charles Town. The scene, had it been stripped of its sterner aspects, and had the element of war been absent, would have been beautiful and inspiring, for drill and discipline had rendered the division a magnificent body of men. Men, women and children, of all ages, both black and white, lined the streets and gazed with wonder upon the oncoming Yankees. They evidently thought that John Brown's avengers had come at last. On past the court house and out beyond the field where the famous execution took place we marched with faultless step and perfect alignment, while all the air seemed vocal with the strange but appropriate melody. It was the lot of the writer to march that day in those ranks and well does he remember the strange thoughts and feelings which came crowding in upon him as the bands played "John Brown's Body" and the thousands of loyal voices vigorously sang the grand old song. 'Twas indeed an inspiring scene and, if the brave old martyr in spirit form hovered about our lines that day, he must surely have thought that he did not sacrifice his life in vain after all, despite the obloquy and ridicule cast upon him by those who could not appreciate his motives.

Whether the survivors of the war for the Union are willing to admit it or not, I believe that that hatred of slavery and love of liberty that animated the grand old hero of Harpers Ferry entered very largely into the sentiment which controlled them on every battlefield from Sumter to Appomattox. I could never see why there should be any attempt or desire to conceal this motive. Was not the liberation of four millions of human beings, the freedom of every man henceforth under the Stars and Stripes and the opening up of our country to a career of human progress and advancement hitherto unknown, a cause worthy the sacrifice of even life itself? Was not the spirit of a martyr who, when asked if he would surrender and trust himself to the mercy of the Government, could reply, "No, I prefer to die here!" a noble one? Did any soldier show greater heroism at Gettysburg, at Atlanta or in the Wilderness? Is anybody really ashamed of old John Brown, the John the Baptist of our Civil War? The war, indeed, is quite generally believed in the South to have started at Harpers Ferry. I recently received a letter from a prominent Virginian, one who fought under General Robert E. Lee,[3] in which occur these significant words, "I served all through, from Harpers Ferry to the surrender."

---

3. A graduate of West Point and a distinguished engineer during the Mexican–American War, Robert E. Lee led the Federal force that recaptured the Harpers Ferry Arsenal from John Brown in 1859. A colonel of the First United States Cavalry in 1861 and one of the most gifted officers in the army, Lee resigned his commission on April 20, 1861, to become a general in the Confederate army and commander of the Army of Northern Virginia. Lee served as president of Washington College in Lexington, Virginia, from 1865 until his death in that city on October 12, 1870. Warner, *Generals in Gray*, 179–83; Heitman, *Historical Register*, 1:625.

We went into camp just beyond Charles Town and then, soldier fashion, began our tours of sight seeing. The whole country, for miles around, soon became overrun with "boys in blue." The next day I visited the court house, in company with a party of comrades, and the seat upon which Brown sat during the trial was pointed out to us. We thereupon indulged in a mock trial, at the close of which, instead of sentencing our pseudo prisoner to be executed as a traitor, we handed him down to the grateful recognition of posterity as a hero who gave his life for a great principle. Leaving the court house we mingled freely with the citizens, nearly all of whom had been eye-witnesses of the John Brown episode, and gave them some points that were probably not brought forward at the famous trial. Later in the day a hot-headed secessionist attempted to raise a Confederate flag in the town, but some Union soldiers and many of the inhabitants objected, and during the controversy that ensued the man was shot. This incident demonstrated the fact that there were heroes upon both sides who were willing to die for what they believed to be right.

Many were the strange experiences that were afterward related about the campfires. One of the most interesting of these was the exploit of two soldiers in Company D—Privates James Lewis[4] and Moses Woodbury.[5] The two soldiers, then but sixteen and eighteen years old respectively, wandered a mile or so from camp in search of something to eat. Army rations were then plenty, but they longed, as the men of both armies did at all times, for

4. Lewis enlisted on June 26, 1861, in Co. D, Twelfth Massachusetts, and was wounded at Second Bull Run and Antietam. Missing in action at Gettysburg, he was exchanged and then reenlisted as a veteran volunteer on January 1, 1864. Lewis was wounded a third time at Cold Harbor, then was transferred as a sergeant to Co. G, Thirty-ninth Massachusetts, on June 25, 1864. He was discharged on account of his latest wound on March 8, 1865. He died in Boston on July 14, 1903. *Massachusetts Soldiers*, 2:26; 4:86; *Boston Directory* (1904), 1056.

5. Woodbury enlisted in Co. D, Twelfth Massachusetts, on June 26, 1861, and served his three-year term before being mustered out on July 8, 1864. Colonel Bates said that "he is brave as the bravest, and in action enthusiastic, entering into the spirit of the fight as though it were his greatest delight. At the battle of Fredericksburg he was complimented on the field by me for his splendid conduct." He died January 19, 1912, in Dallas, Texas. *Massachusetts Soldiers*, 2:29; Thompson, *Swampscott*, 162; *Dallas Morning News*, January 20, 1912.

something which had been cooked in civilized fashion and that could be eaten with knives, forks, spoons, dishes and other useful but then absent accessories of civilized life.

Passing on the way many houses that had apparently been stripped of everything eatable, they at last came to a humble dwelling that showed evidences of having thus far at least partially escaped the visits of predatory bands. After satisfying themselves that no guerrillas were in the neighborhood, they approached near enough to see an old man, with long white locks, at work in the yard, trying to mend a broken down farm wagon. He could not surely be a dangerous rebel they thought and so they walked boldly up and asked for something to eat. The old man looked up when he heard their voices and then, as his eyes fell upon their blue uniforms, with a wild shriek and a look of alarm, he fell backward upon the ground in a fit. His wife and daughter came to the door and, adding their cries and moans, the affair became an exciting scene.

Here was a new experience for these young soldiers, but they were equal to the occasion. They immediately took the old man up in their arms and, carrying him into the house, placed him upon a bed. Then while loosening his clothing and vigorously rubbing his limbs, they applied such restoratives as the family possessed and after a while the man came to. His mind wandered at first and he talked incoherently of the war then in progress, of his two sons away in the Southern army and of the Yankees who had come to burn and destroy. Lewis and Woodbury tried to reassure him and in this they succeeded so well that in a short time the old man, as well as the wife and daughter, had become convinced that Yankees were not so very bad after all, if their visitors could be taken as fair samples.

The feelings of the family appeared to be undergoing a radical change and it was not long before the much-wished-for dinner was ready. While seated at the table the members of the family successively discoursed first upon the false impressions they had had of Northern soldiers and then upon points of fancied resemblance between their visitors and the two boys away serving with General Robert E. Lee. They seemed to be getting on very well and, had the two sons returned at that moment and witnessed the attentions being so freely showered upon the enemy, it is possible there might have been sufficient cause for an exhibition of jealousy.

It occurring to Lewis and Woodbury some time after the dinner was over that possibly it might be drawing near the time when they ought to be returning to camp, some observation was made to that effect, when earnest protestations and invitations to remain longer began to pour in in rapidly succeeding volleys. After a while Lewis barely succeeded in getting an opportunity in the midst of the conversation, which had now become very animated, to ask the time of day. The young lady, while with charming *naiveté* begging them to remain longer, began preparations to leave the house. Unable to resist a Yankee's curiosity, Lewis ventured to ask where the young lady was going, a very impertinent question under ordinary circumstances, but excusable then, inasmuch as suspicions crept into his mind that she might be going to notify guerrillas of their presence.

"O, she's going over to the nearest neighbor's to ascertain the time," replied the female head of the family. "She will not be gone long." "Have you no clock?" asked Lewis. "Yes, we've got one, but it's out of order. It has been stopped for nearly two years," replied the masculine representative of the F. F. V.s [First Families of Virginia]. "Where is it?" asked Lewis. "Perhaps I can fix it." "You!" exclaimed mother and daughter both together. "You fix it?" "Why, yes," said Lewis, "I guess I can fix it if you would like to have me."

So the clock was brought out and Lewis began his task. He possessed some knowledge of clock mechanisms, gained by often having, in his mother's absence, taken the family time-keeper to pieces, just to satisfy his curiosity as to what the thing was made of, and therefore felt confident that if nothing was broken or missing he could soon cause it to resume operations. He carefully removed the machinery and then cleaned, oiled and replaced it, the members of the family meanwhile watching proceedings with a peculiar interest. The daughter was then allowed to go over to the neighbor's for the correct time and so the clear, sharp tone of the old clock, which for half a century or more had charmed the family ear, but which had been so long silent, was heard again. The daughter was the first to speak and her remark covered the ground exactly and left no more to be said except to express thanks to the ingenious mechanic who had set so many useful wheels in motion. "I have heard," said she, "that Yankees can do everything; now I know it."

We left the locality in a few days, but the young soldiers never forgot the kindness of the old Virginian and his family. At the battle of Gettysburg, Lewis fell into the hands of the enemy. With a large number of Union prisoners he was being marched up the Valley toward Richmond and on the way passed the residence of his old-time acquaintance. The old man happened to be standing at the gate, looking at the motley procession, and Lewis waved his hand in salute. Time and the hardships of war had wrought such changes in wardrobe and personal appearance that the old man did not know the young soldier at first, but when Lewis asked, "How is the clock?" he recognized him at once and a moment afterward came running after him with a loaf of bread. This he handed Lewis, after a word of explanation with the guard, and it is safe to say that that loaf of bread and the pleasant recollections which came with it did much to soften the hardships of the months of prison life that followed.

About two weeks afterward we found ourselves in Winchester, a town of about 4,000 inhabitants, mostly "secesh." Some devotees of the "art preservative," belonging to the Thirteenth Massachusetts, took possession of one of the printing offices in town and issued a paper, which treated the misguided people to some very fine Union sentiments. This did not have the effect, however, of entirely removing the prejudice against us and we were compelled to suffer many indignities at the hands of the F. F. V.s.

Winchester contained a medical college among her other public buildings. To this institution were brought the bodies of the men killed in the John Brown raid. Among them were those of two of Brown's sons. These bodies were all dissected, the skeletons preserved and were now stored there, partly in the interests of science but chiefly as a menace to progressive negroes who might take it into their heads to repeat Brown's experiment. Many of us visited the place to look upon these grim reminders of the beginning of the struggle upon which we were now embarked, but with far different feelings from those experienced by previous visitors.

One of the officers of our regiment, having a medical friend at home who appreciated such trophies, secured one of the skeletons and sent it to Massachusetts.

Army rations were plenty, but luxuries were few and far between. Occasionally chickens, turkeys, and geese in the neighborhood, evidently sympathizing with us and desirous of escaping from their disloyal owners, would stray into our camp and beg us to kill and eat them. Not always having the hardness of heart to resist these pathetic appeals, we sometimes yielded. Our brigade commander often remonstrated with these feathered nomads, warning them of the impropriety of their habits and even went so far as to advise their owners to the adoption of measures that would keep them at home. He actually succeeded for a while and camp life became very lonely. Then we were compelled to make clandestine visits to the *fowl* abodes of our favorites and secret excursions to neighboring farmhouses became frequent.

I was sauntering with a companion one day in the vicinity of a two-story house, the male occupant of which was away, "serving his State," when we chanced to meet three geese out for a short stroll. The meeting resulted in an elopement, neither the guard at the door nor the females inside knowing of the departure of the bipeds. These geese had probably never heard of the famous exploit of their ancestors in ancient Rome or else they would have "cackled." Taking one under each arm and my companion taking the other, we made rapid time back to camp.

This was quite early in the morning. Feathers and other uneatable things were removed and then we faced the question, "How shall we bake them?" The other members of the mess were allowed to participate in the discussion and all sorts of expedients were proposed. I suggested jocosely that, insomuch as we lacked facilities for the proper cooking of the fowls, some member of the mess had better go to the very house from whence the geese came and employ the lady or her kitchen servant to bake them for us. "That's a good job for you," said one individual. Of course I protested and claimed exemption on the ground of having already rendered valuable service, but my protest was of no avail. They only pressed the point the more strongly and finally I was *dared* to do it. Then bets were made and after much jargon I set out, with the geese in a camp kettle, upon my perilous errand. I entered the back door of the house, so as to escape the guard and, encountering an aged "auntie" in the kitchen, told her what I wanted, offering her two dollars if she would do the job. As to the yarn I told to cover up what seemed to be a theft, "deponent saith not." In due time, my company—for we asked them all in—dined on baked goose and what was left was hidden away.

In the afternoon our eyes were greeted with an unusual sight. A lady was seen to enter the tent of the colonel. A few moments later the sergeant major was descried springing from one tent to another and then followed a busy scene all over camp, men looking and running in every direction, while in the tent at the head of our company street a suspicious movement was going on in the straw. Soon the colonel came out, escorting the lady, and a tour of the entire camp was made. Every tent was peered into. Never was a Sunday morning inspection more thorough. We were apparently found in good condition to withstand the rigors of the campaign, for the lady departed with a smile upon her countenance that betokened satisfaction and content. She declared to the colonel her firm belief that some other regiment must have decoyed her geese away and sweetly apologized for having even entertained a suspicion that his men had done so. That night a few choice slices of roast goose found their way to regimental headquarters.

I have endeavored to present a few phases of army life in the early part of the war which I hope have not proved entirely uninteresting to my readers, scenes which were, of course, not particularly serious or heroic and which may have proved to be tedious reading to those who are impatient for more exciting details. But I think that such lights and shadows form an essential part of such a picture of army life as I am endeavoring to present and that they serve to make non-military readers, especially, in a measure acquainted with the temper and morale of the men who made up that matchless army which is to stand in history among the foremost fighting forces of the world. To further enlighten those non-military readers, I will now undertake to describe a typical day in camp.

It began before consciousness came—that is, before we woke up—but when the beginning did come there was no fooling about it. Not a bit. No turning over for another nap, no stretching and yawning and debating in our own minds whether it were noble in the mind of man to get up than to wait a while. Its advent was heralded by an abomination called "Reveille," during which that ear-splitting bugle, that ear-piercing fife and that soul-stirring drum all combined to make themselves obnoxious.

The first thing we did, of course, upon getting our peepers open was to curse the drummers. But even in this we were not allowed full scope, for just as the chorus of "big D's" was getting well under way, the shrill cry of the sergeant was heard and, while we were rubbing our eyes, we were *told,* not *asked,* to "Fall in!" As it was not safe or advisable to wait for a second invitation, we generally crawled out from under our canvas dwelling at once and took our places in line, covering up, as well as we could, whatever deficiencies there were in the putting on or buttoning up of our suits of blue. It was always well to give our superiors the impression that we were dressed properly, as it was often a powerful factor in determining whether we merited the punishment of an extra twenty-four hours' guard or a disagreeable tour of fatigue duty.

Having answered "Here!" at the roll call and having escaped being detailed for guard or being sentenced to be shot, we were turned loose for a few moments during which we made our beds. This consisted in two bed-fellows, or chums, getting hold of opposite ends of their blankets and shaking them, after which they were tightly rolled up and strapped upon the knapsacks. It took but a moment to put away the rest of the things, for there were not many of them. Then we took our towels and soap and started on a journey to the brook, that is, providing one ran anywhere within a mile or so of camp. Here we had a good wash. If the brook was lacking and if there were no rivers or lakes in the vicinity, we washed while a comrade poured a slender stream from a canteen and then we poured and he washed.

About this time that confounded bugle broke loose again, followed by the other noises, only more subdued and plaintive than before, and just as we were getting ready for another growl, the sergeant cried, in a suspicious way, "Fall in, sick!" Here was fun, but it takes an abler pen than mine to describe the procession that marched to the surgeon's tent, therefore I am not going to attempt it. Suffice it to say, it included all the "bums" and all the "beats" about the camp, as well as all the really sick and lame. The medicine obtained was of two kinds, blue pills and quinine. The medicine often sought, but not always obtained, was of one variety only—an excuse from duty.

Following close upon the heels of the sick call came the call for drill. In some camps, where the commanders were human and desired that the men might have a moment or two in which to draw a long breath, this was dispensed with. But in the early part of the war, an ante-breakfast drill of half an hour or so was religiously carried out in most regiments, as it was thought it gave the men needed exercise and served to limber up their stiffened joints, thus cheating Old Rheumatism out of some of his victims.

The next number on the program was always somewhat of a puzzle to us unprofessional soldiers, on account of the delusiveness of its title. Why they should designate breakfast as "Peas Upon a Trencher" and then feed us upon hardtack and coffee, with an occasional chunk of "salt horse" thrown in, was something that no fellow could find out. Nor was this all. Candor compels me to say, in order that future aspirants for military glory may not be deceived as we had been, that the meal was not only *sans* peas, but *sans* trencher, too.

After breakfast we smoked our pipes, scoured our muskets and discussed the rumors prevailing in camp, of which there were always plenty, while the picket detail started off for their lonely tour of duty. Then there were a thousand-and-one things to occupy our time and attention till the musical instruments should again summon us to the ranks. Prominent among these were witnessing the ceremonies and listening to the music of guard mounting. I can never forget with what pleasure and interest I used to look upon this imposing and beautiful spectacle. The music of the band, the inspection, the maneuvers of the officers and finally the dividing up of the detail into little squads at the guardhouse and placing of the men upon their posts, all formed a military pageant which was truly unique and, in many respects, grand.

Now came another drill. And it *was* a drill, too, with a vengeance. If a soldier was able to stand upon his feet for an hour after being dismissed, he was looked upon as somewhat of a curiosity by his comrades, for it was during the forenoon exercise that we were initiated into the mysteries of skirmishing. As we frequently encountered fences, stumps, tangled underbrush and thorn bushes, bruised shins and scratches upon all parts of our bodies were among the possibilities. This forenoon drill was one worth remembering.

By this time we were in first-class condition for the next event named upon the bills, which was "Roast Beef!" This dish, however, like the peas of the morning, was present only in the music and we thought ourselves lucky if the company cook, whom we generally designated as "Old Greasy," had not been too lazy to prepare soup or baked beans. However, we cared very little which of the two was served, for we were hungry enough to eat boiled owls and longed chiefly for something soft. But we growled all the same. Of course, to growl was the soldier's prerogative.

After dinner we lighted our pipes and strolled over the camp or lay outstretched under the trees, talking about the novelties and peculiarities of our nomadic life or discussing weightier matters till the bugles blew again and all the drums and fifes set up their din. This meant battalion drill—no ordinary affair, I assure you. The colors were now brought out and the bustle about headquarters showed that the field and staff were coming this time. By and by we were in line. What an imposing array! The companies wheeled, marched and counter-marched and formed in battalion line from all sorts of impossible-looking positions and maneuvers, until it seemed almost certain that we had executed every movement known to the tactics. Sometimes brigade drill took the place of that of the regiment and then the grandeur increased accordingly. I think I can best describe this brilliant military spectacle by quoting a military poet of the Pine Tree State, a man whose name, like that of many of the world's great authors, has been lost in obscurity. He was writing of a Maine muster:

> And now, in many evolutions wheeled,
>   The glittering battalions, file on file,
> Till scientific glory crowns the field,
>   And all the loafers on the fences smile.

We had another short breathing spell, during which we (sometimes) received our mail, bringing letters and papers from thoughtful ones at home.

But the crowning feature of a day in camp was undoubtedly dress parade. For this great preparations were made. Boots were blacked (quite an event in itself!), muskets and brasses were scoured and everything was done which would in any way enhance the splendors of this gorgeous event. The band came out to its place upon the parade ground and began discoursing its sweetest strains and the companies, dressed and equipped at their best, marched out of the company streets in varying and tortuous ways, and, as seen approaching the rendezvous, appeared to be coming from every unexpected quarter. How they could ever be brought into line seemed a real mystery, but the problem was solved at last, as if by magic, and the regiment was in line.

The music had now ceased. The adjutant screamed his customary orders. What a voice he had! The band gracefully wheeled out in front, amid the tumult of drums, and marched down the line, playing its most entrancing waltz. The scene now, as the setting sun was just hiding in the western sky, with all nature in harmony, seemed to combine all there was of romance and beauty in a soldier's life. The musicians reached the left of the line, countermarched and then with a livelier air returned to their place upon the right. The remaining ceremonies were soon carried out, including a drill in the manual of arms and the reading of orders, and the companies returned to camp.

Then came supper, but this was so much like breakfast, holding out the promise of such a feast in its musical invitation and really affording so little, that it requires no special description. But the time about which centered the chief delights of camp life was in the evening. Then the differences of rank seemed to be partially forgotten and the reins of discipline loosened. Visiting was in order. If one unaccustomed to such scenes had entered the camp of an infantry regiment in the evening, he would have been charmed and delighted with everything he heard or witnessed. The merry groups about the blazing fires, laughing and storytelling; the breath of song everywhere floating upon the balmy air, the innocent jest and the childish frolic of the men, trying to drive dull care away and to forget for the moment that they were far from home and friends; the games in progress in all directions; within the tent, by the feeble light of a candle, the more thoughtful soldier penning a few lines to loved ones far away or reading a well-worn book or paper; up there in front of the colonel's tent, the band, delighting all by its delicious music; all these things left an impression upon the mind of the beholder or participant never to be erased. The general effect of all this weird beauty was strangely fascinating. No wonder that the veteran of today takes so much delight in trying to reproduce the scene in the modern campfire.

At half past nine came "Tattoo." Then all was changed. This was the soldier's bedtime. The drums and bugles heralded the hour in their familiar way, the various companies assembled in front of the tents for the evening roll call and then the day in camp was ended.

No, not quite ended, for in half an hour came another call. This was the strangest and most fascinating of all. What soldier can ever forget "Taps" or how lonely it made him feel to hear them? Sometimes, long after those in his own regiment had died away, he could hear them, wonderfully weird and musical, in camps far away in the distance. Then he blew out his candle and sank to sleep, perchance to dream of his home, with the war all over and with comforts all about him.

The foregoing presents the outline of a day's experiences in camp. North and south, east and west, the scene was everywhere the same, whether among the wearers of the blue or the wearers of the gray. If the non-military reader thinks he would like such a life, he can enlist when the next war comes. The pay is thirteen dollars a month, with board, lodging and clothing thrown in and there are opportunities for study, travel, and promotion.

CHAPTER 7

Early Incidents

The frequent inspection of the camps and various belongings of the soldiers of the Union doubtless had a more important bearing upon their health and morale than did any other established institution of the army. It was, perhaps, a source of hardship to many, particularly to the lazy and the unclean, but no one ever seriously questioned its usefulness or denied its good results.

To the uninitiated, inspection may appear to have been a very trifling affair. It is a small matter, doubtless, in "piping times of peace," when the guardians of the public weal are snugly and comfortably ensconced in barracks. But it is something more than a mere incident of the day's routine among soldiers in the field. Imagine the consternation and bitter agony that prevailed when an order was received requiring inspection to be held in an hour and this when we had been floundering about in the mud for days and sometimes even for weeks. It was no boys' play then, for the reputation of each individual as well as that of the organization to which he belonged was at stake. Then, it must be remembered, we had not a very large supply of emery paper, oil, brushes and blacking, articles that are indispensable in a well-ordered army household. These were provided, of course, either from the company fund, the pocket of the captain or that of the soldier himself, but it was simply wonderful to see how suddenly and mysteriously such things would disappear during the march.

One would naturally suppose that, in the absence of blacking, greased shoes would "pass muster." But they would not in the early part of the war, at any rate. At least it was so in the regiment to which I belonged. I have good reason for feeling sure upon this point, for I made a test case of it once and got detailed for two hours' police duty to reward me for my presumption.

Verily the veteran of the war still keenly remembers how hard he had to labor to prepare himself for inspection; how he rubbed his brasses until there was no such thing as mistaking the "U.S." upon his belt or the eagle upon his coat buttons; how he scrubbed his musket until it would not soil even a lady's fingers and until the inside of the barrel glistened like burnished silver; and how he desperately and often vainly endeavored to make his rough and heavy "gunboats" appear like patent leathers. The sometimes needed admonition, too, according to the temper of the inspecting officer, still lingers in his memory.

But to no man in the army did the order to appear upon inspection bring such absolute terror as it did to the company cook. It was a serious matter indeed to "Old Greasy." In his work of preparation he had to begin at the very beginning. He was usually not up in the drill and his clothing and equipments were sometimes in worse condition even than raw material, if viewed from a military standpoint. His musket was usually a veritable bed of rust, his suit of blue besmeared with grease and his shoes, if he happened to have any, were a sight to behold. The exacting nature of his labors in the cookhouse made it hard for him to keep his paraphernalia of war in order. Sometimes he was excused from inspection, but this made it all the worse for him when his captain did order him out. Of all the ludicrous things that came under my observation during the war, I can remember nothing which, in actual drollery, exceeded the figure cut by the company cook as he stood awkwardly in line upon inspection, his face bearing a look of real agony and his whole body trembling beneath the stern and reproachful gaze of the inspecting officer, as if he were saying beneath his breath, with barely suppressed sobs, "You couldn't do any better yourself if you were in my place."

Almost everybody, of course, has heard of the man who had no shoes, but who, when ordered out upon inspection, appeared with his bare feet blacked in a manner that would cause any "professor" of the box and brush to be wild with envy. Yet few regard the yarn as true. It was, nevertheless, a fact, and it showed rare fidelity to military requirements, although it provoked a good deal of merriment at the time.

Some men could never see any utility in white gloves. They could imagine how nice they might be in the militia, but in actual service, knocking about in all kinds of weather, in swamps and forests, they appeared to be sadly out of place. There was one purpose, however, for which they were eminently useful. That was for wear upon inspection—not by the men in the ranks (they seldom had any, being obliged to use theirs for rags in cleaning their guns)—but by the inspecting officer. They were handy then in determining the amount of rust that had adhered to the end of a ramrod after it had been in contact with the bottom of a gun barrel.

A story was told while the army was under command of General George B. McClellan[1] that bore somewhat heavily upon the alleged characteristics of that officer. It was said that President Lincoln, while on a visit to the camps, reproved a soldier for having a rusty musket. "The gun may be dirty," replied the man, "but if you will just step down to my tent I'll show you a shovel that you can see your face in." This yarn was made to do much service in various parts of the South, wherever it appeared to be necessary to find fault, and its application to McClellan, therefore, cannot be certified.

We had a sergeant in our company who had seen service in the English army, and, of course, our battles were mere skirmishes when compared with those in which he had been prominently engaged. He had fought at Balaklava and Sevastopol and I do not know on how many other bloody fields. He used to tell one story which was designed to show how those who had charge of supplies

1. McClellan was a colleague of Robert E. Lee in the Corps of Engineers during the Mexican-American War, where he received two brevets. He was a captain in the First United States Cavalry when he resigned on January 16, 1857, to pursue business interests. Appointed major general of Ohio volunteers on April 23, 1861, he was elevated to command the United States Army on November 1, 1861. Kimball's story about a shiny shovel referred to McClellan's slow and methodical approach to war, best illustrated by a Southern editor who wrote: "We must dig, dig, dig, or McClellan will dig into Richmond. The spade can only be conquered with the spade, and the shovel will always defeat the musket." Relieved after Antietam, McClellan resigned on November 8, 1864, on the very day he ran against Lincoln in the presidential election. Defeated by Lincoln, he eventually was elected New Jersey governor and died in Orange, New Jersey, on October 29, 1885. Warner, *Generals in Blue*, 290–92; Heitman, *Historical Register*, 1:656; *Boston Herald*, July 19, 1862.

in the Crimea escaped censure for supposed dereliction. An officer was sent out there from the War Office in London to see how matters were going on. He came to the regiment in which our sergeant was serving. The colonel knew he was coming, and as a device for covering up certain marked deficiencies in flesh among the men, occasioned by scarcity of supplies, he taught them a new thing in drill. This was to press their tongues into their cheeks at a given signal, the idea being to make them appear fat. The officer from London came and, as he passed down the line, the colonel gave the signal that had been agreed upon for "right cheek bluff" and, as he passed up, that for "left cheek bluff." Thus all was made to appear lovely and the commissary escaped censure.

Does the reader remember that glorious sequel of the weary march—the roaring, crackling, cheering campfire? How after the long tramp through dust or mud, freed from weight of knapsack, grip of belt and from the score of other checks to breath and motion, we scampered to field and forest like children fresh from school in quest of seasoned twigs and smooth, dry rails and, piling them high upon the blazing fire, watched the hissing flames till all save home was forgotten? Ah, those were bright moments in our soldier life! We can never realize how much fence rails added to the *comforts* of the bivouac. What good-natured rivalry took place in gathering them! How we ran to get ahead of the Ninth New York and the Eleventh Pennsylvania and the other rival regiments of the brigade and yet secretly rejoiced to see them, too, get a liberal share!

Talk about the delights of rich furnishings and open grates or of the warmth and convenience of the furnace register; what are they when compared to the real comfort and the real satisfaction of the soldier bivouacked in the field—his coffee drank, his hard bread eaten, his pipe lighted, his body outstretched upon the grass with feet to the fire and head resting upon his blanket roll, with as keen a sense of comfort and of the adaptability of his surroundings as any lolling occupant of the most opulent dwelling? And what shall we say of that fire more than we have said and repeated a thousand times? What is there, anyway, so fascinating about a fire? Are we fire worshippers? I have often thought that soldiers in the field showed strong leanings that way. I have in mind a couple of stories about fence rails which may interest the reader and cause him to give those blessed though inanimate things a kindly thought.

In Upper Maryland and the Shenandoah Valley we had General Abercrombie as a brigade commander who, though naturally a good-hearted man, was nevertheless too much warped by Regular Army discipline to allow us to follow unchecked our manifold inclinations. Among other unpleasant restrictions imposed was a very strict order against burning fence rails. Just think of it. Imagine men living in the open air and confined to the green logs of the forest for fuel! We arrived in camp one night after a hard march, in the midst of a drizzling rain, while this very obnoxious order was in force. We stacked our muskets, unslung our knapsacks and were preparing to extract what comfort as we could from our misery, when Captain David Allen, Jr.[2]—a good deal of a wag, by the way, but one of the bravest men in the Army of the Potomac, afterwards giving his life for his country in the depths of the Wilderness—having been detailed as officer of the day, made us a little speech. He reminded us in stern tones of the order then in force, and declared with tremendous emphasis of carrying it out to the letter. "Men," said he, "I want you to distinctly understand that while I am about here I am determined that fence rails and all other private property of citizens shall be respected." And then he added, *sotto voce*, "I shall be around here about fifteen minutes." I need not tell the reader what followed.

The hero of the other story was our beloved Colonel Fletcher Webster. We turned into an open field one rainy night, just at

2. Prior to the war David Allen, Jr., had belonged to the American Guard, and friends remembered that he "made military science his study." After the fall of Fort Sumter, Allen raised over a hundred volunteers, who called themselves the Dale Guards, and formed most of them into Co. K, Twelfth Massachusetts, prior to his commission as captain dated June 26, 1861. Wounded at Antietam, he was promoted to lieutenant colonel of the regiment on October 8, 1862. Allen was detailed to the staff of General John C. Robinson and, in a letter written on April 28, 1864, said confidently, "The army is in fine condition, and we are all hopeful and confident of success." He was killed a week later on May 5, after the fighting was over at the Wilderness, when he rode over to check on his old comrades in Co. K. Pringle, *History of Gloucester*, 117, 158; *Massachusetts Soldiers*, 2:61; *Cape Ann Light and Gloucester (Mass.) Telegraph*, May 21, 1864.

Lieutenant Colonel David Allen, Jr.
Courtesy of the U.S. Army Heritage
and Education Center

sunset, in the vicinity of Thoroughfare Gap. It had been a long, tiresome march, with mud and the rain all the way, and our clothing was drenched to our skin. We sat down, some of us, upon our knapsacks, waiting for the arrival of the teams, for those were the days of Sibley tents, before we improved upon that old adage of Scripture to "take up thy bed and walk" by shouldering also the house. Pardon me, comrades, if I stop here in the midst of my story just long enough to pay one passing tribute to those old Sibleys. So much like an Indian's wigwam, so roomy and so grand! What a tremendous leap that was from their towering magnificence down to the dugout, what afterward became so unpleasantly familiar as the "shelter." Well, to resume my story. I need only say our misery can be imagined. There was slim prospect of either dry clothing or hot coffee. That "order" was still in force. No fire, because the woods were afar off and the boys were weary. Besides, we did not know at what moment in the near future those teams would come up, and each man wanted to be there when they did arrive to look out for his own. They began to brood over the disagreeable features of their situation and indulge in unfavorable comments upon what they regarded as unnecessary solicitude for the welfare of their foes.

Webster paced back and forth with bowed head as if in deep thought, evidently thinking—as he always was, God bless him—how he could make his boys happy and comfortable. "Let the 'old man' alone," said a tall sergeant, "he'll think up some way to get us out of this predicament." All at once he brightened up as though a pleasant thought had entered his mind and, glancing toward the fence, exclaimed, "Why, boys, *those are not rails!*" We all looked in the direction indicated, and sure enough they were not. They were round, unsplit, unhewn *poles!* We wondered why we had not discovered that before. How stupid! The men charged with a shout upon the fence. In less time than it takes to tell it we had plenty of nice fires and all the boys were happy. A sergeant of my company said that old Abercrombie might "go to thunder with his order against burning rails—poles are just as good!" The general arrived soon after, but his expostulations were in vain, for the colonel argued the point with the ability of a lawyer and the fact was well enough established for present purposes that rails were one thing and poles were another.

Heavy showers were never welcome to soldiers upon the march, loaded down as they usually were, and bad as the roads were any-way, but I remember one of these outpourings that actually had something commendable about it. One of our companies, H, was acting as provost guard for the brigade. It was marching a short distance in rear of the column and, when the rain came on, was directly opposite a small cabin and its attendant outbuildings. A sudden and irresistible impulse to gain cover seemed to seize ev-eryone at once and with a rush Company H—all except the cap-tain, who, by virtue of his office as provost marshal, was mounted and at that moment a little in advance—made for the shelter of the buildings. Before proceeding far, the captain discovered that he was alone in his glory, without a command, and then he, too, concluded to seek the seclusion granted by the cabin.

Company H was now all safely housed and the rain was de-scending in first class shape. It seemed as if it had never rained harder. Some of the men were in the wood shed, others were in the barn, a few, including the officers and sergeants, were in the cabin, while a small *coterie* of congenial spirits, among whom was a favorite soldier nicknamed "Old Reliable," had taken refuge in the hen coop. But "Old Reliable" and his chums were sadly disap-pointed, for large bodies of troops had been passing all day and the only sign of life found in the *fowl* interior was a big, strapping fellow in Confederate gray, a tired out specimen of Stonewall Jackson's Foot Cavalry, who cheerfully yielded to the inevitable.

The men of Company H had not been under cover long, when one of the general's aides rode up in front of the cabin and informed the captain that the brigade had halted for the night and the provost guard was wanted at headquarters. The captain, always prompt to obey an order, rain or shine, called upon his men to fall in. The men were naturally slow in taking their places in line, as it was still raining heavily, those in the hen coop hanging back so long that the captain finally concluded to march off without them, after detailing one of the sergeants to remain behind to see that they came directly to camp as soon as they saw fit to leave their shelter. The sergeant was also ordered to report their names for punishment.

The rest of the company had been in camp some time and the rain had ceased to fall, when the hen-coop squad came in with their prisoner. The sergeant was ordered to detail them to guard the Johnny through the night and he at once divided them into reliefs of one man each and prescribed the usual two hours as the period of duty. He was ordered to take charge of the matter himself and to see that all the regulations applicable in such cases were strictly complied with.

At twelve o'clock it became "Old Reliable's" turn to go on. The vigilant sergeant, after posting his man, sat down before the fire. The sentinel soon noticed that his superior officer had planted his back against a tree and had fallen fast asleep. Feeling a little sleepy himself, "Old Reliable" began to wonder if there was not some way he could combine duty with his own nocturnal desire. At last he hit upon a novel expedient—why not turn in with the reb and both have a good nap. So he unrolled his blanket, tucked one edge of it under the Johnny, got under the remainder himself, crawled up as closely as he could, spoon fashion, threw one leg and one arm over his prisoner and both were soon in the land of dreams.

"Old Reliable's" two hours and a little more had passed, when he was awakened by someone trying to arouse the sleeping sergeant. He sprang to his feet and, when the man with three stripes upon his arm arrived with another hen-coop culprit to relieve him, was pacing back and forth in the exact method laid down in the regulations. Months afterward, Company H was assembled about a huge campfire when someone happened to mention the hen coop affair. "Old Reliable," at the solicitation of those who sat near him, told how he guarded the reb that night. Someone had the courage to suggest that the new method of guarding prisoners should be recommended for general adoption. But the captain refused to do so.

A year and four months from the organization of a regiment to its first battle is a long time—it seemed much longer to us than it can possibly seem to the reader of these lines if he were not an actual participant in the war—but it must be remembered that, with the exception of the First and Eleventh Regiments, very few of the three years men from this state had a much earlier "baptism of blood" than did the men of my organization. We had an excellent drill master and when there was an opportunity for battalion and company drills we were kept pretty steadily at it. In the spring of 1862 we paid much attention to firing volleys. We got so after a while that it was worth a long journey to see and hear us fire a volley. All the hammers would strike the nipples together and the combined discharges sounded like the report of one piece. Our reputation in this regard began to spread through the division and one day our new brigade commander, General George L. Hartsuff,[3] came over to witness this wonder for himself.

We were drawn up in line near camp and our colonel made us a little speech, reminding us of the honor of having the general for a spectator and all that sort of thing. He cautioned us to keep very cool and "wait for the word." We were put through a little battalion drill and had a short tussle with the manual. Then we were

3. A graduate of West Point in 1852, Hartsuff spent the first months of the war on staff assignments before his promotion to brigadier general on April 15, 1862. He assumed command of Abercrombie's brigade on May 1, 1862, and led it until wounded at Antietam. Unable to resume field command, Hartsuff remained in the service and retired on June 29, 1871, as a major general. He was a lucky man, surviving the sinking of the *Lady Elgin* on September 8, 1860, and wounds received in the Seminole Wars and at Antietam. General Hartsuff died in New York City on May 16, 1874. Warner, *Generals in Blue*, 3; Heitman, *Historical Register*, 1:507; *Cape Ann Light and Gloucester Telegraph*, May 17, 1862; *Springfield Republican*, October 11, 1871; *Boston Journal*, May 18, 1874.

supposed to be limbered up and ready. Now we were to show what we could do. We loaded. "Ready, aim, recover arms, aim, fire!" Oh dear! It was the old, old story. Some nervous fellow fired a little before the word, than half a dozen more did the same thing and the whole regiment discharged their pieces in about this order. For fully five minutes the fusillade was kept up. After it began to seem barely possible that the guns were all let off, everybody drew a long breath, the colonel turned very red and General Hartsuff asked, in an inquiring tone, "Have you all got through?" Then as he turned to ride away, he added, "If that is what you call a volley, I don't want to hear any more."

One day in the spring of 1862, Hartsuff's brigade was on the march towards Fredericksburg. The day was intensely warm. We came to a pump beside the road and, as was usual in such cases, the men crowded about it to fill their canteens. So general did the movement become that there was danger that the whole brigade would become disorganized and the march impeded. The commanding officers of the various regiments endeavored to disperse the crowd and to induce the men to move on, but in spite of their efforts the number of thirsty men was constantly increasing and every moment becoming more determined.

Something had to be done and so General Hartsuff himself rode in among the crowd and with drawn sword commanded the men to disperse. This they finally did, after many angry looks and words, the roughest expression coming from a member of the Ninth New York. Several days after, the story came out in this way. Colonel John W. Stiles[4] had occasion to complain to General Hartsuff of some insulting epithet applied to him by a man in another regiment, when Hartsuff retorted, "Yes, but that wasn't so bad as the epithet one of your men applied to me the other day. He said

4. John W. Stiles closed up his business interests after Fort Sumter fell, and on May 27, 1861, he led the Ninth Regiment, New York State National Guards, to the nation's capital. His regiment received the new designation of Eighty-third New York, and he commanded it until his resignation on January 18, 1863, "his health entirely shattered." When Stiles died in New York City on September 16, 1885, the Boston press noted that the colonel "had many friends among Massachusetts veterans representing commands with which his regiment was associated." *New York Tribune*, September 17, 1885; *Boston Journal*, September 18, 1885.

I was 'a God damned Dutch son of a bitch.' But the fellow was greatly excited and I easily forgave him for his rashness."

We men of the Twelfth Massachusetts always regarded ourselves as fortunate in being brigaded with the Eleventh Pennsylvania Regiment. The strong attachment of a faithful dog for its master has always seemed to me to involve one of nature's secrets, difficult to explain or understand. Of the many cases that have come under my notice, the most curious and remarkable was that of a dog named Sally which for four long years followed the fortunes of the Eleventh Pennsylvania. She was brought into camp near Chester, Pennsylvania in May of 1861 and being a chubby little pup then, playful and pretty, immediately became a great pet of the men. Sally at once joined heartily in all the frolics of the soldiers.

I never knew, but certain it was that at first she was just a little shy of us Massachusetts men. I thought at the time that possibly this might be accounted for by the fact that she was born in a neighborhood that had at some time been visited by commercial travelers or peddlers from Yankeedom. After a while, however, she consented to receive our attentions and was always sure of a dainty breakfast from any Massachusetts tent into which she poked her nose—that is, if we were not worse off than dogs ourselves. The Eleventh was commanded by one of the bravest men I ever knew—Colonel Richard Coulter,[5] a veteran of the Mexican War—who soon became known throughout the brigade as "Dick Coulter" and in course of time we began to speak of Sally as "Dick Coulter's dog."

Many a time at dress parade did I go over to the camp of the Eleventh to see the important part that Sally always took in that imposing pageant. With the long line at "parade rest," the drum

5. Coulter served in the Mexican-American War as a private before becoming a prominent Pennsylvania attorney. He served as lieutenant colonel of the Eleventh Pennsylvania for its three-month enlistment and colonel when the regiment was reorganized for three years' service. Always present where the battle was most furious, Coulter was wounded at Fredericksburg, Gettysburg, and Spotsylvania, in addition to having three horses shot underneath him. He was mustered out on July 1, 1865, and returned home to Greensburg, Pennsylvania, where he died on October 14, 1908, leaving an estate valued at $2 million. Bates, *Martial Deeds of Pennsylvania*, 673–76; *Philadelphia Inquirer*, October 15 and 20, 1908.

corps slowly marching down the front, the colonel with folded arms calmly looking into the faces of the men and Sally lying at the feet of the color bearer, as if she loved to be in the shadow of the flag, the scene was an impressive one. On the march Sally followed close behind the colonel. In the long marches, no matter how many of the men fell out, she never straggled. When the brigade came into camp the Eleventh was always sure of being represented by a colonel, a flag and a dog.

At Cedar Mountain, Rappahannock Station, Thoroughfare Gap, Second Bull Run, Chantilly, South Mountain and Antietam she demonstrated that dogs can be brave and true. In this latter bloody battle she was wounded, but imitated many of her betters by remaining on the field until the fight was over. It was soon enough then for her to have her wound attended to and her sympathy for her brave protectors, who were lying torn and bleeding, was manifested in many ways peculiar to the canine. Men related afterward how Sally "came and licked their wounds."

One day in the spring of 1863, a division review took place. The men were ordered to appear at their best. Our regiment resolved to outdo all others in its cleanliness. So they visited all the sutlers and bought their entire stock of paper collars and white gloves, creating such a corner in the market that there were none left for the other regiments of the division. The review came. The regiment appeared, gorgeously adorned, their muskets shining in the sun, the men marching with that erect and firm tread born of a consciousness of superiority. Thus the other less fortunate battalions were made to feel chagrined and unhappy. But the men of the Eleventh were not content to suffer without striking back. Just as the long line was formed and the bands were playing "Hail to the Chief," with the reviewing officers and their brilliant staffs riding down in front, Sally appeared and followed along in front of the whole division, having a paper collar around her neck and a white glove on each paw. The joke was good-naturedly appreciated and roars of laughter were heard long after the men broke ranks.

At Fredericksburg Sally's record was bad. She was probably wiser than some of the generals, foresaw that the whole thing was to be an ignominious failure and became demoralized. She ran

Lieutenant Colonel
Benjamin F. Cook. Courtesy
of the U.S. Army Heritage
and Education Center

away in the face of the enemy, but no one in the brigade ever blamed her for it. At Gettysburg Sally atoned for her disgraceful behavior at Fredericksburg. Sally refused to retreat. She held her ground and was not seen again till July 4th, when it is supposed her patriotic instincts led her back into "God's country" in order that she might celebrate the glorious Fourth. Sally came through the rebel army and was seen between the picket lines. Captain Benjamin F. Cook,[6] though exposed to great danger in so doing,

6. In 1851 Cook joined Co. G, Eighth Massachusetts Militia Regiment, the company commanded by his father. He received a commission as first lieutenant in Co. K, Twelfth Massachusetts, on June 26, 1861, receiving promotions to captain, major, and lieutenant colonel, the latter taking effect May 6, 1864. When he was mustered out on July 8, 1864, a notation on his discharge papers read: "Brave and fearless in action, strict disciplinarian; one who knows his business and does it." One of his men recalled: "He gave us to eat from the last hardtack in his lean old haversack, and he gave us to drink from the last drops in his battered old canteen. He was glad when we were glad, and he sorrowed when we were sorrowful." Cook returned to Gloucester, where he rejoined the local militia, served in the legislature, and was elected mayor. He died September 3, 1915. *Massachusetts Soldiers*, 2:62; *Cape Ann Light and Gloucester Telegraph*, February 22, 1868; Eliot, *Biographical History of Massachusetts*, 8: n.p.; *Boston Journal*, September 4, 1915; *Boston Herald*, September 4, 1915.

went out and escorted her in and was rewarded with the cheers of the whole brigade. In the Wilderness, May 8, 1864, Sally was wounded again. This time her hurt was more severe, being in the neck, and she had to be carried to the field hospital for treatment.

After having her wound operated on and dressed, Sally reported to her regiment for duty. I imagine I hear the reader ask, "Pray, what duty could a dog do in the army?" True, Sally never carried a musket, but she did a great deal to encourage those who had the fighting to do and on one particular occasion did much to check desertion. It is a well known fact that the first thing a great many conscripts did after joining the army was to run away. One tried this in the Eleventh. Sally saw him when he started and interrupted his game by planting her teeth firmly in his flesh, thus reminding him of his duty to his country.

Sally's day came on the 6th of February, 1865. In the battle of Hatcher's Run the faithful creature, after being the constant companion of the men of the Eleventh for nearly four years, was killed by a bullet from the enemy. The boys dug her a little grave, and buried her where she fell under the enemy's fire. The night before her death she howled a great deal, as if she had a premonition of what was coming. She slept among the soldiers of Company D and her most immediate neighbors were a sergeant and three men. In the same fight in which she met her death, the sergeant and one of the men were killed and the other two were severely wounded.

CHAPTER 8

Front Royal

General Banks has been unjustly blamed for the ill-success of his military operations in the Shenandoah Valley and has often been sneered at by cheap critics as "Jackson's Quartermaster." The blame rests rather with those who were higher in authority than he, those who compelled him to face Jackson's powerful force with a body of troops very much smaller and therefore entirely inadequate. The enemy knew every foot of ground and the people residing there were intensely disloyal, so that the Confederate leaders were kept constantly informed of all that was going on. General Banks did the best he could, with the limited number of men given him, and a great deal better than many of his critics could have done under the same circumstances. The fact that General Banks has so patiently borne the abuse that has been heaped upon him and has never since the war spoken in his own defence makes it a pleasure for me to thus speak in his vindication. I believe I am but voicing the sentiment of the veterans of Massachusetts and of all those who served under him in doing so.

Campaigning when all things were propitious was sometimes actually enjoyable—provided the weather was fine—but when everything worked against us, including the weather, personal misery and military failure were sure to result. A campaign decidedly of the latter description was that which took place in the early summer of 1862, having for its object the cutting off of Stonewall Jackson after his famous raid upon General Banks in the Valley of the Shenandoah. The recollection of that trying experience is revived by an old letter that now lies before me, so faded as to be almost illegible. Its description of the sufferings endured, its tone of disappointment and chagrin at the unsuccessful issue of the campaign in question carry me back in memory to that long, severe march and again the wet and hungry thousands are all about me.

Our wagon trains were of tremendous length and the inconvenience of moving and the difficulty of protecting them promised sure defeat when once we should find ourselves close to the enemy. So the work of cutting them down began and it went on until finally only two wagons were left to a regiment. This necessitated the abandonment of tents, cooking utensils (except for the officers) and everything else not absolutely essential to the maintenance of life. Even the bands went home. At first the men grumbled fearfully and it was no wonder that they did, for nearly all of the poetry of army life had disappeared from their midst.

Just before this campaign began or to be explicit, on the 21st of May, a new abomination crept into military life in our division in the shape of the shelter tent. No more the roomy and comfortable Sibley, with its fascinating appearance and complete adaptability to the soldier's needs, but instead a miserable little dog house yelped the "shelter"—a name which was a constant and downright lie. This consisted of three pieces of cotton cloth about five feet square. Two of them were buttoned together over a ridgepole and the third was buttoned on to one end, thus forming a back to the tent. When erected the "shelter" would accommodate three men, but they had to lie close together. If they were tall fellows their feet were unavoidably exposed to the cold wind and rain, unless they were lucky enough to have another strip of cloth or could agree among themselves as to which should give up his rubber blanket for a "fence to the front yard." For the "ponies" it doubtless did very well, but for us "six footers" it was a miserable failure. It was hard—very hard—for us to lie down to pleasant dreams in this insignificant little structure and to be interrupted by either head or foot becoming wet. But, for that matter, the whole body might just as well have been exposed to the elements, for the pitiless rain would often creep in through its thin substance or find its way through the interstices of the ridgepole, where the two sides were alleged to join. *Shelter* tent, indeed!

When on guard or picket we usually slept without other covering than our rubber blankets and, in bad weather, threw down a few fence rails or rolled a couple of logs together and lay down upon them to keep our bodies from unpleasant contact with the wet ground. On the march, when night came on, it was seldom that any attempt was made to establish a regular camp and shelter tents, even, were not always pitched. We usually bunked down wherever it was handy or convenient, wrapped ourselves up in our overcoats and blankets and threw our ponchos over us, covering both head and heels. This protected us from the rain and also from the dew, which was almost as bad, that is if the drainage had been taken into consideration when the spot for the "bed" was selected.

Another useful institution—the company cook, with his camp kettles, his baking pans and his spiders—had to go at this time and we were reduced to the alternative of having to either spend several hours each day over the smoky fires preparing our own food or starve. Very few, however, showed any inclination to choose the latter and although we chafed considerably at first over having to perform what we then thought to be menial service, we finally broke in all right and in time became good cooks as well as disciplined soldiers. We learned to cook from dire necessity, just as papooses learn to swim when thrown overboard. Verily, the stern realities of war were rapidly finding their way into our army life.

Officers were no better off than the men when the army was on the move, as the teams were usually far behind. In the matter of food they were even in worse condition, for sometimes they could get nothing from the commissary. It was no unusual sight to see captains and lieutenants and even colonels enjoying the hospitality of private soldiers. This, however, had one useful effect. It established good fellowship and in time of trial this was of immense importance in maintaining regimental pride and in bringing about that community of feeling and interest necessary for effective blows and united actions.

Our food was now given to us raw. For cooking utensils, we had tin plates and dippers. The former were used both for frying pans and to eat from and the latter for boiling soup and coffee and sometimes rice and beans. When we halted anywhere long enough thousands of little fires would spring up as if by magic and the process of cooking would go on. Frequently two fence rails would be placed near together, a fire would be built between them, and scores of dippers and plates would thus be accommodated. But this plan had one serious disadvantage. Sometimes, in the night especially, some blundering fellow would stub his toe against one of the rails, fall headlong, upset a whole company's coffee and be greeted with a volley of oaths too terrible to be even thought of. These tin plates were also used as shovels sometimes. They came in very handy for throwing up little rifle pits to protect us from the bullets of the enemy. It had a good effect, too. It removed some of the soot. Many men used halves of canteens instead of plates and these were a little better in some respects; they were hollowed out more.

Our bills of fare were not very extensive, of course, but what we lacked in variety we tried to make up in wonderful names. For instance, a mixture of fried pork and soaked hardtack became "skillygalee," "lobscouse," "squaw-boo," "McClellan hash" and other equally unspellable names, while our list of boiled dishes, usually made from the same materials with the very infrequent addition of desiccated vegetables and things confiscated from adjoining plantations, was extended almost *ad infinitum* and often quite *ad nauseam*. Fresh meat, when not made into soups was broiled over the coals. For this purpose, ramrods, bayonets and sharpened sticks were brought into requisition.

It would seem a hard life and yet, after we got used to it, it was not so very hard—when we had enough to eat. We scarcely missed butter, milk and other delicacies of life at home and, although the ground did not furnish so good a bed as those we now enjoy, we got accustomed even to that hardship, too. As an illustration, I may say that on my first night at home, after three years of service, I lay upon a feather bed until nearly morning in a vain attempt to get to sleep and finally had to crawl out of bed and lie upon the floor. Then I fell asleep immediately. It was some time before I got thoroughly accustomed to civilized methods.

We were lying near Fredericksburg, Virginia when these calamities and many smaller ones happened. We had been designated on our arrival there as the "bandbox brigade" by our distinguished corps commander, the unfortunate General Irvin McDowell.[1] This not very pleasing salutation, coupled with his ill luck at the first battle of Bull Run, and what we began to regard even at that early day as his failure to do his duty in not marching to the support of McClellan's army upon the Peninsula, caused us to cherish a hearty dislike for him. It will thus be seen that in addition to the discomforts we now began to experience with so much force and their demoralizing effect upon us, we lacked confidence in our leader, a very necessary thing to the success of a campaign. There was one bright ray of light among us, however. General E. O. C. Ord,[2] who commanded the division, and General Hartsuff, who commanded our brigade, possessed our highest confidence and respect.

McDowell put us into training, too. He caused us to carry our knapsacks on battalion drill and sent us off upon long sham marches just to limber us up. All this, he pretended to believe, would increase our strength and add to our effectiveness as soldiers, but its actual result was to increase our disgust for his methods rather than our *esprit de corps*. We sometimes had the laugh

1. An officer in the adjutant general's office when the war began, Irvin McDowell was quickly elevated to brigadier general on May 14, 1861. He commanded the hastily organized Union army at Bull Run, but despite his defeat he was promoted to major general on March 14, 1862. Assigned to command the Third Corps of the newly established Army of Virginia, he participated in the second Union defeat at Bull Run. When a mortally wounded Union officer claimed that he was dying because of McDowell's treachery, the general asked for a court of inquiry into this and other allegations. Although exonerated, he never again served in the field; he remained in the army and retired in 1882. General McDowell died in San Francisco on May 4, 1885. Warner, *Generals in Blue*, 297–99; Heitman, *Historical Register*, 1:664; *Boston Journal*, May 6, 1885.

2. A brigadier general in 1861, Ord commanded Union forces at the small skirmish at Dranesville, Virginia, and parlayed that into a promotion to major general on May 2, 1862. When he was assigned to command the division containing the Webster Regiment, one of those Massachusetts men remarked that "we will be well taken care of in every respect." By mid-June Ord had left, requesting a transfer from McDowell's command and beginning a career that saw him command a corps in 1863. He died in Havana, Cuba, on July 22, 1883. Warner, *Generals in Blue*, 349–50; Heitman, *Historical Register*, 1:759; *Cape Ann Light and Gloucester Telegraph*, May 31, 1862; *Boston Evening Transcript*, June 16, 1862; *New York Herald*, July 24, 1883.

on the "old man," however, in spite of his shrewdness, for many
of the boys stuffed their huge knapsacks with straw, leaving their
legitimate contents hidden away in camp. When passing corps
headquarters, where the general with his peculiar head gear usually gazed complacently upon us as we went sweating and puffing
by with a sort of "I've-got-you-this-time" air, we indulged in many
an inward smile while distorting our faces and cramping our limbs
in feigned torture from our heavy loads.

On May 23d the division was reviewed by a distinguished party
from Washington, including President Lincoln,[3] Secretary of War
Edwin Stanton[4] and the French Minister[5] and we longed for a
chance to tell "Uncle Abe" how we played it on the general with
the straw. Although we got no opportunity to do so and no chance
to rehearse our wrongs or to complain of the indignities that had
been heaped upon us, we got some compensation in imagining
how the humor-loving president would have laughed could he
have heard the straw story.

On the 25th orders came to march and at four in the afternoon,
stripped of everything not thought absolutely necessary for the actual maintenance of life and in not a very amiable frame of mind,
we took the road. A few of the boys, thinking it would be another
false start, got caught by the straw dodge and also moved out with

3. In January 1862 Lincoln had issued an order commanding the Federal
forces to commence offensive operations on February 22, an edict that was
promptly ignored. When McClellan planned a campaign against Richmond
by way of the peninsula of land between the York and James Rivers, Lincoln
remained unconvinced of its prospects for success. While McClellan slowly advanced toward Richmond, Lincoln came personally to visit McDowell's corps
that had been assigned to defend Washington. Unimpressed with McDowell's
ability, within a month Lincoln brought John Pope on board to lead the Army of
Virginia in a vain attempt to organize a viable Federal force in northern Virginia.
Dictionary of American Biography, 11:253.

4. A successful lawyer in Ohio, Pennsylvania, and the District of Columbia,
Stanton was appointed attorney general by President James Buchanan. He returned to private life until January 15, 1862, when he succeeded Simon Cameron
as secretary of war. One assessment stated that Stanton "was generally conceded
to be able, energetic, and patriotic." Perhaps his greatest weakness was the tendency to retaliate against those he deemed not aggressive enough in prosecuting
the war. Stanton died on Christmas Eve, 1869, in Washington, D.C. *Dictionary of
American Biography*, 17:517–21.

5. Henri Mercier was the French minister.

rather too light cartridge boxes and haversacks for a campaign, but they managed to keep the knowledge of their discomfiture from the officers until such time as opportunity offered to repair these defects in their military make-up. We traveled northward until three o'clock the next morning, when we bivouacked in a filthy camp that had been abandoned by the enemy a few weeks before. At eight we resumed our march and soon arrived at Aquia Creek Landing on the Potomac, a distance of twenty miles from the starting point. We were on our way to the Shenandoah Valley, where we were expected to "bag" Jackson, who had routed Banks and was now endeavoring to escape to Richmond. A large fleet of steamers was lying in the river to take us to Alexandria.

At nine o'clock we went on board the boats, it falling to the lot of the regiment to be assigned to the *South America*. We began steaming up the Potomac and had proceeded but about a mile when the first ill omen came. This was in the sudden and complete breaking down of the *South America*'s machinery. We were then transferred to the *Vanderbilt*, a large steamer drawing rather too much water for ordinary river navigation, but a splendid boat otherwise for the transportation of troops. She was fairly loaded before receiving the *South America*'s passengers and now the crush was simply terrible. Men were wedged in so closely among horses and munitions of war that it became impossible to move about and exhibitions of bad temper toward each other and angry denunciations of the officers in charge of the expedition were frequent. Then we had no coffee to drink and nothing but hardtack and raw pork to eat—enough to make soldiers cross at any time.

The *Vanderbilt* had proceeded slowly about twelve or fifteen miles up river when a peculiar grating sound, accompanied by the audible shaking of the boat causing our nerves to tremble, showed that the old experiment of trying to run a steamer overland was being tried again. After a persistent trial the attempt had to be abandoned and the *Vanderbilt* came to a final stop. Several times she tried to proceed, but only became more firmly imbedded in the mud at the close of each attempt, until at last it was found to be impossible to move at all. Here was accident number two. We began at once—soldier fashion—to discuss the cause of the mishap and to look about for the inevitable culprit. Someone finally

discovered that the pilot was to blame and it was also charged that
he had made the attempt to run the boat over the river's bank in
the interest of Jeff Davis's Confederacy rather than in those of the
science of navigation. Whether this was really true or not we never
knew, but we did hear some time afterward that he was retired
from the service and given secluded quarters in Fortress Monroe.

We spent the remainder of that forenoon and all of the afternoon and evening in discussing the interesting (?) events of our
connection with McDowell thus far and in speculating as to the
prospect of catching Jackson. Early in the morning more steamers and several tugs arrived and the *Vanderbilt's* passengers were
transferred. We now started up the Potomac with every prospect
of being able to reach Alexandria. One of the new arrivals was the
Nantasket, whose familiar name and appearance to Massachusetts
men caused shouts of delight on every hand.

At 11 A.M. on the 27th, after a rapid and delightful sail up the
beautiful Potomac, we landed at Alexandria. The rest of the day
was passed away pretty much as each soldier pleased and the Marshall House, where the gallant Ellsworth was killed, the old slave
pen then used as a guard house and other points of interest were
visited. A few of the men liked the old slave pen so well that they
concluded to remain a while after their companions had left, but
this is a part of the unwritten history of the expedition. At 9 P.M.
we were loaded upon freight cars for a journey to Manassas Junction. The train moved out, for a few moments everything looked
propitious and the bagging of Jackson seemed certain. Then, all
at once, something about the engine went to smash and our hopes
and expectations were again crushed. Here was accident number
three. It took until after midnight to repair the difficulty, but we
were finally able to proceed slowly and arrived at Manassas Junction shortly after daylight on the 28th. We marched about a mile,
with stiffened limbs, and then went into camp.

At 5 A.M., after a good night's rest, we set out again for that
rather indefinite point where we were to intercept Jackson. We
passed through the little towns of Gainesville and Haymarket and,
on getting a mile or so beyond the latter, concluded to try railroad-
ing again. For some unexplained reason—perhaps it was because
of the fear that another accident might possibly happen—we were

only carried about five or six miles by rail this time, when we were ordered to pursue our journey by "Foot and Walker's Line," a more natural method, after all, for soldiers. We had a good opportunity to study the wonderful scenery of the Blue Ridge while passing through Thoroughfare Gap and a short distance beyond its southern opening, just as the sun was going down, we went into camp—that is, if lying upon the ground with little or no covering but our blankets can be called going into camp.

At daylight on the 30th, with no breakfast and with slim prospects for dinner, we moved on. We marched through White Plains and Salem and after a hard tramp, during which we encountered a terrific thunder shower, we reached Piedmont Gap and lay down upon the ground supperless. The division was now together. It consisted of the brigades of James B. Ricketts,[6] George L. Hartsuff and Abram Duryee,[7] four batteries (twenty-four guns) and two regiments of cavalry.

The hungry men took the road again at five o'clock next morning and soon reached Piedmont Station. Here a train was found loaded with supplies for Shields's[8] division. The temptation was

6. Although a graduate of West Point, class of 1839, Ricketts has been characterized as "unexceptional" in his prewar career. Wounded and captured at Bull Run, he was freed in a prisoner exchange then promoted to brigadier general on April 30, 1862. He commanded a division until injured at Antietam and did not resume field command until the 1864 campaign. Disabled by a wound received at Cedar Creek, Ricketts died from long-term consequences of his wound in Washington, D.C., on September 22, 1887. Warner, *Generals in Blue*, 403–404; Heitman, *Historical Register*, 1:830.

7. A longtime militia officer in New York, Duryée recruited a regiment of Zouaves designated the Fifth New York in 1861. He was appointed brigadier general on August 31, 1861, but did not serve in the field until Pope's campaign. After recovering from multiple wounds received in this and the Battle of Antietam, Duryée found that command of his brigade had been given to an officer with less seniority. He resigned on January 5, 1863, and returned to New York City, where he died on September 27, 1890. Warner, *Generals in Blue*, 133–34; Heitman, *Historical Register*, 1:390.

8. A general in the Mexican-American War, James Shields had represented two different states in the U.S. Senate prior to an appointment as brigadier general on August 19, 1861. A lackluster performance in the Shenandoah Valley against Stonewall Jackson led to his resignation on March 28, 1863. He eventually settled in Carrollton, Missouri, where he was chosen senator from yet a third state. Shields died while on a speaking tour in Ottumwa, Iowa, on June 1, 1879. Warner, *Generals in Blue*, 444–45; Heitman, *Historical Register*, 1:883.

very great and, in the partial belief that these supplies might never reach Shields, who had already moved on toward Port Republic, and in the full knowledge that we sorely needed them, General Ord ordered their confiscation. The commissary in charge stoutly protested, but he was compelled finally to yield and we thus came into possession of three days' rations. It is needless to say we were in need of food that morning—we were actually starving—but we could not enjoy it as fully as we might had we not felt that possibly we were eating bread which our comrades needed as much as ourselves. After leaving knapsacks—what few there were in the division—and what other surplus baggage we still had at Piedmont Station, we pushed on. It now began to rain heavily. We had a hard march of twenty-four miles, our route lying through Manassas Gap, and at a late hour in the evening we halted within a mile of Front Royal. It had continued to rain all day and, of course, we were drenched to the skin. In the evening, it being pitch dark, we walked a long distance on the edge of a precipice—"Dismal Hollow"—where a single misstep, as we afterward learned, would have precipitated us a hundred feet to the rocks below.

On Sunday, June 1st, we marched through the town of Front Royal in the midst of a drenching rain and that night lay upon the wet ground just beyond the place with less to cover us than we had hitherto had. We were completely tired out and could therefore sleep even with the rain pouring on our uncovered faces, with our clothing drenched and our skin, as it were, parboiled, but it must not be supposed we were in any degree insensible to our sufferings. We felt them keenly and hundreds succumbed to the inevitable, filling all the hospital tents there were in the division and overflowing into a number of buildings in the town.

The next day we crossed the north fork of the Shenandoah, it still raining, and advanced to Sulphur Springs, within four miles of Strasburg. Here we found the river a raging torrent and the bridge gone. Jackson was reported upon the other side, troubled as much, probably, as we were by the rain and flood.

On the 3d we marched to Buckton, about four miles. Here we obtained a ration of fresh meat—nothing else—other supplies being exhausted. Jackson was reported by deserters and prisoners from his command as in full retreat up the Valley and the movements upon our side, particularly those of Shields and Fremont, gave some promise of his being cut off. We had a large number of prisoners in charge that we had picked up on the march, but these fared better than we did in the matter of food, the people living along the road supplying them quite liberally.

On the 4th, fearing that the bridge we had just crossed at Front Royal, a fine structure 150 feet long, would also be carried away and we be thus left in a bad position for obtaining supplies, we hurried back there that night. The rain came down in torrents, as it had continued to do with little cessation for nearly a week. We found the bridge still in position, though in imminent danger, and the division passed safely over. A few hours after the last regiment crossed, however, it was swept away. At Front Royal we found that a mail had arrived in our absence and for a little while the men forgot their hunger and discomfort in reading letters and papers from home.

On the 5th the knapsacks and extra baggage left at Piedmont arrived and a foraging party succeeded in bringing in a number of sheep. So our sufferings were lessened a little. It continued to rain, however, and but for the huge campfires which we kept burning everywhere we would doubtless have all succumbed to the hardships of our situation.

June 6th, in the morning, a party of soldiers who had been left on picket upon the other side of the river attempted to cross upon a raft which they had built, but when midway in the river their frail raft was swallowed up by the strong current and they were drowned in plain sight of their comrades. Among those who found a watery grave in the Shenandoah River was poor Sergeant John Brown, who had borne our pleasantry so good-naturedly and possessed the love and esteem of all his comrades.

The next five days were passed in alternate feast and famine, in alternate rain and clouds and sunshine—the latter being brief and infrequent, but each time hailed with a cheer—and on the 11th a trio of blessings arrived, consisting of rations, fair weather and the paymaster. Then joy came and gloom departed. Our campaign had been a failure and Jackson had escaped, but we had learned to suffer together for the cause for which we were contending and the bonds of comradeship and fraternity that existed among us had been welded and strengthened never to be broken. Thus the hardships and the failures of those early campaigns of the war were not wholly fruitless, for they served to give temper and discipline to an army the superior of which the world has never seen.

As actual results of the campaign, thousands of poor fellows had fallen under the hardships and privations of the march and the hospitals of Washington and Alexandria became filled with fever-stricken soldiers. More men were prostrated by disease than would have been killed and wounded in a pitched battle had we met Jackson's army of 30,000. Yet in spite of our reverses and notwithstanding our dissatisfaction at the mismanagement that had been shown, we came out of the Front Royal campaign stronger than when we entered it, for we had learned many valuable lessons and there had grown up within us a determination to strike an effective blow if ever our leaders gave us a chance to accept the gage of battle.

General Hartsuff always placed himself on a level with his men when danger was to be encountered or suffering borne. I remember one night at Front Royal when this fact was impressed very forcibly upon my mind. It was a terrible night. Rain fell in torrents and the men had no shelter at all, not even shelter tents. We were in a grove of pine trees and it was pitch dark. I started off to find some water and, picking my way through the woods, had not gone far when I tripped and fell over a prostrate form. He raised himself a little, when I discovered that it was General Hartsuff. I mumbled a few words of apology, to which he replied in the kindest manner possible, expressing his great sorrow that the men had to suffer so much, never hinting at his own condition as he lay there with not so much as a blanket to shield him from the storm.

CHAPTER 9

Cedar Mountain

The 17th of June found us again at Manassas Junction, where we began immediately to smooth war's wrinkled front. President Lincoln came down to us on the 19th and doubtless he was deeply impressed by the evidences of hardship and loss apparent on every hand. In the items of scarcity of proper supplies and the discomfort and suffering occasioned by almost constant rains, it was the toughest campaign we ever experienced.

I remember passing, one hot day in 1862, the mansion of a wealthy Virginian whose sympathies were strongly with the other side. Colonel Webster was riding some little distance in advance of the column and, as he arrived opposite the house, the blinds were suddenly closed with a loud slam, indicating that the lordly descendant of the Cavaliers was not over and above pleased with the approach of the Yankees. This act greatly amused the colonel and he laughed until he grew red in the face. Then, evidently having hit upon a pleasant expedient by which the recreant Southerner could be reminded of his abandoned loyalty, he allowed the regiment to pass on until the colors came opposite the house. The order to halt was then given and the men were brought to the "front." While they were wondering "what was up," the band came down from the head of the column and formed in front of the house.

"Now, Mr. Martland," said the colonel, addressing the bandmaster, "I want you to see if you can't warm this old fellow up a little. He's probably a proud descendant of England—most of these high-toned Virginians are—so suppose you give him 'America,' to start with; that's partly English, you know." And the concert began with the soothing strains of "My country, 'tis of thee," the regiment lustily singing the last verse, but only a slight tremor was noticeable in the blinds—none of them were opened.

"Now try 'Yankee Doodle,'" said the colonel. "Perhaps that will remind him of the way his forefathers and ours fought together in the war of the Revolution." So "Yankee Doodle" was played, but still there were no evidences of life within the mansion.

"I think he must be a hard customer," said the colonel. "It may be that the 'Star-Spangled Banner' will fetch him. Try that." And the beautiful strains of that grand old song were sent out with a sweetness that should have moved the old man's heart if it had been as hard even as stone, but still the blinds were unyielding.

Then the "Red, White and Blue," "Hail Columbia" and other patriotic airs were in turn tried, but still the old Virginian remained obstinate. Even "Carry Me Back to Old Virginia" had not the slightest apparent effect.

Just as we were beginning to think that we would be obliged after all to give it up as a bad job, Martland struck up "Home, Sweet Home" and the piece was rendered with a degree of beauty and feeling that would be hard to excel. As the last notes died away the blinds flew open and the door, too, and the old Virginian stepped out upon the piazza with a broad smile upon his face. He had surrendered, apparently, only because he felt obliged to, but now that the "ice was broken" he became genial and even hospitable. The officers of the regiment were invited in and such refreshments as the house afforded were offered them, while the wish of the men, quite loudly expressed, that the old flag be put out, was complied with. With the Stars and Stripes floating from an upper window and the old man standing at the gate laughing, we moved on.

We were very short of rations at one time and arrived in camp one night with empty haversacks after an unusually long and tedious march through heat and dust. The teams, as usual, were far behind. We were naturally desirous of obtaining a supply of food in some way and it was not many minutes after knapsacks were unslung before the boys were reconnoitering the country far and near. As I was a little "off color" at this time as a forager, I remained behind under orders from my messmates to fill the canteens, gather up some wood and start a fire. I was thus in a favorable position for a comprehensive survey of the whole theatre of operations. And such a scene! The landscape everywhere seemed to be dotted with men in blue, producing a very picturesque effect as contrasted with the green of the fields and the brown of the pastures, while occasionally the sounds that rent the air gave token of victory over two-footed fowl and four-footed beast.

I now put a few extra sticks of wood upon the fire in anticipation of there being need of a larger one than usual and, as I stooped to do so, I was a little startled by the clatter of hoofs close beside me. Raising my head, my eyes rested upon the face and form of a citizen in butternut mounted upon a fiery charger. He seemed to be boiling over with rage and excitement and demanded somewhat sternly, "Where is your commanding officer?" "Over there," I answered, pointing to where Colonel Webster stood. Then, in order to ascertain what was up, I crept a little nearer and overheard this conversation:

CITIZEN: Sir, some of your men are down in my pasture chasing
   my sheep!
WEBSTER: Is that so? Are you sure they are my men?
CITIZEN: Yes, they are your men.
WEBSTER: Well, if they are my men you need have no fear.
   The boys have had a long march and they are very tired. I don't
   believe they can catch them.

The Southerner stormed and swore after the manner of the F. F. V.s, but it was of no use. The colonel was provokingly cool and discoursed with as much earnestness, fluency and apparent sincerity on the utter improbability of his men being able to catch sheep when they were so tired as he would have done had he been arguing the case in court.

Finally the farmer rode away, half convinced, apparently, that the Yankee colonel was right, but seemingly somewhat puzzled by the line of reasoning to which he had listened. Added to this, the facility which had been shown in the use of the Queen's English had had a mystifying effect upon him, for the case had been argued from nearly every standpoint and words of ponderous size and terms not often heard in those parts had been freely used. Turning to one of the men, as he was leaving the camp, the farmer asked: "Who in the deuce is that officer?" "That officer?" replied the man. "Why, don't you know? That's Daniel Webster's son." "Daniel Webster's son!" ejaculated the Virginian with an oath. "You don't tell me that! I thought he talked pretty well. Are all the damned Yankees coming down here to fight us?" "Yes," replied the soldier, "they are all coming if they are needed. We are only the advance guard." The farmer rode slowly away from camp in a thoughtful mood and probably before he had entirely recovered his equilibrium the Webster Regiment was regaling itself with mutton.

On the 26th of June, 1862, the anniversary of our muster in, a new leader appeared upon the scene in the person of a bumptious individual, General John Pope,[1] who said, "I come to you from the West, where we have always seen the backs of our enemies —from an army whose business it has been to seek the adversary, and to beat him when he was found; whose policy has been attack, and not defense." We now found ourselves in Hartsuff's brigade, Ricketts's division, McDowell's corps and Pope's Army of Virginia. We were lying at Manassas Junction when this new organization was effected. President Lincoln and Secretary of State Seward had visited our camp a few days before and this fact, with the new consolidation, led us to surmise that some new movement was afoot. What this movement was to be we were able to form a pretty shrewd guess, for affairs on the Peninsula pointed it out to thoughtful minds with tolerable accuracy. Colonel Webster was at this time absent on leave and the regiment was commanded by Lieutenant Colonel Bryan.

1. An engineer officer with creditable service in Mexico, John Pope was commissioned brigadier general on June 14, 1861, although the appointment may have been influenced by his being related to Lincoln's wife. His forces captured New Madrid and Island No. 10 on the Mississippi River, these successes leading him to be placed in charge of the army defending Washington in June 1862. Soundly defeated at Second Bull Run and having lost the confidence of his army, Pope was sent off to Minnesota to quell the Sioux outbreak. He never again led troops in the field and died in the Ohio Soldiers Home in Sandusky, Ohio, on September 23, 1892. Warner, *Generals in Blue*, 376–77; Heitman, *Historical Register*, 1:798.

It must be confessed we were not very favorably impressed with General John Pope. Men situated as we were do not like to be told that they haven't amounted to much heretofore, that they are inferior to other bodies of men and that a reformation must take place at once, particularly when they do not feel themselves to blame for the alleged bad condition of affairs and bad management. It isn't in human nature to like that kind of treatment or to be inspired with confidence in a commander who adopts such tactics. Neither can the most be gotten out of men in that way. And yet this is precisely what General Pope did tell us—by inference, if not by actual words. His plan of campaign was great, too, as witness this: "I propose to defend Washington, not by keeping on the defensive, nor by fortifying in front of the enemy, but by placing myself on his flanks, and attacking him day and night as soon as he has crossed the Rappahannock, until his forces are destroyed."

In view of what was even then befalling General McClellan upon the Peninsula, with three times as many men in his army as we had in ours, this program looked humorous, to say the least. The soldiers of the Union were sensible, thinking men and they did not like the tone of Pope's grandiloquent orders, whatever they might think of his ability to carry them out.

But enough of this. In commenting as I have, I have only been voicing the sentiment of the men at the time and history has shown that they were right in thinking as they did. Personally, General Pope was a brave, loyal man and his faults were errors of judgment only. I saw him twice under fire—at Cedar Mountain on the evening of August 9th and at Bull Run on the afternoon of August 30th—and can testify that he bore himself as a true soldier should. We were as loyal as ever, notwithstanding the many causes for uneasiness, and that the Army of Virginia succeeded no better in that ill-starred campaign was not the fault of the private soldiers or of the subordinate officers, as everyone knows.

On Independence Day, Ricketts's division started out on its campaign. Marching had then become a familiar pastime, as, up to that time, our regiment had tramped 750 miles. We camped that night at Dranesville. Next morning at seven o'clock we took the road again, halting a while at Buckton, and then pressed on to New Baltimore. Here we remained till the 22d, when we moved down to the Rappahannock River in one of the worst storms I ever encountered. General Pope reviewed our division here on the 1st of August and we thus had an opportunity to "size him up." A soldier of the Thirteenth Massachusetts gave a pretty accurate expression of the verdict by saying, "He's a handsome man, but I don't see the General!" On the 8th we took the road again, bivouacking at night in a forest.

At daybreak, August 9th, we moved forward two or three miles, halted, and here the roar of artillery told us that the battle was already on. Stonewall Jackson, reinforced by A. P. Hill,[2] was crossing the Rapidan River, with the intention of annihilating Banks at Culpeper before supports could arrive. Pope ordered Banks forward to meet the enemy, in the order telling him, in his bumptious style, "There must be no backing out this time, General." Banks's two divisions, numbering about 8,000 men, under Generals Christopher C. Augur[3] and Alpheus S. Williams,[4] arrived at Cedar Mountain, eight miles south of Culpeper, about noon, and attacked the enemy vigorously. Reliable writers have asserted that Jackson had with him at this time 35,000 men of all arms. It is probable, however, that only part of this force was actively engaged at Cedar Mountain.

2. Ambrose P. Hill served in Mexico and the Seminole Wars, but resigned on March 1, 1861, and became colonel of the Thirteenth Virginia. Appointed brigadier general on February 26, 1862, Hill became perhaps the best division commander in Lee's army. He did not perform so well after elevation to corps command and was killed at Petersburg on April 2, 1865. Warner, *Generals in Gray*, 134–35; Heitman, *Historical Register*, 1:529.

3. Augur, who graduated from West Point in 1843, had an undistinguished career. Promoted to major of the Thirteenth United States on May 14, 1861, he commanded the corps of cadets at West Point and was commissioned brigadier general on November 12, 1861. Augur led a division at Cedar Mountain, where he was badly wounded, commanded a corps, and oversaw the defenses of the capital. He retired from the army in 1885 and died in Georgetown, D.C., on January 16, 1898. Warner, *Generals in Blue*, 12; Heitman, *Historical Register*, 1:175.

4. A graduate of Yale, Williams served as a lieutenant colonel of a Michigan regiment in the Mexican-American War and had a successful law career in that state. Commissioned brigadier general on August 9, 1861, he was elevated to division command during Pope's campaign but never achieved higher responsibility, being overlooked because he was not a Regular Army officer. Elected to Congress from Michigan, Williams died in Washington, D.C., on December 21, 1878. Warner, *Generals in Blue*, 560; Heitman, *Historical Register*, 1:1039.

When Banks approached, he found Jackson strongly posted in front and around the sides of the mountain. Part of the way up lay his artillery. Jackson could plainly see nearly every movement made by his antagonist from his elevated position. Only a very little of our line was screened by forests. Early in the afternoon Jackson's skirmishers advanced. They were met by bluecoats half way between the two armies. About five o'clock a heavy column of the enemy swept down upon General Samuel W. Crawford's[5] brigade. His men bravely met the storm and, after pouring volley after volley into the advancing enemy, rushed forward on a counter-charge with loud cheers. They pressed on into the woods where the enemy had rallied to meet them and were there met with such a withering fire that their thin ranks melted away like snow under a warm sun.

Banks handled his men with great skill and, being stung to the quick by his superior's imprudent remark, had fallen upon Jackson's force so savagely that that redoubtable leader was for once in his life deceived as to the strength of his opponent's forces. So Stonewall hurried Hill's troops forward, when Banks, who had been getting the best of the fight all the afternoon, was in turn forced back to his first position. General George Gordon's[6] brigade was now brought to Crawford's support. The musketry

5. Crawford graduated from the University of Pennsylvania medical school in 1850 and next year joined the army as an assistant surgeon. After serving on the western frontier, he was a member of the Fort Sumter garrison. Crawford gave up the medical profession for a commission as major in the Thirteenth United States. Promoted to brigadier general on April 25, 1862, he led a brigade at Cedar Mountain and a division at Antietam, where he was wounded. Given command of the Pennsylvania Reserve Corps the following spring, he led that division to the end of the war. He retired from the army on February 19, 1873, and died in Philadelphia on November 3, 1892. Warner, *Generals in Blue*, 99–100; Heitman, *Historical Register*, 1:337.

6. George Gordon graduated from West Point in 1846 and was wounded twice in the Mexican-American War. He resigned in 1854 to begin a law career. Commissioned colonel of the Second Massachusetts on May 24, 1861, Gordon was commissioned brigadier general on June 9, 1862, and began an undistinguished career in which he served in various capacities in Virginia, South Carolina, Arkansas, and Florida. He returned to Boston, resumed his legal career, and wrote several books on Civil War topics. General Gordon died at Framingham, Massachusetts, on August 30, 1886. Warner, *Generals in Blue*, 177–78; Heitman, *Historical Register*, 1:465.

fire was terrific, while artillery thundered all along the line. John Geary's[7] brigade and all the troops to the left of Gordon were heavily engaged. Men were falling rapidly. Death was enjoying a perfect carnival and the air was weighted down with the screams and groans of the wounded and dying.

The fight was kept up until night. Just before dark Jackson advanced a heavy column against the left of the Union line, and our men were steadily forced back. They were overlapped and outflanked, but they fell back sullenly—in sections, beginning with the left—keeping up their fire and doing all that men could do to check the victorious foe. A new position was gained in the rear and all the ground upon which fighting had taken place now fell into the hands of the enemy. They thereupon heralded the battle as a great Confederate victory. Great indeed! "If it costs them this much to win victories upon other fields as it did at Cedar Mountain," remarked a correspondent, "they cannot afford many."

Here we joined Banks's hard-pressed troops, but why our division, numbering at least 5,000 men, should have been kept lying all that afternoon within a few miles of the field, where we could plainly hear the rattle of musketry and not be hurried to Banks's assistance, has not to this day been explained. General Franz Sigel's[8] corps, after a longer march than ours, had reached the field

7. John Geary held a series of jobs prior to being commissioned lieutenant colonel, then colonel of the Second Pennsylvania in the Mexican-American War. He was elected mayor of San Francisco and served as territorial governor of Kansas prior to the Civil War. Commissioned colonel of the Twenty-eighth Pennsylvania on June 28, 1861, he was promoted to brigadier general on April 25, 1862. Wounded once at Bolivar Heights and twice at Cedar Mountain, he commanded a division in the Army of the Potomac and in General Sherman's army. After the war Geary was elected governor of Pennsylvania and died in Harrisburg on February 8, 1873, after completing his second term in office. Warner, *Generals in Blue*, 169–70; Heitman, *Historical Register*, 1:450.

8. Sigel graduated from a German military academy and began a promising military career, but he was forced to flee after the insurrections of 1848 and ended up teaching school in the United States. Popular in the German community in St. Louis, Sigel was appointed brigadier general on August 7, 1861, and major general on March 22, 1862. Despite a few minor successes early in the war, Sigel never developed into a dependable division commander when transferred to the Eastern Theater. Sigel resigned on May 4, 1865, and had a relatively ordinary life thereafter. He died in New York City on August 21, 1902. Warner, *Generals in Blue*, 447–48; Heitman, *Historical Register*, 1:886.

and, as darkness closed in, affairs were in better shape. General Rufus King's[9] division of McDowell's corps was not present, but Pope had now in hand about 17,000 men, a force nearly equal to Jackson's.

We marched on to the field in "all pomp and circumstance of glorious war" and, as our Falstaffian lieutenant colonel was then "in good voice" and in command, the rebel commander doubtless thought our whole army was closing in around him. I well remember that bright, moon-lit night and the impressions we received as we formed our line of battle. The ground had been fought over many times that fateful afternoon and the dead of both sides lay where they fell, their up-turned faces giving us a momentary feeling of horror as we passed. Shells were screaming over our heads and bursting all about us, but in spite of the fact that this was the first time we had been under fire, our men kept their places and moved steadily forward. I even remember what I was thinking about in that trying moment. In Banks's corps were the Second Massachusetts, the Fourth and Sixth Maine batteries, the Tenth Maine and Fifth Connecticut regiments—all organizations with which we had served in Banks's corps—and the feeling that came to me strongest was one of satisfaction that we had now an opportunity to come to their assistance.

While moving rapidly forward, a battery of artillery, with unmanageable horses and excited men, tore through our brigade and created some confusion, but we soon got back into order again and pushed on. We halted at last in front of a scattered forest and were ordered to lie down. Shells were plowing the ground and ricocheting over us, but, although the effect was a trifle disquieting, few men were hurt by them and everybody was in good humor. A loud laugh would follow the ducking of heads and the squirming of a part of the line as the dreaded missiles went by.

9. A graduate of West Point in 1833, King served only three years before he resigned and became a successful newspaper editor. Appointed minister to the Papal States by Lincoln, he instead accepted a commission as brigadier general on May 17, 1861. A sufferer from epilepsy, King proved to be a failure as a division commander in Pope's campaign. He resigned his commission on October 20, 1863, and began a civilian career as unremarkable as his military one. He died in New York City on October 13, 1876. Warner, *Generals in Blue*, 269–70; Heitman, *Historical Register*, 1:600.

After we had gotten into line upon the field, Pope, McDowell, Banks and others, with their staffs, rode a short distance to the front to reconnoiter. Suddenly there was a clatter of small arms among the trees in our front. Many of us raised ourselves on our knees, but many more sprang to their feet so as to be ready to return the fire should word be given. Out of the grove dashed the generals, amid the laughter of our men. Cautioning us not to fire, they passed quickly through our ranks. Eight of our men were wounded by the flying bullets and Captain Nathaniel B. Shurtleff, Jr., who was standing six or eight feet in front of his company, trying to see what was going on among the trees, was struck in the breast and killed. We then fired a volley, which doubtless prevented a further advance of the enemy, and we afterward learned that the generals in question had been making a reconnaissance to discover, if possible, the enemy's position and while doing so had been charged upon by a body of rebel cavalry. A pretty narrow escape for a distinguished *coterie!*

I was looking directly at Captain Shurtleff and wondering at his coolness when he fell. He was the first man I had seen struck down and his death made a deep impression upon me. He was the first man to enlist under Fletcher Webster and now became the first to fall. Although I was not a member of his company—he commanded Company D—I had all along regarded him as deeply conscientious in all things and as a thoroughly loyal, true and brave soldier. He was the son of the late Doctor Nathaniel B. Shurtleff,[10] an ex-mayor of Boston.

In a letter to his father, Lieutenant Arthur Dehon spoke of his first experience under fire: "The rifle firing lasted from fifteen to twenty minutes and the enemy were within fifty yards. . . . We were under fire about two hours and a half and only five men left

10. A graduate of Harvard College in 1831, Nathaniel Shurtleff was a true Bay State man—six paternal ancestors had been on the *Mayflower*. He obtained a medical degree from Harvard Medical School in 1834. A member of various historical and scientific societies, the doctor wrote and edited a number of histories. An old-fashioned antiquarian, it was generally said that "if you want to know anything about Boston, go to Dr. Shurtleff." Shurtleff was elected mayor in 1868 but otherwise avoided the political field. But once did he leave Boston during his adult life, so it was natural that he should die in his hometown, on October 17, 1874. *Boston Daily Advertiser*, October 19, 1874.

Captain Nathaniel B.
Shurtleff. Courtesy of the
U.S. Army Heritage and
Education Center

the ranks, none from my company. . . . I did not feel frightened
or want to run, but I could not help stooping to avoid the shells,
though they were not half so bad as the rifle balls. The crack of the
rifles made me feel a little nervous, but I was too much taken up
with the company to be scared."

Our brigade commander, General Hartsuff, in another part of
the field late in the night, gave us a little shell talk. Shells were flying over our heads in a lively manner and our boys were bowing
gracefully to each visitor from the Confederate battery, while the
general rode up and down the line, occasionally cautioning us
to stand steady: "Men," he said, "remember that it takes a man's
weight in lead, even, to kill him; and, as for shells, I am not able
to give the exact statistics, but they are comparatively harmless,
anyway, and it is foolish to dodge. When the sound of their passing
reaches us, they are beyond us and incapable of doing us harm."

The general was sitting on his horse at the time and, just as he wound up his little speech, a terrible monster, with unearthly screech, whizzed by and down he went on the animal's neck, while the whole brigade burst out laughing. When the merriment subsided, he rode away, saying, "Well, boys, I couldn't help it. I was always taught to be polite."

Most of the shells at this time came from a battery posted about 200 yards from us. Its position was where the forest ended in a sharp point, which made it easy for our artillerymen, posted upon rising ground behind us, to get its exact range. We could see shells burst directly over it and among its guns and occasionally a caisson would blow up. Their loss in men and horses must have been heavy. Indeed, we saw abundant evidence of this next day, when we passed over the spot. Dead men and dead horses were lying about in considerable numbers and the ground was covered with debris. We heard afterward that it was Captain William J. Pegram's battery.[11] The boys in gray who served its guns were brave fellows.

Late at night the rebel artillery slackened its fire—firing had been pretty general all along the line—and General Sigel advanced. Then it became quiet in our section of country and about 3 A.M. we "turned in" for a little sleep. We were glad the racket was over, as it was getting monotonous.

When we awoke, soon after the sun had risen, we found that the Johnnies had fallen back. We cooked our coffee, munched a few hardtack and then many of us went sightseeing. We first studied the process of burying the dead, thus learning how it was likely to be with us later on, and then visited a hospital near where we had been lying. This was established in and around a small dwelling and large numbers of men, in a condition impossible to describe, lay about, pale and bleeding, many of them moaning piteously. There were men there belonging to the Second Massachusetts and Tenth Maine, some of whom we knew personally. We did what we could to assist and encourage the poor fellows and came away,

11. William J. Pegram enlisted in Purcell's Virginia Battery in 1861 but was elected lieutenant shortly thereafter. He was commissioned captain in 1862, major in 1863, lieutenant colonel in 1864, and colonel of artillery in 1865. Mortally wounded at Five Forks, he died on the battlefield on April 2, 1865. "Reunion of Pegram Battalion Association," 33.

Captain Andrew J. Garey.
Courtesy of the U.S. Army
Heritage and Education Center

leaving them to the tender mercies of the surgeons and ambulance corps. It was a long time before those agonizing cries ceased
to echo in my heart and the sight of those terribly mutilated bodies left off haunting me in my dreams.

We went into camp on the battlefield that forenoon and remained till 2 A.M. of the 13th. It was like living in a graveyard and I
was glad when the order came to move. Instead of going forward,
however, as we had expected, we marched back to Culpeper. We
remained in Culpeper two days only, when we retraced our steps
past Cedar Mountain and kept on till we reached the Rapidan.
The road over which the enemy had passed was lined with broken-
down wagons and other evidences that their retreat had been a
hurried one.

Reaching the river, our batteries shelled the opposite shore, and
we remained here till 9 A.M. of the 16th, when certain of Stonewall
Jackson's movements, which I need not here mention, convinced
General Pope that his purpose of "seeking the enemy" had better be abandoned. He thereupon ordered a retreat and the move
began, not hurriedly or precipitately, but with the dogged perse-
verance and determination to resist the enemy, if he pursued us,
so characteristic of the American soldier.

Before leaving Fort Warren our sergeants were given old-fashioned navy boarding cutlasses to carry *in lieu* of regulation swords. These cutlasses were only about twelve inches long, but in consequence of their clumsy brass hilts and thick blades, were quite heavy. No one blamed the boys for being anxious to get rid of them and they did disappear very rapidly, no one knowing where or how. Sergeant Andrew J. Garey,[12] of Company H, placed his in a tree one night at Cedar Mountain and in January of 1864, seventeen months afterward, while passing the same spot, he found it again. It had remained, evidently untouched, all that time, while the spot had doubtless been visited many times by bodies of troops of both sides. Garey was a captain then and had no further use for such antiquated weapons, but he seized his old friend with ardor and possibly has it yet. The incident excited much interest at the time, for while the cutlass rested there its owner had marched more than 1,000 miles and had participated in at least four of the greatest battles of the war, to say nothing of many smaller ones.

12. Andrew J. Garey buried his wife in 1861 and shortly thereafter enlisted as a sergeant in Co. H, Twelfth Massachusetts, on June 26, 1861. Promoted to second lieutenant and then to first lieutenant on August 11, 1862, Garey was elevated to captain on December 21, 1862. Wounded at Spotsylvania, he was mustered out on July 8, 1864, as captain of Co. I. Commissioned captain of Co. G, Fourth Massachusetts Heavy Artillery, on August 23, 1864, Garey served until mustered out on June 17, 1865. He died in Weymouth, Massachusetts, on November 27, 1896. Cook, *History of Norfolk County*, 106–109; *Massachusetts Soldiers*, 2:50; 6:36; *Boston Journal*, November 28, 1896.

CHAPTER 10

Second Bull Run

If we had been in Gordonsville immediately after the battle of
Cedar Mountain, we would have noticed great activity among the
rebel leaders and could easily have seen that some great move
was in contemplation. A concentration was taking place of all
the Confederate forces that could be safely withdrawn from Mc-
Clellan's front. Jackson and A. P. Hill were already there or beyond and General James Longstreet[1] arrived as early as the 13th
of August. General Lee himself came three days later and, freed
from anxiety as to McClellan's movement upon Richmond, that
great general now determined to "annihilate" Pope before "Little Mac" could come to his assistance. Pope had been reinforced
on the 14th by the divisions of Generals Isaac Stevens[2] and Jesse

1. A graduate of West Point in 1842 and a veteran of the Mexican-American
War, Longstreet resigned his commission as major in the Paymaster Department
and was commissioned brigadier general in the Confederate army on June 17,
1861. Promoted to major general on October 7, 1861, and lieutenant general on
October 9, 1862, he became one of the most successful and dependable commanders on either side during the war. Wounded at the Wilderness, he returned
to surrender at Appomattox; after the war he stirred controversy among his former comrades by supporting the Republican Party. Longstreet died at Gainesville, Georgia, on January 2, 1904. Warner, *Generals in Gray*, 192–93; Heitman,
Historical Register, 1:640–41.

2. After graduating first in his class at West Point, Stevens served in the Corps
of Engineers and was wounded in Mexico. He resigned in 1853 to become governor of Washington Territory and also served as a congressional delegate, but his
outspoken support of the proslavery Democratic Party in 1860 led the Lincoln
administration to question his credentials. Belatedly appointed colonel of the
Seventy-ninth New York on July 30, 1861, he won his star on September 28, 1861,
and commanded a brigade in South Carolina. Transferred to the Army of the

Reno[3] and now had an army of 40,000 with which to oppose the 60,000 graycoats assembled in his front.

Before the arrival of these two divisions, Pope had maneuvered so skillfully that the Confederate leaders were deceived as to his strength and thus a few days' valuable time was gained. Had Jackson and Hill moved upon us immediately after the battle, with all their available forces, and had Longstreet been made to follow with greater speed, a disaster well-nigh irreparable would doubtless have resulted to the Union cause. Pope's men were not lacking in fighting qualities, but they would have been taken at an immense disadvantage. They were largely inferior to the enemy in numbers. They were far from their base of supplies. They were in the heart of the enemy's country. Nearly every planter was a secessionist spy—with the exception of John Minor Botts of Culpeper,[4] of honored memory—and every situation would have been made known as promptly as possible to the Confederate chief.

Fortunately, however, when Lee's "annihilation" of Pope began, Stevens and Reno from North Carolina and King from Fredericksburg had arrived and General Samuel Heintzelman's[5] corps

---

Potomac, Stevens was killed at Chantilly on September 1, 1862. Warner, *Generals in Blue,* 475–76; Heitman, *Historical Register,* 1:923.

3. An 1846 graduate of West Point, Reno served in the Ordnance Department until the Civil War, but did win two brevets in Mexico. Commissioned brigadier general on November 12, 1861, he commanded a brigade in North Carolina prior to his promotion to major general on August 20, 1862. Reno was killed at South Mountain on September 14, 1862, while commanding the Ninth Corps. Warner, *Generals in Blue,* 394–95; Heitman, *Historical Register,* 1:823–24.

4. Botts was a well-known Virginia lawyer and politician who espoused unpopular Unionist views during the secession crisis. A bitter opponent of Jefferson Davis and the Virginia governors, Botts was jailed on March 2, 1862, when Davis proclaimed martial law. Released on parole two months later after incarceration in a demeaning "negro jail," he purchased a farm in Culpeper County and remained out of the public limelight during the war. He died on January 7, 1869, in Culpeper. *Dictionary of American Biography,* 2:472–73.

5. A graduate of West Point in 1826, Heintzelman performed rather routine service in Mexico and on the frontier prior to his commission as colonel of the Seventeenth United States on May 14, 1861. Promoted to brigadier general within days and major general on May 5, 1862, Heintzelman never lived up to his potential. After Pope's campaign he was diverted from field command, served until his retirement in 1869, and died in Washington, D.C., on May 1, 1880. Warner, *Generals in Blue,* 227–28.; Heitman, *Historical Register,* 1:521.

and other troops from McClellan's army were hurrying forward, so that when Lee got ready to move, he found a more formidable task upon his hands than he had anticipated. Pope did not "annihilate" so easily after all.

Our retreat from the Rapidan had but just begun, when our beloved colonel returned from his visit to Massachusetts. We joyfully welcomed him back and, while regretting that he had not been with us in our first battle, he was pleased with the good reports in circulation as to the regiment's behavior.

Pope's retreat began at 11 P.M. on the 18th of August. We found the road strewn with abandoned war material and burned wagons. Immense trains preceded us and marching at first was difficult. We moved at a snail's pace for a mile or two and then had to wait for the roads ahead of us to be cleared. This proved not only tiresome, but aggravating. Meanwhile, Jackson, who was unhampered because his trains were behind him, led the Confederate advance and was making preparations to seize the fords of the Rappahannock. When daylight came we could see great clouds of dust in the west, showing the progress of his columns. The moment was an exciting one, for there was not a thoughtful soldier in Pope's army who did not know that a race was in progress which involved the safety of the capital itself. Our only hope was that McClellan could get enough of his men up from the Peninsula to save it.

We passed through Culpeper on the 19th. We had been in the town so much that we had become somewhat acquainted with the people. They had appeared to be even friendly, but now we found that their attitude toward us had undergone a complete change. The women insulted us in every way they could. Standing upon the sidewalks and in doorways, they made grimaces as we marched past and quoted from Pope's grandiloquent orders.

We reached the Rappahannock at night, crossed on the railroad bridge at Rappahannock Station and, sleepy and tired after our exhausting march of twenty-five miles, were soon asleep on the bank of the stream. Next day our brigade re-crossed the river and went into line of battle. Those ominous dust clouds were still visible south and west and heavy firing could be heard. Early on the morning of the 21st, the rebels came up and shelled our position and our batteries—Captain James Thompson's[6] and Ezra Matthews's[7] Pennsylvania and James A. Hall's[8] and G. F. Leppien's[9] Maine—vigorously replied. Above us, however, at Waterloo Bridge and Kelly's Ford, the firing was heavier and more incessant.

On the 22d the artillery duel continued. A funny incident occurred about noon. A large herd of cattle, belonging to the enemy, took it into their heads to secede and came into our lines. The Johnnies made frantic efforts to prevent their desertion, but the creatures were determined to come, so we promptly hauled them over to the commissary. Something funnier than this, however, happened that evening at Catlett's Station, a few miles in our rear,

6. James Thompson, "an esteemed Irishman" and a veteran of the Crimean War, raised men to fill what would become Pennsylvania Independent Battery C and was commissioned captain on August 24, 1861. Wounded at Gettysburg, Thompson was mustered out on June 30, 1865. He died in Pittsburgh on March 13, 1906. Bates, *History of Pennsylvania Volunteers,* 5:869; McKenna, *Under the Maltese Cross,* 21; Pennsylvania Veterans Burial Cards, 1929–90, Bureau of Archives and History. Harrisburg.

7. Ezra Matthews enlisted in the Twenty-third Pennsylvania on April 21, 1861, and served as a private, corporal, sergeant, and adjutant before being mustered out on July 31, 1861. He was commissioned captain of Battery F, First Pennsylvania Artillery (Forty-third Pennsylvania), a part of the Pennsylvania Reserve Corps, on July 8, 1861. Promoted to major on April 11, 1863, he was discharged for disability on July 18, 1864. A prominent banker and brigadier general in the Pennsylvania National Guard militia, he died in Philadelphia on November 8, 1885. *History of the Twenty-third Pennsylvania,* 8, 18; Bates, *History of Pennsylvania Volunteers,* 1:971, 995; *New York Tribune,* November 10, 1885.

8. James A. Hall was commissioned first lieutenant of the Second Maine Battery on November 30, 1861, and captain May 22, 1862. He was wounded at Gettysburg and had two horses shot under him. Hall was promoted to major of the Maine artillery battalion on July 19, 1863, and lieutenant colonel on September 9, 1864. After being mustered out on July 22, 1865, he was commissioned colonel of the Second United States Veteran Infantry on August 15, 1865, and was mustered out March 1, 1866. Hall was brevetted a brigadier general effective March 13, 1865. He died on a train between Syracuse and Utica, New York, on June 11, 1893. Heitman, *Historical Register,* 1:489; *New York Tribune,* June 12, 1893.

9. Although he was a native of Philadelphia and product of the best schools in Prussia, George F. Leppien's "fame belongs to Maine." Commissioned captain of the Fifth Maine Battery on November 11, 1861, he frequently acted in higher capacities. The chief of artillery for the Army of the Potomac said that "no better battery than Leppien's could be found in the U. S. service, either volunteer or regular." Leppien lost a leg at Chancellorsville, was promoted to lieutenant colonel on May 18, 1863, and died of his wound at Washington, D.C., on May 24, 1863. *Portland (Me.) Daily Advertiser,* June 27, 1863; *Philadelphia Inquirer,* May 26, 1863.

where the ubiquitous General J. E. B. Stuart[10] got possession of Pope's headquarters belongings, together with a large amount of public property. But as this joke was on us, we didn't laugh as loud as we did over the capture of the cattle.

It rained heavily—artillery fire is a sure rain-maker—and next morning, the 23d, it was found that the river had become greatly swollen. The bridge was at best a rickety affair and our engineers now reported that there was imminent danger of its collapse. So Hartsuff's brigade was brought over to the north bank again. Longstreet had now arrived and one of his famous batteries, the Washington Artillery, shelled us vigorously, but Thompson, remaining on the south side till the last, kept the rebel infantry at bay, although skirmishers several times advanced. When all were over, our batteries took position, the rebs came out into view and for an hour or two there was plenty of music. Hall was particularly active and I remember a young gunner of the Fifth Maine Battery, wearing a red smoking cap, who hit the mark so often that the boys of my regiment loudly cheered him. It was great sport. We had already become accustomed to shells and did not mind them much.

Shells were bursting with alarming frequency and the men were lying upon the ground for protection. All the while Colonel Webster had been sitting on his horse, deeply absorbed in a book he was reading, his only noticeable movement being when he occasionally raised his hand to turn a leaf. After a while one of the general's aides rode up and ordered him to march his regiment away to another part of the line. He signified his readiness to obey the order and, putting the book into his pocket, he turned to the men and said: "Well, boys, here we go again. We'll be pretty well acquainted with the geography of Virginia when this campaign is

10. A graduate of West Point in 1854, Stuart served on the frontier until circumstances led to his presence at Harpers Ferry during John Brown's raid. He resigned his commission as captain of the First United States Cavalry on May 14, 1861, and was commissioned colonel of the First Virginia Cavalry. Rising to the rank of major general, which he attained on July 25, 1862, Stuart was the Civil War's preeminent cavalry commander, although his reputation was tainted by an unnecessary raid during the Gettysburg campaign. General Stuart was mortally wounded at Yellow Tavern and died on May 12, 1864, in Richmond, Virginia. Warner, *Generals in Gray*, 296–97; Heitman, *Historical Register*, 1:933–34.

over." We took the road and marched ten miles in the direction of Warrenton, bivouacking at night in the woods.

At daylight on the 24th, without breakfast, we started again and marched eight miles toward Waterloo. General Richard Ewell[11] was now on the north bank of the river and we expected to "bag" him, but, as usual in this unlucky campaign, the rebels were too smart for us and got away. It began to look as if Pope was about to "find his Waterloo" with a vengeance, for there appeared to be very little system in any of his movements.

On the 25th we moved on a few miles farther and the next day started again, but about noon were ordered to retrace our steps. We got back to Warrenton at night on the 27th and, our division being ordered to Thoroughfare Gap to dispute the passage of Longstreet's corps, left for that place, arriving there, after a hard march, at 3 P.M. on the 28th. Jackson had passed through two days before and was now making things lively about Manassas Junction.

Quite a lively fight began at once, as the head of Longstreet's column had already got through when we came upon the ground. Company H of our regiment and the whole of the Eleventh Pennsylvania deployed as skirmishers and advanced into the gap, forcing the enemy back some distance and capturing a few prisoners. Our batteries poured shells into the narrow defile, but the enemy soon appeared in such strength that General Ricketts was convinced that it was better for him to rejoin the main column while he could. So back we started.

One funny incident happened during this fight. A man named Cooper,[12] in charge of the stretcher bearers, was ordered into the

11. Richard S. Ewell graduated from West Point in 1840 and spent his career on the frontier and in Mexico before resigning as captain of the First Dragoons on May 7, 1861. Commissioned brigadier general, major general, and lieutenant general, the latter effective May 23, 1863, Ewell was a good example of an excellent commander promoted beyond his capabilities. Following the fall of Petersburg and Richmond, he was captured at Sayler's Creek on April 6, 1865. He died on his farm at Spring Hill, Tennessee, on January 25, 1872. Warner, *Generals in Gray*, 84–85; Heitman, *Historical Register*, 1:410.

12. Joseph Cooper enlisted in Co. A, Twelfth Massachusetts, on May 18, 1861, and was missing in action at Second Bull Run. He returned and was discharged on February 14, 1863, but enlisted a second time in Co. H, Seventeenth Massachusetts, on February 14, 1864. He was mustered out as a corporal in Co. B on July 11, 1865, and died on July 27, 1868, in Newburyport, Massachusetts. *Massachusetts Soldiers*, 2:6, 332; Massachusetts Death Records, 1840–1915, MVR.

woods during the melee. He paraded his men with much ceremony in front of the regiment and insisted upon their moving
forward in regular order, meantime carrying his stretcher as if it
were a flag. The incident was greeted with roars of laughter, but
Cooper did not intend it for a joke and loudly expostulated with
the regiment for its levity. He had been in the British army in the
Crimea and hoped we would "allow" him to "know how to do such
things properly."

Late that night we stopped for a few hours' sleep in a large field
near Gainesville and at daylight discovered that a large body of
rebs was snoozing less than a quarter of a mile away. We took the
road very quietly (it was surprising to see how still the boys could
be!) as soon as this unwelcome discovery was made and tramped
on toward Manassas Junction, where Jackson had been operating
some time, the sound of his guns having been ringing in our ears
for a number of days. General King had had a collision with him
only the evening before.

We halted a couple of hours at Bristoe Station and, as we were
all very hungry, rations were distributed and greedily eaten. It
may be well to say here, what the reader may have already sur-
mised, that rations during those terrible marches, day and night,
were as scarce as robins in winter. The heat, too, was often intense
and pure drinking water hard to find. My package of army letters
covering this period, from which my facts are largely drawn, give
ample evidence upon this point. Many wagons carrying supplies
fell into the hands of the enemy, many others were destroyed to
prevent this sad fate and all were often so far from the troops as to
be inaccessible. Then Jackson accomplished a wholesale destruction of supplies at Manassas Junction, but our suffering from this
cause came later on.

Shortly after leaving Bristoe, we fell in with General Fitz John
Porter's[13] men and our spirits began to brighten a bit, as now

13. A graduate of West Point in 1845 with gallant service in Mexico and on
the frontier, Fitz John Porter was commissioned colonel of the Fifteenth United
States at its initial organization on May 14, 1861, but his ability quickly led to a
promotion to brigadier general in 1861 and major general in 1862. An excellent
organizer and field commander under McClellan, he and Pope shared a mutual
hatred that eventually led to Porter's arrest "for disloyalty, disobedience, and
misconduct in the face of the enemy." He was unjustly dismissed from the army

it seemed likely that McClellan was to be on hand in sufficient force to prevent future disaster. Heavy firing was going on in the direction of Groveton and we pushed on till ten o'clock in the evening, when we halted in the rear of King's division, now commanded by General John P. Hatch,[14] on the Sudley Springs Road near Groveton, but a short distance north of the Warrenton Pike. Being nearly worn out by our long marches, it did not take long for those who were lucky enough not to be detailed for guard or picket to fall asleep.

We were awakened by the roar of artillery at daylight on the 30th. The forenoon passed without any incident of importance, as far as Irvin McDowell's troops were concerned, but Stevens, who had been heavily engaged with Jackson's forces the day before, advanced a part of his division to convince General Pope that the rebels were not running away. It was one of the unaccountable, as well as provoking, things of the campaign that Pope was continually troubled with an idea that the Confederates were either planning or executing a retreat.

Our division was to support the divisions of Generals Philip Kearny[15] and Joseph Hooker[16] on the right and we moved into

on January 21, 1863, after being found guilty by a court of officers some of whom had done much more to undermine Pope than had Porter. General Porter spent the remainder of his life trying to restore his good name. He died in Morristown, New Jersey, on May 21, 1901. Warner, *Generals in Blue*, 378–80; Heitman, *Historical Register*, 1:799.

14. John Hatch graduated from West Point in 1845 and, after creditable service in Mexico, filled positions on the frontier until 1861, when he received a commission as brigadier general on September 28. Assigned to lead the cavalry under General Banks in the Shenandoah Valley, Hatch was demoted by Pope to command an infantry brigade. Wounded at South Mountain while leading a division, he spent the remaining war years on humdrum assignments. Hatch retired from the army in 1886 and died in New York City on April 12, 1901. Warner, *Generals in Blue*, 216–17; Heitman, *Historical Register*, 1:511.

15. After graduating from Columbia University and inheriting a million dollars in 1836, Kearny entered the French army and became a cavalryman. He came home to serve in the Mexican-American War and lost an arm at Churubusco. Kearny traveled the world and again served in the French cavalry before returning to be appointed a brigadier general on May 17, 1861. Promoted to major general on July 4, 1862, Kearny was killed at Chantilly on September 1, 1862. Warner, *Generals in Blue*, 258–59; Heitman, *Historical Register*, 1:586.

16. A graduate of West Point in 1837, Hooker served in Mexico and amassed more brevets for gallantry than any other lieutenant in the army. After resigning in 1853, Hooker eked out a living on the West Coast until he rejoined the army

position to do so. Two of Porter's divisions occupied the centre, supported by Hatch, while the Pennsylvania Reserves, under General John Reynolds[17] (temporarily attached to McDowell's corps), held the left. Sigel's corps and the divisions of Stevens and Reno were placed in reserve. There was a good deal of desultory fighting, mainly by the artillery and skirmishers, while these dispositions were being made. Shortly after noon, Kearny and Hooker advanced against Jackson and a desperate fight ensued. The red and white diamond men were successful at first, but were finally repulsed. Ricketts's division was not called in, although upon the ground and ready for action.

About 4 P.M. Porter became engaged with Jackson's left centre and Hatch was also ordered in at the same point. The fighting was desperate, Porter's loss being heavy. His two small divisions, commanded by Generals George Morell[18] and George Sykes[19] (Charles

---

as a brigadier general on May 17, 1861. A dependable and audacious leader, Hooker rose through division and corps command to lead the Army of the Potomac in 1863. Following his defeat at Chancellorsville, Hooker took two army corps west to reinforce the army at Chattanooga, Tennessee. After a subordinate was promoted over him in 1864, he asked to be relieved of field command. Hooker retired in 1868 and died at Garden City, New York, on October 31, 1879. Warner, *Generals in Blue*, 233–35; Heitman, *Historical Register*, 1:540.

17. John Reynolds graduated from West Point in 1841 and spent his prewar career in garrison duty except for the Mexican campaign. He was commandant of the cadets at West Point at the outbreak of war but was quickly commissioned brigadier general on August 20, 1861. He was captured while serving under McClellan on the Peninsula. Assigned to lead the Pennsylvania Reserves, he was soon elevated to command the First Corps, having been promoted to major general on November 29, 1862. Reynolds was killed on July 1, 1863, while leading the advance of the Army of the Potomac. Warner, *Generals in Blue*, 396–97; Heitman, *Historical Register*, 1:825.

18. After graduating first in his class at West Point, Morell resigned after only two years to seek his fortune in railroads and the law. He was commissioned brigadier general on August 9, 1861, and major general on July 25, 1862. Morell was as devoted to Fitz John Porter as Porter was to George McClellan, so when that thread unraveled from the top he found himself shifted off to secondary assignments. He left the army on December 15, 1864, and died at Scarborough, New York, on February 11, 1883. Warner, *Generals in Blue*, 330–31; Heitman, *Historical Register*, 1:724.

19. Following his rather uneventful career after graduating from West Point 1842, Sykes led a battalion of regulars at First Bull Run, after which he became a brigadier general on September 28, 1861. A solid career as brigade, division, and corps commander (with promotion to major general on November 29, 1862) was ruined late in 1863 when he was deemed not aggressive enough. He was sent

Griffin's[20] brigade not being in action), lost 2,151 out of 6,500 engaged, while Duryee's Zouaves, one of Porter's regiments, suffered the largest loss at Second Bull Run in killed and wounded of any regiment in Pope's entire army. And Pope preferred charges against Porter for not preventing the advance of Longstreet! I do not propose to enter into the Pope–Porter controversy, but will simply say that I could never believe that an officer who could fight as Porter did at Gaines Mill and Second Bull Run, could be guilty of cowardice or of lack of disposition to sustain his superior officer.

Longstreet now took a hand. General John Reynolds's division had been weakened to provide reinforcements for other parts of the line and Longstreet, discovering this, made a determined advance. It was his purpose to get possession of the Warrenton Pike and thus double up Pope's left. Longstreet seemed to be carrying all before him and it was at this critical moment that our brigade, under Colonel John W. Stiles of the Ninth New York—General Hartsuff having been absent from us several days on account of sickness—was ordered in. We had left our knapsacks in a grove over toward the right a few hours before and when the order came to advance we were all ready for a rapid move. We had had little or nothing to eat that day, but as this had been the case every day for two weeks we did not growl very much, although when the courier came with the order we were just kindling fires, intending to boil coffee. A cheer went up and every man sprang into his place. Waist belts were tightened (it was fast becoming an open question whether we could much longer keep them from slipping down to our heels unless Uncle Sam gave us more to eat!), cartridge boxes were examined and guns capped. As the colonel ordered his men

---

off to ponder his fate in Kansas for the rest of the war. Sykes died at Fort Brown, Texas, on February 8, 1880. Warner, *Generals in Blue*, 492–93; Heitman, *Historical Register*, 1:941–42.

20. Graduating from West Point in 1847, Griffin served as an artilleryman in Mexico and on the frontier until appointed to teach artillery tactics at West Point in 1860. After commanding a battery at First Bull Run, Griffin was elevated to brigadier general on June 9, 1862. He became a solid division commander at Fredericksburg and beyond. Commissioned major general on April 2, 1865, he commanded the Fifth Corps in the closing days of the war. Griffin died at Galveston, Texas, on September 15, 1867. Warner, *Generals in Blue*, 190–91; Heitman, *Historical Register*, 1:478.

to fall in, he alighted from his valuable black horse upon which he was at the moment sitting—a gift from his Harvard classmates—and in a cheerful voice called out to John Peach,[21] his groom, "John, bring up my war horse." Peach led the bay horse up and the colonel mounted him, quietly remarking that the one he had been riding was "too good to be sacrificed to the gods of war." The men were soon moving forward in line of battle, as straight as if on parade, and as they neared the enemy Webster gave the order, "Double-quick, march!" He then cried out in a voice full of satisfied feeling, "Now, boys, we've got a chance!"

We were soon on the move. We could be seen by thousands of troops to the right and left and they cheered us loudly, which gave us great encouragement. We met hundreds of wounded men from the commands of Porter and Reynolds, many of them being Duryee's men in Zouave uniform.

We halted finally on the eastern slope of Bald Hill. The Twelfth Massachusetts occupied the right, the Thirteenth Massachusetts the left of the brigade line. The Eighty-third New York (Ninth Militia) and Eleventh Pennsylvania were in the centre. Firing began. There was a line of graycoats lying down in the tall grass in our front and it was hard to get their range, but their bullets reached us very readily. "Fire to the left!" cried Colonel Webster and the word was repeated along the line.

The battle was becoming furious. Down to our left the rattle of musketry was a continuous roar and high above it could be heard the rebel yell. We poured our bullets to the left oblique as fast as we could. Men were falling by the score. Someone cried out, "Webster is killed!" I looked around just in time to see Adjutant Thomas P. Haviland[22] take him in his arms.

21. John Peach enlisted at the age of fifteen in Co. I, Twelfth Massachusetts, on June 26, 1861. Seriously wounded at Antietam, he received a discharge for disability on November 14, 1862. He enlisted again for ninety days in the Eleventh Unattached Company of Massachusetts Militia on May 11, 1864, and was mustered out on August 15, 1864. He eventually settled in Malden, Massachusetts, and died there on August 19, 1924. *Boston Herald*, August 20, 1924; *Massachusetts Soldiers*, 2:59; 5:219.

22. Thomas P. Haviland was commissioned adjutant of the Twelfth Massachusetts on June 26, 1861. Taken prisoner at Second Bull Run and exchanged, he resigned on March 8, 1863. Appointed major and paymaster on February 23, 1864, Haviland served in that capacity until April 30, 1866, when he was mustered out.

Then my attention was attracted to Captain Richard H. Kimball[23] of my company. He had been struck in the forehead and was falling to the ground. I cried, "Kimball is killed, too!" All in the company uttered a cry of grief and then expressed a determination to avenge his death. We all liked our captain. He was a thorough soldier—brave and true—a native of Portland, Maine. Before joining the Twelfth he had been in the employ of Moses Pond,[24] a dealer in stoves and furnaces on Blackstone Street, Boston, and belonged to the old Boston City Guards.

It did not seem more than twenty minutes—so swiftly does time fly in battle—from the time we opened fire before the troops to our left gave way. All was now confusion. We kept our line to the last—even till the enemy, who had gained the rear, was seen marching up in line. As we faced to the right and started from the spot, I saw a rebel battleflag directly behind Company K, our left company.

The rebels (Richard Garnett's,[25] and afterward George Pickett's[26] division) kept steadily on with fixed bayonets, but few of

---

Major Haviland died in Germantown, Pennsylvania, on July 27, 1885. *Massachusetts Soldiers*, 2:3; 6:764; *Boston Journal*, July 30, 1885.

23. Admitted to the ranks of the Ancient and Honorable Artillery Company in 1859, Richard Kimball was commissioned captain of Co. A, Twelfth Massachusetts, on June 26, 1861. He was wounded at Cedar Mountain and killed at Second Bull Run on August 30, 1862. His last words were supposedly, "Now, boys, fire to the left, and fire low." Roberts, *Ancient and Honorable* 2:324; *Massachusetts Soldiers*, 2:8; *Portland Daily Advertiser*, October 15, 1862.

24. Moses W. Pond entered the stove business in the mid-1850s. A prominent member of Boston charitable societies, during the war he acted as superintendent of the Discharged Soldiers Home. Pond died in Boston on May 18, 1883. *Boston Journal*, May 19, 1883.

25. Richard Garnett graduated from West Point in 1841 and served in Florida and on the frontier until May 17, 1861, when he resigned as captain of the Sixth United States to accept a position in the Confederate army. Appointed brigadier general on November 14, 1861, he served under Stonewall Jackson until a quarrel between them resulted in Garnett's transfer to Longstreet's corps. He was killed in the climactic charge at Gettysburg on July 3, 1863. Warner, *Generals in Gray*, 99; Heitman, *Historical Register*, 1:447.

26. After graduating from West Point in 1846 and serving in Mexico, Pickett served in the western territories until his resignation on June 25, 1861. He was not commissioned brigadier general until January 14, 1862, but performed well until wounded at Gaines Mill. Pickett is best remembered for two failures—the famous charge at Gettysburg in 1863 and the defeat at Five Forks in 1865. He

Captain Richard H. Kimball. Courtesy of
the U.S. Army Heritage and Education
Center

them firing. Sixty-three of our regiment were captured and
seventy-five were killed and wounded. We fell back firing, and
soon reached a house, behind which we rallied. Then we fell back
some distance, in good order and with colors flying. We came finally to a line of Regulars. Here we halted and formed upon their
left. General Abner Doubleday[27] of Hatch's division, McDowell's

died in Norfolk, Virginia, on July 30, 1875. Warner, *Generals in Gray*, 239–40;
Heitman, *Historical Register*, 1:790.

    27. After graduating from West Point in 1842, Doubleday served in the artil-
lery unremarkably until the attack on Fort Sumter in 1861 when he fired the first
shot in defense of the American flag. Commissioned brigadier general on February 3, 1862, and major general on November 29, 1862, he commanded a brigade,
then a division in 1862, and took over the First Corps at Gettysburg after the fall

corps, was here and he made us a little speech suggesting that we take position upon a hill farther to the left. We did so and opened fire upon a number of detached bodies of the enemy coming forward, which had the effect of checking their further advance.

A little to the left, yet in front of our position, was a shallow ravine and, believing that water could be found in it, I went out there with a comrade. We hesitated a little as we saw how thickly it was strewn with the dead and dying, but being very thirsty, we persisted in our search for water until rewarded by finding a muddy pool. We were filling our canteens with the foul liquid, my comrade holding his by the strings and pouring the water in from his dipper. The bullets whispered very softly to us as if telling us to go away from the dangerous spot, but we heeded them not until one came and cut both strings of my comrade's canteen as keenly as though done with a knife, letting the receptacle of muddy water fall with a splash. We "left very sudden."

Of course, many movements other than those mentioned took place upon the field. I have referred only to those with which Ricketts's division was in some way connected. This was one of the great battles of the war. When darkness came the battle was over and we crossed Bull Run on the Stone Bridge, our knapsacks falling into the enemy's hands. Here we witnessed a scene of confusion impossible to describe—wrecked wagons and other war material, with excited officers rushing about trying to evolve order out of chaos. That night we marched to Centreville in a drizzling rain, worn out and hungry, but ready still to battle for the Union when an officer should be found who had the ability to successfully lead us.

Teamsters were indispensable to a great army in the field, faithfully caring for necessary supplies of ammunition and food and in safely transporting them from point to point where they were most needed. They probably contributed as much to the success of our arms as did the men in the ranks. How could battles be won or campaigns be successfully prosecuted if the supplies of the army were not skillfully handled? Teamsters sometimes got into

---

of General Reynolds. Not having the trust of his army commander, Doubleday was relegated to busywork in Washington for the next two years. After retiring in 1873, Doubleday moved to Mendham, New Jersey, where he died on January 26, 1893. Warner, *Generals in Blue*, 129–30; Heitman, *Historical Register*, 1:380.

tight places where they had disagreeable experiences and tastes of danger. Clark Cole[28] and I happened to serve together in the great Civil War and one delightful August day, more than a score of years after Pope's ill-fated campaign, he shared some of his adventures during those perilous times:

"On the afternoon of August 29th I was encamped, together with an almost innumerable host of army teamsters, in the rear of the army, when an order came for all empty wagons to go down to Cedar Run and there load up with commissary and quartermaster stores from the cars that had been run down from Warrenton, our former base of supplies. We arrived there shortly before dark and found three or four long trains, containing everything conceivable in the shape of army stores, to the value, probably, of many thousands of dollars. We had ample time and opportunity to have saved much of this valuable property, but either because of some misapprehension of orders or of the absence of them we lay quietly by till morning, when, as the sequel shows, it was too late to accomplish much.

"Soon after daylight we began to bestir ourselves and get ready for work, but no officers appeared upon the scene and no one felt authorized to give the word. After a while it was reported that the Johnnies were close at hand and then everyone made a break for the cars. We pulled out shoes, pants, blankets and everything we could lay hands upon, in a hurried and aimless way, and it seemed as though after all we would busily accomplish a part of what we had been sent there to do. But just as things appeared to be going on swimmingly, the rebs burst upon us and began pillaging from the rear of the trains while we were trying to clutch the property of Uncle Sam from the forward ends. Finding that this grab game was likely to result more to their advantage than to ours, we set fire to the cars that we could reach and then mounted our mules and drove away.

"Still no officers appeared. We had a plucky little wagon master whom we called 'Dan.' I have forgotten the rest of his name, but

28. Clark R. Cole enlisted on April 20, 1861, as a wagoner in Co. A, Twelfth Massachusetts, and served until mustered out on July 8, 1864. A native of Dayton, Maine, he returned to his hometown and died there on January 21, 1915. *Massachusetts Soldiers*, 2:6; Clark R. Cole Pension Records, RG 15, NA.

remember that he belonged to a New York regiment. We did not
know, in the excitement of the moment, what direction to take,
but Dan was cool and collected and he led the way and preserved
order with as much ability as generals sometimes display in taking
their troops into battle. Soon after we started there were heavy
explosions ahead of us and we could see great columns of smoke
rise suddenly into the air. We naturally thought a great battle was
going on in our very path, but Dan still urged us forward. After a
while we met General Banks, marching at the head of his troops
toward the point we had just left. We then learned that the explosions we had witnessed were caused by the blowing up of ammunition wagons to prevent them from falling into the hands of the
enemy. Many of Banks's soldiers were bare-footed, while we had
left enough shoes burning at Cedar Run to have re-shod his whole
division.

"When we finally reached the rear of the battleground, tired
and hungry, and before we had a moment to rest, we were ordered to immediately proceed to the field hospitals, load up with
wounded men, and take them to the hospitals in Washington.
Some growling was indulged in at first, but when we thought of
the poor fellows lying there mangled and torn by shot and shell,
all caviling ceased. We swung out in a lively but systematic way—
for there was need of haste—under the leadership of our brave
little wagon master Dan and in an hour every wagon was filled
with the sad wrecks of what a few hours before had been strong
and heroic defenders of the Union. I have been placed in many
trying positions, but I never had anything to do that was harder
than that—to put those poor fellows, wounded in every imaginable way, into those rough, springless army wagons, with not so
much as a little straw to lie upon. It was terrible, but the brave
fellows thought it was better than it would be to be left in the enemy's hands and doubtless it was.

"Late in the afternoon of Saturday, as we started upon our journey of more than forty miles to Washington, our ears began to
be greeted with groans and cries of pain and this was kept up
all the way along, the men begging of us continually to stop and
leave them by the roadside to die. We had nothing to give them
to eat or drink—in fact, we had had little ourselves for several

days—and all we could do was to steel our hearts against all their cries of anguish and push on and on. We kept on all that night, being obliged to halt an hour or so occasionally to allow bodies of McClellan's troops to pass us, for they were now hurrying forward to the front.

"All the next day we pressed on as fast as we could, but could not make much headway, as the roads were badly blocked and our mules were nearly worn out. The cries of the men were growing less loud and frequent, for they were becoming weaker, and occasionally one was taken out and left by the roadside dead.

"Sunday night was a particularly trying one. We were then nearly exhausted ourselves. Soon after dark I picked up a contraband fleeing from his master and, ascertaining that he could drive, I put him in the saddle. After telling him to water the mules and the wounded men if he should happen to cross a stream, I got up on my wagon box and went to sleep, sitting bolt upright. I was so nearly worn out that I could sleep anywhere then, for I had not closed my eyes for thirty-six hours. I slept soundly for several hours, despite the groans of the wounded and the noise and curses of the thousands who were continually passing us in both directions.

"After a while I awoke and, finding that the stupid negro had driven through a stream without heeding my instructions, I said and did some things in my wrath that I will not speak of now. I'll leave you to imagine what they were and will only say that my opinion of 'our colored brother' was not at the time a very exalted one. We finally reached Washington the next day and turned the wounded men over to the hospital authorities after being forty-eight hours without food and care. We had not had anything to eat ourselves for sixty hours and the same may be said of the mules."

CHAPTER 11

Maryland Campaign

Lee's easy victory at Second Bull Run made the Confederates confident, created consternation throughout the loyal North and badly rattled the officials in Washington. But the men in blue, knowing that eventually the right man would be found to lead them and that the right course would then be pursued, were still firm and reliant. The only serious complaint heard was that so many precious lives were being needlessly sacrificed.

Now that the battle was over, we keenly missed many familiar faces—among them that of our beloved colonel. We ascertained that Adjutant Haviland had remained with him and that his wounds, in his left arm and chest, were thought to be mortal. We earnestly desired his rescue from the Confederates and Lieutenant Arthur Dehon, whose father was a warm personal friend of both the colonel and his distinguished father, expressed his willingness to attempt it. The lieutenant, mounted, went on to the field with the surgeons, as permission had been obtained from the Confederates to render what aid we could to the men whom we had left in their hands.

Soon after entering the Confederate lines, Lieutenant Dehon was detained as a prisoner, but when Doctor Lafayette Guild,[1]

---

1. After graduating from Jefferson Medical College in 1848, Lafayette Guild accepted a position as assistant surgeon in the army and served on the frontier until the outbreak of war. Dismissed from the army on July 1, 1861, he was commissioned surgeon in the Confederate army and was appointed medical director of the Army of Northern Virginia on June 27, 1862. He remained as such until the war's end and died in San Francisco on July 4, 1870. One writer estimated that "for every soldier who laid down his arms at Appomattox at least six had passed through the kindly hands of Lee's efficient medical corps." Schroeder-Lein,

Medical Director of Lee's army, heard of the incident and of the lieutenant's errand, he promptly ordered his release and provided him with a pass. After a long search Lieutenant Dehon found the colonel's body. It had been buried in a shallow grave, but he disinterred it, removing the earth with his own hands, having no spade or other instrument, and, strapping it upon the back of his horse, returned to the Union lines in safety.

From this point his body was taken to Alexandria, where it was embalmed. Then it was brought to Boston, in charge of Mr. George J. Abbott[2] of the State Department. Here it lay in state twenty-four hours in Faneuil Hall, guarded by the Independent Corps of Cadets and visited by thousands. On the 9th of September, there was an imposing funeral and an eloquent eulogy was pronounced by Reverend Chandler Robbins[3] in the old stone church in Church Green, Summer Street.

At the services in Marshfield, Massachusetts an incident occurred which shows how Colonel Webster was beloved by even the humblest people. In the years when he was Surveyor of the Boston Custom House an old lady used to sit upon the steps of the building with fruit to sell. Webster, when passing in and out, always spoke kindly to her and bought from the contents of her basket. In the town of Marshfield lived a poor, simple-minded fellow, whom people were in the habit of avoiding. He almost invariably met Webster at the station on his return from the city, because the colonel always had a kind word for him. When the colonel's body was borne from the Webster mansion to the tomb, followed by a large number of the residents of the town, on foot and in carriages, the old lady who had sold fruit on the Custom House

---

Encyclopedia of Civil War Medicine, 119; Heitman, *Historical Register*, 1:483; "Medical Director of Lee's Army," 447.

2. George J. Abbott had been the personal secretary of Daniel Webster during his term as secretary of state. Abbott stayed in the State Department and died in January 1879 while serving as consul at Goderich, Canada. (*Troy, N.Y.*) *Times*, January 30, 1879.

3. Reverend Chandler Robbins graduated from Harvard, then went on to Cambridge and graduated in 1833 from the divinity school there. He succeeded Ralph Waldo Emerson at the Second Unitarian Church and received a doctor of divinity degree from Harvard in 1855. Robbins died at Weston, Massachusetts, on September 11, 1882. *Boston Journal*, September 11, 1882.

steps and the simple-minded man whom Webster had so often befriended appeared, plainly clothed, walking side by side in the funeral cortege. They had come unbidden to pay their humble tribute to their departed friend.

All that was mortal of big-hearted Fletcher Webster was interred at Marshfield beside the body of his brother Edward, who had died in the service of his country in Mexico, and thus the two defenders of the Constitution were united in death with its great Expounder.

> Here rest the great and good. Here they repose
> After their generous toil. A sacred band,
> They take their sleep together, while the year
> Comes with its early flowers to deck their graves,
> And gathers them again, as Winter frowns . . .
>   They need
> No statue nor inscription to reveal
> Their greatness. It is round them; and the joy
> With which the children tread the hallowed ground
> That holds their venerated bones, the peace
> That smiles on all they fought for, and the wealth
> That clothes the land they rescued—these, though mute
> As feeling ever is when deepest
> Are monuments more lasting than the fanes
> Reared to the Kings and demigods of old.

It is commonly supposed that Colonel Webster died soon after receiving his wounds. This is not the case, however. He lingered till the next morning and all that night the pitiless rain beat down upon him. But he was not entirely without human sympathy.

On the morning after the battle, the Confederate brigade commanded by General Garnett was resting at the roadside after its hard service of the previous day when a soldier of the Nineteenth Virginia, Jesse Burley[4] of Company H, came up and began to relate his adventures. He had been over a portion of the field where

---

4. Jesse A. Burley enlisted in Co. H, Nineteenth Virginia, on March 1, 1862, and was hospitalized several times prior to being killed at Antietam. Jordan and Thomas, *19th Virginia Infantry*, 59.

the savage encounter of the previous day had taken place and had found the dead and dying upon every side, friend and foe being strangely intermingled, showing that the death grapple had been fierce and at close quarters. He had gazed in horror upon the mangled forms of the slain and listened with well nigh broken heart to the piteous moans of the dying.

It was not a desire for plunder or the promptings of idle curiosity that had drawn this man to such a terrible place. No, the motive was a deep and grand one. It had its foundation in one of the noblest attributes of man—a desire to relieve human suffering. Men with ghastly wounds were everywhere crying for help, while to many none came but the kindly Angel of Death. Some were calling aloud in their delirium for friends, though loved ones were far away. For hours, this noble fellow had been carrying water to cool the parched lips and fevered brows of friend and foe alike.

Lying in that part of the field where his brigade had so gallantly charged the evening before, he found a wounded colonel of the Union army, evidently dying, but who seemed to be bearing his terrible sufferings with more than ordinary fortitude. No word or murmur or complaint came from his lips, but he lay calmly awaiting his final summons, knowing perfectly well that his wounds were mortal and that death was very near. When the kind-hearted Southerner had rendered him attentions, giving him water, bathing his wounds and covering his form with a rubber blanket, the officer expressed his heartfelt thanks. Then, as the soldier bade him be of good cheer and turned to go, the colonel took from his finger a ring and gave it to the man in gray, wishing in this way to further show his gratitude. The ring was an old style bloodstone seal ring, on it the letter "W," above which was a horse's head. The man, now with the light heart which always follows the performance of a good deed, hurried forward to rejoin his company.

Major George T. Jones,[5] quartermaster of the Nineteenth Virginia and acting quartermaster of Garnett's brigade, was about

5. George T. Jones was commissioned captain on July 19, 1861, in the Nineteenth Virginia and major on October 4, 1862, and spent the war on quartermaster duty. He surrendered at Appomattox on April 9, 1865, as a member of Pickett's division. Jordan and Thomas, *19th Virginia Infantry*, 78; *Appomattox Roster*, 71.

setting out for Gordonsville to bring up supplies, so Burley handed him the ring for safe keeping and very earnestly implored him to visit the place on his way back and see if any more could be done for the comfort of the wounded officer. The quartermaster, with great difficulty, found the colonel in the place described, but he was past all human help. Death had ended his terrible sufferings. On a bush near by he found hanging a little slip of paper, on which was written, "Colonel Fletcher Webster, Twelfth Massachusetts Volunteers." As Lieutenant Haviland, the last of Webster's comrades to leave him and who bravely stood by until carried away a prisoner, knows nothing of this little tag, it is fair to presume that it was written and placed there by the Confederate soldier.

Major Jones gazed on the inanimate form before him for a moment, knowing full well whose son it was who had so bravely given his life for the Union cause. "Then," as he said in a recent letter to me, "in the kindest of feeling," impelled by his "great respect for the Webster name," he took his penknife from his pocket and, leaning over the lifeless form of the good and brave colonel, he cut a button from the breast of his coat as a souvenir. Not caring to remain longer in the midst of such a terrible scene, Major Jones hurried on to rejoin his train. He did not again see the soldier to whom Colonel Webster had given the ring, as only seventeen days afterward, at the Battle of Antietam, Burley was struck down by a Federal bullet while bravely fighting in the ranks of his regiment.

During the winter of 1863, while Lee's army was lying upon the heights of Fredericksburg, a question arose in the Nineteenth Virginia as to the rightful ownership of Webster's ring. It was claimed by a relative of Burley's,[6] then serving in Company H, while Major Jones was intending to forward it to the widow of its late owner. The matter was finally left to the decision of Captain John T. Ellis,[7] then commanding the company, and the ring was turned over to Burley's relative. Jones then bought it from him for its appraised

6. It is impossible to positively identify Burley's relative.
7. A graduate of the Virginia Military Institute in 1848, John T. Ellis received his commission as captain of Co. H, Nineteenth Virginia, on July 1, 1861. Promoted to major on April 29, 1862, and lieutenant colonel on September 14, 1862, he was killed at Gettysburg on July 3, 1863. Jordan and Thomas, *19th Virginia Infantry*, 67.

value, the price being determined by a jeweler, a soldier in the regiment. He thereupon sent both ring and button to his son, Louis, who ever afterward carefully guarded and preserved them all through the trying vicissitudes of the war and the many years that have followed.

In the month of March, 1878, Mrs. Webster[8] received a letter from Louis T. Jones, who stated that he had just seen an extract from a Northern newspaper giving an account of the burning of the Webster mansion and that she was the widow of Colonel Fletcher Webster of the Twelfth Massachusetts. Jones explained that he had a finger ring in his possession, evidently a family keepsake, which he desired to return to her. A short time after confirming her address to Jones, Mrs. Webster received the ring and it proved to be a valued heirloom of the Webster family. When the collection of material for the *History of the Webster Regiment* began, I wrote to Mr. Jones for further particulars and he told the story of the button and offered to send it either to Mrs. Webster or to me. Mrs. Webster kindly waived her claim in my favor and I received it by mail on the 10th of January, 1883. I at once presented it to Fletcher Webster Post 13, Grand Army of the Republic, of Brockton, in whose custody it still remains. The button is mounted on a passé-partout, surrounded by a maroon velvet mat. Underneath, in a panel, appears its history, briefly told, together with a statement as to its presentation. The whole is elegantly framed in gilt.

Those who loved Colonel Fletcher Webster remember how much better than bugle or band was his "Close up, boys!" Tumbling through deep mud holes into the darkness, wading through creeks into the swamp, crowding through thickets into the forest, "Close up, boys!" sounded out clear and musical, never failing to start the echo of a cheer when the good cheer itself was quite marched out. The men were proud of him. He was indispensable

8. Caroline Story White was joined in marriage to Daniel Fletcher Webster by Reverend S. K. Lothrop in Boston on November 29, 1836. Described as "a healthy, buxom, lively person," Caroline received a pension on April 17, 1863, that she used to raise her children. This pension was increased to $100 per month by act of Congress following the loss of the Webster mansion in 1878. Caroline was an invalid in her later life and died in Roxbury, Massachusetts, on August 7, 1886. Fletcher Webster Pension Records, RG 15, NA; *Boston Journal*, August 9, 1886; *Boston Daily Advertiser*, August 9, 1886; *Boston Herald*, February 17, 1889.

to the commissary when the beef was over salt, shoes over worn or blankets lost. His charity covered a multitude of cold and aching places. He had a way of looking out for them quite home-like. He rarely took discipline into his hands, but his rebuke was more severe than courts martial were elsewhere. No one marched them so slowly, spoke to them so kindly or met them so cordially, yet none was more respected. As the scenes are shifting so quickly and our earthly labors are not finished, out of the shadows and silence we can still hear the old voice, "Close up the ranks, steady, forward!!"

To return to my narrative, late in the afternoon of September 1st, in a furious thunderstorm, we reached Chantilly, where the Confederates were being held in check by the divisions of Kearny and Stevens. We came on the double-quick and formed in the edge of a wood, our right resting on the Fairfax Turnpike. The battle was raging furiously, but as we were placed in reserve we suffered no loss. We were lying behind a rail fence, waiting for the expected attack of the enemy. It was early in the evening, but as there were no indications of an immediate advance of the rebs, I obtained permission to leave the ranks for water.

Soon after dark I took the canteens of a number of my comrades and started off. I crossed the pike and a short distance beyond found a running stream. After filling the canteens I filled my dipper, now black with soot. While re-crossing the pike, an officer, a stranger to me, closely enveloped in a military cloak, asked, "Have you any good water, my man?" "Yes, sir," I said, "but my dipper is rather sooty." He drank eagerly, and then laughingly remarked, "If we don't have any worse things than black dippers to put up with, we can consider ourselves lucky." Then he added, "We've got a good position here, and I feel sure that we can hold them this time."

Something in his manner gave me confidence and I told him that I hoped so, too. I was disgusted with the way matters had been managed lately; I had no confidence in either Pope or McDowell and I railed pretty freely over the blundering at Bull Run. This he seemed greatly to enjoy and even assisted me in describing the battles and movements of the various corps, particularly the fight of the 30th of August, in which McDowell's corps was so badly worsted. After a while I turned to go and as I did so he inquired my name and regiment. I gave him both and then visions of the punishments laid down in the Articles of War for too freely criticizing commanding officers arose in my mind and I became just a little disconcerted, inasmuch as I did not know to whom I had been talking. I touched my cap and made a stammering apology, to which he replied with a laugh, "O, that's all right. I like to hear a man speak his mind once in a while." I ventured to remark, as a parting salutation, "I hope we will not have another Bull Run affair here."

"I don't mean that we shall," said he. "We'll have no more such blunders as were made there. I have placed your division in the edge of this forest, so that they may have perfect command of this open ground. Then I have batteries in good positions and plenty of troops to call in if we need them."

This emphatic use of the pronoun "I" did the business for me and I was sure then that I had "put my foot in it." But I summoned what little courage I had remaining and in a faltering voice asked, "May I ask with whom I have had the honor of conversing?"

"I am General Hooker and I've been put in command of your corps."[9] I told him I was very glad to hear it. He bade me a cordial good-night and I hurried back to the regiment. The news I brought did more good than would have resulted had the water I brought been the drink of the gods and had every one of those weary, wet and hungry fellows partaken of it. For an hour or so more they crept to the side of the road, singly and in groups, to get a peep at the new commander of the corps, whom we now knew for a surety and to our intense satisfaction had succeeded the disliked and inefficient McDowell, rumors of which had been whispered through the ranks for several days.

We were at this time a pretty used up lot. My own wardrobe was frightful and I was never in worse condition outwardly than just after the Second Battle of Bull Run. I had lost my knapsack during the fight and my Bible, too—the latter an irreparable loss—and consequently started on the retreat toward Alexandria in the most dilapidated condition imaginable. I was barefooted and had been

9. Although Kimball probably met Hooker that night, the latter did not take over official command of the First Army Corps until September 6, 1862.

for a week, thanks to the Government contractor who had made the soles of my last pair of shoes of shoddy instead of leather. The disagreeable insect which all who read this will recognize, even though its disgusting name is not recalled,[10] had disputed with me as to the possession of my shirt and drawers and these had been given up as a result. My blouse had become torn and greasy and ditto my pants—particularly below the knees—so that they hung in shreds about my ankles. I had used my cap as a "holder" in handling my smutty dipper when full of soup or coffee and to remove the greasy fry pan from the fire, so that its condition may be better imagined than described. My condition generally would have secured me unquestioned admission into the society of tramps. Everybody, particularly in the Army of Virginia, was more or less dilapidated and yet, so wonderfully did that buoyancy of spirits that has always characterized the American soldier show itself, complaints were few.

I remember a neat little satire that I first heard sung on the march to Hall's Hill the next day after the battle of Chantilly. It was sung with great gusto to the air of "Louisiana Lowlands." One verse was as follows:

> It was down in old Virginia not many months ago,
> McClellan made a movement, but he made it mighty slow,
> Old Jackson found it out, and he pitched into his rear,
> But he couldn't make it work, for he found Phil Kearny there,
>   In the old Virginia lowlands,
>   Lowlands, lowlands,
>   In the old Virginia lowlands low.

Whether it was intended as a thrust at "Little Mac" for his Peninsular failure or as a jab at Pope and everybody in general over McClellan's shoulders I never knew, but it is beyond dispute that an army that could sing such a song as this, so heartily at such a time, could be depended upon to fight wherever and whenever they were given an opportunity.

10. Kimball was obviously referring to the ubiquitous, wingless, bloodsucking louse, the persistent companion of all soldiers North and South.

We were plodding over the road towards Hall's Hill and the enemy was following only a few miles back. Suddenly I heard much shouting on ahead and soon learned the cause. It was a simple event which in ordinary times would attract no attention at all—only the passage of a well-dressed citizen upon the road-side—but in the army it was different. There it was sufficient at any time to rouse the men to a high pitch of excitement and interest. The sight of a man in citizen's dress at once excited the envy of all the boys in blue who beheld him and in no other way could that feeling be shown better than by shouting very loudly. Well, the shouting continued and after a while the representative of civil life came in sight. Could I believe my eyes? He was no other than one of my acquaintances at home—a companion of my boyhood![11]

I called his name and, hearing it above the clatter of tongues, he came nearer to the moving line. Still I kept repeating his name and after a while he recognized me among the dirt-begrimed mass. I obtained permission to fall out and then soon learned that my friend was a clerk at the headquarters of one of the generals. He had been out with the army but a short time, having recently graduated from college. He said he was on his way to Alexandria and was greatly surprised to hear that he would be more likely to bring up in Richmond than on the Potomac if he kept on much longer that way. He was hungry, so I concluded to teach him a culinary lesson. It excited astonishment in him to observe the comparative ease and rapidity with which I prepared the coffee, boiled potatoes, broiled fresh meat and roasted green corn, but to me such things had become familiar work. He ate heartily to "give the house a good name" and then we plodded on together. In talking over old times we enjoyed ourselves very much. To me, especially, it was one of the happiest experiences of my army life and the light of his presence remained with me long after his bodily form had disappeared. My friend is now pastor of a Boston church.

In the early evening of September 2d, we were lying at Hall's Hill, in the vicinity of the forest which commanded the approaches

11. This individual cannot be positively identified.

to Washington from the south. The men were scattered about in groups, discussing the events of their ill-starred campaign and indulging in comments that were decidedly uncomplimentary to those who had been responsible for its mismanagement. We did not know, of course, the exact significance of all that had happened, but being mainly thinking men, we were able to form pretty shrewd guesses as to where the real difficulty lay.

Suddenly, while these mournful consultations were in full blast, a mounted officer dashing past our bivouac reined up long enough to shout, "'Little Mac' is back here on the road, boys! God bless 'Little Mac!'" The scene that followed cannot be described. From extreme sadness, we passed in a twinkling to a delirium of delight. A Deliverer had come! A real "rainbow of promise" had appeared suddenly in the dark political sky. The feeling in our division upon the return of General McClellan had its counterpart in all the others, for the Army of the Potomac loved him as it never loved any other leader.

The advent of McClellan restored confidence, but the situation was still alarming. On the 4th the rebs came near capturing our regiment's wagon train and thus stripping us entirely of the comforts of life. They already had our knapsacks. As they were reported as heading toward the fords of the Upper Potomac, it looked as if they intended to "wipe us out" if we did not "get a move on."

While at Hall's Hill I went sightseeing—forgetting that I was quite a "sight" myself. I climbed the ramparts of a fort, where a grand view could be had of the surrounding country. The fort was garrisoned by nine months men, in all the splendor attainable in such service. I soon noticed that I was being watched by an officer in full uniform, with everything about his trappings bright, new and clean and two gaily-dressed ladies, but did not dream that my presence could be objectionable until sharply reminded that such was the case by hearing the officer tell an orderly to "Go up there and drive that dirty soldier away." I will leave the reader to imagine what was said in reply. I found a pair of brogans, however, that some fastidious nine-months man had discarded for more dainty footwear and so my visit to the fort bore some fruit.

My only fear as we approached the gay capital of our country was that the fashionable people of that city would gather in the streets to see the troops pass through. In that case my only hope of escaping the penalties of the law against indecent exposure lay in the fact that there were many more "in the same box." Luckily my division went through in the night. At half-past 10 P.M. on the 5th of September, we set out upon the Maryland campaign, crossing the Potomac on the Chain Bridge. Army wagons and battalions of artillery continually blocked the way and progress was slow. The streets of Washington were filled with a struggling mass of animals and men, wagons and guns, the soldiers cursing as only soldiers can curse when in heavy marching order they find their way obstructed. We floundered wearily, apparently aimlessly, about, now making room for the passage of long trains of white-capped army wagons, which appeared anything but picturesque at this time, and now crowded to the sidewalks by double lines of guns and caissons and it was almost daylight when we finally came to a halt only a few miles north of the city. It was a short march, but an extremely tiring one. Luckily, during one long halt, I had gotten a good nap in a gutter with my head upon the curbstone.

At 5 A.M. on the 6th, this time with an open road, we set out again. Making seventeen miles with scarcely a halt, we reached Mechanicsville. We remained here the rest of that day and all of the next and were made happy by the receipt of new uniforms, shelter tents and everything we needed. General Hartsuff, our gallant brigade commander, who had been absent on account of sickness, here rejoined us.

On the 8th we took the road again and made good progress. Next day a new regiment, the Sixteenth Maine, joined our brigade. We were on the march almost continuously in one direction or another till the 14th, when we reached Frederick. Here we were received with enthusiasm by the people. They gave us food and in other ways manifested their pleasure because of our arrival. They had had a taste of Confederate occupation and did not relish it. They remembered us, we having passed the previous winter there. We remained an hour in the streets amid a continuous ovation. Then on over the old Hagerstown Pike to Middletown, a distance of eight miles, we marched with scarcely a halt and by three o'clock in the afternoon were facing Turner's Gap in the South Mountain. General D. H. Hill[12] was there, with what appeared to be a strong force, to dispute our passage.

We were pleased with our corps commander, "Fighting Joe" Hooker, and as he led us down the road to our position we passed General McClellan. He sat proudly upon his magnificent horse, watching the troops as they filed by, and thousands greeted their beloved leader with the wildest enthusiasm. We threw our caps into the air, cheered, yelled and danced in turn, until it seemed as if all organization and order was in danger of being forgotten. Even the noble animal which the general bestrode came in for a share of the adulation, men actually throwing themselves upon the ground beneath him and hugging his legs. It was the most pronounced case of hero worship it was my good fortune to witness during my whole three years of army life. All the while the worthy recipient of these attentions sat upon his horse like a statue, pointing toward the smoke of the enemy's guns as it rose lazily from the mountain summit. The meaning of this appeal was fully understood and it called forth continuous cheers. It was if he were saying to us, "There lies your way." I could think of nothing but Napoleon surrounded by his legions. Now, as I think of that scene, I am convinced that no general in the Union Army ever possessed so fully the love of the men as did George B. McClellan.

Whenever General McClellan appeared among his troops, from the crossing of the Potomac at Washington to the grapple with Lee at Antietam, it was the signal for the most spontaneous and enthusiastic cheering I ever listened to or participated in. Men threw their caps high in the air and danced and frolicked like schoolboys, so glad were they to get their old commander back.

12. A graduate in the West Point class of 1842, Daniel H. Hill served with distinction in the Mexican-American War, but resigned on February 28, 1849, to become a mathematics professor. The outbreak of war found Hill serving as superintendent of the North Carolina Military Institute. Promoted from colonel of the First North Carolina to brigadier general in 1861 and major general on March 26, 1862, he proved a dependable division commander, but the last two years of the war saw Hill relegated to insignificant posts as a lieutenant general. He died in Charlotte, North Carolina, on September 24, 1889. Warner, *Generals in Gray*, 136–37; Heitman, *Historical Register*, 1:529.

It is true that McClellan had always been fortunate in being able to excite enthusiasm among his troops, but demonstrations at this time took on an added and noticeable emphasis from the fact that he had been recalled to command after what the army believed to be an unwise and unjust suspension.

As we neared the mountain, we found that Reno and Hatch were fighting their way up the steep side, inch by inch upon the Sharpsburg Road, and the rattle of musketry was continuous. Hooker led us to the right, on the old road to Martinsburg, and when the sun went down we were in line of battle at the base of the mountain. Soon we began our tedious ascent, over jagged rocks and through almost impenetrable underbrush. "Handsome Joe" playfully reminded us that we need not be cautioned not to fire too high this time. We climbed 700 feet to a position near the summit, often having to pull ourselves along by the aid of roots and anything we could get hold of. The enemy's skirmishers disputed our progress, but we crept on, swinging toward the right and driving them before us, until, late at night, we were told that we had gained their rear. We then rearranged our lines and laid down for a little sleep. Owing to the fact that it was difficult for the enemy to get our range, our loss was small, Clark Parker[13] of Company E being the only man killed in our regiment. The *esprit de corps* of this fine body of troops was now particularly high. The men felt that if any shadow of discredit had attached to them on account of the disaster at Manassas, it had been swept away by the brilliant flank movement at South Mountain.

Daylight on the 15th revealed the fact that the enemy had fled, leaving their dead unburied and many of their wounded fell into our hands. From these it was learned that the troops who had held the position, curiously enough, were a part of the same division that had routed us at Bull Run only sixteen days before. More curious still, one of the regiments—the Nineteenth Virginia—had left

13. Parker enlisted as a private in Co. E, Twelfth Massachusetts, on June 26, 1861, and was killed in action at South Mountain on September 14, 1862. Following the Maryland campaign, Clark Parker's remains were recovered and shipped to Boston, where they were buried after an impressive funeral service at Reverend Hepworth's Church of the Unity. *Massachusetts Soldiers*, 2:33; *Boston Evening Transcript*, November 20, 1862.

a number of knapsacks behind. On examination, many of ours were found among them and a number of our fellows recovered their own! One recovered a pistol which he lost at Manassas and several found photographs, etc. In some of the knapsacks, however, silk underwear and other articles were found, which, most likely, were either purchased or confiscated at stores in Frederick. While waiting here the commissary distributed what supplies he had on hand. The allowance to our regiment was one box of hard bread—fifty pounds—about two crackers apiece!

The impression those upturned faces of the enemy's dead made upon my mind can never be effaced, but more vividly than all the others do I remember the heroic determination expressed in the features of Colonel John B. Strange,[14] of the Nineteenth Virginia, as he lay, sword in hand, in advance of what was apparently their line of battle. A noble specimen of manhood, it seemed a pity that such men should be sacrificed in an effort to uphold a relic of barbarism in the nineteenth century and to divide a people which the Fathers of the Republic had intended should be one.

14. A graduate of the Virginia Military Institute in 1842, Strange was selected as lieutenant colonel of the Nineteenth Virginia on May 2, 1861, and reappointed to the same rank when the regiment was reorganized on April 29, 1862, before his death at South Mountain. General Garnett wrote of the deceased colonel: "His tried valor on other fields and heroic conduct in animating his men to advance upon the enemy with his latest breath, and after he had fallen mortally wounded, will secure imperishable honor for his name and memory." Jordan and Thomas, *19th Virginia Infantry*, 97; *Official Records*, ser. 1, vol. 19, pt. 1, 895.

CHAPTER 12

Antietam

The attempt to induce the people of Maryland to join the Confederacy, a part of Lee's program in crossing the Potomac, having utterly failed, the political sky began to look brighter. There yet remained, however, much hard fighting to be done, but the second 300,000 were coming and the future, from a military standpoint, was full of promise.

The enemy having fallen back from the passes of South Mountain, by 9 A.M. on the 15th of September we were sweeping down its western face, full of enthusiasm over our easy victory and forgetful of weariness and hunger in the delirium of the moment. On through Boonsborough to Keedysville we swiftly marched, making the air vocal with songs and answering the echoes of the guns in front with shouts of wild delight.

Near Keedysville the pace slackened. Brigades and divisions were filing right and left into open fields and the increasing roar of the guns showed that the enemy was making another stand. Our men now became more silent and gazed thoughtfully in the direction of the firing. Such seriousness always preceded a battle, but it was not due to lack of determination, nor did it indicate a disposition to falter. "We'll have a tussle with them here," said a tall soldier who was marching beside me. "Yes," I replied, "but the Johnnies will find 'Little Mac' and General Hooker hard men to deal with."

A moment later my comrade, Nathaniel H. Dyer,[1] spoke again. He was usually light-hearted and merry, but now appeared strangely

1. Nathaniel Dyer enlisted on July 6, 1861, in Co. A, Twelfth Massachusetts, and was killed at Antietam while serving as a corporal. He is buried in the Antietam National Cemetery. *Massachusetts Soldiers*, 2:6.

serious and thoughtful. He had a brother in the company and between the two men the closest relations existed. The welfare of each other was their constant thought. If rations were short or duty bore more heavily upon one than the other, the rest of the company were given an illustration of brotherly love which always had its good effect. My comrade now looked around to make sure that his brother should not hear him and said, "George, I don't know why it is, but I cannot get over the feeling that I am to be hit in this fight. If I am and you get out of it all right, look out for Charley,[2] won't you?" "Certainly," said I, "but don't think anything like that is going to happen. Look on the bright side."

The regiment was under command of Major Elisha M. Burbank,[3] Colonel Webster having been mortally wounded at Bull Run August 30th and Lieutenant Colonel Bryan being absent on sick leave. It numbered (nine companies) 325 officers and men. One of its companies, H, was at this time detached as provost guard at brigade headquarters. During the afternoon and night of the 15th the regiment lay in an open field just beyond the town of Keedysville, awaiting orders.

That afternoon and evening were occupied by maneuvers to uncover the enemy's position and at a late hour we lay down for a little sleep. The booming of guns, which continued at intervals throughout the night, was not sufficient to keep us awake, for we were very tired.

The 16th dawned clear and cool. Heavy firing in front roused the men of the First Corps even before the sun. The day seemed to promise great results. Rations and ammunition were hastily issued

2. Like his brother, Charles F. Dyer enlisted in Co. A, Twelfth Massachusetts, on July 6, 1861. He lost a leg at Fredericksburg and was discharged for his disability on March 17, 1864. Dyer died in Bryantville, Massachusetts, on March 30, 1917. *Massachusetts Soldiers*, 2:6; *Boston Herald*, December 27, 1862; Charles F. Dyer Pension Records, RG 15, NA.

3. Elisha M. Burbank had become colonel of the Sixty-fourth New York State Militia in 1846 and retained that office when that regiment was reorganized into the Thirteenth Regiment on July 5, 1847. This lengthy militia experience led to his commission as major in the Twelfth Massachusetts on June 26, 1861. Burbank died at Frederick, Maryland, on November 30, 1862, of wounds received at Antietam. *History of the 13th Regiment*, 11; *Massachusetts Soldiers*, 2:3; *Boston Evening Transcript*, May 13, 1861; *Boston Daily Advertiser*, December 4, 1862.

and the movement toward the right began. Besides the forty rounds that the cartridge boxes contained, each man put twenty more into his haversack. We made a wide detour to avoid being seen by the enemy, crossed Antietam Creek by the bridge known as No. 1 and the column then filed sharply to the left, soon coming out into a large cornfield near Joseph Poffenberger's house. Here the brigade halted, formed line of battle and began preparations for supper. The march had been a short one, but much time was consumed in waits and measures and the day was far spent. The men were comparatively safe in this position, as only occasionally did shells burst in their midst and they were out of range of the enemy's infantry.

McClellan had carefully reconnoitered the enemy's position and had decided upon his plan of battle. The work he had assigned to Hooker was to turn the enemy's left. This rested upon the Potomac and stretched away to and beyond the Dunker Church. Ricketts's division was placed in an open field on the left of the corps. General George Meade's[4] Pennsylvania Reserves came next and beyond them were Doubleday's men. The latter had good positions for artillery and improved them fully.

When all was ready the forward move began. The enemy had become aware of our intentions and was ready to meet us all along the line. A rattling skirmish fire, heaviest in Meade's front, showed that the ground was to be stubbornly contested. When darkness closed in, a halt was made, lines were readjusted and batteries placed in every available position for the harder and bloodier work of the morrow. Strong picket lines were thrown well out and in a cold, drizzling rain we lay down to sleep near the cornfield which was next day made so famous. All through that long, cold, dismal night the crack of rifles greeted the ears of Hartsuff's

4. George G. Meade graduated from West Point in 1835 and served only one year before resigning his commission, but he was reinstated in 1842 and served on engineering duties until the war. Commissioned brigadier general on August 31, 1861, he led a Pennsylvania brigade until wounded at Glendale. Meade was elevated to division command after Pope's campaign, to corps command as a major general (on November 29, 1862), and finally to command of the Army of the Potomac on June 28, 1863. He served in this capacity during the rest of the war and died in Philadelphia on November 6, 1872. Warner, *Generals in Blue*, 315–17; Heitman, *Historical Register*, 1:700.

troops. Occasionally Doubleday's artillery thundered out its defiance, only to be answered by the heavy roar of the enemy's guns as they savagely belched forth their acceptance of the challenge. Everything betokened a desperate battle on the morrow and no one who lay that night among Hartsuff's men will ever forget the terror, the anxieties, and the discomforts of his experience. Hooker, our intrepid corps commander, slept that night in a barn upon the Hoffman farm, and before retiring is said to have remarked to those about him, "To-morrow we fight the battle that will decide the fate of this Republic."

The company in which I was serving numbered at this time thirty men. We had borne our full share of the hardships and losses of Pope's ill-starred campaign. Our captain had been killed at Bull Run on the 30th of August. Our first lieutenant, William Greenough White,[5] a noble fellow, had been stricken down with slow fever early in Pope's campaign. We left him behind when the advance was made up to Cedar Mountain. He would gladly have gone with us, but was too sick and reluctantly entered the brigade hospital tent. We bade him an affectionate good-by, for we all loved him. The nurses who had charge of him told us afterward what trouble they had to keep him in bed, so great was his desire to leave and to follow on after us.

When Lee cut loose from Richmond and turned his whole army upon us, we were forced to retire, but we fell back fighting inch by inch. The sound of the guns came nearer and nearer the tent where our lieutenant lay. After a while he heard it and his keepers could keep him no longer. He rose like a lion from his lair. Demanding his uniform and sword, he left while the other sick ones

---

5. White received his commission as first lieutenant of Co. A, Twelfth Massachusetts, on June 26, 1861, and was killed at Antietam. He was described as "a young man of great capability for business and . . . deeply imbued with a taste for historical study. At the call of duty he did not hesitate to relinquish his prospects of mercantile success, and the enjoyments of home, to take his portion of the inevitable dangers of the field." White's obituary gave a few details of his last hours: "While fighting bravely he fell wounded by the bursting of a shell. His faithful friends Corporal [John] Jeffrey and Sergeant [Eben P.] Thompson immediately bore him from the field. He died in a few hours, and was calm and conscious to the last, giving directions as to the disposal of his effects and of his body." *Massachusetts Soldiers*, 2:10; "In Memoriam," 193; *Boston Post*, September 29, 1862.

were being hurriedly herded into ambulances for transportation to Washington. He started in the direction from which the firing came. Alone and unassisted he hurried forward. His desire to be with us, his love of country, his manly pride and the heavy roar of the guns, every moment sounding louder and nearer, nerved him on and gave him unnatural strength. When he came up we gave him a cheer and he wept like a child, so glad was he to be with us once more.

We were being whipped, but were constantly ready to fight and fight again and the arrival of our lieutenant gave us fresh courage. Our chagrin gave way to enthusiasm and we did our best to hold Lee in check till McClellan could get up from the Peninsula to help us. We reached the Rappahannock and made a stand. Here we held the enemy a few days, when we started off on our long march to Thoroughfare Gap to try to keep Longstreet from coming through. Our lieutenant had been as active as any of us and we all felt his influence and loved him more than ever. But the poor fellow's strength began to leave him in a few hours after we set out and finally he fainted and fell in the road. The surgeon took him from us again and sent him to the rear in an ambulance. He finally reached a hospital in Washington, where he had a relapse of the fever.

Now that Bull Run and Chantilly and South Mountain had passed into history and our brave captain and many of our men were "sleeping the sleep that knows no waking," we were face to face with the army of Lee upon the soil of Maryland. It was the night before the great ball at Antietam Creek was to open. The moon, which for a number of nights had been lighting our weary way over the mountain and through the forests of the land of the Calverts, had now withdrawn her face. Evidently the heavens thought it more in keeping with the scene and the time to draw a curtain of clouds over our heads and to shut us up in blackness.

We were just lying down for a little sleep, with our rifles beside us and our equipments on—for we were very tired—when an unusual stir and bustle, with handshaking and "God bless yous," announced the presence of our lieutenant. He had again broken away from his keepers, but was no more fit to endure the rigors of campaigning than before. His face was pale, his eyes were sunken and his limbs weak, but his soul was on fire. News of an impending battle had taken him from his bed and brought him to us again in spite of the protests of doctors and nurses. We shared our rations with him, for he had none, and rolled him up in blankets and overcoats and he slept between two comrades as peacefully as a child.

With the first gray gleam of light on the morning of the 17th of September, the men of the Twelfth Massachusetts were awake and ready for any duty—any sacrifice their country might require of them. No need of the roll of drums—reveille was sounded by the roar of 200 cannon and the clatter of thousands of muskets—and the men of the grand old Army of the Potomac sprang to their feet, ready for the work of the day. This began at once on our part of the field. Meade's brave Pennsylvanians, in three brigades, led the advance through smoke and fog. The artillery a little west of Hoffman's poured a perfect storm of shot and shell upon the point toward which Meade was moving. His infantry pressed bravely on. Ricketts, with his first and third brigades, followed. Hartsuff's brigade was left behind as a reserve. On the right, Doubleday advanced. The enemy skirmishers sullenly retired, and soon the rattle of musketry began in earnest.

The storm broke most furiously about the point of the wedge that Meade was driving into the enemy's line. His men went down by hundreds and soon a continually increasing stream of wounded began to pour toward the rear. The Reserves were doing nobly. They faltered not before the withering fire that broke upon them from behind trees and rocks and fences, but pushed on and on. They reached a rise of ground in advance of the rest of the line that formed a natural breastwork for the enemy. Here harder work was encountered and there was need of help. Ricketts's two brigades now moved forward, took position upon Meade's left and poured a perfect storm of bullets upon the stubborn Confederates. It was more than they could stand and they broke from their cover and went streaming back. A cheer went up from thousands of Union throats and the whole line advanced again. On they went, through fields of waving grain, over fences, across the open ground and through the grove past Miller's house. The flying Confederates reached the shelter of the woods behind the

Dunker Church and made a stand. Here the progress of the Union line was checked.

On the right, Doubleday had gained the ridge near Poffenberger's house. There had been sharp work all along the line and the ground over which the advance had taken place was strewn with the dead of both armies. No further progress seemed possible for the present, but the line was straightened and preparations were made to hold what had been gained. The fog lifted and the opposing forces were able to gaze into each other's faces.

In the forest just back of the Dunker Church the division of General John B. Hood[6] was forming. They came forward to the edge of the forest and opened a terrific fire. What remained of the old division of Stonewall Jackson also advanced and renewed its savage attack upon the men of the First Corps. The ordeal was a trying one, but the heroic Unionists bore it patiently for a time and rapidly returned the fire. Soon Stuart's batteries gained positions from which they were able to deliver an annoying and destructive crossfire and Hooker's men wavered. There was nothing to shield them from Stuart's guns. They were in the open field. Troops that will stand as firm as the hills when attacked in front will become uneasy under a fire upon their flank; they then get the impression that they are being surrounded. So it was now with Hooker's men and they began to give way. Hood saw this and pressed his splendid division forward. The Confederates advanced with a loud yell and the Unionists fell back in some confusion to the woods out of which a half hour before they had easily driven the enemy.

On a slight rise to the left of Poffenberger's, where they had been anxiously watching the furious battle that had been going on, stood Hartsuff's brigade. We had been ready at any moment to advance and now that the Union line seemed to be melting away and the victorious Confederates were advancing, we knew

6. A graduate of West Point in 1853, Hood was only a first lieutenant in the Second United States Cavalry when he resigned his commission to enter the Confederate service. Appointed a brigadier general on March 3, 1862, Hood enjoyed a reputation as a fighting general and was rewarded by promotions to major general and lieutenant general. Severely wounded twice, he proved unable to halt the Union juggernaut of 1864 in the Confederate heartland while commander of the Army of Tennessee. Hood died in New Orleans on August 30, 1879. Warner, *Generals in Gray*, 142–43; Heitman, *Historical Register*, 1:540.

that we would soon be needed. "Attention!" rang along the line and scarcely had we assumed that position when Captain William Candler,[7] of General Hooker's staff, rode up and ordered us forward. The men never obeyed a summons with greater alacrity. We moved down the slope steadily and with as good a line as we would have maintained had it been a parade. At the foot of the rise men began to fall, for the enemy's skirmishers had gained the cornfield and Stuart's shells had already begun their destructive work. We wavered but little under this opening of the storm and, as we passed General Hooker, his eyes grew brighter and his handsome face bore a smile as we swept on. "I think they will hold it," he remarked to one of his staff.

We soon reached a narrow farm road, on both sides of which were heavy fences, the rails or poles running through the posts and, as we could not throw them down, we had to climb over them. The Confederate skirmishers had already gained the large cornfield on the opposite side; bullets were flying. Many of the Twelfth were killed or wounded while climbing the fences. On the other side the line was re-formed. Companies K and E were thrown out as skirmishers, under Captain Benjamin F. Cook, and the regiment moved forward again. It was soon discovered that one company of skirmishers was sufficient and Company E returned to the line.

On we swept through the waving corn, reaching far above our heads, the bullets of the enemy doing deadly work at every step and shells bursting all about us, while the yells of the foe, more exultant because of their easy victory at Harpers Ferry two days earlier, pierced every Union ear and nerved every loyal heart. On, on we pressed, closing every gap made by the enemy's missiles. Before proceeding far, we struck the enemy's skirmish line and

7. William L. Candler was appointed first lieutenant of Co. A, First Massachusetts, on May 28, 1861. Although he had been an aide to General Hooker since the Peninsula campaign, he did not receive his official appointment to captain of United States Volunteers until November 10, 1862. Candler resigned on May 12, 1863, following Hooker's failure at Chancellorsville and finished the war as an aide on the staff of Governor Andrew. Brevetted three times for his wartime service, Candler died in Brookline, Massachusetts, on December 20, 1892. *Massachusetts Soldiers*, 1:4; 6:758; Hebert, *Fighting Joe*, 131; *Worcester (Mass.) National Aegis*, June 18, 1864; *Boston Journal*, December 21, 1892.

brushed it away. As we moved forward, our brave first lieutenant, tall and erect as a statue, was a conspicuous figure in the line. He was as cool as he would have been had he been leading his company in review. To us he seemed the very embodiment of an ideal soldier. Men were falling every moment. My limbs trembled at every step, for fear had taken a strong hold upon me. Only by thinking of the requirements of duty and of the ridicule to which I would be subjected from my comrades should I fail, was I able to keep my place in the ranks. Some men never had this fear in going into battle. I confess I never entered one without it.

At last we gained the other edge of the cornfield and were here met by a perfect storm of bullets, while shells and canister flew about us furiously or went screaming over our heads to the rear. Here another fence was encountered, but this one was easily removed. Lieutenant White was struck in one of his feet by a bullet. It was a bad wound, as two of his toes were cut away, but he halted only a moment while we were pulling down the fence. Major Elisha Burbank advised him to go to the rear, but he only smiled and said he was "worth a dozen dead men yet." I was holding a rail above my head in both hands, in the act of throwing it behind me, when a piece of shell or a solid shot wrenched it from my grasp with such violence that my arms were benumbed.

We finished leveling the fence and moved forward again. Beyond this point the ground rose slightly, culminating in a small knoll some fifty yards from the fence. The fire had been increasing every moment until now it seemed terrible. We started up the slight rise and our lieutenant followed, limping. Second Lieutenant George W. Orne advised him to go to the rear. He raised himself to his full height and somewhat scornfully replied, "I shall not leave the company."

We gained the crest of the little knoll. Our main line had not yet fired a shot. Being now upon open ground, high enough to afford a view of our surroundings, what a scene was that which opened up about us! Directly in front, not more than 100 yards away, was Hood's whole division moving towards us. With their saucy battleflags gaily floating above them, those gray-clad heroes presented a magnificent spectacle. To their left, in more scattered order, behind fences and rocks and trees, were Stonewall

Jackson's men. Farther still in the same direction were Stuart's batteries, pouring a heavy crossfire upon the little knoll upon which we were standing.

When the men of the Twelfth reached the summit of this knoll, they found themselves actually face to face with the enemy. They needed no order, for their duty was a plain one. Every musket was leveled at once and fired simultaneously and the effect was distinctly noticeable. So near was the foe it is undoubtedly true that every bullet did its work. The enemy wavered and recoiled before this fearful storm of lead, but soon rallied and returned the fire and the men of Massachusetts met their onslaught with a fortitude not excelled on any battlefield of the war.

How terrible was the shock and how our men went down! What screams and groans followed that first volley! Then we loaded and fired at will as rapidly as we could. Our officers cried, "Give it to them, boys!" and the men took up the cry, too. There was a pandemonium of voices, as well as a perfect roar of musketry and a storm of bullets. Shells were bursting among us, too, continually. In the wild excitement of battle, I forgot my fear and thought only of killing as many of the foe as I could. The tall soldier at my side, who had told me on the march that he felt as though he was to be hit in this battle, had already fallen. He lay at my feet with a mortal hurt. His brother dragged him back a few paces and then returned to his place in the ranks. A few moments more and my brother, too, was wounded, though not so badly. When I had assisted him to a stump a short distance to the rear, he crept behind it and told me to "go back and give it to them."

Our ranks were terribly broken now, but the line was kept up and we fought on. Our second lieutenant had gone to the rear, his right shoulder being torn from its socket by a piece of shell. Lieutenant White still remained. His eyes glowed with the joy of battle and he seemed to be everywhere imparting courage and stimulating the efforts of his men. By-and-by he was struck again. A piece of shell had stripped the flesh from the upper part of one of his arms. The shock was severe enough to throw him to the ground, but he quickly rose again and his voice was heard as before above the din of battle. I looked at his face to see if he showed evidences of pain and was met with a cheery smile. By this time our ranks had become fearfully decimated and the lieutenant began moving those who were yet in line nearer the colors. "Let us die under the flag, boys!" he cried.

My ramrod was wrenched from my grasp as I was about to return it to its socket after loading. I looked for it behind me and the lieutenant passed me another, pointing to my own, which lay bent and unfit for use across the face of a dead man. A bullet entered my knapsack just under my left arm while I was taking aim. Another passed through my haversack, which hung upon my left hip. Still another cut both strings of my canteen and that useful article joined the debris now thickly covering the ground. Having lost all natural feeling, I laughed at these mishaps as though they were huge jokes and remarked to my nearest neighbor that I supposed I should soon be relieved of all my trappings. A man but a few paces from me was struck squarely in the face by a solid shot. Fragments of the poor fellow's head came crashing into my face and filled me with disgust. I grumbled about it as though it were something that might have been avoided. My supply of cartridges was exhausted and I sought for more among the cartridge boxes of the dead. Many others were doing the same and nearly everybody had had experiences similar to mine. There were but few of us left now. The enemy's line, which had looked so magnificent when we opened fire upon it, seemed as ragged as our own. We had fulfilled General Hooker's prediction. We had "held it."

The Massachusetts boys were falling by the score, but still they fought on and kept closing up on their colors as fast as gaps were made in their line. The lieutenant moved what few were left of our company up to the colors. We had some distance to go, for the gaps were wide. The regimental line, such as it was, was reformed. Seven men had fallen while holding the flags. The groans of the dying seemed louder and more dreadful every moment. A piercing shriek was heard behind us. We looked and found that our brave lieutenant had been hit again. This time it was a mortal hurt. His hip was shattered and his abdomen torn open in a shocking manner, but his voice was heard high above the din, "Don't mind me, give it to them!"

General Hooker and General Hartsuff had both been wounded. The latter, while being borne to the rear, begged of those who carried him not to tell his brave men of his mishap, feeling that their love for him and their confidence in his leadership might perhaps create a temporary feeling of discouragement. Not a half dozen officers were left in our regiment. The men did not know or care who was in command. They continued the fight just the same and would have kept on without officers as long as a man was left. After a while a cheer apprised us of the approach of supports. Samuel Crawford's and George Gordon's brigades of General Joseph Mansfield's[8] corps were coming.

Orders came to retire. Captain Benjamin F. Cook took command of what was left of the regiment and we began slowly to retire. The colors of the Twelfth were toward the close of the fight flying from their poles while the latter were stuck in the ground. As the regiment started for the rear, Lieutenant Arthur Dehon, who had brought Colonel Webster's body off the Second Bull Run battlefield, took up our blood-stained flags. They were literally covered with dead heroes—those who had been killed beneath them or had been wounded and crawled upon them to die. He had to pull the dead away and wrenched the staffs from the clutch of those who had last held them aloft. In speaking of the colors, Lieutenant Dehon wrote, "After the color sergeant was shot I ordered three different men to raise the colors up, saw one after another wounded and when the last fell I had not the heart to order another up, so I picked them up and brought them off myself till we were out of danger and then gave them to one of the men." For his bravery in this battle, Dehon was made a captain and aide-de-camp on General Meade's staff.

As we left I looked for my brother, but found that he had gone. Of the thirty men of my company who entered the fight, but seven besides me remained. Four of us took up Lieutenant White. We

8. Joseph K. F. Mansfield graduated from West Point in 1822 and began a distinguished career in the Engineer Department, including three brevets in the Mexican-American War. A colonel in the Inspector General Department from 1853 to 1861, he was commissioned brigadier general on May 18, 1861, and served in a series of minor assignments. Commissioned major general on July 18, 1862, and appointed to command the Twelfth Corps of McClellan's army in the Maryland campaign, Mansfield was wounded at Antietam and died of his wounds on September 18, 1862. Warner, *Generals in Blue*, 309–10; Heitman, *Historical Register*, 1:688.

Colors of the Twelfth Massachusetts Volunteers. Courtesy of the
U.S. Army Heritage and Education Center

placed him on a blanket and started for the rear. We had to pick our way among the dead and dying. The groans of the wounded were terrible. It was hard to disregard the appeals for help that came from every quarter. The enemy had been reinforced and it now seemed as if they were bound to annihilate what remained of our brigade. Shot and shell plowed the ground about us and went crashing into the troops that were pressing forward to continue the work which we had so well begun. It seemed almost a miracle that we were not hit, for the air was full of flying fragments of iron and whistling bullets. But we hurried on with our precious burden, anxious to get our poor lieutenant to a place of safety where the surgeons would care for his wounds.

We had to go through the cornfield again. The tall stalks had now been trodden down and the dead lay thickly everywhere. Hundreds of wounded men were slowly creeping toward the rear or, unable to get any farther, were lying down in despair to die. We passed many whose faces were familiar—those who had long been dear to us—and now realized more fully than before what heavy losses we had sustained. We stopped occasionally for a moment's rest and, when we tenderly raised our wounded officer and resumed our journey, he cheerily sang:

> O, carry me along, carry me along,
> Carry me till I die.

At last we reached Poffenberger's and laid our dying friend at Surgeon John M. Hayward's[9] feet. The doctor examined his wounds. The lieutenant talked lightly of his hurts and with his own hands replaced the torn flesh. This exhibition of heroism was too much even for professional self-control and the surgeon turned aside and burst into tears. We took an affectionate leave of our dear

9. A graduate of Harvard Medical School in 1858, J. McLean Hayward was commissioned assistant surgeon of the Twelfth Massachusetts on June 26, 1861. Promoted to surgeon on April 29, 1862, he resigned April 22, 1863, and returned home to be married two months later. Doctor Hayward died in Wayland, Massachusetts, on March 8, 1886. Harrington, *Harvard Medical School*, 2:959; *Massachusetts Soldiers*, 2:3; *Boston Evening Transcript*, June 22, 1863; *Boston Journal*, March 10, 1886.

Surgeon John M. Hayward. Courtesy
of the U.S. Army Heritage and
Education Center

friend, for we had to return to the ranks. He thanked us one by
one for the service we had rendered him and whispered a final
message to those who loved him at home.

Those who were with him when he died told us he was brave to
the last. He died late in the afternoon. One of his lower limbs was
very painful just before he breathed his last. An attendant was rubbing it. "Does this rubbing do you any good, lieutenant?" "No,"
said he, "but that cheering does," for just then our troops had
gained an advantage. His body was sent home and buried in the
family lot at Mount Auburn. The funeral, at St. Paul's Church, was
attended by the Independent Corps of Cadets, to which organization he had belonged when he joined the Webster Regiment. He
was twenty-two years old and a son of Ferdinand White,[10] a Boston
merchant. He was a Latin School boy and resigned a desirable
position in the office of a prominent State Street banking firm
when the war came. Everything that life seemed worth living for
appeared to be opening up before him, but he sacrificed all.

When the Webster Regiment reached the rear it numbered
but thirty-two and was not again engaged that day, although the
officer in command tendered its services to support a battery. A

10. Ferdinand E. White was a prominent commission merchant and auction-
eer with offices on Long Wharf. When he died on January 4, 1853, at the age
of sixty-four, one editor eulogized him as "a man who was highly respected and
beloved by a large circle of friends, and who was justly ranked as one of our most
honorable and upright merchants." *Boston Evening Transcript*, January 5, 1853;
Boston Daily Atlas, January 6, 1853; *Boston Journal*, January 10, 1853.

number of the men left the ranks when the regiment fell back to help off wounded comrades, so none were captured by the enemy. We lost 220 killed and wounded out of 325 carried into action, or 67 per cent according to official figures. I have always claimed, however, that we lost over 80 per cent. We had nine companies in line, the missing company numbering 70 men or more. It is fair to suppose that the official loss was based upon the whole ten companies. But base the loss upon the nine companies actually in line, and it makes our loss over 80 per cent or, as I figured it some years ago, 84.732 per cent.[11]

Major Burbank, who commanded us, died of wounds received and all of our officers but four were either killed or wounded. The other officers killed or who died of their wounds were Assistant Surgeon Albert A. Kendall,[12] First Lieutenants William G. White and Lysander Cushing[13] and Second Lieutenant George W. Orne. The fighting was terrific, as everyone knows. Let me simply say that a letter which I wrote to a friend on the 30th of September, 1862, says my company (A) had twenty-two men killed and wounded out of thirty and of the eight who escaped unhurt five had missiles strike either their clothing or equipments. This was no accidental or forlorn hope affair, but a square stand-up fight. The other regiments of the brigade were not so much exposed as

11. The report to the adjutant general of regimental casualties generally bears out Kimball's claim. This report from Lieutenant Colonel Bates, inexplicably published in the press as "Kimball," shows a loss of 53 killed, 161 wounded, and 5 missing, for total casualties of 219. As Kimball noted, there were no losses in Co. H. *Boston Daily Advertiser,* September 30, 1862.

12. Albert A. Kendall graduated from the New York University in 1852 and began the practice of medicine. He guided his local Masonic chapter during the first year of the Civil War but received a commission as assistant surgeon of the Twelfth Massachusetts on April 29, 1862. It was said that Doctor Kendall was "killed by a chance shot at Antietam, while binding up the wounds of his soldiers." A fellow Mason traveled to Maryland, located the rudely inscribed headboard, and brought Kendall's body home for burial in Newton Lower Falls. Binney, *Dalhousie Lodge,* 15; *Massachusetts Soldiers,* 2:3; *Boston Daily Advertiser,* October 1, 1862.

13. Lysander F. Cushing was commissioned second lieutenant in Co. G, Twelfth Massachusetts, on June 26, 1861, and promoted to first lieutenant on June 25, 1862. He was killed at Antietam on September 17, 1862, leaving a widow and two toddlers back in Marshfield. *Massachusetts Soldiers,* 2:43; Lysander Cushing Pension Records, RG 15, NA.

we were and escaped with lighter losses. The Sixteenth Maine was assigned to special duty and did not enter the fight.

The circumstances were in no way exceptional. It was not an ambuscade. The Twelfth Massachusetts did not fall into a trap. It was one of the fairest tests of bravery upon any battlefield of the war. It abundantly proved the regiment to be possessed of the highest discipline and to have the best of fighting qualities. They honored themselves and reflected immortal honor upon the First Army Corps at Antietam.

It was reported at the time that General McClellan called an aide to his side and asked what troops those were upon the knoll beyond the cornfield. He had been watching Hartsuff's brigade through his glass and noticed their fast decreasing number. His questions were answered and he is said to have given the order, "Have them relieved at once," and then to have remarked, "They will stand there till every man of them is shot down."

But we gave as good as we received, as is shown by the losses of the Confederate regiments opposed to us. One of them, the First Texas of Hood's division, had 46 killed and 141 wounded out of 226 present in action or a percentage of 82.3, the highest percentage of loss in any one battle by any regiment, North or South, in the Civil War, except as mentioned above.

Do these losses not afford a glimpse of the desperate character of the fighting that took place in the great war for the preservation of the Union and are they not sterling evidence, if any is needed, of the valor of the American people?

CHAPTER 13

Fredericksburg

Antietam was doubtless a drawn battle, but as the determined fighting of the Army of the Potomac served to greatly strengthen the confidence of the loyal masses and to check the enthusiasm of the Confederates, it may be considered, in its effect at least, a Union victory.

The 18th was devoted to burying the dead and caring for the wounded. For this purpose a truce had been agreed upon and the men of both armies detailed for the work mingled freely together and talked of their experiences. A few hours before seeking each other's life, now a "touch of nature" had made them kin. I searched the field hospitals for my brother and found him in a barn with a large number of wounded men belonging to my regiment. He was badly hurt, but was doing as well as could be expected.

The Confederates re-crossed the river that night and we moved across the battlefield again and went into camp. On all sides there were evidences of the terrible struggle. It made us shudder as we passed the lane near Poffenberger's and the cornfield and knoll beyond, where our regiment was so nearly annihilated. The little band of survivors was but a shadow of the regiment which that fateful day so bravely faced the hottest fire it encountered in its entire term of service. Every one of us had lost tentmates and friends and, when we pitched our shelter tents that night and began life anew, each little group felt like a family of mourners returning from the burial of the idol of the household.

On the 21st came a new colonel, in the person of James L. Bates,[1] formerly captain of Company H. On the 5th of August preceding,

1. Commissioned captain of Co. H, Twelfth Massachusetts, on June 26, 1861, Bates was promoted to the post of major of the Thirty-third Massachusetts on

Colonel James L. Bates.
Courtesy of the U.S.
Army Heritage and
Education Center

he had been commissioned major of the Thirty-third Massachusetts and on the 9th of September, on the recommendation of
General Hartsuff, was made colonel of the Webster Regiment. He
was a man of dignified bearing and of unblemished character and
as an officer of his rank had few equals in the army. He was also
of a kindly, even affectionate, disposition and enjoyed the respect
and esteem of the men.

August 5, 1862. Following the death of Colonel Fletcher Webster, Bates received
a commission as the new colonel of the Twelfth Massachusetts on September 9,
1862. Wounded at Gettysburg, he continued in command of the regiment until
it was mustered out on July 8, 1864. Bates was brevetted brigadier general effective March 13, 1865. He died in South Weymouth, Massachusetts, on November
11, 1875. Colonel Bates never forgave his Civil War opponents, saying proudly,
"When the graves of treason are to be decorated with those of loyal men, then
pass my grave by undecorated." *Massachusetts Soldiers*, 2:3, 48; 3:538; *Boston Journal*, November 15, 1875.

"Father Abraham" ran up to see us on the 2d of October and the army had a grand review. We had been filtered through the battle of Antietam, previous to which we had been coquetting at divers times and places with the gallants of the sunny South, so that now our regiment numbered but 119. Sundry new regiments had a short time before joined the corps and, when the various organizations were drawn up in line for review, the distinction in numbers was painfully apparent. The older regiments looked strange beside the more recent arrivals and the officers and men of the former looked upon their younger companions and wondered how so short a time should have wrought so great a change. We, too, but a few months before, had made an imposing appearance. We could not realize that death and wounds and disease could do so much in so short a time.

While busy with thoughts of this nature, the roll of drums to our right announced the approach of the reviewing party. Nearer and nearer they came and higher and higher arose our expectations, for our curiosity was raised to a high pitch. By-and-by he arrived opposite the regiment upon our right and loudly did the drums roll, for it was a new regiment and had a large drum corps. He rode slowly down in front, in a sort of indifferent way, and soon our feeble drum corps took up the signal.

As he arrived opposite our right, he suddenly checked his horse, rode nearer our line, removed his hat (which he had worn while passing in front of the new regiment) and moved at a walk down toward the left, scanning eagerly each man's face as if searching for that of a friend. I shall never forget his look of tenderness. We felt as if he expressed the gratitude of the country for the victory of Antietam and the sorrow of surviving friends for the loss of so many brave men. "Old Abe's got a big heart," whispered a man at my side. It was ample compensation for all we had suffered to touch the heart of this great and good man.

General Nelson Taylor,[2] promoted from one of the regiments of the Excelsior Brigade, took command of our brigade on the 8th

2. Nelson Taylor served as a captain of New York troops in the Mexican-American War, settled in California, where he held several minor offices, and returned to the East, where he graduated from Harvard Law School in 1860. Commissioned colonel of the Seventy-second New York, he was promoted to

and, after several marches up and down the Potomac, we crossed on pontoons at Berlin Station on the 30th. We marched through Lovettsville, Waterford and Hamilton and to our surprise found many Union people on the way. Lee's failure in Maryland had evidently made them bold. A few days afterward, General McClellan rode by. We cheered him to the echo and this was the last we saw of our idolized leader, as at Warrenton, on the 7th of November, he was relieved by General Ambrose Burnside. That night was dismal enough and in addition to our other troubles there was a heavy fall of snow, accompanied by quite a blizzard. Then for some unexplained reason we were put into General Zealous B. Tower's[3] brigade, thus being taken away from our chums, with whom we had marched and fought so long.

We came up with the enemy at the Rappahannock, had consultations with them across the river and on the 23d, after apparently aimless perambulations up and down the country, it raining and blowing most of the time, we arrived at Brooks Station, near Aquia Creek. We called our camp here, not inappropriately, "Starvation Hill." Indeed, starvation—or short rations, the next thing to it to men living out of doors in November—was the rule during Burnside's administration. I remember a day called "Thanksgiving," which was celebrated four days after our arrival, when everything I possessed that was eatable was a handful of beans. To cook these I had neither pork nor salt. So I parboiled them, crawled away to a lonely nook, ate them with as much relish as I could muster, thought of the "land flowing with milk and honey," of the groups about the ancestral fireside, of the many friends who would gladly have shared their bountiful store with me and (shall I confess

brigadier general on September 7, 1862, and performed well at Fredericksburg, but resigned on January 19, 1863. Taylor enjoyed a long and profitable law career until his death in South Norwalk, Connecticut, on January 16, 1894. Warner, *Generals in Blue*, 495–96; Heitman, *Historical Register*, 1:948.

3. After graduating first in his class at West Point in 1841, Tower spent his prewar career in the Engineer Department, including three brevets in the Mexican-American War. Commissioned brigadier general on June 12, 1862, he fell badly wounded at Second Bull Run and could never again hold an active field command. At Fredericksburg Tower's brigade was commanded by Colonel Peter Lyle of the Ninetieth Pennsylvania. Tower retired from the army in 1883 and died in Cohasset, Massachusetts, on March 20, 1900. Warner, *Generals in Blue*, 510–11; Heitman, *Historical Register*, 1:966.

it?) cried like the big baby that I was. An attack of homesickness, which afflicted me at this time, probably superinduced the unmanly shedding of brine.

The weather was cold for the season and many men were frostbitten. We were glad, on the 9th of December, when orders came to move. Anything was better than lying there cold and hungry. At 7 A.M. on the 11th we reached the Rappahannock, a mile and a half below Fredericksburg. Union batteries on Stafford Heights shelled the town all that day. From high ground in our vicinity we could see shells burst in the streets. Still the enemy's sharpshooters held their position, as everybody knows, until driven out by brave bluecoats who crossed in boats.

General John Gibbon[4] had now succeeded General Ricketts, General John F. Reynolds had succeeded General Hooker and we were a part of General William B. Franklin's[5] grand division. The engineers had some trouble in laying bridges at the point where we were to cross, as well as opposite the town, being annoyed by sharpshooters and losing ninety men. It was intended that Franklin should begin crossing by daylight on the 11th, but it was 4 P.M. before the movement began and then only General Charles Devens's[6] brigade of the Sixth Corps was thrown over the river. Our division did not cross till the morning of the 12th.

4. A graduate of West Point in 1847, Gibbon served in the artillery, including five years teaching courses at his alma mater while he wrote *The Artillerist's Manual,* a text approved by the War Department. Appointed brigadier general on May 2, 1862, Gibbon advanced successively from brigade to division to corps command, receiving two serious wounds, and being promoted to major general on June 7, 1864. Gibbon remained in the army and spent a number of years on Indian campaigns in the West. He died at Baltimore on February 6, 1896. Warner, *Generals in Blue,* 171–72; Heitman, *Historical Register,* 1:452.

5. Graduating first in the class of 1843 at West Point, Franklin became an engineer, and the Civil War found him in Washington, D.C., where he had been supervising construction on the Capitol and Treasury Buildings. Commissioned brigadier general on May 17, 1861, and major general on July 4, 1862, he rose steadily to corps command, but his career stalled when Burnside blamed him for the failure at Fredericksburg. Relegated to relative obscurity for the remainder of the war, Franklin found greater success in business and died in Hartford, Connecticut, on March 8, 1903. Warner, *Generals in Blue,* 159–60; Heitman, *Historical Register,* 1:434.

6. A graduate of Harvard Law School in 1840, Charles Devens became a noted politician, militia officer, and orator in Massachusetts. Commissioned major of

That entire day was spent in getting the troops over and placing them in position. A most uncomfortable day it was, too, the cold and damp chilling us through and through. Fires, of course, were not allowed. But what can be said of that night, with the temperature below the freezing point? The reader must imagine our discomfort.

That old proverb which declares "self preservation" to be "the first law of nature" often found its illustration, strangely enough, in the army. Sick men, of whom there were always necessarily many, hindered the army more than they helped it. Hence when the "icy breath" of winter came and campaigning became difficult if not impossible, the men naturally began to lay their plans for comfortable quarters to shield them from the cold blast. Among prime requisites in these preparations were axes and shovels and, as these were often scarce articles with us, we naturally clung to them tenaciously when we were lucky enough to get them.

When the campaign began, we were about to construct our winter cabins and consequently had a supply of these coveted implements. In my company a consultation was held before starting out upon the march and it was resolved not to throw away our shovels and axes unless absolutely compelled to do so. Men volunteered to carry them and expressed a determination to stick to them at all hazards, at the same time prophesying that the campaign would come to naught and that we should need them soon in building our quarters. So the battle of Fredericksburg presented, among other strange spectacles, that of a company in which a number of men stood for hours in front of the enemy's rifle pits with axes and shovels stuck into the ground in front of them and vigorously banged away at the foe.

When morning came a heavy fog enveloped everything, so that we could not see 100 feet in any direction. We munched our

the Third Battalion, Massachusetts Volunteer Militia, on April 15, 1861, Devens was promoted to colonel of the Fifteenth Massachusetts on July 24, 1861, and elevated to brigadier general on April 15, 1862. Wounded three times, Devens did little after his final wound at Chancellorsville and was mustered out on June 2, 1866. His law career culminated in his appointment as attorney general in the Rutherford B. Hayes administration. He died in Boston on January 7, 1891. *Massachusetts Soldiers*, 2:133; 5:304; 6:761; Warner, *Generals in Blue*, 122–23; Heitman, *Historical Register*, 1:370.

hardtack and waited for the battle to begin. We had a pretty fair idea as to the plan of operations, having studied the situation and looked upon the heights occupied by the enemy for two days, and while we felt that the whole thing was in the nature of a forlorn hope, we were still, as always, ready to obey orders. At 11 A.M. the fog lifted.

We moved forward into a large plowed field and threw ourselves upon the ground to await orders. The atmosphere now being clear, a heavy fire of both artillery and musketry began. The sun thawed the frozen ground upon which we were lying and the whole field soon became a sea of mud. Our situation was very uncomfortable, but lying flat in the mire was preferable to standing up and stopping bullets and fragments of shells.

A heavy battle was going on to our left, where Meade's division was hotly engaged. Away to our right, too, at the base of Marye's Heights, the roar of musketry was incessant, while the thunder of heavy guns in all directions was almost deafening. Even behind us our own batteries were in full play and while we lay there we wondered if any of us would ever get out alive.

The Thirteenth Massachusetts and other regiments, deployed as skirmishers, had been keeping up a lively fire all the morning. When Meade made his successful charge, the remaining regiments of Taylor's brigade and a portion of General David Birney's[7] division of the Third Corps were thrown forward as a diversion in his favor. The battle now became furious. The enemy opposite us—Jackson's troops—was posted behind the embankment of the Richmond and Fredericksburg Railroad. Taylor's men persisted in their work until their ammunition was exhausted.

About 1 P.M. our brigade was ordered forward to relieve Taylor. The brigade was commanded by Colonel Peter Lyle[8] of the

7. A lawyer prior to the war, David Birney was commissioned lieutenant colonel of the Twenty-third Pennsylvania, a three-month regiment, and became colonel when it reorganized as a three-year unit. Commissioned brigadier general on February 17, 1862, he succeeded to command Philip Kearny's division and was promoted to major general on May 20, 1863. After being promoted to corps command, Birney died of malaria in Philadelphia on October 18, 1864. Warner, *Generals in Blue*, 34–35; Heitman, *Historical Register*, 1:220.

8. From his youth Peter Lyle "manifested a deep interest in military tactics," and he became captain of a Pennsylvania military company in 1846. This interest

Ninetieth Pennsylvania. It advanced in perfect order in the midst of a storm of bullets and bursting shells. Soon Taylor's regiments were met retiring and to allow them to pass to the rear we were obliged to sacrifice our formation. The Twelfth Massachusetts was on the right of the brigade and when the advance was resumed the other three regiments took a left oblique direction, while we, a moment later, started straight forward. We were carrying our arms at right shoulder shift and our line was perfect, save when broken by men falling, but these gaps were quickly closed and we kept moving on. Occasionally Colonel Bates's magnificent voice could be heard above the din, as he calmly said, "Steady, men! The stock of the musket against the back of the head!" We marched down to within 100 yards of the railroad cut, when the order to halt was given and we opened fire. We could get but an imperfect view of the enemy because of the smoke from our own guns, which, in the hazy atmosphere, hung closely about us. The regiment kept on firing, however, until ammunition was nearly gone. Men fell rapidly, but those who remained closed in upon the colors and the line was kept nearly perfect.

My position, upon the right of the company, brought me next to the color guard and I did not have a shovel in front of my feet and ankles, a circumstance which I had cause to regret for many months. Corporal George W. Childs,[9] of Company F, one of the guards, was killed and fell against me. It staggered me for a moment. Then I felt something strike the calf of my leg and in the excitement thought it was a blow from Childs's musket, which fell from his hands as he went down. I fired again and, while loading for another shot, put my hand upon the spot where I felt the blow and found that blood was flowing from it. Then Charles F. Dyer,

---

in militia affairs continued throughout his continued election to office in the Second Regiment, Pennsylvania National Guards. He led the Nineteenth Pennsylvania, three months' service, as colonel and retained that rank when the regiment mustered in during the fall of 1861 as the Ninetieth Pennsylvania. Wounded at Antietam, Lyle was mustered out November 26, 1864, and was brevetted brigadier general effective March 13, 1865. He died in Philadelphia on July 17, 1879. *Philadelphia Inquirer,* July 18 and 19, 1879; *Harrisburg Patriot,* July 18, 1879.

9. George W. Childs enlisted in Co. F, Twelfth Massachusetts, on June 25, 1861. Appointed corporal, he was wounded at Antietam and killed in action at Fredericksburg. *Massachusetts Soldiers,* 2:36.

my rear rank man, asked, "Did that hit you, George? It hit me, too, the same one." I laughed and, after repeating the old saw about two birds and one stone, suggested a trip to the rear. We started, but Dyer soon found that the bone of his leg was broken and he had to lie down where he was. Captain Erastus L. Clark, who commanded my company, rushed up and, seeing that we were both *hors de combat,* told us to go to the hospital as fast as we could. Seeing that my comrade could not walk, I started, using my musket for a crutch. The reader will remember two brothers—Nathaniel and Charles Dyer—mentioned in my Antietam chapter. He will also remember that on the march to that battlefield I promised Nathan, who was killed there a day or two later, that I would "take care of Charley." I had kept my promise as well as I could, but now could do no more.

It was a common thing for an exploding shell or a charge of canister to wipe out a file of men and sometimes a whole platoon, for that matter, but this was the only case that came under my notice during the entire war wherein I was sure that two men were placed *hors de combat* by a single bullet.

I had not hobbled far when I met the Sixteenth Maine on their way to relieve us. It was their first battle, but they were coming forward in as good a line as though it were their twentieth. Not a man faltered. When the men that were left in the Twelfth Massachusetts looked around and saw them coming, someone cried, "Three cheers for old Maine!" and they were given and answered with a will. I crawled into a ditch so that they could pass over me and remained there a while to watch the proceedings. Every regiment in the division was now out of the battle except these two.

Colonel Adrian Root,[10] in command of the brigade in which the Sixteenth Maine served, told Colonel Bates that he was going to charge and asked him to join in the movement. The Webster Regi-

---

10. Commissioned lieutenant colonel of the Twenty-first New York on May 20, 1861, Root became colonel of the Ninety-fourth New York on May 2, 1862. Wounded and taken prisoner at Gettysburg, Root and a portion of his regiment were paroled on the battlefield. He ended up at Camp Parole in Annapolis, where he assumed command of that installation and continued in that position until the war ended. He was mustered out July 18, 1865, as a brevet major general and died in Buffalo, New York, on June 4, 1899. Heitman, *Historical Register,* 1:845; *Watertown (N.Y.) Daily Times,* June 7, 1899.

ment was out of ammunition, but the order to fix bayonets was given and the two regiments dashed forward. They met a heavy fire as they neared the railroad embankment, but kept on and, although a large part of the enemy stubbornly defended the position, it was finally carried and 200 Confederates were captured. The gallant assailants pressed forward into the woods. I became so enthusiastic over this successful movement that I almost forgot my wound and hurried to the rear to carry the good news and, if possible, secure reinforcements. Assuming unwanted importance, I appealed to a number of officers, but from each one received the same answer, "We cannot advance unless we get orders." But no such orders were given, although the general in command at that point must have seen this breach in the enemy's line. Who knows but that the battle of Fredericksburg might have been won if advantage had been taken of this and of Meade's successful charge?

It being impossible for these two regiments to maintain their advanced position, with the enemy on three sides, they were finally obliged to withdraw. Just as they reached the edge of the woods where a little while before they had had a hand-to-hand encounter with a body of South Carolinians, a large force of the enemy was seen moving up from the left with the intention of cutting them off. Captain James Thompson's Pennsylvania battery poured canister into these troops at short range with such vigor that their scheme was foiled.

These two regiments were loudly cheered when they took their places in line. Their losses were heavy, that of the Twelfth Massachusetts being 14 killed, 88 wounded and 3 missing, out of 258 taken into the fight, and the Sixteenth Maine had 90 killed and 134 wounded.

Major Abner Small,[11] in his excellent *History of the Sixteenth Maine,* relates a number of interesting incidents of the battle,

11. Abner Small enlisted in Co. G, Third Maine, a three-month regiment, in June 1861 and rose from private to sergeant. Commissioned adjutant of the Sixteenth Maine in May 1862, he served in that office and on the brigade staff for over a year. Captured near Petersburg on August 14, 1864, Small was promoted to major of his regiment on October 31, 1864. He was released from captivity on February 22, 1865, and was mustered out on June 5, 1865. Major Small died at Oakland, Maine, on March 13, 1910. Small, *Sixteenth Maine Regiment,* 231–32; *Boston Journal,* March 14, 1910.

from which I select two. While a member of the Sixteenth Maine was climbing the breastworks at the railroad embankment, a stalwart rebel, placing his musket against his face, fired. The man's face was only blackened and burned, for there happened to be no bullet in the weapon and, before Johnny could recover from his surprise, the Maine man sprang upon him and killed him by a bayonet thrust. Corporal Benny Worth,[12] of Company E, Sixteenth Maine, was only fifteen years old. Early in the day his face was fearfully lacerated by a piece of shell. He refused to go to the rear and remained with his company all through the fight. At the close of the battle his commanding officer warmly praised him for his conduct. The young corporal replied, "That's what I came here for."

In one of the companies of the Sixteenth Maine a young woman was serving in the ranks, her sex unsuspected. She went into the battle. Her lover, a soldier in the same company was mortally wounded. She remained too long beside him and was captured. The *Richmond Whig* not long afterward contained this paragraph:

> Yesterday a rather prepossessing lass was discovered on Belle Isle, disguised, among the prisoners of war held there. She gave her real name as Mary Jane Johnson, belonging to the Sixteenth Maine Regiment. She gave as an excuse for adopting her toggery that she was following her lover to shield and protect him in danger. He had been killed, and now she had no objection to return to the more peaceful sphere for which nature, by her sex, had better fitted her. Upon the discovery of her sex Miss Johnson was removed from Belle Isle to Castle Thunder. She will probably go North by the next flag of truce. She is about 16 years of age.

A soldier in my company had confiscated a Dutch oven weighing fifteen or twenty pounds at a house near the battlefield. He thought of the nice things he could bake in it and therefore took

12. Private Benjamin F. Worth joined Co. E, Sixteenth Maine, on August 14, 1862, was captured at Gettysburg, was wounded August 18, 1864, and was mustered out June 5, 1865. Kimball seems to have overestimated the extent of Worth's Fredericksburg injury. The quotation from Small's book reads: "Young Worth was struck in the head by a fragment of iron, shedding the first blood of the Sixteenth. Stunned and bleeding, heedless of advice to go to the rear, he went through the fight, and at its close, smilingly said, while rubbing his bruised head, 'This is what I came for.'" Small, *Sixteenth Maine Regiment*, 80, 126, 272.

it along with him. Yankees are great fellows to plan for future comfort. He carried it through the whole fight and the fight for us was no small affair either, as it included the firing of sixty rounds and a bayonet charge upon the enemy by which they were driven a long distance. Had that man been a farmer at the breaking out of the war, he would undoubtedly have brought his plow to the front with him instead of leaving it in the furrow.

Joseph D. Todd,[13] of my company, had lost his voice and was suffering from other results of a severe cold. He was excused from all duty by the surgeon. When we crossed the river he went to the wagon train, got his musket and fell into the ranks. He was killed early in the fight. His name is upon the Soldiers Monument in Haverhill, Massachusetts, from which place he enlisted.

There were many instances of personal bravery. Captain John Ripley,[14] of Stoughton, died from his wounds and Lieutenant Arthur Dehon, of Boston, the young officer who had rescued the body of Colonel Webster and who so distinguished himself at Antietam, was killed. Lieutenant Colonel David Allen, Captains Edward P. Reed,[15] Charles T. Packard,[16] Erastus L. Clark, Edwin

13. Joseph D. Todd enlisted as a private on June 26, 1861, in Co. A, Twelfth Massachusetts, and was killed at Fredericksburg. *Massachusetts Soldiers*, 2:10.

14. On May 7, 1861, John Ripley marched over seventy men of the aptly named Ripley Rifles from Stoughton through the streets of Boston. The local press noted that none were "less than five feet, nine and a half inches in height, and their average weight is 153 pounds." Ripley received a commission as captain of Co. I, Twelfth Massachusetts, on June 26, 1861. Wounded at Cedar Mountain and Antietam, Captain Ripley was struck a third time in the abdomen at Fredericksburg and died as a result on December 20, 1862. *Boston Herald*, May 8, 1861; *Massachusetts Soldiers*, 2:59; *Boston Evening Transcript*, December 22, 1862.

15. Edward P. Reed received his commission as first lieutenant in Co. G, Twelfth Massachusetts, on June 26, 1861, and was promoted to captain on June 25, 1862. At Antietam "he received a bullet through his hand, a slight graze on the foot, and his life was saved by his rubber overcoat folded in his haversack, through which a bullet passed. His canteen was literally riddled with bullets." He rushed into battle at Fredericksburg "with his right arm in a sling and in his left hand his sword" and was wounded again. Reed was promoted to major on May 6, 1864, and was mustered out at that rank on July 8, 1864. He became a prominent businessman after the war and died in Boston on May 28, 1894. *Massachusetts Soldiers*, 2:46; *Boston Journal*, May 29 and 30, 1894; *Boston Daily Advertiser*, May 30, 1894.

16. Packard was a sergeant in the North Bridgewater Dragoon Company upon its organization in 1853 and captain of the Protector Fire Company in that same town before the war. He received a commission as second lieutenant

Hazel[17] and Francis B. Pratt,[18] and Lieutenant Calvin Walker[19] were wounded.

The Webster Regiment received many compliments, among them this from the report of Colonel Charles Tilden,[20] of the Sixteenth Maine, to Colonel Root, commanding the First Brigade, Second Division, First Army Corps, "I shall be remiss did I fail to mention the bravery and heroic conduct of the Twelfth Massachusetts, Colonel Bates commanding, which regiment we were ordered to relieve. It was with difficulty we gained their front, so determined were they in doing their whole duty."

---

in Co. B, Twelfth Massachusetts, on June 26, 1861, and was promoted to captain on August 20, 1862. Wounded at Antietam and Fredericksburg, where he lost an eye, Captain Packard was mustered out on July 8, 1864. He died January 25, 1873. Kingman, *History of North Bridgewater*, 294; *Boston Traveler*, September 9, 1858; Lathrop, *Massachusetts Reports*, pt. 2, 301.

17. When Co. K, Twelfth Massachusetts, was originally organized under state law, Edwin Hazel was appointed fourth lieutenant but "gallantly gave up his commission and took a musket" as first sergeant under federal regulations on June 26, 1861. He was promoted to second lieutenant on May 3, 1862, and captain effective September 1, 1862. Wounded at Antietam, Fredericksburg, and Gettysburg, Hazel was mustered out on July 8, 1864. He died on January 30, 1919, at the Danvers State Insane Asylum. Pringle, *History of Gloucester*, 166; *Massachusetts Soldiers*, 2:3, 63; Edwin Hazel Pension Records, RG 15, NA.

18. Francis Pratt was commissioned second lieutenant of Co. H, Twelfth Massachusetts, on June 26, 1861, first lieutenant on October 6, 1862, and captain on November 30, 1862. Wounded at Fredericksburg, Pratt was mustered out a captain of Co. C on July 8, 1864. He died in East Weymouth, Massachusetts, on February 16, 1915. *Massachusetts Soldiers*, 2:52; *Boston Journal*, February 17, 1915.

19. Calvin Walker enlisted in Co. K, Twelfth Massachusetts, on June 26, 1861, but was soon promoted to sergeant. He received commissions as second lieutenant on August 11, 1862, and first lieutenant on January 1, 1863. Wounded at Fredericksburg, Walker was discharged on account of his wounds on July 18, 1863. He committed suicide in Boston on February 7, 1871. *Massachusetts Soldiers*, 2:67; Deaths Registered in the City of Boston for the Year 1871, MVR.

20. A lieutenant in the state militia, Charles W. Tilden received a commission as first lieutenant in Co. B, Second Maine, on April 27, 1861, and was promoted to captain on June 24, 1861. He received a new appointment on June 23, 1862, this time to lieutenant colonel of the Sixteenth Maine and was advanced to colonel on January 8, 1863. Captured at Gettysburg, he escaped from Libby Prison. He rejoined his regiment on March 24, 1864, and was brevetted brigadier general effective March 13, 1865. Tilden died on March 12, 1914, at Hollowell, Maine. Small, *Sixteenth Maine Regiment*, 227–28; Hunt and Brown, *Brevet Brigadier Generals in Blue*, 618.

Major Edward P. Reed.
Courtesy of the U.S.
Army Heritage and
Education Center

On January 20, 1863, the Army of the Potomac, under command of General Ambrose E. Burnside, started in mid-winter upon one of the most remarkable marches in history. The press of the country had called for an onward move. Everywhere men recognized as leaders of public opinion clamored loudly for active operations. People affected by the war's interruption in business were becoming impatient and exceedingly restive. Wall Street was making itself felt as it never had before. Everywhere the old cry was raised again, "Why doesn't the Army of the Potomac move?" The great pressure brought to bear upon the military authorities at last had its effect and, against his better judgment, though smarting under his defeat at Fredericksburg a little more than a month before and anxious to vindicate his honor as a soldier and his ability as a commander, Burnside set out upon the extremely doubtful experiment of a winter campaign in Virginia.

The army at this time was in winter quarters in the vicinity of Falmouth and it may be truly said that never at any period of its glorious career was the brave old Army of the Potomac so thoroughly disheartened by its reverses. The terrible experiences upon the Peninsula, the defeat at the Second Bull Run and the bloody repulse in front of the Gibraltar of the Rebellion (the well-nigh impregnable Marye's Heights) had rapidly followed each other. Amid all the bitter discouragements crowded into those darkest days, from the disastrous defeat of McClellan in front of Richmond to the time of which I write, there had been but one ray of light, but one reward for all the weary marches, for the outlay of money, for all the noble and brave men who had been slain in battle and for the thousands whose bodies had been torn by shot and shell. Antietam alone stood out like a bright star of hope and promise through the black cloud that overhung the country. The First Army Corps lay in camp near Fletcher's Chapel. The men had built log huts, covering them with shelter tents, and with the huge fires night and day, the frequent arrival of the mail carrier bringing letters and papers from home, a liberal allowance of rations and little to do except to picket the river bank, their situation was beginning to be pleasant and comfortable, if that remark is ever true of a soldier's life. The Webster Regiment was ensconced in a little valley, just large enough to contain the rude cabins, and they were sheltered from inclement winds by slight elevations on all sides. Directly through the camp there ran a limpid brook, its waters adding greatly to health and comfort.

Naturally enough the men were very reluctant to leave their winter home, for they had surrounded themselves with many of the comforts of civilized life. Many of the huts had floors, bunks, tables and benches to obtain material for which barns and fences were made to suffer and some of the more aesthetic had surrounded their rude habitations with evergreen and cedar. They had christened their camp "Smoky Hollow" in compliment to the immense clouds of smoke which issued from the mud-covered chimneys and persisted in hugging the ground when the air was heavy. But it is a soldier's business to obey, even though he knows "someone has blundered," and so when orders came to move they buckled on their armor, loaded themselves down with extra rations and ammunition and started with a growl of dissatisfaction upon what they knew was to be a wearisome and they felt was to be a fruitless march. We learned afterward that it was intended that the army should move rapidly to fords above Fredericksburg, cross the Rappahannock and annihilate Lee. How much of this brilliant programme was accomplished can be gleaned from the following letter:

Camp Near Fletcher's Chapel, Va.,
February 12, 1863

Dear Father—I am back again in the old log shanty after one of the hardest and muddiest marches I ever experienced. We broke camp three weeks ago yesterday noon and marched fourteen miles which brought us above Falmouth some two or three miles. We halted in the dark, it being between eight and nine o'clock, on an open and muddy plain, with no wood to be had, either trees or rails. It commenced raining and the rain increased, with a high and cold wind blowing. We could not put up our shelter tents and so we lay down on our rubber blankets and rolled ourselves up in our woolen blankets and tents. Before morning we were lying in two or three inches of water—everything wet, cold and muddy. We could not be quiet, so we got up and began walking around in the mud, stamping our feet, thrashing our arms and blowing on our fingers, trying to keep warm, but meeting with very poor success.

Oh, the curses that night breathed on the move, the war, the generals, the Government and everything of like ilk! They were awful. Then the many sad thoughts on the whole affair were as plenty as the curses. Home and all its comforts came up vividly to our minds. The worst home ever known, filled with the greatest miseries ever experienced by the most wretched of mortals, would be a paradise of comfort compared to our situation at that time.

The next morning, as soon as it was light, the colonel mounted his horse and hunted up a better place in a wood about a mile off. He came back and, with a sorrowful face and a cold, shivering voice, ordered us to pack up for a better camping ground. We wrung the water from our blankets and tents, as well as we could with our benumbed hands, and packed up. Our packs were very heavy, every thread of clothing on our bodies was wet and we were trembling and moaning with the cold. Some of us had gloves and mittens, but they were worse than useless, being sopping wet and muddy. Oh, father, you cannot imagine how terrible were our sufferings and how discouraged we were.

Just as we had got about ready to move, up rode Colonel Lyle, our brigade commander. 'Fall in' and 'Forward' were the orders. Such a despondent and disconsolate look as our colonel put on I never saw before and, if you ever saw anyone mad enough to curse and kill all mankind, you can get a partial idea of the temper and disposition of the soldiers of our regiment and, in fact, of the whole brigade, when we got into line. Well, in this manner, in this frame of mind, heavily laden with our wet clothes and blankets, covered with mud, nearly freezing with cold, we commenced our march. The mud in the road was above our ankles and so sticky that we could hardly lift our feet. Before we came to a halt the mud had increased in depth, so that it was nearly to our knees. In some places it was so sticky that it pulled off our shoes every few minutes. In other places it was more shallow but as slippery as ice and men were continually falling down and being helped up by their comrades, yet so saddened were the men no one thought of laughing.

By the next morning the mud became over knee deep. We marched that day (Wednesday, the 21st) between four and five miles, to a wood about five miles from Kelly's Ford, where we have since learned, it was intended that we should have crossed the river. But Providence interfered and thwarted the plan, for the storm increased, and it looked as though it would continue for a week—and, in fact, it has continued even till now, as we have had but two days since wherein the sun has shone at all and then not all day. It is now snowing hard and it rained all last night. Our shanty leaks and the floor is muddy and wet. I am crouched up in an inner bunk, writing between droppings of water. But to my story.

Well, it was so muddy and the traveling so bad that it took thirty-two horses to drag an artillery caisson and three regiments of soldiers and eight mules to pull an army wagon loaded lightly with hard bread, over the river road, where it was level. Dead horses and mules lay strung along the whole line of march for miles with broken-down wagons and other wrecks beside them. Broken-down pontoon wagons and material of every description, with boxes of ammunition and packages of army supplies of every kind, lay thickly everywhere. I should think it would cost the Government millions of dollars to replace what has been so foolishly lost. It was impossible to draw the wagons, especially over the hills, and most of the hills were small mountains with very steep sides. The route seemed nothing but a succession of hills the whole distance.

But what is saddest of all, hardship and exposure killed a number of soldiers. Three of our own brigade died and six or seven in the division. In one spot, on the top of a hill, I counted five new graves, and in two other places I saw three or four others. So you can get a glimpse from this of how awful the march was, but no one can realize all its horrors until something like it is experienced.

We lay in the woods mentioned above a day and a half. General Sickles's[21] division was detailed to corduroy the road to the river so that they could get the artillery and the pontoon and wagon trains back again, for they had unfortunately gone thus far. The tired and dissatisfied soldiers had to wade miles in the mud carrying spades and axes in addition to their own wet luggage and, when they were weary enough to lie down and never care whether they arose again or not, had to go to work trying to build a road. Oh, it was awful!

Friday orders came to pack up and return to our old campground. So we started off and after going only a quarter of a mile we came to a halt and there in the mud we stood for an hour with everything on, as we could not drop our knapsacks and guns. We were waiting for our turn to go forward or rather watching for a chance to do so and our uncomfortable position, added to annoyances which always come when the road is blocked up ahead, greatly increased our ill temper and made us very uneasy and impatient. We finally got started and this time it was a march indeed—almost a run—it seeming as if one brigade and division was vying with another to see which could get ahead and get into camp first. Soon straggling commenced, owing to the rapid pace and muddy footing and, before we had got six miles, regiments became reduced one-half or two-thirds of their real strength. When the various regiments arrived at the old camps, especially those which had long distances to go, there was no formation and

21. A lawyer, murderer, and congressman (quite the career path!) when the war began, Sickles was commissioned brigadier general on September 3, 1861, and placed in command of the Excelsior Brigade. Elevated to division and corps command, he became a major general on November 29, 1862, and lost a leg at Gettysburg, where he won a Medal of Honor. He never again held a field command, but after the war he held a number of political appointments and served again in Congress. Sickles died in New York City on May 3, 1914. Warner, *Generals in Blue*, 446–47; Heitman, *Historical Register*, 1:886.

no order at all. A colonel and his staff would come in together, then an officer, with a sergeant or a corporal or private, and now and then groups of three or four of one grade would come in together, so that from that night (Friday) till the next day at dress parade they kept coming in singly and in squads, covered with mud and loudly cursing.

When our regiment arrived at Burnside's headquarters, it was detailed to go down to the river to a point opposite Fredericksburg and help get the artillery along. We went there, but were not needed, much to our satisfaction, but we had the fun of seeing the rebels caricature Burnside and his army "stuck in the mud" and they hallooed to us from the other side that if we would come over they would help us lay the pontoons and then whip us afterward. We were unable to say or do anything and had to bear their taunts as best we could, feeling, under the circumstances, that we were fit subjects for ridicule.

All this time since Friday morning or the night before we had nothing to eat, our rations giving out, and it was not convenient to furnish us with more, but on the way back we came across the Sixth New Hampshire Regiment and they kindly gave us hard bread—in fact, in a soldierlike manner, they gave us as much as we could stow away in our haversacks—so we got along. Now we are once more back again in the old camp and I think we shall not move again in a hurry. It is still snowing hard and the ground is well covered. Various rumors are afloat in camp about the other two Grand Divisions going south and west and our Grand Division going back to Washington.

The experiences of every regiment in the army on this disastrous march are shadowed forth in the foregoing vivid description written by John Darrow,[22] a brave boy who had enlisted when but eighteen years of age and afterward laid down his life while fighting in the Wilderness. Scarcely can the young men of to-day realize with what suffering and what sacrifice of life and treasure our country was redeemed from the curse of human slavery and the supremacy of the Union established.

22. John N. Darrow—"Johnny" to his comrades—enlisted as a private in Co. A, Twelfth Massachusetts, on June 26, 1861. He was advanced to corporal on November 1, 1861, and sergeant on March 1, 1863, but was killed in the Wilderness on May 6, 1864. *Massachusetts Soldiers*, 2:6.

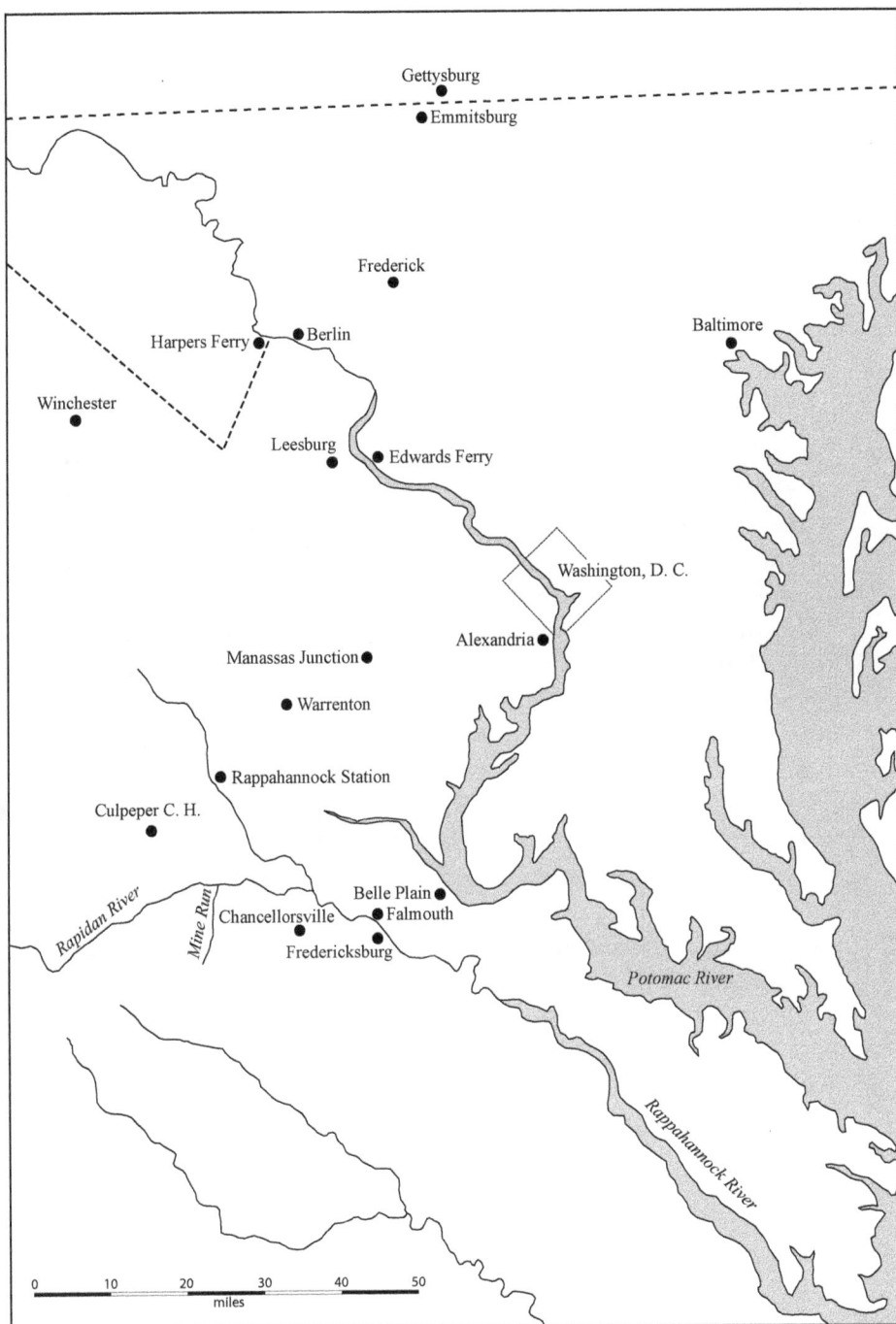

Theater of Operations, 1863.

CHAPTER 14
Gettysburg

The only furlough I obtained while in the service was a pass of forty-eight hours from Portsmouth Grove, Rhode Island hospital in the spring of 1863. I came on to Boston alone. Leaving the cars at the Providence depot, I started across the Common on my way up town. I was busy with thoughts of the great events I had witnessed, the exciting scenes I had passed through, mingled with bright anticipations of meeting with loved ones whom I had not seen for two long eventful years, and I became so intensely wrapped up in this occupation that I was doubtless wholly unmindful of all around me. I can remember even now, as I stood upon Flagstaff Hill, where the Boston Soldiers' Monument now towers toward the sky, how I looked off in the direction of Brookline and imagined I could see a skirmish line of the enemy advancing, while farther away upon the hills it looked exactly as though guns were frowning upon me. Whichever way I turned my eyes it was the same. I did not—I could not—realize that at last I stood on Boston Common, a spot which had dwelt in my thoughts day after day and my dreams night after night. True, it had only been two years, but it seemed an age. I do not know how long I had been there, when an aged man, with long white hair, brought me to my senses by a tap upon my shoulder and the question, "Does it look natural?"

On May 22, 1863, I was back again after five months' absence in hospitals at Wolf Street in Alexandria, Virginia and Portsmouth Grove. The regiment was then in camp at Belle Plain Landing. I was glad to be once more with my comrades, for in spite of the fact that there were many hardships yet to be endured, there was, nevertheless, a glitter of romance about the life we were leading that made it peculiarly fascinating.

My brother had also returned to the company and had much to tell me, as he had been in Burnside's Mud March and Hooker's Chancellorsville campaign. At the battle of Chancellorsville, the men of the Twelfth Massachusetts had found themselves in a peculiar situation, i.e., deployed as skirmishers in the rear of Stonewall Jackson's position. It was on the 3d of May, after Stonewall's furious attack upon the Eleventh Corps and the rout of its German soldiery. The regiment had been sent to the extreme right of Hooker's line and was now advancing over the very ground where Jackson's troops had charged.

No organized bodies were met, but straggling squads were found in plenty and the larger part of a picket line was captured. After a while the regiment had more prisoners than they themselves numbered, including two officers. Many amusing incidents and situations were encountered in that somewhat eventful experience. Colonel Bates himself came across two rebs quietly enjoying a bath and made them fall in with their unfortunate companions, in extremely meager attire, causing an explosion of merriment in spite of the hardships all were undergoing and the weariness that all felt.

But the most laughable incident was that related by John B. Whalen,[1] of Company B. He reported that he came unexpectedly upon three rebs sitting upon a log and naturally was a little disconcerted at first by the sudden encounter, especially as he found himself so far outnumbered. After glaring at him a moment, one of the rebs inquired, "Do we-uns belong to you-uns or you-uns to we-uns?" "I guess you-uns belongs to me-uns," said Whalen, and the three responded promptly to the brave fellow's summons to "come on," soon after being turned loose among their companions in captivity.

1. John B. Whalen enlisted as a private in Co. B, Twelfth Massachusetts, on June 26, 1861. He was taken prisoner October 10, 1863, exchanged at Annapolis on November 26, 1864, and mustered out December 26, 1864. He died March 9, 1897, in Boylston, Massachusetts. *Massachusetts Soldiers*, 2:16; Death Register for the Town of Boylston, Massachusetts, 1897, MVR.

An old yarn, to the effect that Wellington or some other distinguished commander, before beginning a battle, was wont to inquire if Private McCarty was in the ranks, often did duty when fun was necessary to existence. Now that I had returned, the first thing I heard on my entering the camp was: "Now let the battle begin!!" shouted in stentorian tones by one of the principal wags of the company. It may be barely possible that General Hooker had not been waiting for me to get back, but one thing is certain, the battle did begin very soon after my arrival and the preliminaries, in the shape of long and rapid marches, began in earnest, too, right away.

Not during the whole period of our Civil War did the conspiracy to overthrow the Union assume such gigantic and threatening proportions. To say nothing of their influence upon the army itself, the disasters of Fredericksburg and Chancellorsville had had a very depressing effect upon the country at large. Many hitherto earnest supporters of the Union cause were heard to declare that final rebel success seemed to be at last among the possibilities. Volunteering had almost ceased in the loyal States and the unpopular draft, always a breeder of discontent among a people, had been resorted to. Loud threats of open resistance to the enforcement of the conscription law were uttered in a number of Northern cities and this, coupled with the fact that drafted men always at best became but indifferent soldiers, made the real strengthening of our army from this source a matter of extreme doubt. The price of gold, in those days a true barometer of public feeling, advanced to an exorbitant figure. Much talk was heard of the possible recognition of the Southern Confederacy by European powers and rebel sympathizers were everywhere not only loud-mouthed in their denunciations of the Government but were daily becoming more and more defiant in their attitude. The cloud which overhung the country was indeed becoming blacker day by day.

Regarded purely from a military standpoint, the situation was anything but promising. Lee had been heavily reinforced by the return of Longstreet's divisions from Suffolk. In addition to this, large bodies of conscripts had already been incorporated into his army, while we had not yet received a man from that source. He was now more confident than he had ever been before of his ability to defeat any force the Federal commander might place in his path. His army, too, was enthusiastic. It had become accustomed to look for victory, for all along, up to this point, despite its temporary checks, the preponderance of advantage had been with it.

Once in position north of the Potomac, Lee felt sure that he could, by avoiding the mistakes of his former Maryland campaign, gain a firm foothold. He declared that either Washington or Baltimore or Philadelphia should be the reward of his followers— perhaps all three cities might fall into their hands. From either one or all of them he would dictate terms of peace to his discomfited antagonists. France and England would then come to his assistance and the blockade of Southern ports would be broken.

The authorities in Washington were more thoroughly alarmed than they had ever been before and with reason, too, for the situation of affairs was daily becoming more serious. Some great leader, thought they, must be found capable of solving the gigantic problem that now presented itself or some new element of strength must be evolved upon which to rely in the great emergency. But the experience of the preceding two years had not been such as to afford any special promise either of the appearance of a modern Moses or of the development of any hitherto unknown elements of power. They were finally compelled to be content with such leaders as they already possessed and to commit the fate of the Republic to the keeping of the patriotic soldiers of the same army that had all along confronted Lee.

But unknown to the officials at the capital—unknown even to the soldiers of the Army of the Potomac themselves—there had already sprung up that very element of strength and power that was needed. It was found in a truer comprehension of the danger which threatened the country, now daily gaining ground among the common soldiers, followed by a firmer resolve on the part of each man than had ever been felt before to fight with greater determination and to die if need be rather than that the enemy should succeed. The grand old Army of the Potomac was never more actuated by a higher principle upon any former occasion, never was more eager to meet its foe, never more determined to rescue its imperiled country than in the campaign made necessary by the advance of Lee into Pennsylvania.

At 3 P.M. on the 12th of June, three weeks after my arrival, the First Corps started out upon the Gettysburg campaign. Fifteen hours later it was at Rappahannock Station, twenty-five miles from its starting point. At 5 A.M. on the 14th it was put in motion again and reached Manassas Junction at 2 A.M. next day. Then, after a halt of four hours, it pushed on to Centreville, arriving there at 2 P.M. Centreville is forty-five miles from Rappahannock Station and seventy miles from Belle Plain Landing. These three days of work will serve as a specimen of that performed by the Army of the Potomac in the now-famous Gettysburg campaign, though other corps may have had even longer and harder marches than ours had. With such rapid movements and such skillful handling of the army as was displayed by General Hooker, it is no wonder that Lee was deceived and mystified.

On the 17th, with the thermometer at 102½ in the shade, we took the road for Leesburg. Seventy men were that day prostrated by sunstroke in our brigade alone, while a greater nuisance than the burning rays of the sun, in the shape of Major John S. Mosby's[2] bushwhackers, hovered about our flanks. A great deal had been written in defense of their method of warfare, but I want to say that our boys never had any feelings but contempt for it and them. The only chivalry worthy of mention displayed by the Confederates was that which shone out so abundantly in the manly way in which their organized bodies of soldiers faced us upon so many battlefields.

We crossed the Potomac on pontoons at Edwards's Ferry on the 25th and two days afterward, not far from the spot where we began our career, we "celebrated" our second anniversary. Verily one of the promises of the recruiting officer, that we should have "study, travel and promotions" had been kept. We had had "travel"—1,476 miles of it—in the two years. But we couldn't complain, as our excursions were personally conducted.

I had a letter in my pocket containing twenty dollars. It was ready for mailing, but no opportunity had occurred to send it

2. Graduating from the University of Virginia in 1852, John S. Mosby left a law career to enlist as a private in the First Virginia Cavalry in 1861. An accomplished scout, Mosby was appointed captain on March 15, 1863, and organized a company of partisan rangers, called "bushwhackers" by his opponents, tasked with harassing Federal supply lines and outposts. Promoted to major on March 26, 1863, on June 21, 1864, he was made lieutenant colonel and organized the Forty-third Virginia Cavalry Battalion. He ended the war as colonel of the Forty-third Virginia Cavalry and died in Washington, D.C., on May 30, 1916. Krick, *Lee's Colonels*, 259; *Richmond Times Dispatch*, May 31, 1916.

away since writing it. Noticing a woman at the roadside watching us pass, whose face seemed to show honesty and feeling, I stepped out of the ranks and accosted her by asking if she would be kind enough to mail my letter. At the same time I told her that it contained twenty dollars and that I did not like to trust it to teamsters and others. She consented to accept the trust and in due time the letter arrived safely at its destination. There was a vast difference between the women of Maryland and those of the Old Dominion in their feeling toward Union soldiers.

While the Army of the Potomac was being concentrated about Gettysburg, it was known that Hooker had resigned and much discussion took place among the men as to the next commander. It has often been stated that a rumor prevailed at the time that McClellan had been again called to command. I distinctly remember that such a rumor did prevail and also remember the enthusiasm that the belief caused. Many men fought under the impression that "Little Mac" was at their head and very few of the men in the ranks knew that the command had actually been given to General George G. Meade. Newspapers were scarce and, as the army was constantly moving and as corps and division headquarters were widely separated, very little opportunity occurred to learn the news.

On the 30th we were at Marsh Run, two miles north of Emmitsburg and within five miles of Gettysburg. We were in bivouac awaiting orders and it was here that Charles F. Weakley, a brave boy of slender form and modest appearance, living with his father in the mountains in the vicinity, joined us. He came to Sergeant Anson B. Barton,[3] of Company A, while the sergeant was filling his canteen from a stream. He was brimful of patriotism, wished to do his share and wanted to join us and "fight the rebels." He had seen the enemy marching northward and the sight had nerved him to a high pitch; he had been with a battery the day before, riding upon a caisson, but the cannoneers had driven him away. The sergeant tried to dissuade him from what seemed so rash a purpose, reminding him of his lack of physical strength, of his tender age

3. Barton enlisted in Co. A, Twelfth Massachusetts, as a private on June 25, 1861. Missing in action after Second Bull Run, he was transferred to the Veteran Reserve Corps on February 19, 1864, and was mustered out June 28, 1864. Barton died May 25, 1897, in Abington, Massachusetts. *Massachusetts Soldiers*, 2:5; Deaths Registered in the Town of Abington for the Year 1897, MVR.

and of the probable anxiety of his mother because of his absence from home. But the sergeant's arguments were of no avail. The boy was determined to become a soldier.

Barton brought the little fellow into camp, where Captain Clark asked him the usual questions. The captain was convinced that he meant business and took him to Colonel Bates. The unusual incident attracted attention among the men and quite a crowd gathered about headquarters. Here a "scene" was witnessed, for the colonel was a tender-hearted man, as well as a brave officer, and he pleaded with the little fellow to return at once to his mother as earnestly as he would have done had the boy been his own son. Ordinarily the colonel was not averse to receiving recruits, but this one held out such slim promise of utility as a soldier that he would much rather have sent him home as an object more properly fitted for maternal care than for food for powder. But the little fellow was persistent and convinced the colonel that he meant business. He was deaf to all entreaties, would not listen to reason and seemed determined to crush the Rebellion there and then.

So Colonel Bates turned him over to Captain Clark, with the remark, "Well, you may take him into your company, but we cannot muster him in now, as the books are back in the teams." The boys of the company took kindly to the little fellow, giving him some friendly advice as to the new life upon which he was entering and, in the course of the day, by dint of close search, a musket, roundabout, haversack, canteen, blouse and cap were secured for him.

We had forgotten his name, but in 1885 Adjutant Charles C. Wehrum[4] secured it from Lieutenant George A. Whitman[5] of

4. Charles C. Wehrum lived the American dream. A native of Bavaria, he landed alone in New York City at the age of eleven but eventually ended up in Boston, where he enlisted on June 26, 1861, in Co. E., Twelfth Massachusetts. Appointed first sergeant and wounded at Antietam, Wehrum was promoted to second lieutenant on November 30, 1862, first lieutenant on February 18, 1863, and adjutant on March 31, 1863. After being wounded at Gettysburg, he was promoted to captain on February 4, 1864, and was mustered out as captain of Co. A on July 8, 1864. Returning to New York, he served on the Board of Education and belonged to many societies and cultural organizations prior to his death in that city on March 11, 1908. *Massachusetts Soldiers*, 2:35; *New York Times*, March 12, 1908.

5. George Whitman enlisted April 20, 1861, as a private in Co. A, Twelfth Massachusetts. He was promoted to sergeant on August 31, 1862, first sergeant

New York, who found it in one of his old army letters. I then communicated with Surgeon General Robert Murray[6] and was given the record of the General Field Hospital of the First Army Corps, Gettysburg, Pennsylvania, which showed that Weakley was treated there for "gunshot wounds right arm and thigh."

I investigated further and was informed by Surgeon General John Moore[7] that Weakley was treated in Mulberry Street Hospital, Harrisburg, Pennsylvania, from July 24 to October 30, 1863, when, according to the record, "he was discharged from the hospital and sent home, never having been enlisted or mustered into service."

I ascertained also that young Weakley enlisted after his Gettysburg exploit and that as he died in the service, his father, Mr. Charles Weakley[8] of Shippensburg, Pennsylvania, received a pension. I thereupon wrote to the Pension Commissioner and was informed that "Charles F. Weakley enlisted December 18, 1863,

---

on September 7, 1862, and second lieutenant on September 9, 1862. Transferred to Co. I on October 7, 1863, Whitman was discharged for disability on April 16, 1864. *Massachusetts Soldiers*, 2:11.

6. A graduate of the University of Pennsylvania in 1843, Robert Murray was commissioned assistant surgeon on June 29, 1846, and served through the Civil War as surgeon with the rank of major. Promoted successively to lieutenant colonel, colonel, and assistant surgeon general, Murray was appointed surgeon general on November 23, 1883, and retired August 6, 1886. He died in Baltimore on January 1, 1913. Heitman, *Historical Register*, 1:738; Kelly and Burrage, *American Medical Biographies*, 840–41.

7. John Moore graduated from New York University in 1850 and was commissioned assistant surgeon June 29, 1853. Promoted to surgeon with the rank of major, he served at that rank during the war. Advanced to lieutenant colonel, Moore was appointed surgeon general on November 18, 1886, and held that office until his retirement on August 16, 1890. He died in Washington, D.C., on March 18, 1907. Heitman, *Historical Register*, 1:722; Kelly and Burrage, *American Medical Biographies*, 813; *Washington (D.C.) Evening Star*, March 19, 1907.

8. Charles Weakley of Adams County, Pennsylvania, married Juliana James of Frederick, Maryland, in the St. James Evangelical Lutheran Church in Gettysburg on January 14, 1836. The following year Charles petitioned the local court to be allowed to declare insolvency. By 1860 the Weakley family was living in Emmitsburg, Maryland, and consisted of Charles, his wife, Juliana, and their children Rebecca, Charles, Nicholas, Francis, Catherine Ann, and Thomas. The census taker noted Charles Weakley as having forty dollars of personal property. *Gettysburg Times*, January 20, 1986; *Gettysburg (Penn.) Adams County Sentinel and General Advertiser*, October 9, 1837; 1860 Census, Maryland, Frederick County, Town of Emmitsburg, RG 29, NA.

in Company G, Thirteenth Pennsylvania Cavalry, and served until November 23, 1864, when he was found drowned near camp, his drowning being due to epileptic seizure." Evidence submitted to the Pension Office showed that he was born in Carroll County, Maryland on September 2, 1841.

It thus happens that he was older than we at the time supposed. He was unusually slender and youthful in appearance and this probably accounted for our mistaking him for a boy. Of his heroism, however, there could be no doubt, and I think his name deserves a place beside that of that other citizen hero, John Burns[9] of Gettysburg, who also fought July 1, 1863, in the ranks of the First Army Corps.

We were awakened early in the morning of Wednesday, July 1st. General John Buford[10] had visited Reynolds at Emmitsburg the night before and the two chiefs had doubtless located A. P. Hill's corps and other bodies of rebel infantry, which were then concentrating at Gettysburg, with tolerable accuracy. By six o'clock the First Corps was in motion. General James Wadsworth's[11] division

9. A veteran of the War of 1812, John Burns attempted to join the army at the outbreak of the Civil War. He first tried enlisting in C. H. Buehler's three-month company but was rejected on account of his advanced age. He tried a second time to enlist in Edward McPherson's company of the Pennsylvania Reserve Corps but was again rejected. During the first day of fighting at Gettysburg, Burns fought as a volunteer with Federal regiments west of town and was shot in the leg and arm. Lionized as "the Hero of Gettysburg," Burns was a popular figure in that town until his death there on February 4, 1872. *Gettysburg Star and Sentinel*, February 9, 1872.

10. John Buford graduated from West Point in 1848 and saw extensive service on the frontier in the Second Dragoons, designated the Second Cavalry in 1861, in which he served as captain. Promoted to brigadier general on July 27, 1862, he was wounded at Second Bull Run and became a solid cavalry commander. Buford's determined defense at Gettysburg on July 1, 1863, was a key to the eventual Union victory. He died in Washington, D.C., on December 16, 1863. Warner, *Generals in Blue*, 52–53; Heitman, *Historical Register*, 1:260.

11. One of the wealthiest men in New York State, Wadsworth served as a volunteer aide to General McDowell at Bull Run and received a commission as brigadier general on August 9, 1861. Assigned as military governor of the District of Columbia in 1862, he led a division of the First Corps in 1863 and a division in 1864 when that corps was consolidated into the Fifth Corps. One of the oldest generals to serve in the field, Wadsworth was mortally wounded in the Wilderness on May 6, 1864, and died two days later in a Confederate hospital. Warner, *Generals in Blue*, 532–33; Heitman, *Historical Register*, 1:992.

took the lead. Then came Abner Doubleday's, followed by ours, General John Robinson's.[12]

Everybody made sacrifices during the war—some a leg, others an arm—but one of the biggest offerings upon the altar I ever witnessed, outside of life itself, was Captain Erastus L. Clark's moustache. The captain was a gay fellow, proud of his personal appearance, especially proud of his moustache, but a soldier every inch and as brave as a lion. No matter how hard the march, that moustache was always in proper shape, each particular hair waxed and curled in the most approved style. It was at once an object of wonder and envy on the part of every other officer with whom he came in contact; and deservedly so, for it was really a massive and handsome affair. It was none of your black moustaches, giving the wearer the appearance of a Jack Cade or a Captain Kidd, but was of that peculiar golden hue so popular with the ladies. George Armstrong Custer[13] was never prouder of his curls than was Captain Clark of that upper lip appendage. Well, everything went well with Captain Clark and his moustache until July 1, 1863.

The regiment was on the march, Buford's guns were heard and our pace quickened. Our assistant surgeon—a brave little fellow, even if he was a doctor—with such short legs and large piercing eyes and heavy black moustache and long-legged boots that we used to call him the "Jack of Clubs," happened to be riding beside

12. Dismissed from West Point prior to graduation, John C. Robinson was commissioned second lieutenant in the Fifth Infantry on October 27, 1839. After service in Mexico and on the frontier, Robinson was a captain in the Fifth United States when promoted to colonel of the First Michigan on September 1, 1861. Elevated to brigadier general on April 28, 1862, he commanded a brigade that year and a division in 1863 and 1864. General Robinson lost a leg at Spotsylvania but remained in the service until his retirement on May 6, 1869. A lieutenant governor of New York and national commander of the G.A.R., he was awarded a Medal of Honor for his gallantry at Spotsylvania. He died at Binghamton, New York, on February 18, 1897. Warner, *Generals in Blue*, 407–409; Heitman, *Historical Register*, 1:838–39.

13. Graduating last in his West Point class of 1861, Custer served in staff assignments until he skipped from first lieutenant to brigadier general on June 29, 1863. A distinguished cavalry commander for the remainder of the war, Custer was commissioned major general on April 15, 1865, in recognition of his exceptional career. Appointed lieutenant colonel of the Seventh Cavalry in 1866, he was killed on June 25, 1876, at the Little Big Horn River. Warner, *Generals in Blue*, 108–10; Heitman, *Historical Register*, 1:348.

Captain Clark. The captain appeared sadder than usual that morning. "Doctor," said he, "am I not a brave man? Do I not always do my duty?" "Yes, captain. Why do you ask such questions?" "Because," replied the captain, "I don't want you to think me afraid or superstitious. I want to tell you that we are going to have a fight to-day. I shall be wounded. Look for me to-night, doctor, among the wounded. Remember!!"

When Lieutenant John Calef's[14] guns of Battery A, Second United States Artillery rang out on the morning air, the First Army Corps was quietly plodding on toward Gettysburg, all unconscious of the proximity of the foe. The sound of the guns infused new life into the weary marching column. Men closed up into their places, stragglers returned to the ranks, faces brightened up, hunger and weariness were forgotten and the brave fellows, voluntarily and without orders, quickened their pace. They knew not then who was in general command, neither did it matter. The enemy was upon loyal soil and the country was in great peril—this was enough to awaken the utmost energies of every man, from the highest to the lowest.

A detail was made that morning for a guard for the ammunition train and it fell to my lot to march with this detachment. Captain Edward P. Reed of my regiment was in command of those from our brigade. We had not gone far when the roar of Buford's guns burst upon our ears. "How's that for Pennsylvania?" someone cried. The troops all along the road for miles broke into a wild cheer. I had heard the thunder of artillery many times when approaching the enemy, but never saw such enthusiasm awakened by it before. Evidently a great spirit of devotion and a firmer determination to conquer had taken possession of the men.

We pushed on rapidly, after a while the din of battle increased and we knew that General Wadsworth had fallen upon the enemy.

14. John H. Calef graduated from West Point and was commissioned second lieutenant in the Fifth United States Artillery on June 17, 1862. Transferred to Battery A, Second United States Artillery, on October 6, 1862, Calef's guns opened the Battle of Gettysburg. He finished the war as first lieutenant and regimental adjutant, stayed in the service, advanced to the rank of lieutenant colonel, and retired on August 10, 1900. His summer home was in Gloucester, Massachusetts, but Calef died in St. Louis on January 4, 1912. Heitman, *Historical Register*, 1:274; *Springfield Republican*, January 5, 1912.

Doubleday, too, pitched in as soon as he reached the ground and when our detachment, relieved from its care of the train, turned into the open field at Nicholas Codori's house, the battle was at white heat. We could see the troops moving forward upon the ridge, the smoke from their rifles hanging about them in clouds and the cheers of the brave boys rising above the roar of the guns. Robinson's division, which had rested a while in reserve in rear of the Lutheran Seminary, was now moving into position.

Our detachment halted in a small clump of trees a half mile or so east of the Seminary. The men soon became uneasy and began to ask Captain Reed what they were being kept there for. We could see our regiments and were anxious to rejoin them. The captain did not know positively, but presumed the general intended to use us as provost guards or something of that sort. Our uneasiness increased and finally it became so great that we could hold it in no longer and we broke into loud yells of dissatisfaction. "We want to go to our regiments!" we cried in chorus. General Henry Baxter,[15] who commanded our brigade, heard the racket and rode over where we were to ascertain its cause. "What is the matter here?" he demanded. "We want to go to our regiments," was our answer. "Do you?" he asked and then added with a smile, "Well, if that is the case, you are just the men I want there. Go to your regiments!" Such a scattering as then took place! When the little party belonging to our regiment, which was now in line parallel with the Mummasburg Road, on the eastern slope of the ridge, reached its goal, the boys looked over their shoulders and gave us a cheer that made our hearts rise into our throats.

Our young recruit had kept up with us, for it was a rapid march, that five miles from Marsh Run, and when we turned in from the Emmitsburg Road at Codori's house and double-quicked down across the fields to the Seminary, with a wild shout—so eager were

15. A miller before the war, Henry Baxter was commissioned captain of Co. C, Seventh Michigan, and became the regiment's lieutenant colonel on July 1, 1862. Wounded on the Peninsula and at Fredericksburg, he commanded a brigade in the First Corps at Gettysburg and in the Fifth Corps at the Wilderness, where Baxter was again wounded. Brevetted major general on April 1, 1865, he was mustered out in August 1865. He returned to his prewar profession, except for a short stint as a diplomat, and died in Jonesville, Michigan, on December 30, 1873. Warner, *Generals in Blue*, 25–26; Heitman, *Historical Register*, 1:200.

we to attack the foe—our new friend was as demonstrative as the oldest veteran in the regiment. When we first met the enemy, at the foot of the ridge, facing to the northwest, and the bullets began to fly about us and the shells came screaming over our heads and bursting at our feet, I watched him to see if he would face the terrible storm unmoved. He was as firm as a rock.

We also felt very solicitous for Captain Erastus Clark, as he persisted in remaining in plain sight of our antagonists and his yellow shoe-brush presented a brilliant spectacle that bright summer morning. It seemed to draw more messengers of death and destruction in the direction of Company A than fell to the lot, even, of the company that proudly bore the starry banner aloft. But we could not persuade him to keep shady, for like all fellows with handsome moustaches he would persist in making himself conspicuous, evidently desiring to show the enemy his contempt for the close shave they were giving us.

The enemy at this moment was deploying a skirmish line from the rear of a large red barn over toward Oak Hill. Captain Hazel was ordered by Colonel Bates to lead a line of skirmishers out to meet them. Hazel deployed Company K and they moved forward rapidly and fell upon the enemy with such spirit that the Johnnies scampered back to their cover.

We waited for further demonstrations, occasionally getting in a few shots, and then, it having been discovered that the enemy was moving around Doubleday's right and threatening our rear, orders came to change front forward on the left company and advance to the crest of the ridge. We swept on with a shout. This movement was executed with precision and a little later General Gabriel Paul's[16] brigade took the position we had vacated. As the Johnnies had by this time begun operations in earnest in the direction of Oak Hill, Paul's men, among them the Thirteenth Mas-

16. Gabriel R. Paul graduated from West Point in 1834 and served in Florida, Mexico, and frontier posts until the war found him a major in the Eighth United States Infantry. He served in New Mexico Territory until commissioned brigadier general on September 5, 1862, but his appointment was not confirmed until April 18, 1863. He commanded a brigade at Gettysburg, where he was wounded by a bullet that destroyed the sight in both eyes. Retired on February 16, 1865, General Paul died in Washington, D.C., on May 5, 1886. Warner, *Generals in Blue*, 363–64; Heitman, *Historical Register*, 1:776.

sachusetts and Sixteenth Maine, had plenty of work on hand and they did it. Colonel Edward O'Neal's[17] brigade and other bodies of rebels advanced several times, but the plucky bluecoats held on like grim death.

About noon the descendants of Alexander the Great sauntered in. Alexander Schimmelfennig's[18] and Francis Barlow's[19] divisions were put in line on Paul's right, facing north, but as they did not connect with Paul's men by a mile or so, the latter had their troubles increased, as the Johnnies were bent on getting through the loophole if they could. General Adolph Von Steinwehr's[20] division was left on Cemetery Hill, east of the town.

17. Edward A. O'Neal graduated from LaGrange College in 1836, began a law career, and became one of the most outspoken secessionists in Alabama. He joined the Ninth Alabama and became its major and lieutenant colonel before being promoted to colonel of the Twenty-sixth Alabama. A commission as brigadier general dated June 6, 1863, was rescinded after O'Neal's poor performance at Gettysburg, and he finished the war chasing deserters in Alabama. Elected governor in 1882 and 1884, O'Neal died in Florence, Alabama, on November 7, 1890. Warner, *Generals in Gray*, 226.

18. A veteran of the Prussian army, Schimmelfennig came to the United States in 1853 and began a career in engineering. Commissioned colonel of the Seventy-fourth Pennsylvania on September 30, 1861, and brigadier general on November 29, 1862, he was frequently ill and only an indifferent commander. Schimmelfennig died in Wernersville, Pennsylvania, on September 5, 1865. He is now best remembered as the general who hid in a pigpen following the defeat of Union forces on the first day at Gettysburg. Warner, *Generals in Blue*, 423–24; Heitman, *Historical Register*, 1:864.

19. A graduate of Harvard and a lawyer, Barlow served for three months as a private and lieutenant in the Twelfth New York in 1861 before receiving a commission as lieutenant colonel of the Sixty-first New York on November 9, 1861. Promoted to colonel of the regiment on April 14, 1862, and brigadier general on September 19, 1862, he was wounded at Antietam and Gettysburg. Barlow returned to command a division in 1864 and was promoted to major general on May 25, 1865. He resigned on November 16, 1865, and held a number of political offices in New York until his death on January 11, 1896, in New York City. Warner, *Generals in Blue*, 18–19; Heitman, *Historical Register*, 1:191.

20. Adolph Wilhelm August Friedrich, Baron Von Steinwehr was a native of the duchy of Brunswick. He came briefly to America in the 1840s but returned for good in 1854. Commissioned colonel of the Twenty-ninth New York on June 6, 1861, and brigadier general on October 12, 1861, Von Steinwehr had an undistinguished career as a brigade and division commander. He did little better when sent west with the Eleventh Corps in 1863 and was superseded by a junior officer, leading to his resignation on July 3, 1865. He died in Buffalo, New York, on February 25, 1877. Warner, *Generals in Blue*, 330–31; Heitman, *Historical Register*, 1:989.

Meanwhile Baxter's brigade was not idle. When we reached the crest of the ridge, we found General Alfred Iverson's[21] brigade of North Carolinians advancing from its western slope, their left being opposite our right centre, and we poured a volley into them at short range. As the Twelfth Massachusetts was the second regiment from the right of the brigade, our fire was left oblique. This volley was terribly destructive. General Doubleday reported that it killed and wounded fully 500 men and Iverson's report supported the statement. The enemy recoiled and sought shelter in a ditch at the foot of the hill. We peppered them a while and then our boys began to shout, "Forward!" and "Charge!"

The Eighty-third (Ninth Militia) and Ninety-seventh New York and Eighty-eighth Pennsylvania, on our left, made a charge, the enemy being directly in their front, and our men, seeing this movement, began to cry: "Forward! Forward!!" Colonel Bates, with Companies H and G, was at this moment assisting the Ninetieth Pennsylvania in repulsing a body of the enemy which was moving toward our right from a northerly direction. His attention was so completely absorbed in this duty that he did not know of the charge of the rest of the brigade, but he had previously instructed Adjutant Wehrum that if at any time any movement should appear necessary during his temporary absence from the centre of the line, to order it at once.

We were in the edge of a scattered grove and this probably prevented the adjutant from seeing the charge of the regiments on our left from where he was standing. The left of the brigade was in open ground. That gallant officer, hearing the shouts, came forward to the stone wall behind which we were standing and asked my brother what they meant. He had been wounded and was trying to rest his gun in the crotch of a small tree for another shot, while Captain Clark and myself were urging him to go to the

21. Iverson's military career began as a second lieutenant in the Georgia battalion in the Mexican-American War, which led to a commission as first lieutenant in the First United States Cavalry on March 3, 1855. He resigned March 21, 1861, to accept the appointment as colonel of the Twentieth North Carolina and was promoted to brigadier general on November 1, 1862. Shuttled off to relatively minor assignments after Gettysburg, he grew oranges after the war. Iverson died in Atlanta on March 31, 1911. Warner, *Generals in Gray*, 147–48; Heitman, *Historical Register*, 1:565.

rear. My brother said, "They are going forward" and pointed toward the left. I don't think the order came through the regularly constituted channels. It was sort of spontaneous and voluntary movement on the part of the men, who were brim full of fight. Everybody in the regiment was shouting "Forward!" and the advance was inevitable. The adjutant then sprang over the wall and, waving his sword, cried, "Forward, Twelfth!"

Away we went like a whirlwind, nearly all of us, except Companies H and G, (I think there were about fifty) and were soon in the midst of the enemy. Although the three regiments named were a little ahead of us, we nevertheless took quite a number of prisoners and brought them in. Altogether, the larger part of Iverson's brigade was captured, with three stands of colors from the Fifth, Twentieth, and Twenty-third North Carolina regiments, by our brigade. Captain Cook delivered them over to the Provost Marshal of the Eleventh Corps. But a provoking circumstance in connection with this movement is that General Baxter, in his report, from some unexplainable reason, failed to mention our part in the affair and we were thus robbed of credit that certainly belonged to us. Fancy, if you can, a movement like that under their very noses and the Webster Regiment not in it!

Coolly placing himself behind the stone wall, our little recruit had opened fire upon Iverson's troops with the precision and rapidity of an old soldier. After a while he was wounded, but he continued to load and fire. When that part of the regiment which faced Iverson voluntarily charged, our young hero followed us, limping, part of the way down to the enemy's line. I did not see the little fellow again, but was told by members of the company that he kept on firing until again wounded, this time in his right arm. When the regiment was ordered back north of the town, our young hero had to be left on the field with other wounded. But little was known of him afterward, except that he was seen among the wounded by one of the regiment, who glanced into the hospital when the army advanced on the morning of July 6th. He was then suffering terribly and was begging to be taken to his mother.

While we were disarming the enemy and starting them toward the rear, I became engaged in conversation with a group of a dozen or more Tar Heels. Here is where I came to grief. "Where will you send us?" and similar questions were asked of me. Excessive loquacity at inopportune moments has always been one of my prominent faults and I was easily detained answering superfluous questions for some time, until the regiment went back to its old position. Finally when I did come to my senses, I found myself alone "in the enemy's country." When they noticed my return of reason, they laughed aloud and coolly informed me that I might as well remain with them and take a trip south, which was a "durned sight better country" than the regions I had been describing. I was in a dilemma, sure enough, but had no idea of accepting their pressing invitation. I quickly determined to take my chances of instant death rather than perish by the slower method of disease and starvation in prison, so began to walk slowly backward, meantime keeping up the conversation, until I got to a good starting point, when I set out, as fast as my long legs would carry me, toward "God's country." They cried "Halt!" and threatened to fire, but I boomed ahead. I informed them in not very elegant terms that they might go straight to a very warm country. Some of them did fire, but their bullets whistled harmlessly by.

A force of the enemy had now reached an advanced position on our left, where three lines of battle were seen in the distance moving obliquely toward the left or left centre of the First Corps, and my brigade, which was now doing business at the old stand, was exchanging shots with it. I soon came into the path of this fire. Then, to make matters still worse, bullets were coming with provoking regularity from north of the Mummasburg Road and shells were bursting all about me. It looked as if it was to be a tight squeeze. I did not relish the idea of being hit by my own friends, so I put my handkerchief on my bayonet and held it aloft in order that they might not take me for a bloodthirsty secessionist. The faster the bullets came the faster I ran. I had gotten within about 150 feet of my regiment—on the last lap, as it were—when I felt that peculiar sensation that I had felt at Fredericksburg— this time, however, in my left groin—and I went down like a log. I tried to get up again to resume my journey, but it was no go. I was wounded this time so that I must postpone running and walking matches for a while. Of two comforting facts, however, I was certain. The bullet that did the mischief was a Southern one and the wound was in that part of the body which is usually regarded as proper to present to an enemy.

I was seen by men in the regiment and Sergeant Uriah Macoy,[22] of Company F, whom I recognized by his long red beard, motioned to me to lie low. I unslung my knapsack and placed it upright against my head as a barricade. Strapped on the outside was a sheet-iron frying pan and for an hour or so bullets struck this as often as once a minute. I did not expect to get out of it alive and it has always seemed to me rather strange that I did.

22. Uriah Macoy enlisted in Co. F, Twelfth Massachusetts, on June 25, 1861, as a corporal. Promoted to sergeant on July 13, 1862, he was captured at Gettysburg and paroled on March 8, 1864. Advanced to first sergeant on May 10, 1862, he was mustered out on July 8, 1864. Not content to sit at home, Macoy received a commission as captain of Co. C, Sixtieth Massachusetts, a one-hundred-day regiment, on July 11, 1864. Promoted to major on July 30, 1864, he was mustered out a second time on November 30, 1864. Long associated with the Brockton police force, he died in that city on March 28, 1888. *Massachusetts Soldiers*, 2:39; 5:94, 101; *Boston Journal*, March 30, 1888.

CHAPTER 15

Behind Enemy Lines

After a while the fire slackened and finally ceased altogether. Then came a period of terrible suspense. Had our men been beaten? The mystery was finally solved by the appearance of large bodies of the enemy, which swept over me with yells of triumph. On came cavalry, infantry and artillery and I thought I would surely be crushed beneath the wheels of the guns or the hoofs of the horses, but I escaped death.

Following the organized bodies came groups of stragglers, who plied me with questions. It was evident that the rebels had been told that they were only to have militia to fight. On my telling them that the First Army Corps of the Army of the Potomac had held the position, they appeared to be astonished. One burly Southerner, after telling me that I lied and saluting me with very opprobrious epithets, raised his musket to brain me. As he did so a general, handsomely uniformed and attended by a large staff, burst upon the scene. "What are you doing with that man?" he demanded. "He has lied to me. He says he belongs to the First Army Corps," replied my would-be assailant. "So he does," said the general. "Don't you see the badge on his cap? Go away and let him alone. Go to your regiment."

I lay there, wondering why I did not die, till late in the afternoon. I was growing weaker every minute from loss of blood. Finally four drummer boys came, gave me a biscuit and some water and not only warmed my heart, but renewed my courage by expressions of sympathy. They proposed to carry me to a hospital, too. So taking my blanket they placed me on it and, though I was as much as they could stagger under, they succeeded in landing

me on the floor of the front hall at the residence of Reverend Doctor Henry L. Baugher,[1] then president of Pennsylvania College, in
the suburbs of town. The first familiar face that I saw there, out
of fifteen or twenty wounded men belonging to the First Corps,
was that of my brother, who had been hit just before the regiment
started on its charge.

Some of the Johnnies could not resist their well-known propensity to add to their meager stock of luxuries and everywhere the
work of rifling the dead went on. Watches, money and clothing
of all kinds were being gathered in faster than all the quartermas-
ters in the rebel army combined could have issued them. Coming to what they supposed was the dead body of a member of the
Twelfth, a man always famous among his comrades for his excellent outfit, they entered with zest upon the work of relieving the
prostrate soldier of a pair of boots. The poor fellow lay perfectly
unconscious from loss of blood and exhaustion and one boot
was removed without awakening him. But when the next one was
tried, it happening to be upon his wounded leg, their little game
was rudely interrupted by a sharp order from the now-aroused
man to quit. Quit they did, for they uttered a cry of alarm at what
they supposed to be a dead man come to life and ran away like
frightened deer.

The day's fight was over. The harvest of mangled human forms
had been gathered in and cries of anguish rent the air as our assistant surgeon who that morning had ridden beside Captain Clark
flew from one sufferer to another in his work of mercy and love.
By-and-by he caught sight of a beckoning finger. As soon as he
could he went to him who thus mutely called. He found an officer
frightfully wounded, his face so disfigured and bloody as to be
unrecognizable. The officer tried to speak, but could not. Finding
the doctor did not know him, he pulled open his coat and pointed
to a badge, which told the whole story. It was Captain Clark.

1. A graduate of Dickinson College in 1826, Henry L. Baugher became a
professor at Gettysburg College in 1832 and in 1850 was selected as its second
president. Baugher was described as "a fine scholar, an excellent executive officer, and a man who took deep and fervent interest in advancing the cause of
education." He died in Gettysburg on April 14, 1868. *History of Cumberland and
Adams Counties*, 2:349; *Philadelphia Inquirer*, April 15, 1868.

His prediction had become true. But saddest of all, that moustache was gone and with it a portion of his upper lip and face. The men of the captain's company who led him to the rear are the authority for the report that he remarked on the way out, "I would much rather have lost my life than my moustache." As corroborative of my statement that Captain Clark was a brave man, it may not be out of place to mention the fact that, soon after the war, he fought a duel at the South. He became involved in a quarrel with a Mississippian and sent him a challenge. For weapons the Southerner chose Bowie knives and stipulated that the encounter should take place in a dark room with locked doors. They met and hacked each other to pieces.

This is really all I saw of the first day's fight at Gettysburg, but I knew then and investigations have since strongly confirmed my conclusions, that it was one of the liveliest fights on record. The gallantry displayed by the First Army Corps and Buford's cavalry that day was not exceeded anywhere by any other body of troops in the whole war. Buford's force numbered 2,200; the First Corps, 8,200. These 10,400 men held their ground six and one-half hours against three divisions of the enemy—those of Robert Rodes,[2] Henry Heth[3] and William Pender[4]—numbering in the aggregate

2. After graduating from the Virginia Military Institute in 1848, Robert Rodes taught there for a few years before switching to a career as a civil engineer. He became colonel of the Fifth Alabama and was promoted to brigadier general on October 21, 1861. A highly respected brigade and division commander, he was advanced to major general after Chancellorsville. Rodes was mortally wounded at Winchester on September 19, 1864. Warner, *Generals in Gray*, 263.

3. After graduating last in his class at West Point in 1847, Henry Heth became a captain in the Tenth United States on March 3, 1855, and resigned that position to become colonel of the Forty-fifth Virginia. Promoted to brigadier general on January 6, 1862, and to major general rank from May 24, 1863, Heth led a division through the remainder of the war. As a civilian he sold insurance before his death in Washington, D.C., on September 27, 1899. Warner, *Generals in Gray*, 133; Heitman, *Historical Register*, 1:526–27.

4. A graduate of West Point in 1854, Pender resigned as adjutant of the First Dragoons to become colonel of the Thirteenth North Carolina. Promoted to brigadier general on June 3, 1862, Pender had been wounded four times before he was made a major general on May 27, 1863. Mortally wounded at Gettysburg on July 2, 1863, he died at Staunton, Virginia, on July 18. Warner, *Generals in Gray*, 233–34; Heitman, *Historical Register*, 1:781

22,000, and did not give way till General O. O. Howard's[5] retreat made it necessary. Rodes's loss at Gettysburg was 2,853, Heth's 2,349 and Pender's 1,936, a total of 7,138—the bulk of which was incurred on the first day.

The loss of the First Corps at Gettysburg—nearly all the first day and not including General George Stannard's[6] Vermont Brigade—was 3,476 killed and wounded, and 2,190 missing, the loss in prisoners being principally due to the fact that the two divisions of the Eleventh Corps could not or did not keep General Jubal Early's[7] division away from our rear. Early's loss the whole three days was only 827. His division numbered 5,000. Buford's plucky troopers lost 418 of their number. These figures, which are those given in the *Century War Book*, show the stubborn character of the fighting that day on Seminary Ridge.

The loss in officers throughout the First Corps was heavy. In the Webster Regiment, Colonel Bates was wounded in the neck, but remained on duty throughout the fight. Adjutant Wehrum was

5. Oliver O. Howard graduated from Bowdoin College in 1850 and from West Point in 1854. Only a first lieutenant in the Ordnance Department, he resigned on June 7, 1861, to accept a commission as colonel of the Third Maine. Promoted to brigadier general on September 3, 1861, he lost an arm at Seven Pines but was advanced to major general on November 29, 1862. His Eleventh Corps was driven from the field at Chancellorsville and Gettysburg, but he eventually rose to command the Army of the Tennessee in 1864. Howard received both a Medal of Honor and Thanks of Congress and retired November 8, 1894. He died at Burlington, Vermont, on October 26, 1909. Heitman, *Historical Register*, 1:546–47; Warner, *Generals in Blue*, 237–39.

6. A foundry owner and colonel of the Fourth Regiment of Vermont Militia in 1861, George J. Stannard became lieutenant colonel of the Second Vermont on June 20, 1861, and colonel of the Ninth Vermont on July 9, 1862. Promoted to brigadier general on March 11, 1863, he sustained four wounds during the war, the last costing him an arm. After resigning on June 28, 1866, Stannard held some minor political posts, and he died in Washington, D.C., on June 1, 1886. Warner, *Generals in Blue*, 471–72; Heitman, *Historical Register*, 1:915.

7. Jubal Early graduated from West Point in 1837 but served only a year in the Third Artillery before resigning on July 31, 1838. A major in the First Virginia in the Mexican-American War, he was a lawyer when he accepted the post as colonel of the Twenty-fourth Virginia. Promoted to brigadier general effective July 21, 1861, major general on January 17, 1863, and lieutenant general on May 31, 1864, Early was an able leader until given an independent command in the Shenandoah Valley in 1864. He died in Lynchburg, Virginia, on March 2, 1894. Warner, *Generals in Gray*, 79–80; Heitman, *Historical Register*, 1:393.

wounded in one of his arms and captured, but on the third day ran through the enemy's skirmish line and reached the regiment on Cemetery Hill. Lieutenants Francis Thomas[8] and Charles G. Russell[9] were killed. Captains J. Otis Williams,[10] Erastus L. Clark, and Edwin Hazel and Lieutenants George H. French[11] and Cornelius

8. Francis Thomas (identified by the U.S. Army Heritage and Education Center as Frank Thomas) enlisted in Co. H, Twelfth Massachusetts, as a sergeant on June 26, 1861, at the age of seventeen, the first of five brothers to serve in the war. Advanced to sergeant major, Thomas received commissions to second lieutenant on September 9, 1862, and first lieutenant on September 11, 1862. According to General Baxter, Lieutenant Thomas was acting inspector general on his brigade staff and had "passed through the battle nobly and with honor to himself, but while passing through the streets of Gettysburg was struck by a shell, killing him instantly." His division commander said: "He was unwearied on the march, faithful and diligent in the performance of his duties, fearless in action, and beloved by all who knew him. Brothers and sisters should have been proud to call *him* brother, and parents should thank God who gave them such a son!" *History of Hingham*, vol. 1, pt. 1, 344; *Massachusetts Soldiers*, 2:53; *Official Records*, ser. 1, 27, pt. 1, 308; Burr and Lincoln, *Town of Hingham*, 408–409.

9. A member of the Boston Light Infantry, Charles Russell was elected captain by the company with Nathaniel Shurtleff as first lieutenant. When Shurtleff's father and his rich friends donated $500 to the company, Russell waived his election in favor of his lieutenant. When the Twelfth Massachusetts was organized, there were too many lieutenants, so Russell agreed to an appointment of sergeant major. He was promoted to second lieutenant of Co. D on September 6, 1861, and first lieutenant on September 18, 1862. Russell was sent on recruiting service from June 1862 to May 1863, returning to the regiment only to be killed on July 1, 1863, at Gettysburg. His widow claimed that he had been killed beside General Reynolds when that officer fell and that Russell had been in line to become a lieutenant colonel. Neither claim could be verified. *Boston Evening Transcript*, April 29, 1861; *Massachusetts Soldiers*, 2:3; Charles G. Russell Pension Records, RG 15, NA.

10. A graduate of Harvard in 1840, Joseph Otis Williams obtained a law degree from that institution in 1843. He was noted as the only secretary of the Pierian Sodality to record its minutes in verse and as secretary of the fiftieth-anniversary celebration of the Hasty Pudding Club. Williams had been a member of the New England Guards since at least 1852 when he enlisted as first lieutenant in Co. D, Twelfth Massachusetts, on June 26, 1861. Promoted to captain on October 8, 1862, he was wounded at Antietam and Gettysburg and discharged for his wounds on June 11, 1864. Commissioned captain in the Eleventh Veteran Reserve Corps on July 18, 1864, he received his discharge on June 30, 1866. Williams died at New Bedford, Massachusetts, on April 3, 1875. *Boston Courier*, August 18, 1845; *Salem Register*, March 22, 1852; Evans, "Pierian Sodality," 431; Brown, *Harvard University in the War*, 16; *Massachusetts Soldiers*, 2:29; 7:284; *Boston Daily Advertiser*, April 17, 1865.

11. French enlisted in Co. B, Twelfth Massachusetts, on June 26, 1861, as a sergeant. Promoted to second lieutenant on September 11, 1862, and first

Batchelder[12] were wounded. Captain John S. Stoddard[13] was taken prisoner and escaped, but Lieutenants Warren Thompson,[14] John H. Russell,[15] Edward Lewis[16] and James B. Sampson[17] were

lieutenant on December 21, 1862, he was wounded at Antietam and at Gettysburg, where he lost an arm. French resigned on October 28, 1863, as a first lieutenant of Co. H to accept the same rank in the Veteran Reserve Corps. He was discharged on September 23, 1866, and worked in the Treasury and Naval Departments before his death in Washington, D.C., on September 29, 1914. *Massachusetts Soldiers*, 2:13; 7:176; *Washington Evening Star*, September 30, 1914.

12. Cornelius Batchelder enlisted as a sergeant in Co. D, Twelfth Massachusetts, on June 26, 1861. Commissioned second lieutenant on March 9, 1863, and first lieutenant on February 4, 1864, Batchelder was wounded at Gettysburg and mustered out on July 8, 1864. He died on September 14, 1899, in Boston. *Massachusetts Soldiers*, 2:24; *Boston Herald*, September 16, 1899; Deaths Registered in the City of Boston for the Year 1899, MVR.

13. John Stoddard enlisted as first sergeant of Co. F, Twelfth Massachusetts, on June 25, 1861. Promoted successively to second lieutenant on May 13, 1862, first lieutenant on December 14, 1862, and captain on July 23, 1863, he was wounded at Antietam and evaded captivity at Gettysburg by his "native shrewdness and strategy." He was killed at Spotsylvania on May 10, 1864, while leading his men. It was said of Stoddard that "he proved himself faithful, and an officer of unusual capacity, while his kind and considerate regard for his men, and his ever genial disposition, made him a favorite with all, wherever he was known." *Massachusetts Soldiers*, 2:41; Kingman, *History of North Bridgewater*, 255.

14. Warren Thompson was commissioned second lieutenant of Co. I, Twelfth Massachusetts, on June 26, 1861, and promoted to first lieutenant on June 24, 1862. Captured and paroled at the surrender of Harpers Ferry on September 15, 1862, he was captured again at Gettysburg. Thompson "gave an illegal parole and went home," being regarded as a deserter by the army. He returned on May 2, 1865, under the presidential proclamation of amnesty for deserters and was mustered out May 12, 1865. *Massachusetts Soldiers*, 2:60.

15. Russell enlisted in Co. B, Twelfth Massachusetts, as a sergeant on June 26, 1861, and was soon promoted to first sergeant. Promoted to second lieutenant on July 8, 1862, and first lieutenant on October 8, 1862, Russell was captured at Gettysburg and confined in Libby Prison. After four unsuccessful attempts, he escaped on November 22, 1864, and was mustered out as first lieutenant of Co. F on January 3, 1865. Russell died on November 1, 1896, at Lynn, Massachusetts. *Massachusetts Soldiers*, 2:16; *Thirty-first Annual Encampment*, 108.

16. Edward Lewis enlisted as a corporal in Co. H, Twelfth Massachusetts, on June 26, 1861. Appointed sergeant, then sergeant major on May 10, 1863, he was captured at Gettysburg and confined in Libby Prison. Freed in a prisoner exchange, he was promoted to first lieutenant on October 29, 1863, then mustered out on July 8, 1864. A deacon in the Old South Church, Lewis died on March 15, 1893, in South Weymouth, Massachusetts. *Massachusetts Soldiers*, 2:51; *Boston Journal*, March 16, 1893

17. Sampson enlisted as a sergeant in Co. F, Twelfth Massachusetts, on April 27, 1861, and was quickly elevated to sergeant major. Commissioned second

Lieutenant Frank Thomas.
Courtesy of the U.S. Army
Heritage and Education
Center

carried to Richmond. The large number reported as missing in the Twelfth is accounted for by the fact that they fought on the first day, north of the town, and when ordered back to Cemetery Ridge found their line of retreat nearly cut off by the enemy, who overlapped both flanks of the First and Eleventh Corps.

Look wherever the student of history may, he will find only acts of heroism at Gettysburg. No case of faltering or cowardice will meet his eye. It was a battle which added nothing but luster to American valor. At Gettysburg the old maxim, that when the hope and strength of a people lie in the masses, guided by intelligence

lieutenant on January 16, 1863, he was captured at Gettysburg and confined at Libby Prison. After being transferred to a prison in Columbia, South Carolina, Sampson "ran past the guard with two other fellow-captives, and reached Union lines in safety, after a perilous journey of three hundred miles." He died in North Bridgewater, Massachusetts, on February 11, 1865. *Massachusetts Soldiers*, 2:40; Kingman, *History of North Bridgewater*, 255–56; *Boston American Traveler*, February 18, 1865.

Captain J. Otis Williams.
Courtesy of the U.S. Army
Heritage and Education
Center

and patriotism, received a fresh illustration. It was emphatically a soldiers' battle. No stirring appeal of an idolized leader, no expectation of personal advantage spurred them on to action. The men who held subordinate positions and the men who carried muskets and who served upon the guns, saw only their duty to their country. This was their only incentive.

Everywhere throughout the North, the loyal voice of woman was heard while her busy fingers were ever at work, either at home or in hospital relieving the soldier's needs and lessening his sufferings. I never realized this so fully as just after the Battle of Gettysburg. Here woman's kindly ministrations in my behalf began.

My wound being pronounced mortal by a rebel surgeon who came in—Doctor Frazer[18] of Galveston, Texas—it seemed like a

18. Kimball seems to have confused the story of Doctor Frazer. This is undoubtedly Dr. Henry D. Fraser of South Carolina, who studied at the state medical college and completed his education in Paris. Fraser remained with the

waste of time and effort to endeavor to thwart the busy Reaper, so I came to the conclusion that there was nothing left for me to do but to die and doubtless I would have made a quiet exit.

That night I sank almost to death's door and, had it not been for the unremitting attentions of Miss Alice K. Baugher,[19] the doctor's daughter, my name would have appeared in the mortality list. A couple of ounces of lead had played sad mischief with my groin and hip. They afterward told me that I had lain some time unconscious. I knew very little of what was going on, as weakness from loss of blood and lack of food had very nearly landed me where pain and sorrow are no more. When I became sufficiently conscious to see the faces about me, I became alarmed, for the doctor who was bending over me wore a suit of gray and I was troubled at finding myself in the hands of the enemy. Casting my eyes, however, in another direction, I espied Miss Baugher. Then assurance came, for I knew she would permit no violence or cruelty. Shot and shell could not frighten her. Like a true woman she clung to her post and did her duty with as much courage and fidelity as any soldier out upon the line of battle. This loyal lady—as brave and as devoted for the time-being as was Florence Nightingale of Crimea fame—with the limited resources at her command (for the rebels had stripped the family of nearly everything the day before), used every means in her power to woo me back to life. I remember that every time I opened my eyes in my brief periods of returning consciousness during that eventful afternoon her kindly face was looking down upon me. It was like being watched over by a guardian angel, while heaven and earth appeared to be melting away, and it brought to my mind such vivid realizations of the sympathy of the women of the North that it finally nerved me back to life. The Confederate surgeon, too, during the next two days, could

---

Confederate wounded following Lee's retreat from Gettysburg and oversaw some seven hundred patients. He died in Charleston, South Carolina, on February 8, 1895. *Reports and Resolutions of South Carolina*, 680; "Paper by Dr. B. F. Ward," 537; South Carolina Death Records, 1821–1955, South Carolina Department of Archives and History, Columbia.

19. Alice K. Baugher was born in August 1838 and remained unmarried her entire life. A music teacher, she was a member of the choir at the dedication of the National Cemetery at Gettysburg on November 19, 1863. Miss Baugher died in Gettysburg on November 18, 1914. *Gettysburg Star and Sentinel*, November 11, 1914.

not have done more for his own men than he did for us and used to remark, "We're all human, don't be afraid."

During the second and third days of the battle I was better and could watch this good and brave lady as she moved rapidly from one prostrate form to another—there were twenty or more of us lying in the hallway and lower rooms—and though shells were frequently bursting about the grounds, the fragments crashing against the walls of the building and tearing the limbs from the trees in the yard, she paused not in her noble work nor shrank from any danger, however great. Once, during a heavy cannonade on the second day, she accompanied her father to a neighboring field and brought in a supply of straw for us to lie upon. During the afternoon of July 2d General Lee paid us a visit to watch the progress of the battle from the upper floor of the house and in passing through stepped over me very carefully.[20] The look she gave him left no doubt in my mind as to her sympathy with the loyal army and her contempt for rebels. Verily, the boys in blue are not the only heroes of Gettysburg.

During the succeeding two days, with the great battle going on all about the building where our little party of wounded men were lying, our experiences were novel and interesting. We were behind the scenes, as it were, in one of the greatest dramas ever enacted upon this continent. Bodies of the enemy were almost constantly passing to and fro and we were kept fully informed as to the progress of the fight, our information, of course, causing us great anxiety, being all favorable to the Confederates. Shells were bursting all about us or screaming over our heads. Officers of high rank came into the building frequently and talked with us.

While the battle was raging, Sergeant William R. Carr,[21] of Company I, was lying wounded in a house in the suburbs of the

20. In speaking of this incident, Colonel Benjamin F. Cook gave some additional details: "Kimball was lying at the foot of the stairs and a rebel officer stooped to move him out of the general's path. Lee said, 'Let the poor boy lie there.' In coming down the stairs, Lee stopped, put out his hand and brushed aside his tangled hair and asked, 'Whose mother's boy are you?' On being told his name and home, Lee said, feelingly, 'How many more mothers' sons, like you, will have to be sacrificed before this terrible war will cease?'" *Boston Daily Globe*, June 29, 1913.

21. William R. Carr enlisted as a private in Co. I, Twelfth Massachusetts, on June 26, 1861, and was promoted to sergeant. Wounded at Gettysburg, he died of

town, inside the rebel lines. There were a number of others there, including several of the enemy. Carr had a wound which all believed to be mortal. He lay near the door, when a Confederate surgeon came along. Looking in, he asked, "Are there any Confederate wounded here?" "No, sir," replied Carr, in an emphatic way. "Perhaps you didn't understand my question," said the surgeon, as he peered farther into the room and thought he saw men in gray. Now was the plucky sergeant's opportunity, and summoning all the strength he could, he replied in a voice showing great determination, "There are no *Confederate* wounded here and you have no Confederacy yet. You are fighting desperately for it, but will never get it. There are a lot of *rebel* wounded here, if that is what you mean."

This was great excitement for a moment, as many feared the effect of the sergeant's heroic utterance, and those of his comrades who could drew near, fearing that bodily harm might come to him. But the surgeon soon allayed all fear by gently leaning over the prostrate form of the sufferer and, taking his hand in his, saying, in a voice showing deep emotion, "I want to shake hands with you. You are a brave man!" A few days after this, in the night, Carr awoke the comrade lying at his side. "Joe," said he, "my leg is bleeding." "Then it must be attended to," was the reply and a nurse was dispatched for the surgeon, but that officer was so long in reaching the room that an unbidden Messenger entered before him and took the brave spirit of Sergeant Carr where war is no more.

On the third day our little party occupied a house within the rebel lines, a short distance from the spot where Longstreet formed his attacking column. Not having had our wounds properly attended to and being almost wholly without food, it can readily be seen that our situation was anything but pleasant. And yet, bad as this was, we were compelled to endure something a great deal

---

his wounds on July 14, 1863, and is buried in the Gettysburg National Cemetery. Joseph W. Thayer of Co. H was in the house with Kimball and Carr and placed this encounter with the rebel surgeon on the morning of July 2. He also said of his comrade, "Carr knew that his wound was likely, sooner or later, to cause his death, but he was nevertheless brave and cheerful." *Massachusetts Soldiers*, 2:55; *Gettysburg Compiler*, August 18, 1909.

worse, in the shape of tantalization and insult from the hordes of sneaks and bummers who were continually prowling about the building. Among the bluster to which we were compelled to listen came the following.

"You-uns will hear plenty of music pretty soon, Longstreet's a going to charge," said a blatant rebel captain, who had hung about us like a leech for a day and a half, while his regiment, the Eighth Georgia, was preparing to advance with the attacking column. "Oh, give us a rest!" cried an indignant boy in blue, lying helpless upon the floor. "What do you know about it?" "I know this about it, Yank. In a little while you'll hear a big gun. That's only the signal, though, the fun is to follow. Then the artillery will open all along the line. Then Longstreet will charge and, if any of your fellows are left alive when his men get there, they'll have to git." And our Falstaff, having delivered himself of this bombastic utterance, strutted back and forth with the air of one who had settled the whole business with a wave of his hand.

"What does the reb mean?" we whispered to one another. "Can it be possible there is any truth in what he says? Do you suppose he knows anything about it or that if such a movement is contemplated their whole army knows it?" asked a sergeant who was lying beside me.

We felt certain, anyway, that the rebels were up to some mischief, so many hints of it had been given and it was so still everywhere. Those of us who could crawl got to the doors and windows. We were a sorry looking set of fellows—torn by shot and shell, covered with blood and dirt, our faces haggard with weariness and suffering—but the grand old Army of the Potomac contained no men who were more anxious for success. In anxiety, in agony even, we watched and waited for hours.

At last the signal for the onslaught came. It was the sharp report of a Whitworth gun and as its echoes died away in the distance we could see thousands of men everywhere scrambling for their places in the ranks and behind the breastworks. Batteries came galloping up from the right and left, taking position on the ridge and immediately opening fire and staff officers were carrying orders in every direction. It was an exciting moment. The portentous silence of the morning had been oppressive and we were glad it was now broken. The cannonade was terrible. We were almost deafened by the roar of cannon, for more than a hundred rebel guns had opened their mouths and were spouting tons of iron at every discharge. The windows of the building we occupied were rattling as though an earthquake was upon us and the very ground beneath seemed to tremble. In a short time, emerging from a straggling forest in the distance, we distinctly saw the heads of three columns of infantry.

Our eyes were now strained to their utmost to watch the movements of this new force. Slowly it came out into the open ground. It halted and dressed its lines. Here and there a slight wavering, as if shaken by the wind, showed they were stripping for action. Officers were riding up and down and in and out among them and their wild cheers showed they were determined to do or die. They waved their hats and caps above their heads, as if in answer to the appeals of their leaders. All this time we did not speak to each other, so intently were we watching the enemy. We held our breath and waited, each busy with his own thoughts. After a while the great "entering wedge" moved forward. Then cheers and yells broke out all along the line of battle. It was a scene which for grandeur and heroic interest was never before equaled on the continent and how mighty were the interests involved. The fate of the Republic itself—aye more the progress of mankind—hung trembling in the balance.

I had often seen great bodies of troops in motion, but never anything like that. Steadily, with the regularity of a machine they swept on. Added to this was our anxiety for our comrades. Could they live through such a cannonade? Would they be able to hurl back the mighty charging column, so terribly in earnest? Yes, in spite of our fears, we knew they would. We knew the temper of the men upon whom the destiny of the Republic now rested.

Even while we speculated thus, the guns of the Union made answer. Every loyal gun was now pouring shot and shell upon the advancing enemy. We could no longer see them, so closely were they enveloped in clouds of dust and the smoke of bursting shells. The volume of sound now increased a hundred fold and it seemed every minute that it would be more than our ears could bear. It was terrific beyond anything that can be imagined by those who never witnessed an artillery battle of magnitude. It was my lot, just before the battle of Fredericksburg, to lie behind Burnside's guns massed on the heights of Falmouth, while they rained shot and shell into the town and onto the hills beyond. I thought that cannonade was terrible. But it was boys' play compared with the one we were now witnessing.

Above all the roar of conflict we could hear the rebel yell of that reckless charging column. It was shrill and continuous, like the whistling of the wind in a storm. Finally the fire of the rebel artillery slackened a little as there was now danger of their killing their own men, but the battle was becoming more furious, for the rattle of musketry had begun and the clatter of small arms was continuous. The roar of the guns on Cemetery Hill and from every available point in the Union line continued with increasing fury, but still, above it all, that rebel yell! Would it never cease? The rebels back of us and from every elevated point far and near were watching their forlorn hope and officers of high and low degree gazed anxiously into that vortex of carnage. Occasionally they would point in this direction or that and staff officers would gallop away to distant parts of the field as though preparations were being made for a general advance. Our anxiety increased every moment, but we were still hopeful. As long as there was no abatement in that terrible musketry fire we knew our boys were standing their ground. We dared not think of the thousands of brave fellows who were going down every moment.

But the climax came at last. That piercing yell had died away and nothing could now be heard but the din and roar of battle. This continued for some time and then, as the sun is wont to burst through the clouds and scatter the mists and darkness, only more suddenly, came the full, round hearty hurrahs of our comrades. We needed no interpreter to tell us the meaning of those cheers. They were louder even than had been that rebel yell and we answered them with a will from our position inside the rebel lines. Rebel officers standing about the building tried to stop us, but we only screamed the louder, for we were beside ourselves with joy. Wounds and hunger were forgotten and tears flowed down our grimy faces. We cheered again and again. A few of my companions, in that supreme moment, snapped the slender cord that held them to earth and their spirits took flight to a world where wars never come. This was all that marred the scene—all that lessened our joy.

"Ah, here they come!" we all cried out at once. Yes, sure enough, they were coming. But they were not coming back in the order in which they advanced. Far from it. They were pouring back to the shelter of their guns in the wildest disorder—swarming over every foot of ground in defeat and confusion—broken and completely demoralized. No order and no formation anywhere. It was a terrible rout—a wild stampede for safety. The descendants of the Cavaliers had dashed themselves upon Plymouth Rock and been hurled back. For some time wounded men had been streaming in from the scene of the encounter in large numbers and for hours, till far into the night, the mournful procession kept moving on. It was a sickening sight and one I can never forget. It soon became silent again. Despair rested on the face of every rebel we could see. Chaos ruled everywhere. The enemy had staked their all on the throwing of the dice and had lost. A final exciting moment was when the enemy's pickets were withdrawn and the men in blue appeared, which happened to be our own brigade, with General Baxter riding proudly at its head.

After the battle was over and the rebels had dismissed their dream of Southern invasion, the wounded men were brought forth from their hiding places in private houses and out-of-the-way nooks and corners and were placed in public buildings and churches and immense field hospitals. Then ensued an era of womanly devotion and noble, self-sacrificing effort in behalf of the wounded soldiers of the Republic, the scope of which people far away from the scene did not and never can realize. Hundreds of noble women from Gettysburg and all the surrounding country labored incessantly for weeks in alleviating human suffering, giving their time and money freely to the good work, and many mothers and wives to-day in all parts of this now united country owe the lives of their dear ones to the devoted efforts of these good Samaritans of the Keystone State.

Early one Sunday morning, I found myself lying upon one of the platform cars of a long train bound north and this journey, painful though it was, proved to be the most eventful of my life.

Soon after leaving Gettysburg we began to encounter crowds of sympathizing people at every crossing and station and the kind expressions, the moistened eyes, the uncovered heads and the showers of hearty "God bless yous" that were rained upon us as we continued on our journey made a deep and lasting impression upon every loyal heart upon the train. I shall never forget that ride or how the good-hearted Pennsylvania women flocked about the cars at every stopping place and wept over us as though we were their own sons and brothers. "This is a country worth fighting for," exclaimed a New York soldier at my side and this remark expressed the feeling of every one.

But great as had been the demonstrations all along the route, we were destined to witness even greater ones. We arrived in Baltimore just as people were on their way to the churches. The long train with its heavy load of human wrecks stopped in the street opposite a building used as a temporary tarrying place for soldiers. Well-dressed ladies on their way to a Catholic Church near by surrounded us in a moment. Others who had got beyond retraced their steps. Hundreds of others still who had already entered the sacred edifice came out and never in my life did I witness such a strange scene, the women being foremost in everything. We were tenderly lifted from the cars and, as fast as we could be accommodated, we were carried into the building. Wounds were dressed and refreshments served. The regular attendants had plenty of willing helpers that day.

As I lay upon the sidewalk awaiting my turn, an elegantly attired lady leaned over me to inquire if she could do anything to help me. Controlled by embarrassment, I declined her proffered help with thanks. But she would not leave me. She declared that it was her intention to dress my wound. Here was a dilemma indeed and the only way I could see out of it was to tell her of the wound's location. This, I thought, would deter her from any further importunity, but, to my surprise, it had just the opposite effect. Earnestly, reprovingly, almost indignantly, she declared her disbelief in what she termed sham modesty when human suffering was to be relieved. At her command a stretcher was brought and despite my mild remonstrance I was conveyed to the interior of the building. Here she performed her friendly service with as much skill and heroism as the most experienced nurse could have commanded and, when my wound had been cleansed, my soiled and bloody garments exchanged for new ones, my appetite satisfied with steaming hot coffee and toast and I lay comfortably upon a bench while her fan was waving gently to and fro before my face, I fancied there was not a king in the wide world who felt any better or happier than I.

Born and raised in a New England town where Catholics were almost unknown, my religious training, what little I had received, had led me to look upon them as somewhat exclusive and shut up within themselves. I had read, of course, of their charitable work and of their great devotion to suffering humanity, but I had the mistaken idea that all, or nearly all, of their efforts were in behalf of those of their own way of thinking. But I took it all back there and then and thought that if the religious teachers of my boyhood days could have been upon the spot, they, too, would have said with me that, after all, accidents of race and creed are of little account when the real welfare of humanity is at stake.

After a while we were placed again upon the cars and, amid the benedictions of the crowd, now increased to a multitude, the train moved slowly away. All the way to Philadelphia the scenes we had witnessed between Gettysburg and Baltimore were repeated at every town and village. So heavily did the atmosphere about us seem freighted with the good wishes of the people that but for an occasional jar caused by the brakes we might have fancied ourselves borne along upon the wings of the people's gratitude or something equally as airy. It was worth all we had dared and suffered to receive such an ovation. The whole population seemed roused to the highest pitch now that their homes were no longer exposed to the ravages of the invader and when we arrived in Philadelphia the kindness we had experienced in Baltimore was repeated, although our wounds did not require so much attention and the stop was not so long as at the former city.

On leaving Philadelphia the ovations continued till Jersey City was reached, but we were not in a condition to appreciate them so fully, for the officials who had charge of the party, probably thinking that we deserved better accommodations, had placed us in regular passenger cars. No longer having an opportunity to lie down, we suffered terribly. One poor fellow, who sat or rather leaned in the seat with me, bled to death upon the way. I have forgotten his name. At Jersey City our party was divided, part of it going to hospitals in the vicinity, while others continued on farther north. In due course of time I found myself an inmate for a while in the hospital on Bedloe's Island in New York Harbor. The great draft riot was going on in the city and there was need of men to quell it. It was even rumored that the rioters contemplated a raid upon Fort Wool, located upon Bedloe's. Great consternation prevailed in consequence and the wounded men, such of them as could move about, were enrolled for service. This novel battalion, many of them with an arm in a sling, was mustered every morning and held subject to orders from the military commandant of the city. The boys just longed to get a chance at these enemies for whom they had a greater contempt than for the real rebels themselves.

I was soon sent to McDougall Hospital, at Fort Schuyler, New York. It was my good fortune to be placed in a ward presided over by a lady, who, for great sacrifice in leaving a home of affluence, devotion to the sick and wounded under her charge and sincere efforts to lead her patients to remember the Christian teachings of their fathers and mothers, deserved to be given a place among the many true and noble women of the war. Her name was Miss Julia M. Goddard[22] and her home was in Worcester, Massachusetts. I heard, after leaving the hospital, that she had married a clergyman and resigned her position as nurse. She had a sunny disposition and was always manifesting her sympathy for her suffering friends. I remember a remark made by my brother when we first arrived. He was struck with her pleasant expression, which was such a novelty to him then, that it moved him to say, "She looks good enough for butter to melt in her mouth."

One day while confined at McDougall Hospital, a boy belonging to the Seventeenth Pennsylvania Cavalry was lying upon a cot

22. Julia Goddard married Franklin D. Austin on May 1, 1865. She tried unsuccessfully to obtain a pension based on her nursing service and died in Los Angeles on December 11, 1925. Massachusetts Marriage Records, 1840–1915, MVR; California Death Index, 1905–39, California Department of Health and Welfare, Vital Records, Sacramento; Julia M. Goddard Pension Records, RG 15, NA.

dying. I was summoned from sleep by Miss Goddard and bidden to hurry to his bedside. I arrived there to find that he was still conscious and that he knew death was near. I had talked with him during the afternoon before and had found him ready for the great change that awaited him. I had endeavored to learn his last wishes and the names of those he loved. He had given me his mother's name, but he begged me not to tell her of his fate, as he feared it would break her poor heart to know that he had died so far from home and among strangers.

The little fellow had enlisted without her knowledge, running away from home. He was the only boy left to her now, an older brother having already fallen in defense of his country at Gaines Mill. His father had died before the war, leaving the mother to manage the farm alone with such assistance as her two boys could render. What would she do when both were dead? These thoughts troubled the little fellow more than the gaping wound in his breast or the dread of setting out upon the unknown journey upon which he was entering.

I endeavored to comfort him as well as I could. Miss Goddard, as true a Christian as ever lived, read to him from the Bible by the dim light of a candle and prayed for him and for that poor mother far away. I can hear his voice now as he faintly whispered "Amen" at the close of the prayer. A moment later he sat upright in his bed, being given unnatural strength, and while wildly swinging his arms as if wielding a saber, cried, "Forward! Give it to them, boys!" Then he fell back upon his pillow and, while I was sitting upon one side of his cot holding one of his hands and the lady was sitting upon the other holding the other hand, he breathed heavily for a moment and then was gone. All was over now. Another poor widow was childless and another noble martyr had fallen.

Two men entered the ward with a stretcher and the body of the boy was borne to the dead house, where so many had been carried before him and so many more were yet to be taken. Then I sat down and did what he had requested me not to do. I wrote to that poor mother the words that I knew would break her heart, for I thought it better that she knew the truth. The lady added a few affectionate lines and the morning boat that carried the body to the city, to be buried beside those of his comrades in Greenwood

Cemetery, carried also the fatal letter to the stricken mother in her far-off Pennsylvania home.

Such sights as these, terrible as they are to sensitive natures, show war as it is. They strip it of its false coloring. They throw off every cloak which poetry and fiction have wrapped around its horrid form and cause it to stand forth in all its ugliness and deformity. When we consider that this was only one of hundreds of thousands of similar cases, we get some glimpse of the fearful price we paid for the restoration of the Union and the uprooting of slavery.

CHAPTER 16

Mine Run

The fall of 1863 found the Army of the Potomac lying between the Rappahannock and the Rapidan. Search history where you will, you will not find a better army anywhere, all things considered, than the brave old Army of the Potomac. The men comprising it had all the requisites of good soldiers. Its defeats were rarely the fault of the men themselves. It was always ready to go wherever led—to do whatever was required of it. Blind leadership threw that army against fortifications, as at Marye's Heights, or the chances of war placed it in the path of well-nigh irresistible columns, as at Gettysburg. Defeat followed defeat, idolized leaders were removed and new ones substituted, political influences thwarted its carefully laid plans, Washington interference paralyzed its well-directed efforts, yet loyalty to the cause for which it struggled and the inherent honor of the men themselves would carry it bravely through every crisis in the country's affairs.

Of the many tests that were given of its manhood and courage none stand out more prominently, in my opinion, than that at Mine Run. To men who had endured the severe marching and great hardships that followed the memorable battle of Gettysburg it was in a peculiar sense a trying campaign. It was undertaken late in the season and the weather had begun to be uncomfortably cool. The ranks had been recruited, but the newcomers were an untried element among those who had already acquired the title and character of veterans. Many of its best and bravest had fallen at Gettysburg and thousands had since that battle succumbed to the diseases which always followed in the wake of active campaigns. Two large army corps had been detached to aid in raising the siege of Chattanooga and, added to all these depressing circumstances, the draft riots in the Northern States and the apparent unwillingness of men who had remained at home to come to the assistance of those who were in the field had its natural effect. But despite all these adverse influences, the grand old Army of the Potomac remained as true as steel and as constant as ever and undertook the Mine Run campaign with all its old-time spirit and enthusiasm. It was even anxious to strike one more effective blow before the coming of winter and consequent bad roads should make all further movements impracticable.

The enemy, who still manifested almost constant activity, gave us little opportunity for rest and our men were suffering greatly from the long period of exposure to which they were being subjected. By November the weather had become quite cold and life out of doors was almost unendurable. Campaigning even then was not quite over and winter quarters existed only in the most ardent anticipations. Wrapped in overcoats, the men gathered about the huge campfires during the long, monotonous hours and drearily talked of the hardships they had already undergone or gloomily prophesied of those still to come. Hard marching and desperate fighting during the preceding summer had sadly decimated regiments and batteries, while the men who remained, bronzed and toughened as they were by exposure, bore every look of veterans.

A soldier's stomach, when he is upon active duty, always demands a large share of his attention and now, stimulated by the cool air and the rough life they were leading, appetites at times became almost ungovernable. Rations were up to the usual standard, as a general rule, yet not in excess of needs, for the army was far from Washington and it was not easy to transport supplies. Railroad communication with the capital was frequently interrupted, too, by prowling bands of guerrillas, who constantly threatened every unguarded point between us and the Potomac.

Every organization contained men with extreme appetites— those who seemed to suffer from the gnawings of hunger continually. In Company D, William F. Emerson,[1] whose home was

---

1. William F. Emerson enlisted as a private in Co. D, Twelfth Massachusetts, on June 26, 1861, and died in Andersonville Prison on April 7, 1864. Kimball's

in Wolfboro, New Hampshire, most effectually filled this role. He was a good soldier and popular with his comrades, but his inability at this particular time to control his stomach or rather to keep it from rising in actual rebellion against the meager diet which Uncle Sam was wont to dole out to his defenders while they were engaged in an active campaign, subjected him to a great deal of good-natured chaffing. Emerson, however, never lost his temper because of this; neither did the boys get out of patience with him. On the contrary, many a cracker found its way into his open hands from allowances that in the first place were no larger than his, but which had evidently been more providently guarded.

Emerson had as a tentmate a soldier nearly his opposite in character—a man of a sensitive nature, delicate and refined in his tastes and a very small consumer of army stores. Indeed, it was often said in the company that if all of the men of the Army of the Potomac were like him, bases of supplies might be abolished and the army might go forward practically unhampered by troublesome baggage.

It was undoubtedly very fortunate for Emerson that he had such a tentmate—at the time of which I write particularly so—for then the little fellow was slightly "under the weather" and had even less appetite than usual. He had been worked during the preceding summer a little beyond his strength, but he tugged away as long as he could, not giving up until his slender limbs utterly refused to longer bear the punishment that was being inflicted upon them. Then he was obliged to answer sick call. The surgeon thought him not actually afflicted with any of the dreaded diseases inseparable from army life and even hinted that something in the nature of homesickness might be the disturbing cause. In this opinion a number of the boys coincided and sympathy was very generally felt

---

recollections and the published report of the Massachusetts adjutant general are at odds over the timing of Emerson's capture. Kimball emphatically places his capture after the Mine Run campaign, the retreat from which began on December 1, 1863. The adjutant general reports him taken prisoner on November 4 "near Rappahannock River." At this time the regiment was well north of the Rappahannock at Catlett's Station on the Orange and Alexandria Railroad. If Kimball is correct, and there is no reason to question his story, the adjutant general's report should probably list his capture on December 4 rather than November 4. *Massachusetts Soldiers*, 2:25; Cook, *History of the Twelfth Massachusetts*, 110, 119–20.

and expressed for him. Little groups would form about the sufferer, some suggesting one thing and some another. All these suggestions were impracticable, however, on account of the absence from our vicinity of first-class hotels and other appurtenances of civilization; but while everyone knew that there was but one cure for homesickness, it was thought that the simple mention of some of these unobtainable delicacies might excite the fading spark to renewed life.

Emerson was always an interested spectator of these manifestations of sympathy and at their close would drawl out in his peculiar tone, "Neow let me tell what I think. I think a light diet is the thing for you, Charley.[2] I've seen jest such cases as yours afore and I don't believe it's good for you to overload your stomach."

This remark always excited a quiet laugh among the bystanders, in which even Charley himself would often join, for all readily saw the "cat in the meal" that inspired the suggestion. Charley finally refused army food altogether, but no one thought it necessary to inquire as to what became of his daily allowance. It soon became necessary to send him away to the hospital, Company D thus losing a good soldier and Emerson a source of supply for his abnormal appetite.

The Mine Run campaign was begun on the 26th of November —Thanksgiving Day that year. It was Meade's plan to rapidly concentrate the army at Robertson's Tavern and Parker's Store, about six miles south of the Rapidan in the heart of the great Wilderness. Rations were issued and the march was begun at 6 A.M. After a tramp of sixteen miles the river was reached. The movement was admirably managed. Divisions and brigades were kept well together, notwithstanding the fact that the men were heavily burdened with extra rations and ammunition. Before dark, the First and Fifth Corps crossed the Rapidan at Culpeper Mine Ford, the Third and Sixth at Jacobs's Mills Ford and the Second at Germanna Ford. All were now south of the river and the first great object of the campaign had been attained. The army now pushed on toward Robertson's Tavern, but darkness coming on, numerous mishaps occurred in the dense forests and but little further

2. Emerson's tentmate cannot be positively identified.

progress was made. Meanwhile Lee had been apprised of what was going on and began operations to meet the danger which threatened him.

Early on the morning of the 27th the Army of the Potomac was again in motion, the cavalry, under General David M. Gregg,[3] and the Second Corps, under General Gouverneur Warren,[4] taking the lead. By eleven o'clock Warren was in the vicinity of Robertson's Tavern and, finding a large force of the enemy there, a brisk skirmish ensued. The First Corps joined him and the Third and Fifth Corps also came up. Skirmishers were sent out all along the front and throughout the remainder of the day fighting took place at irregular intervals, the loss in some of the regiments being quite severe. It was not Lee's intention to fight a battle now outside of his intrenchments; he was only maneuvering to ascertain Meade's strength and purposes. His experience at Gettysburg had taught the Confederate chief a useful lesson—it had made him cautious. So when night came on he fell back to his strongly intrenched line on the west bank of Mine Run.

At daylight on the 28th Meade moved forward. It rained heavily and consequently the movements of the day brought much suffering to the troops. Lee was found behind his earthworks and, after reconnoitering the position, Meade formed his line of battle. It was six miles in length, the first line being occupied by the Second

3. David M. Gregg graduated from West Point in 1855 and was a first lieutenant in the First Dragoons at the outbreak of war. Promoted to captain and transferred to the cavalry, he was commissioned colonel of the Eighth Pennsylvania Cavalry on January 24, 1862, and brigadier general on November 29, 1862. A solid commander, Gregg resigned unexpectedly on January 3, 1865, and spent most of his postwar years in Reading, Pennsylvania, where he died on August 7, 1916. Warner, *Generals in Blue*, 187–88; Heitman, *Historical Register*, 1:476.

4. Gouverneur K. Warren graduated from West Point in 1850 and served as a topographical engineer and mathematics instructor at the academy. Commissioned lieutenant colonel of the Fifth New York on May 14, 1861, and colonel of that regiment on September 11, 1861, he was advanced to brigadier general on September 26, 1862. Promoted to major general on May 3, 1863, he was chief engineer of the Army of the Potomac and is credited with saving the critical Union position on Little Round Top. He commanded the Second and Fifth Corps but was unfairly relieved of command after Five Forks and resigned from volunteer service on May 27, 1865. Warren remained in the Regular Army and died in Newport, Rhode Island, on August 8, 1882. Warner, *Generals in Blue*, 541–42; Heitman, *Historical Register*, 1:1003.

and Sixth Corps, two divisions of the First Corps and a part of the Third Corps. All was now ready and the men were calmly waiting for the word. Pickets were placed well out toward the enemy and everything betokened a day of bloodshed on the morrow.

The morning of the 29th dawned with clear skies, revealing no change in the military situation. The enemy was still waiting for Meade to attack, as grimly and defiantly as ever. Hardly a word was spoken all that day among the men save when one soldier thoughtfully reminded another of the desperate chances to be taken in the coming assault. The silence became oppressive. All could plainly see that the odds were heavily against them, for Lee's engineers had rendered his position almost a Gibraltar. Our skirmishers had driven those of the enemy into their rifle pits and the long lines of blue-clad heroes were advanced to within half a mile of the mouths of the enemy's cannon. That night they rested on their arms and many a boy in blue closed his eyes to think and dream of friends in far-off Northern homes for what he thought might be the last time.

At three o'clock on the morning of the 30th every man in the grand old Army of the Potomac was awakened. The moon shone her pale light upon the scene, unconscious of the bloody work about to begin. Everywhere men were getting ready. Now and then the sharp report of a Union gun would be heard and a scream-ing shell would be sent on its ugly errand to the enemy's works. The occasional replies that were received showed that the rebels were still there, while the nearer crack of rifles gave evidence that the pickets of both armies were alert. Storming columns, in some cases two and in others three lines of battle deep, were formed under cover of hills and clumps of trees. Skirmishers were pushed forward and the men now waited for the great ball to open.

While they waited, personal preparations were made for the encounter, which everyone knew was to be desperate. "It's to be another Fredericksburg," was a common remark. "With this differ-ence, that this time we will drive them," was the constant answer. Knapsacks were removed, little keepsakes taken out and carefully stowed away in breast or hip pockets, belts tightened, money and valuables handed over to the chaplain and others whose duties were to keep them in the rear and ammunition was prepared

250   A CORPORAL'S STORY

for rapid handling. In General John C. Robinson's division these preparations were carried forward with the utmost care and coolness, hundreds of men writing their names upon little slips of paper and pinning them upon their breasts in order that they might be recognized if found among the dead.

All this time couriers and staff officers were galloping in every direction with orders. As was the case with Pickett's heroes at Gettysburg, the men were plainly told what was expected of them. Warren was to dash upon the enemy's right at eight o'clock, one hour later General John Sedgwick[5] was to assail the left, while the First and Third Corps were to attack the centre. Many of the men crept forward far enough to get a clear view of the enemy's position. When they returned to their comrades, a simple shake of the head told the whole story, but there was nowhere any faltering. All were ready for the work required of them. All were ready to do their best. What an inspiring scene was that upon the banks of Mine Run that 30th of November! A great army of men, realizing that their country was in danger and ready to die if need be for its deliverance. Where in history is there anything grander?

The hour for action came. Warren's skirmishers dashed forward. The artillery opened. The word for which all had been waiting was about to be given. But there is delay. Warren, whose engineering skills had saved Little Round Top and with it Gettysburg to the Union cause, had become convinced that the scheme was well-nigh hopeless—that the enemy's position could not be carried without fearful and unwarrantable slaughter—and Meade, the cautious but brave commander, had acquiesced in the opinion and had decided to abandon the attempt. The Army of the Potomac fell back from the face of the enemy at Mine Run without a battle, but it was only to renew the attempt to defeat him at some other time and under more favorable conditions. It

5. A graduate of West Point in 1837, Sedgwick spent his early career in Florida and in Mexico and as major of the First Cavalry after March 8, 1855. He succeeded Robert E. Lee as colonel on April 25, 1861, and became a brigadier general on August 31, 1861. Promoted to major general on July 4, 1862, after being wounded at Glendale, Sedgwick was wounded again at Antietam. Assigned to command the Sixth Corps, Sedgwick was killed at Spotsylvania on May 9, 1864. Warner, *Generals in Blue*, 430–31; Heitman, *Historical Register*, 1:872.

was not because it was afraid to fight. It had demonstrated to the country that it could be relied upon for an effective blow whenever occasion should offer.

It was weary work, marching and maneuvering in the forest, but Private William Emerson held on remarkably well, the only thing about him which showed any signs of giving out being his supply of pork and hardtack. While lying behind Mine Run, Emerson devoured his last crumb. The retreat began on the 1st of December and while the move back to the old stamping ground was rough on all, it was particularly rough on Emerson, for he was wild with hunger and moaned piteously over his hard fate. When the Rapidan had been left a few miles in our rear, the men of Company D were rejoiced to learn that Emerson had met with a bit of good luck. He had somehow obtained a pint of raw beans and, although no suitable opportunity to cook them was likely to occur before reaching camp, all hoped that his appetite might be sufficiently fed upon expectancy to allow him to pull through.

The First Corps brought up the rear of the infantry and the enemy's cavalry followed closely, hugging both our flanks. It made occasional halts, but they were of short duration and offered meager opportunities for culinary operations. Emerson, however, improved each shining moment during these brief cessations of the tramp by building fires and making desperate attempts to boil his beans. He had neither pork nor salt with which to render them palatable, but this was of small moment, for he was hungry enough to devour them raw had he been able to do so. Sometimes the water in his dipper would merely become warm and at others it would show actual signs of boiling, but the inevitable cry of "Forward!" from the colonel would salute Emerson's unwilling ears at the crucial moment and set him to grumbling louder than ever. Then he would pour out the water and trudge on. The boys, of course, did not neglect these opportunities to chaff him unmercifully.

At last, during a halt which had been a few moments longer than usual, Emerson announced with great satisfaction that his beans had begun to crack open. This news was received with delight by the men of Company D, who had begun to be a little tired of his complaints. But alas! just then the inevitable order came, "Fall in! Forward!" It was now noticed that Emerson intended to remain behind. His commanding officer emphatically remonstrated, reminding him of the proximity of the enemy, and the boys all kindly entreated him to come on, but hunger had made him desperate. He turned a deaf ear to everything and everybody, exclaiming in a tone which showed that reason no longer held sway over his mind, "I'll eat them now if I have to eat them in hell!"

The weary march continued till at last the Rappahannock was reached, where we went into camp. Many stragglers came in, but Emerson was not among them. No one had seen him since many miles back he was left watching his half-cooked beans. The night wore on and morning came, but still no tidings of the missing man. Day succeeded day and he was finally given up as lost. One day an official document came to headquarters announcing that Emerson had been received as a prisoner of war at Andersonville, Georgia. Hideous echoes of his fearful declaration had remained in our minds since that fruitless December march and now we were not surprised to hear that his fate was likely to become scarcely less horrible than it would have been had he literally eaten his beans in the dark abode of which he had spoken.

On the 7th of April, 1864, poor Emerson succumbed to the hardships and privations of prison life at Andersonville and his body, fearfully wasted by disease and starvation, was buried with the 13,000 other human wrecks outside of that frightful inclosure, which will ever remain there as evidences of rebel cruelty and neglect. Let us hope that what poor Emerson did to bring about a restoration of the Union and a better order of things and what he suffered in the cause of his country and mankind, may weigh in his favor in that great day when God shall judge us all for the deeds we have done in the body.

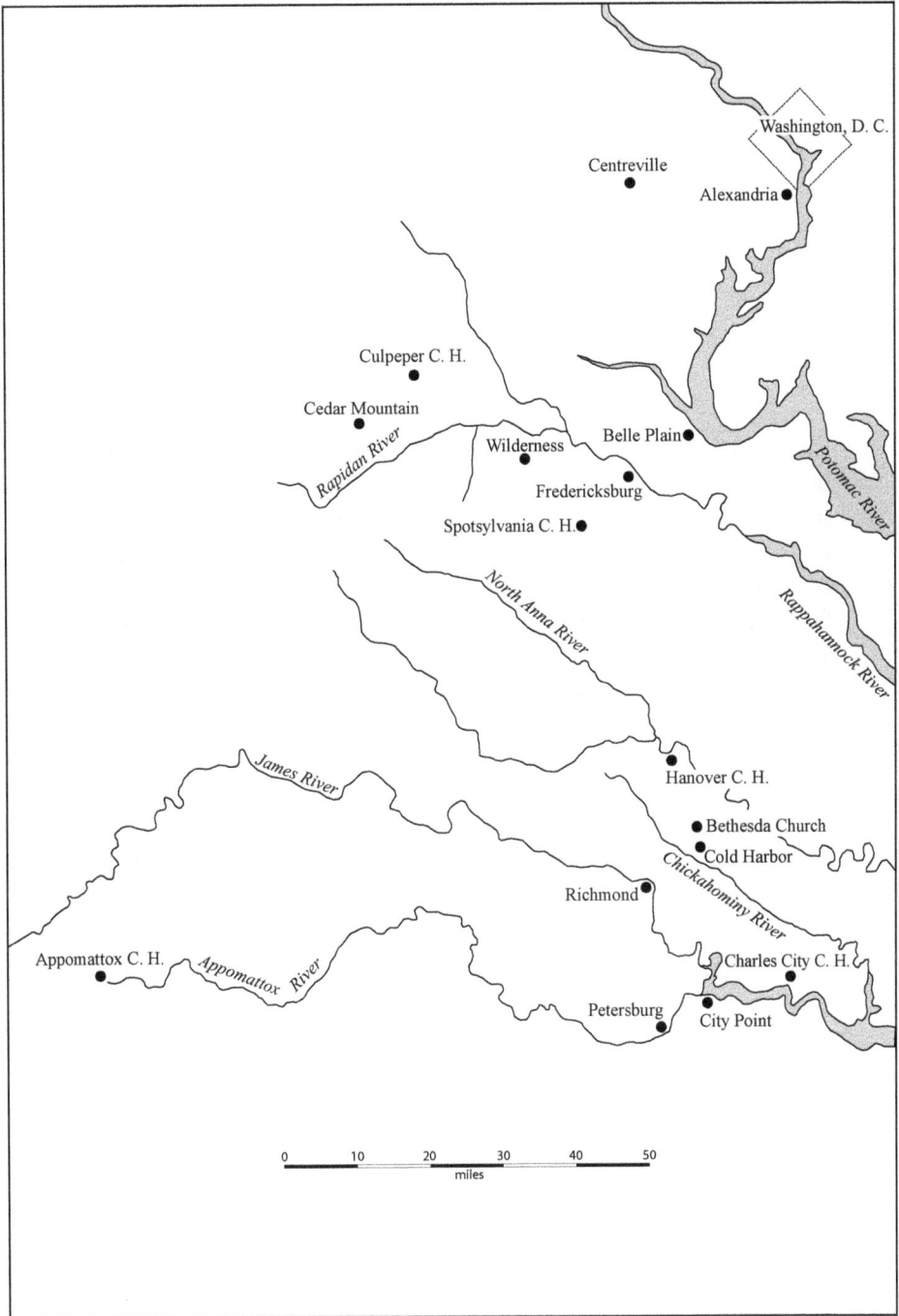

Theater of Operations, 1864.

CHAPTER 17

Grant's Campaign

Ever since entering the service it had been my ambition to return home with the regiment—or what was left of it—when its term of service should expire. I wanted to march through the streets of dear old Boston again with the war-worn survivors of the gallant organization which, on that July day three years before, had so fanned the fires of patriotism, so stirred the hearts of the people, so thrilled those loyal throngs that lined the city's streets by their glorious burst of song and their ringing cheers. I wanted to be among those who should return our tattered flag to the heart of Massachusetts through the hands of the beloved governor who had intrusted it to our safe keeping and be awarded the "well done" of her grateful people.

Accordingly, by the latter part of November, 1863, having sufficiently recovered from my wound, I left McDougall Hospital, where I had been so kindly cared for, for the front. I spent three or four unhappy weeks at Camp Distribution, near Alexandria, Virginia. It was intended that our time should be fully occupied, so that we might be kept out of mischief and to that end we were marched out every morning to work upon the fortifications. The working party usually numbered about 400 when it left camp and about 75 when it arrived at the fort where the work was to be done. About 325 men usually found their way by circuitous routes to Camp Convalescent, where the day was passed in partial seclusion, while some wandered off to neighboring camps and houses and a few even to Alexandria itself. It is true we were marched away under guard, but how can a dozen guards see everybody who drops into clumps of bushes?

I had a great desire to go to Washington and set about studying up a plan to attain my wish. I had no money—"nary a red"—and the thought struck me that it would be a good idea to apply for a pass to visit Washington "to get my pay," although I knew I could not get it even if I did go there. Although I had not been paid for over a year, I did not have the necessary papers. However, it would do for a pretext. So I put in for a pass to visit Washington "to get my pay." The pass came and, barring the tramp over and back and the lack of money to spend, I had a pleasurable day. On my return to camp, I reported to the officer in command that I had been unable to find the paymaster and asked for another pass.

The next morning pass number two came. I had another day's fun and again reported my inability to find the officer I was after, adding that I had been misinformed by a clerk on my former visit. Passes three, four, five and six were obtained by slightly varied yarns and it came to number seven. Here my career came to an end, my commanding officer probably having his suspicions excited. But I had a good opportunity, in my six visits "to get my pay," to study Washington and I escaped work with the pick and shovel, too.

I reached the Webster Regiment on the 10th of December. I found it at Kelly's Ford, on the Rappahannock. There were many strange faces in camp now—faces that I had not thought of finding there, for in my absence the draft had been enforced and the Twelfth Massachusetts, in common with other regiments, had received its quota of conscripts. But a few of the tried and true of earlier days remained and the old home feeling came back again as I took my place in the ranks.

The boys were building huts for winter quarters when I joined them, but before they were completed we were ordered to Cedar Run, a distance of fifteen miles. Here we built a second set of houses, but with a similar result, as on the 2d of January we were ordered to Cedar Mountain, to which point we marched in a furious snowstorm. We had become too shrewd by this time to be easily fooled and concluded to wait a while before beginning again. Accordingly we spread an abundance of green boughs, which, contrasting with the "beautiful snow," gave our camp a picturesque appearance and if we lacked some of the real comforts of life we reveled in aestheticism.

Sure enough, an order came to move again and in a few days we marched to Culpeper, where we were put into buildings of the Adams Express Company. The medical authorities soon discovered, however, that we were not good housekeepers and another move became necessary. This time we built our miniature city upon the Sperryville Pike, just outside of town. Here we erected our third set of log cabins, but no extra work was put into them for reasons that are only too obvious. The wiseacres had their inning again, for lo! on the 5th of February the whole army moved down to the Rapidan. This movement was in the nature of a "call" upon our friends the enemy, though it must be confessed that it was rather unseasonable weather for "social functions" and the distance, too, down and back, was forty-five miles. But it gave our "buds" a chance to "come out" and, after exchanging civilities with the Johnnies at Raccoon Ford, which had the effect of still further intensifying our strained relations, we returned again to our old camp on the Sperryville Pike.

About this time a welcome visitor came—to me thrice welcome —in the person of Paymaster Lyman S. Hapgood.[1] My two trips to dry dock for repairs had sadly interfered with the usual round of muster and pay days and, as it had been fourteen months since any of Uncle Sam's greenbacks had found their way into my poor empty pockets, my finances were in a wretched state.

"The Army of the Potomac is a very fine one and has shown the highest courage. Still, I think it has never fought its battles through." This is what General Grant is reported to have said upon his arrival in Washington in March, 1864. In the light of history the remark was a true one. It also bespoke the character of the men, for when fighting had once begun in the Wilderness it never really ended until the surrender at Appomattox. The glorious old Army of the Potomac thus demonstrated to the world that all it had needed during its long years of hard fighting and comparative failure was a leader imbued with its spirit. The men were

1. A member of the Ancient and Honorable Artillery Company, Hapgood was appointed additional paymaster on June 1, 1861, and was mustered out on December 1, 1865. One of the employees in his Washington office was Walt Whitman. Hapgood died March 27, 1896, in Boston. Roberts, *Ancient and Honorable*, 2:364; Heitman, *Historical Register*, 1:499; *Boston Herald*, March 29, 1896.

ready, but they never had until now a chief who could fight battles through to decisive results.

General Grant came to us on the 24th of March, while we lay in and around Culpeper Court House, and with his advent came a consolidation of army corps. Ours was united with the Fifth and General Warren was placed in command. We had no objection to the Fifth Corps or to General Warren, but the elimination of our organization, of whose record we were justly proud, seemed like an act of unnecessary cruelty. We were graciously allowed, however, to retain our division and brigade organizations and to continue to wear our First Corps badges.

Our camp was about two miles from Culpeper, in which village Grant established his headquarters. On the 26th of March, Generals Grant, Meade and Warren reviewed the new Fifth Corps. It was our introduction to the hero of the hour. Our impressions, on the whole, were favorable, although he flashed by us so quickly, with his staff so far behind, that we could hardly realize that we had seen him at all. Such was our introduction to the hero of Fort Donelson and Vicksburg.

After the review was over the men gathered in little groups about the campfires and discussed the new commander. The tenor of comment, as near as I can remember, was in the main that of confidence, but the belief seemed to be quite general that the Western armies, under Grant, had not up to that time been called upon to face such brave troops and such skillful generalship as had the Army of the Potomac. "Let him try Lee awhile," remarked one soldier, somewhat derisively. "He'll sing a different tune inside of three months."

We were not then fully aware of the persistent and systematic fighting habits of our new general, although we were familiar, of course, with his brilliant career in the West. But somehow we seemed to think that other qualities than those he had already shown were needed to fit him to cope with Lee, particularly that of greater strategic skill. This was the natural outcome of our belief that we had borne harder knocks than had our Western brethren. But we soon learned that Grant could plan as well as our adversary and fight as well, too, and, as the Army of the Potomac turned southward after its bloody repulse in the Wilderness, all caviling ceased and a feeling of entire confidence took possession of the men. It was to be a hard campaign, but it promised to put an end to the war and that was what we wanted. The whole situation was summed up in a remark then heard upon every hand, "It is to be a Kilkenny fight, but our cat has got the longest tail."

Grant always rode a blooded horse and his staff and other followers found it difficult at times to keep up with him. The Thirteenth Massachusetts relates with much gusto an incident which occurred when they first were reviewed. The brigade was in line waiting, when off in the distance they beheld a solitary horseman coming at break-neck speed. As he drew near, the commander of the brigade saw that it was Grant. "Attention!" he cried and the order was instantly obeyed. Grant rode at slightly reduced speed, drums were beaten, arms presented and flags were lowered and then he was off again as rapidly as he came. By and by Meade and the staff came along, their horses panting, and rode methodically down the line. As the last one reached the left of the regiment, the men burst out into a loud laugh.

I distinctly remember the good impression I got of Grant one beautiful April day in Culpeper, when, having a day of liberty, I sallied forth to get a peep at him and waited for hours about his headquarters until he should show himself. He came out finally and sat down in front of the house and, walking slowly by several times, I was able to study his face almost as much as I wished to. He was smoking, of course, and to my mind bore more of the appearance of a man spending a few days' leisure in the country than of a great commander charged with a mighty responsibility. He was in undress uniform and had I not seen him at the review and thus become somewhat familiar with his face, I would not have been able to distinguish him from others about the house. He was even less pretentious than many of his staff. While I was passing for the last time, he called his orderly and ordered his horse to be saddled. His tone and manner were so unaffected and natural that I became delighted with the man and hurried back to camp to tell my comrades. "Well," said one, "that's all well enough, but what do you think of him anyway?" My reply was something like this, "To tell the truth, boys, there isn't much style about him, but he is a man of business, you can depend upon that."

In May the spring campaign began. At midnight on the 3d of May we broke camp and marched to the Rapidan. At noon next day that stream was crossed at Germanna Ford. Then began a series of battles that lasted up to the very day our term expired.

We still had fifty-two days to serve, but our thoughts now traveled homeward and we reminded each other of the welcome fact that the day was not far distant when we would greet wives and mothers and other dear ones. We were living in the future while conscious of a present that gave small promise indeed of the fulfillment of our desires. We dreamed of our homes when sleep permitted and talked of them incessantly amid the roar of artillery and the rattle of musketry. Many, oh how many of those good, brave fellows were to find graves in the depths of the forests that lay in our bloody pathway to the James River! How many of them were to die that the nation might live, with the love of kindred and friends so strongly moving them to heroic deeds! As I write, their faces come back to me again and I see them once more as, lighted by love of home and love of country, they press forward at the word, never faltering, never seeking to spare themselves, for to true men honor is dearer than everything else and stronger even than human ties.

I shall not attempt to describe the great battles through which we passed in our journey to Petersburg, but will relate a few incidents that came under my observation. At one time during the fierce fighting, our division was moved to the right to help check an advance of the enemy. When we arrived at the threatened point the troops were in some confusion and one gun of a battery was being slowly hauled to the rear. The officer in charge was weeping as though his heart would break. "Oh, my guns, my guns," said he. "They have taken my guns." Then he appealed to us to help him. Just then Grant rode up. The officer turned to the general and begged him to send in a division of infantry to recapture his lost guns. Grant addressed the officer in a reassuring way, saying, "Never mind. Let them have them. It would cost more men than they are worth to get them back again."

Early in the evening of the first day's fight, we received a small accession to our membership in the shape of a detachment which had been guarding a signal station upon Garnett's Mountain. One of these men was my brother and, as the all absorbing subject among us was Grant, I proceeded right away to enlighten his darkened understanding, supposing him to be ignorant of the personal appearance, at any rate, of our great leader. "I'm not so green as you suppose," said he. He then proceeded to tell us how that the men in the detachment, while stumbling about in the forest in search of the regiment, had accidentally encountered the hero from the West. They had seen a man sitting upon the ground, whittling and smoking, and my brother, who was in charge of the detachment, asked the silent whittler as to the whereabouts of Robinson's division. In the course of the conversation he learned that the man was Grant himself, although he had not mistrusted it on his approach from the unpretentious surroundings. The general kindly directed him to the division and was very cordial in his manner. From that time forward my brother became an enthusiastic admirer of Grant. On the 5th, in the Wilderness, 7 of our men were killed and 50 wounded.

Early on the morning of May 6th, the sun, unmindful of the dreadful day he was ushering in, had just begun to kiss the tops of the trees above our heads. We had been fighting at short range since the first gray streaks of dawning day had shown us the enemy. They lay hidden in the deep recesses of the tangled forest and it was only by the puffs of smoke from their muskets that we knew where to direct our fire. So close were we together that during the preceding night we had actually filled our canteens from the same brook and had talked with them almost face to face. But now all this had changed. We were seeking each other's lives with all the ferocity of savages.

"Adjutant," said Colonel Bates, as he was walking down the line, "come here a moment. Who is that little fellow behind that log?" "That is Sergeant Darrow of Company A," replied Adjutant Wehrum. "Wait a moment," said the colonel. "He is loading. I want you to see how coolly and carefully he aims and fires. I never saw anything like it. He is attending strictly to business. There, he is getting ready. Look now. Oh, isn't that splendid? No waste of powder there. I've been watching that little chap for some time and I noticed yesterday, too, he was doing the same kind of work. Now, Adjutant, I want you to remind me of it when the wagons come up and we can get at the books. Sergeant Darrow shall have the next commission given out in this regiment."

Suddenly there rang out the cry of "Forward!" Taken up and repeated all along the line, thousands of voices echoed and re-echoed the order. Men sprang from their cover and began the advance. On, on, over fallen trees and through almost impenetrable undergrowth, picking their way among the dead, swept the men of the Fifth Corps. All order was lost, so dense was the forest, but we still pressed forward. We fired occasionally and men were falling upon every side. Above the roar of battle rang out the wild cheers of the men. Near the Plank Road, we came upon a battery and shot down the gunners. While checked here a moment, the Second Corps came up and joined us. The men of the Fifth and Second Corps pressed on together, vying with each other in their eagerness to fall upon the enemy. They had rallied and had been heavily reinforced, but it was too late for them to save the roadway.

When the Second Corps made this charge, we were occupying the ground over which Hancock's[2] men advanced and at that moment were deployed as skirmishers and were quite busy exchanging compliments with the enemy. We did not notice, therefore, the approach of this solid column in our rear, until we found ourselves borne along somewhat as the mighty tempest drives the dust in clouds before it. Some of our men wisely threw themselves upon the ground and, after the tempest had passed, dusted the other way, but it was my lot to be engulfed in the miniature whirlpool and in course of time I found myself loading and firing in

2. Winfield S. Hancock graduated from West Point in 1844. Assigned to the Sixth United States Infantry, he served as second lieutenant until promoted to first lieutenant on January 27, 1853, acting during that period as regimental quartermaster and adjutant. Promoted to captain and assistant quartermaster on November 7, 1855, Hancock was in Los Angeles at the outbreak of war. Coming east, he was promoted to brigadier general on September 23, 1861, and to major general on November 29, 1862. Rising from brigade to division and corps command, Hancock became one of the Union's finest generals. Seriously wounded at Gettysburg, he managed to resume command of the Second Corps during the 1864 campaign. Late that year he was sidelined by his wound and relinquished field command. General Hancock remained in the army and ran for president against James A. Garfield in 1880, but lost in a close election. He died at Governors Island in New York Harbor on February 9, 1886. Heitman, *Historical Register*, 1:496–97; Warner, *Generals in Blue*, 202–204.

the ranks of the Seventeenth Maine. Here I was made to feel quite at home by my left-hand neighbor, one of the coolest customers under fire I ever saw. He chatted freely, meanwhile puffing away at his old clay pipe, more smoke seeming to come from its blackened bowl than was proceeding from the muzzle of his musket, until after a while the source of the fellow's comfort received a frightful shock, a missile of some kind parting the stem within an inch of his teeth. The reply of the gentleman from Maine was preceded by a terrible oath, after which, as he rammed home another cartridge, he settled down into his accustomed composure, evidently feeling that he had obtained complete satisfaction from the rebel who had broken his dudeen.

When a halt was finally made and the fighting became regular, we began to get together in companies and regiments. Then it was we missed our little Sergeant Darrow and eager inquiries were made for him, not only by the men of his own company, who knew and loved him best, but by officers and men of other companies in the regiment, for everyone knew the little sergeant of Company A. After a little while Lieutenant David B. Burrell,[3] our company commander, came over to the left of the Plank Road from another part of the line and information was sought from him. "Boys," said he, his eyes glistening with tears, "Johnny is dead." "Dead! Can it be possible?" "Yes, just as we rose up for the advance, you will remember, they gave us a volley. He was shot through the heart and died instantly."

Thus perished one of the best and bravest little fellows that ever fell a martyr in a noble cause. In our hours of despair we turned to our little sergeant. He was ever hopeful, ever true. He was only a boy in stature and scarcely more than a boy in age, being but

---

3. David B. Burrell enlisted as a corporal in Co. H, Twelfth Massachusetts, on June 26, 1861, and was promoted to sergeant and first sergeant before receiving a commission as second lieutenant on November 30, 1862. He was promoted to first lieutenant and killed at North Anna River on May 25, 1864. The Boston press shows his death occurring on May 23, 1864, the Massachusetts adjutant general lists his date of death as March 24, but the regimental history shows it as March 25. Burrell wrote to friends of his desire "to do his duty faithfully, but yet he longed to be with them once more, and enjoy their society away from the noise and strife of war." *Massachusetts Soldiers*, 2:49; Cook, *Twelfth Massachusetts*, 156; *Boston Congregationalist*, July 8, 1864.

eighteen, yet around his slender form clung the hearts of men who were double his years and who stood head and shoulders above him. He inspired in us a love for home and his sweet, pure words and thoughts brought the memories of the dear New England fireside to the strange life we were leading.

During the latter part of the winter of 1863–1864, he was taken sick and they sent him away to Stanton Hospital in Washington, but he was back again with his company before Grant's campaign began. While in the hospital he had been offered his discharge, but he refused to accept it and wrote to his father on April 10, 1864, "I think I am improving. I do not want my discharge now, for my time is most out. It is true I have not been in Boston since I enlisted, but I had rather wait and come home with the regiment."

But the poor fellow was destined never to see again the home he loved so much. He lies where he fell and to this day "no man knoweth his sepulcher." He was born in Boston and attended the Phillips School at the West End. He was also a constant attendant, up to the time of his enlistment, at the Sunday School of the First Universalist Church. While in the company he always carried his Testament and his Sunday School Question Book with him and spent much of his spare time in their study. So great was the love and respect of his comrades, no man, however rough or irreligious, ever made light of him for it. The influence of our little sergeant was one of the great moving forces that gave us nerve to do our work. On May 6th, 5 more of our men gave up their lives and 20 were wounded and, on the 7th, 2 were killed and 4 wounded.

After the Wilderness fighting came the night march from Robinson's Tavern to Spotsylvania, so replete with weird but interesting incidents, with Grant, Meade and Warren at the head of our regiment, for we happened that night to lead the infantry. We left Robinson's Tavern at 9 P.M. and on the way passed Hancock's men sleeping on their arms. How swiftly yet silently we moved in the rear of a large part of the yet unbroken line of battle, answering, in whispers, a thousand times, the question, "Where are you going, boys?" not with definite information, as we knew not whither we were going ourselves, but simply the word "south," for we had discovered that we were leaving the North Star behind us. The men were roused from slumber by the clatter of hoofs, the tramping of feet and the rattle of dippers and side arms and, as we told them we had Grant on ahead, they broke out into loud cheers all along the line. I have heard the army cheer after victory, but I have never heard cheering like that which swept down the marching column then. Hitherto we had fallen back when failing to dislodge the enemy. A man was at the helm now who was discarding such foolish tactics.

At daylight on the 8th we came out of the forest near Todd's Tavern, where we found General Philip Sheridan[4] and his brave troopers. A horseman rode out of the forest and cried out to Adjutant Wehrum, "What regiment is this?" "The Twelfth Massachusetts." "Order them to deploy on the left of the road. What regiment comes next?" "The Ninth New York." "Order them to deploy on the right of the road." "By whose order?" asked the adjutant. "Sheridan!" replied the horseman, as he rode away as rapidly as he came. I shall never forget how sharply each word was bit off by the fiery cavalry leader—Grant's able lieutenant—or how impatiently he cried, "Quick, quick," as he disappeared among the trees. We deployed and immediately became engaged, for General Richard Anderson,[5] commanding Longstreet's corps, having a shorter route, had arrived at Spotsylvania Court House before us. Then came a series of bloody battles, lasting till the morning of the 21st, with the charge at Laurel Hill on the 10th and the dreadful burning of the woods where our poor wounded lay; the efforts

4. Graduating from West Point in 1853, Sheridan was promoted to captain of the Thirteenth United States on May 14, 1861. Commissioned colonel of the Second Michigan Cavalry on May 25, 1862, he became a brigadier general on July 1, 1862, and major general on December 31, 1862. After a successful career in the West, Grant brought Sheridan east to command his cavalry in 1864 and 1865. Following a stellar career, Sheridan remained in the army and eventually attained the rank of full general on June 1, 1888. He died on August 5, 1888, at Nonquitt, Massachusetts. Warner, *Generals in Blue*, 437–39; Heitman, *Historical Register*, 1:881.

5. Richard Anderson graduated from West Point and was a captain in the Second Dragoons when he resigned on March 3, 1861, and joined the Confederate service. Commissioned brigadier general on July 18, 1861, and major general on July 14, 1862, he was a competent division commander and temporarily led Longstreet's corps after that officer was wounded in the Wilderness. Anderson was later assigned to the defenses of Richmond and was relieved the day before Lee surrendered his army. He died at Beaufort, South Carolina, on June 26, 1879. Warner, *Generals in Gray*, 8–9; Heitman, *Historical Register*, 1:164.

all along the line to drive the enemy; the skirmishes, the artillery duels and picket duty so near the foe we could talk to them. Fifteen of our officers and men were killed and 32 wounded in the operations about Spotsylvania.

The regiment was small now. It numbered less than 300 when the campaign opened. General John C. Robinson having lost a leg on the 8th, we were without a division commander. The division was so decimated that it was attached to General Samuel Crawford's. Nearly all the brigades were commanded by colonels and many regiments by captains.

The memory of the sad fate of many of these noble men still lingers with me, but the saddest of all is that of a poor fellow who fell at Spotsylvania Court House on the 10th of May, 1864. I withhold his name for obvious reasons, yet no better or braver boy ever wore the blue. We became acquainted in a hospital in New York soon after the battle of Gettysburg. We had known each other in a general way for more than two years, as we had followed the fortunes of the old First Corps flag over the same roads and through the same battles, but we had not until then shared each other's confidence. Yet now it came about naturally, for we occupied adjoining beds and had little else to talk about but ourselves.

His comrades called him Jack.[6] He was a farmer's boy and when the war came was just making preparations to begin life for himself. In the little village in which he had lived up among the hills of New Hampshire, he had enjoyed the reputation of being a good boy and from his modest manner, his frank and manly disposition, his scorn of everything bearing the appearance of evil and his love of all that was good and pure and true, it was easy to see how he had obtained his good repute. He was an only son and his greatest sorrow seemed to be that he had allowed his father to mortgage the little farm in order to raise money to provide for his tuition at the academy.

Sometimes visitors came through the ward on errands of mercy, but poor Jack lay there so quietly they often passed him by, while the more demonstrative secured all the attention. But his friends at home never forgot or neglected him, as the frequent arrival of

6. This individual cannot be positively identified.

letters and papers and boxes of good things bore ample witness. I shall never forget Thanksgiving Day that year. Jack had such a big box! He sat up in bed and laughed and cried in turn as he took the articles one by one from the box, saving some for himself but giving away a great many more. In a few weeks I was back again with the army, now in winter quarters.

In the spring, just before breaking camp to enter upon the Wilderness campaign, Jack came back, but I found him greatly changed. There appeared to be some sorrow on his mind that was weighing him down and he would pass hours without speaking to anyone, going about the camp in a dejected way, as though thoroughly disheartened by some great trouble or bitter disappointment. After the terrible battle in the Wilderness thousands of brave fellows lay dead, yet we had gained almost nothing and we were all well-nigh discouraged. Jack and I had passed through unscathed and, on the evening of the 7th of May, after three days of continuous fighting, we sat down together and talked.

"I will tell you," said he, "what has happened. I believe I told you while we were in the hospital together who sent me those long letters in the large square envelopes?" "Yes, Jack," I replied. Then, beginning to discover the cause of Jack's despondency, I added, "But you never told me she was anything more than an old schoolmate and friend." "I know I never did and perhaps I had no right to think of her otherwise," said Jack. "But somehow it always seemed to me that some day Nelly and I would be married and settled down." "Did you ever talk with her of all this?" I asked. "No," replied Jack, "I never thought it necessary. You see, we were children together and we grew up in each other's confidence so naturally that no other result than that I have mentioned ever seemed probable. And although I never asked her for a promise of any kind, I always knew she was looking forward to the same future that I was."

"And what has happened now, Jack, to make you so low spirited?" "I am coming to that directly. Do you remember that Fifth New Hampshire sergeant in the next ward who used to come in and see me so often?" "Yes," I replied. "Has he done you an injury? I never liked his appearance."

"No, that is, not intentionally. The doctors were not satisfied with the slow progress I was making toward recovery and one day two of them came in to make an examination of my wound. They gave me ether and, as I was afterward told, removed some pieces of bone from my leg. After the operation I did not rally for a long time and was unconscious so long that a report got outside that I was dead. It so happened that the sergeant left for home that day on a furlough and he carried that report home with him. It was a long time before I could write and the story, of course, remained uncontradicted. The first intimation I had of it was one day when father came walking into the ward. He had come all the way there to carry my body home."

"But there must have been a sudden and radical change in his feelings when he saw you rise up to greet him." "Yes. But he brought news that turned all his joy and mine, too, into sadness. The report of my death had given Nelly such a shock that she had been stricken down with brain fever and her recovery was despaired of. In fact, before my father left me news came that she was dead."

I tried to comfort Jack as well as I could, but he was perfectly uncontrollable and we wept together in silence for a long time. Finally he whispered something about ending all his troubles in the next battle and told me of a terrible dream he had had the night before. I tried to rally him and bring him back to his old-time manhood, but he was in utter despair. Three days after this, we charged the enemy at Laurel Hill, near Spotsylvania. While we were getting ready for the advance Jack came down the line where I was standing. Grasping my hand with a vice-like grip, he whispered, "Good-by" and was off again before I could give him a word. "Forward!" cried the colonel and before we had gone fifty yards we met their canister. We pressed on and opened fire, but it was like attacking Gibraltar with a corporal's guard. In a few moments what was left of the division recoiled and fell back. My first thought was of Jack and I sought for him among his comrades. But my seeking him was in vain. They told me he died nearer the enemy's works than any other man in the division.

CHAPTER 18

Homeward Bound

Picket duty at all times in the Army of the Potomac was exciting and perilous, even when performed but a few miles from camp with no enemy near and no hostile movement in progress. There was a certain indescribable sense of loneliness and imaginary danger attending it at no other time and in no other way experienced. Particularly was this the case at night. Then men with the strongest nerves and not given to undue stretches of imagination, found it difficult to persuade themselves that stumps and trees and lights and shadows were not long lines of advancing men, while to hear a stealthy footfall in each rustling leaf and crackling twig seemed something far more tangible than a flight of fancy. Yet the soldier always knew for what purpose he had thus been placed in the van and, while standing at his post and peering out into the darkness, his trusty rifle ever ready, he felt that somehow to a certain extent the very fate of the Republic itself was committed to his individual care.

This weighty sense of responsibility served to crowd down, in a measure, his own ignoble fears, giving him nerve to stand in his place and, if need be, if he were a true man, courage to die there. But in the midst of active operations, with great bodies of men in motion and with a watchful enemy threatening every point, ready to sweep down at any moment and from the most unexpected quarter upon any part of the line, these emotions and feelings of responsibility were increased a thousand fold.

At no time during my three years of service did picket duty seem more hazardous or more responsible than during Grant's campaign. Late in the afternoon of May 12th, when we had been marching and fighting almost constantly for a week or more and were nearly worn out with hardship, our regiment was ordered upon the picket line. The order found us lying behind rude breast-works that we had constructed in the northern edge of a dense forest. The picket line was five or six hundred yards in front. We reached the position just at dark and the men, as usual, were di-vided into "reliefs." It fell to the lot of my brother and me to be put upon the first relief. We immediately went upon duty.

It was cold, rainy and dark. It being necessary to conceal, as much as possible, our position from the enemy, fires, of course, were not to be thought of. We therefore suffered greatly from the cold for we were drenched to the skin, yet the only resource open to us was to get what exercise we could by moving about upon our posts and rubbing our benumbed hands together.

We were quite near the enemy, so near, in fact, that we could hear their voices and conversation was carried on with them at in-tervals. Among much that was said I remember one question and its answer that illustrates the tenor of the talk, all of which partook largely of the nature of banter. "Have you got any dry powder over there, Yank?" "Yes," someone replied, "come over and see," an invi-tation we were just then very glad our enemy did not accept. Alter-nately stamping our feet and rubbing our hands, peering into the darkness, listening to the plaintive cry of the whippoorwill, wonder-ing if the relief would never come, gazing with feelings of terror upon every moving shadow, starting with apprehension at every sus-picious sound, the weary hours at last dragged on and relief came.

When we had arrived back with the reserve and preparations had been begun for sleep, I proposed, in view of our being so cold and wet and hungry, that I should go back to the position we had left that night and make coffee. To this my brother earnestly objected, but I finally carried my point and, taking the old black coffee pot that had long done duty for both of us, I set out alone. I found the place without trouble, boiled the coffee, drank my share of it and then started to return with his. I thought I should have no trouble in finding the reserve again and therefore walked on confidently through the darkness.

I saw no one, for although thousands of men were within a ra-dius of a few miles, all were asleep save those whose duty it was to keep watch and ward. The occasional reports of muskets along the line gave evidence that the pickets were still vigilant and active. I kept on for a while, until I thought I had gone far enough, and then, beginning to think I had somehow missed my reckoning, I changed my direction more toward the left. I walked on some distance and finally, noticing that the picket firing seemed to come from new and strange directions, I became alarmed and bewildered and finally realized the startling fact that I was lost in the forest. The night seemed, if possible, to grow even darker until all my surroundings became blackness itself. I groped from tree to tree and from rock to rock, occasionally stumbling into the thick and tangled undergrowth. I was nearly wild with fear. I knew I must have wandered outside the picket line. But how? I cannot to this day answer the question.

After a while a new and strange sound struck my ear, softly at first, like the prolonged whispers of the wind, and then, as I advanced nearer to the point from which it seemed to come, clearer and louder, until I heard distinctly the voices of men singing. This gave me new hope and I crept still nearer in order that I might detect the air and the words of the song and, if possible, see the men who were singing it. Until I had ascertained these facts never did music sound sweeter to me. At last there was no longer any doubt. I had got near enough to distinguish both the song and the words but they gave me fresh dismay instead of happiness, for from my position behind a large rock I could see four men, crouching over a smoldering fire, dressed in rebel gray, their muskets leaning against their shoulders and the words they were chanting with repressed voices breathed the spirit of disloyalty and disunion:

> Hurrah, hurrah, for Southern rights, hurrah.
> Hurrah for the bonny blue flag that carries a single star.

I wasted but a moment in determining what to do and then started back in the direction from which I had come as near as I could judge in my excited condition.

As soon as I thought it safe to do so, I changed my course so as to reach a point in our line farther to the right than where I supposed I had crossed it. I had not gone far before I became convinced from the peculiar appearance of the trees and from the great number of fallen branches lying about that I was upon ground where fighting had taken place. I now believed that I was nearing Union pickets and, knowing that if I was heard approaching I would be fired upon, I guarded more carefully each footstep. I wondered if any other evidences of battle were lying about unseen in the darkness and while I thought of this it seemed as though a thousand pairs of sightless eyes were fixed upon me. Having thus set my imagination at work, my uneasiness became greatly increased. Just as I was about to give up in despair and had nearly made up my mind to lie down and wait for daylight, I stumbled and fell over what at first I thought to be a log, but which I found, upon investigation, was a dead soldier. Wishing to learn to what organization the man had belonged, I leaned over the body and lighted a match. I found the body to be that of one of the enemy. The poor fellow had been killed by a fragment of a shell, his head being terribly crushed and mangled. A few feet away lay still another.

I was just turning away in horror from the scene when the sharp report of a musket rang out, seemingly not more than a hundred feet away. The bullet whistled harmlessly by, but fearing a repetition of the firing, which was undoubtedly occasioned by the light from the match, and that perhaps the next discharge might be that of a dozen instead of one musket, I sprang behind a large tree, where I waited a long time. Finding all quiet again, I began creeping toward the point from whence the report had come. When I thought I had got near enough I cried out, "Halloo." In answer came the question, "Who are you?" I replied, "I belong to the Fifth Corps." "What are you doing out there?" asked the picket. "I got lost," I answered and then began advancing toward my questioner, who allowed me to approach.

His firing had called the officer of the guard and a sergeant to his side. I told them my story, which, I was glad to see, they believed. I found that I had fallen into the hands of men belonging to a regiment of Pennsylvania Reserves, which formed one of the divisions of the Fifth Corps. The officer kindly detailed a corporal to escort me to my regiment, where I was immediately recognized, of course, and a moment after was comfortably ensconced under my rubber blanket. But before falling asleep, which I soon did from sheer exhaustion, I mentally resolved that thereafter, when relieved from duty, I would stay with the reserve and not wander away to make coffee.

On the 18th of May, Ewell's Confederate division crept around the right of Grant's army at Spotsylvania Court House and made a wild dash for his supply train. While we lay anxiously watching the furious contest and listening to the rattle of musketry, an incident came under my observation, the recollection of which will linger in my memory like a hideous phantom as long as life shall last. It was the tragic death of an old man, evidently of the poor white order, one of Ewell's sharpshooters.

They were bringing him out of the woods as we came in on the double-quick and they laid him down on the grass near where we halted. We knew as we looked into his pallid face and saw the red spot in his breast where the bullet had entered, that death was very near. He lay in a stupor, breathing heavily. He was an old man, over whose whitened locks more than sixty winters had come and gone. He was about to die among those who knew him not. We looked with pity upon him, for each one thought of his own father in the far-off Northern home. And he, too, might have sons! It mattered not that he was clothed in gray, for thoughts of our own dear homes and the presence of Death leveled all distinctions. They had shot him in a tree and he was stunned by the heavy fall to the ground. He soon came back to consciousness and his great, glaring eyes, set off by heavy eyebrows, looked up wildly into our faces.

Then we gathered closer about him and eagerly waited to catch the words which should come from his lips. We hoped at least to learn his name, that we might place it at the head of his lonely grave. We desired, too, to sooth, if possible, his dying hour. He was such an old man and looked so much like a martyr with his long, white hair and beard. But when consciousness returned and he began to speak, how disappointed and astonished we were for what terrible words he uttered! They were curses, loud and deep, so filled with rage, so charged with hate, so fraught with malice, so laden with wicked blasphemy they seemed like breathings from hell rather than sounds from human lips. All the savagery of war—the cruelty of the prison pen, the fury of the charge and the horrors of the battlefield—seemed summed up and expressed in his bitter words.

Do you wonder that our blood boiled as he boasted of having killed sixteen colonels since the war began? He was just getting ready to take the life of another, and he a Massachusetts man, when the revengeful bullet found its way to his breast. We begged him again and again to tell us his name and the names of those who were to mourn his fate, but he only cursed the more loudly. Then the surgeon came and tendered his kindly offices, but he, too, was brutally and rudely repelled. Thus he stormed and raved and cursed till we almost sickened of the sound of his shrill voice.

Yet we pitied the poor misguided man. Men whispered together of their wives and children and we all eagerly watched for the approach of the Death Angel, knowing that when that great Messenger came all would be well. And so it was, for soon his strength began to leave him and he sank into a stupor again. We tried in vain to rouse him, still hoping he would tell us his name. His breathing was now heavy and irregular and after a while it ceased. Then we slowly turned to go.

But suddenly, like one coming back from the dead, he rallied again and once more opened his great eyes. They had lost their fierceness. They were ghastly and expressionless now. His thin, pale lips parted again and he whispered, "Flora." Then, after a moment's pause, during which he tried to say more but could not, we heard him say, "Georgia." We were glad that in that gloomy, frightful hour of death, there was this one little ray of light, as if an angel from heaven had finally triumphed. So as we stood gazing upon the now lifeless form of the old man, who had seemed to us such a perfect embodiment of that fierce hatred of the North which had instigated and carried forward the cruel war for disunion and slavery, someone said quietly, "The Prince of Peace has finally triumphed over the powers of Darkness." We never knew whether the old man had spoken the name of wife or child, but we supposed his last word was the name of his native state.

On the 21st we made a forced march to Guiney's Station. We were all well-nigh worn out with marching and fighting and during this tramp I was so exhausted that I fell asleep in broad daylight while walking in the ranks. My brother and other men in the company were positive of this, unusual as such things are, as I not only failed to answer when spoken to, but breathed heavily as men do when sleeping. When the regiment finally halted, I threw myself upon the ground and fell asleep, not even removing my equipments.

Next day our brigade made a reconnaissance under Colonel Bates, securing information which determined the subsequent movements of the whole army. For this we were complimented in general orders. Then came three days' operations in the vicinity of Jericho Ford, on the North Anna River, during which we suffered a further loss of 3 killed and 15 wounded, after which we had a long march and a battle near Bethesda Church, losing 2 killed and 9 wounded. We were also among the reserves at the bloody battle of Cold Harbor. During all this time, when not actually fighting, we were almost constantly marching or working upon fortifications. In our battles and skirmishes we took many prisoners.

On the march to Hanover Court House, a man belonging to the Thirteenth Massachusetts was walking by the roadside while Grant and his staff were passing. The man had an old coffee pot in his hand filled with water. The coffee pot was covered with grease and soot and looked anything but inviting. Grant sang out, "Got some good water there, my man?" "Yes, sir," replied the soldier. "I can recommend the water, but not the receptacle." "Oh, that's all right," said Grant in a pleasant way, "the water is just as good." He raised the old black coffee pot to his lips and drank as heartily as though it were a silver goblet. It was the simplicity of General Grant, as well as his great generalship, that endeared him to his soldiers.

On the 11th of June we started on a march of fifty-five miles to St. Mary's Church, skirmishing with the enemy in the White Oak Swamp while *en route,* and on the 15th reached the James River, near Charles City Court House. It is really wonderful that any of us survived that terrible campaign. I had many narrow escapes. In the Wilderness a bullet plowed a furrow in the stock of my musket, at Laurel Hill a grape shot passed through my haversack and there was hardly a battle or skirmish that did not leave a reminder of some kind.

The saddest incidents were the deaths of the brave fellows, who were looking forward so longingly to their return to civil life. It seemed strange, but it was nevertheless a fact, that those who talked most of home were the very ones to fall. Some of the men kept count in different ways of the days they had to serve. At night it was a common thing to hear someone call out the number remaining. Garrett Hartnett,[1] a sergeant in Company I, cut fifty-two notches in a stick when we crossed the Rapidan. Each night he removed a notch, and announced the number that remained. The incident became a matter of general knowledge and we had many a laugh over Hartnett's piece of wood. The poor fellow had but nine notches to remove when, in front of Petersburg, a rebel bullet found its way to his heart.

On the morning of the 16th we crossed the James River in the old familiar steamer *John Brooks* and that night reached the vicinity of Petersburg, where we found the Ninth Corps hotly engaged. Next day and, in fact, every day and every hour up to 3 P.M. of the 26th, when we were relieved from duty, we were under fire more or less severe, which added to our already long list of casualties. Colonel Bates is authority for the statement that in our last fifty-two days' service, we were under fire forty-one distinct times. Such was campaigning under Grant. These were tactics which, had they been pursued with equal vigor at the beginning of the war, would have ended the Rebellion in one campaign.

At Petersburg, we were engaged in constructing rifle pits and rebel sharpshooters annoyed us terribly. We speculated a good deal among ourselves as to where the shots came from, for although the rebel lines in front could be plainly seen, we could not discover the lurking places of these troublesome marksmen. The Eleventh Massachusetts Battery was in position on our right and

---

1. Garrett Hartnett enlisted as a private on June 26, 1861, in Co. I, Twelfth Massachusetts. After being wounded at Antietam, he was promoted to sergeant. He was killed at Petersburg on June 18, 1864. Prior to his death, Hartnett had "regularly paid more than half of his wages to his mother for her support." *Massachusetts Soldiers*, 2:57; Garrett Hartnett Pension Records, RG 15, NA.

they threw their shells into every thicket, tree or hollow that it was thought could hold a sharpshooter, but still our men were being wounded and killed continually. This vexatious state of affairs continued several days.

One day Lewis C. Champney,[2] of my company, after several hours of close watching, called me up out of my rifle pit with the remark, "Get up here and I'll show you where those shots are coming from." We very foolishly stood on top of the loose dirt which had been thrown up in front of us and Champney pointed towards the rebs. "You see that old chimney over there?" said he. "Yes," I replied. "Well," said Champney, "watch for a minute and you'll see a puff of smoke." We kept our eyes on the chimney for a moment. Then came a puff of smoke and a shriek at my side almost instantaneously and Champney fell against me mortally wounded. He was sent to the General Hospital at City Point, where he died a few days after. He was a noble fellow and one of the best soldiers in the regiment. He belonged in Adams, Massachusetts and left a widow. After this occurrence, I went over and related the facts to the officers of the battery and the chimney was soon brought down by a round shot.

At night on the 25th we started alone for City Point, after turning our re-enlisted veterans and conscripts over to the Thirty-ninth Massachusetts.[3] Anxious as we were to reach our homes, there was yet a tinge of sadness in our parting from our comrades who remained, those with whom we had fought so long and with whom we had drank so deeply from the cup of human sorrow and the fountain of human joy. How strong become those ties that bind

2. While other Massachusetts men were at the front, Lewis Champney married Kate Lyons on October 2, 1862, and began a family. He was drafted and mustered into Co. A, Twelfth Massachusetts, on July 14, 1863. Wounded in the abdomen at Petersburg on June 19, 1864, he died at Deport Field Hospital at City Point, Virginia, the following day. Lewis C. Champney Pension Records, RG 15, NA; *Massachusetts Soldiers*, 2:5; *Pittsfield (Mass.) Sun*, July 21, 1864.

3. At Weldon Railroad on August 18 and 19, 1864, the Thirty-ninth Massachusetts was outflanked and driven back twice, losing 10 killed, 32 wounded, and 245 taken prisoner. Of these prisoners, 50 recently had been transferred from the Webster Regiment and 23 would die in rebel prisons. *Massachusetts Soldiers*, 4:47–105.

men together when welded in the fiery furnace of human suffering in a common cause!

"Carleton"[4] at this time wrote of us in the *Boston Journal:* "This regiment, noted for its modesty as well as gallantry and heroic conduct, retired so quietly from the lines that its absence was not generally known till it was far on its way for home. Had its departure been known in time it would have received such demonstrations of respect as have been accorded to none other."

When the Webster Regiment left the rifle pits it numbered eighty-five officers and men. My own company had no officers and numbered but three—my brother, Sergeant William L. Kimball, Cornelius Callaghan[5] and myself. But two of our men re-enlisted and these were not with the company when its term expired. Callaghan had been in the ranks only since the 26th of May. At City Point we embarked on the steamer *Vanderbilt* for Washington. As we marched on board, the band of the Fifty-ninth Massachusetts, which happened to be at hand, struck up "Home, Sweet Home" and the reader can imagine the effect. To say that we were all in tears, from the gallant colonel to the drummer boys, is drawing it mild. Most of us sobbed aloud.

In Washington the men who had been on detached service joined us and a number came in from hospitals. In New York we were given a grand ovation. Our old friends, the Ninth New York State Militia, with which regiment we were so long brigaded and

4. Charles Carleton Coffin was the nighttime editor of the *Boston Journal* in 1860 and personally reported on the Republican Convention in Chicago that year. When war threatened, Coffin declared that he wanted to see battles and became the *Journal*'s foremost war correspondent. He made it a rule "not to criticise, but only to describe," an attitude that gained him access to important events throughout the country. Charles O. Rogers, editor of the *Journal*, gave him free rein, saying, "Keep watch of the campaign. You can tell better than anybody else where you ought to be. Keep the *Journal* ahead." The edition that carried his account of Gettysburg sold 122,000 copies, a huge print run for that time period. After the war Coffin became a popular writer of history, and he died in Boston on March 2, 1896. *Boston Journal*, March 2, 1896.

5. Cornelius J. Callaghan (Callahan) enlisted as a private in Co. A, Twelfth Massachusetts, on June 25, 1861, and was mustered out on July 8, 1864. He died on August 6, 1917, at Chelsea, Massachusetts. *Massachusetts Soldiers*, 2:5; Cornelius J. Callahan Pension Records, RG 15, NA.

which had been at home a month or so, met us on our arrival. Such a scene as ensued can only be imagined. As we swept up Broadway to the armory of the Ninth, where a bountiful spread awaited us, heads were uncovered and the enthusiasm of the people of the metropolis was heartfelt and continuous.

Jennie, an equine native of Vermont, had accompanied the Twelfth Massachusetts to the front in July of 1861. She was the property of Quartermaster George E. Muzzey,[6] of Lexington and served faithfully three years, carrying her owner through all the campaigns in which the regiment participated. Her appearance in camp after a hard march was always a welcome sight to the men, as it signified that rations were at hand. The boys were always fond of Jennie, too, and she seemed to appreciate their attentions. It is undoubtedly true that during her term of service she received more shouts of welcome and ringing cheers than any horse in the regiment, not excepting the fiery, untamed steeds ridden by the successive colonels. When the little squad of men forming what was left of the Webster Regiment was mustered out in Boston, Jennie was there, and she gave her head a toss of approval.

We reached Boston on the morning of July 1st. After a breakfast at the old Beach Street Barracks, the Westborough Independent Company of Militia, Captain C. P. Winslow,[7] with Gilmore's Band, escorted us to Faneuil Hall. The scene as we passed through the

6. George E. Muzzey enlisted on June 2, 1862, in Co. F, Twelfth Massachusetts, and was appointed quartermaster sergeant the same day. Promoted to second lieutenant on October 9, 1862, and first lieutenant on December 7, 1863, he was appointed regimental quartermaster on May 1, 1864. Muzzey was mustered out on July 8, 1864, and died in Lexington, Massachusetts, on December 14, 1896. *Massachusetts Soldiers*, 2:39; *Boston Journal*, December 14 and 15, 1896.

7. Although newspaper and regimental accounts report that C. B. Winslow commanded the Westborough militia, his name was actually Charles P. Winslow. Originally a lieutenant in Co. K, Thirteenth Massachusetts, Winslow stepped aside because the unit had too many lieutenants. Commissioned first lieutenant in Co. E, Fifty-first Massachusetts, a nine-month regiment, he was mustered out on July 27, 1863. Winslow was appointed captain of the Sixth Unattached Company of Militia, a ninety-day unit, on May 4, 1864, and mustered out on August 2, 1864. He immediately formed Co. E of the Fourth Massachusetts Heavy Artillery and was commissioned captain on August 12, 1864, and mustered out again on June 17, 1865. Captain Winslow died in Chicago on December 5, 1910. *Massachusetts Soldiers*, 4:563; 5:199; 6:29; DeForest and Bates, *History of Westborough*, 252–53; 257, 263–65, 324; Charles P. Winslow Pension Records, RG 15, NA.

Quartermaster George E. Muzzey.
Courtesy of the U.S. Army
Heritage and Education Center

streets contrasted strangely with that grand triumphal march at the beginning of our career. Sadness now took the place of enthusiasm. Our little band of survivors was a keen reminder to the throngs that filled the streets of the faces that were missed from firesides. Eyes were dimmed with tears and not noisy demonstrations, but "God bless you, boys!" flowed in upon us from every direction. Nearly all of the ladies were in mourning, for there was hardly a family in our broad land that had not lost dear ones in the terrible war which was then raging.

At the old "Cradle of Liberty" there were the usual speeches and we were furloughed to meet at Boston Common on July 8th. On the spot where now stands the noble monument which the city has erected to the memory of the men who on land and sea gave their lives for the preservation of the Union, we answered roll call for the last time and our service ended as the mustering officer, Lieutenant Patrick H. Moroney[8] of the Fourteenth United States Infantry, uttered those welcome words: "This regiment is hereby mustered out of the service of the United States."

8. Moroney steadily advanced through the ranks of the Tenth and Fourteenth United States until June 27, 1862, when he was commissioned second lieutenant of Co. F of the latter regiment on June 27, 1862. Elevated to first lieutenant on July 11, 1863, he retired on January 26, 1865. Moroney became involved in a scandal involving the signing of false pay certificates in 1869. President Grant remitted the court-martial punishment for imprisonment, but he ordered repayment and dismissed Moroney on July 8, 1875. Heitman, *Historical Register*, 1:727; *New York Times*, November 6, 1869; Simon, *Papers of Ulysses S. Grant*, 26:264.

In withdrawing from the campfire, permit me a personal word. I have made frequent use of the personal pronoun "I." This has been with no feeling of self-exaltation. I did no better than the average young American of today would do if like occasion and like opportunity were to present themselves. Nor do I claim that my regiment, the Webster Regiment, which I have mentioned so frequently, was any better than other organizations. All were good and together they formed one of the grandest armies the world has yet seen.

APPENDIX A

Roll of Honor
Twelfth Massachusetts (Webster) Regiment

Compiled by the editors of this volume, from Massachusetts Soldiers, Sailors, and Marines in the Civil War (1931).
[*k* = killed; *acc k* = accidentally killed; *mw* = mortally wounded; *m* = missing; *pow* = prisoner of war, either in captivity or after exchange; *dis* = died of disease; *dr'd* = drowned]

Name	Company	Date of Death	Manner/Place of Death
Allen, Lt. Col. David, Jr.	F&S	May 5, 1864	*k* Wilderness
Allen, Edward F.	K	Dec. 5, 1863	*pow* Richmond, Va.
Allen, Isaac F.	K	Sept. 17, 1862	*k* Antietam
Allen, Lyman	F	May 10, 1864	*k* Spotsylvania
Allen, William	K	Nov. 3, 1863	*pow* Richmond, Va.
Arnold, Sanford P.	E	Apr. 15, 1864	*pow* Richmond, Va.
Atkinson, John	H	Dec. 6, 1863	*dis* Alexandria, Va.
Atwood, Joshua	B	May 6, 1864	*k* Wilderness
Austin, James H.	I	Sept. 17, 1862	*k* Antietam
Ayers, Benjamin F.	E	Sept. 17, 1862	*k* Antietam
Babbington, Sgt. William	C	July 1, 1863	*k* Gettysburg
Bacon, George	H	June 5, 1864	*mw* Wilderness
Baker, Sgt. John H.	C	June 18, 1864	*k* Petersburg
Bangs, William W.	F	June 27, 1864	*mw* Petersburg
Barber, Cpl. John W.	C	Aug. 1, 1862	*dis* Washington, D.C.
Barnes, John	F	Oct. 29, 1863	*pow* Richmond, Va.
Bartlett, Charles A.	B	May 8, 1864	*k* Laurel Hill
**Bartlett, William H.	E	Dec. 30, 1864	*pow* Salisbury, N.C.

**After transfer to Thirty-ninth Massachusetts Infantry

Name	Company	Date of Death	Manner/Place of Death
**Bartoll, William H.	K	July 1, 1864	*mw* Petersburg
Bean, Charles E.	D	Aug. 30, 1862	*m* 2nd Bull Run
**Becker, Ferdinand	A	Jan. 16, 1865	*pow* Salisbury, N.C.
Bennett, Benjamin F.	F	May 7, 1864	*k* Wilderness
Birkenholz, Henry	A	Jan. 3, 1864	*dis* Culpeper, Va.
Blackman, John H.	H	Dec. 13, 1862	*k* Fredericksburg
‡‡Blaisdell, Lorenzo C.	B	Jan. 15, 1865	*k* Charleston Harbor, S.C.
**Bowen, Samuel C.	A	Nov. 27, 1864	*pow* Salisbury, N.C.
*Brigham, Clarence O.	E	June 22, 1862	*k* Gaines Mill
Brown, Frederick R.	G	Jan. 18, 1864	*dis* Culpeper, Va.
Brown, 1st Sgt. James	D	Dec. 13, 1862	*k* Fredericksburg
Brown, Sgt. John	A	June 6, 1862	*dr'd* Front Royal, Va.
Brownell, Darling M.	B	May 8, 1864	*k* Laurel Hill
Bryant, George W.	I	Dec. 25, 1862	*pow* Richmond, Va.
Buckley, Patrick	A	Dec. 8, 1863	*pow* Annapolis, Md.
Buhl, Peter	B	Dec. 9, 1863	*pow* Richmond, Va.
Burbank, Maj. Elisha M.	F&S	Nov. 29, 1862	*mw* Antietam
**Burnham, Sgt. Isaac	I	Aug. 13, 1864	*pow* Andersonville, Ga.
Burns, George W.	D	Nov. 2, 1862	*mw* 2nd Bull Run
Burns, John W.	H	Feb. 25, 1864	*pow* Richmond, Va.
Burrell, 1st Lt. David B.	A	May 24, 1864	*k* North Anna
**Bushnell, Charles	H	Nov. 17, 1864	*pow* Salisbury, N.C.
Butler, Patrick	A	Dec. 8, 1863	*pow* Annapolis, Md.
Carey, Cpl. Charles E.	E	Sept. 17, 1862	*k* Antietam
Carr, Sgt. William R.	I	July 14, 1863	*mw* Gettysburg
**Carter, Charles L.	B	Feb. 8, 1865	*pow* Salisbury, N.C.
Casperson, Cpl. John P.	D	Sept. 17, 1862	*k* Antietam
**Cassidy, John	B	Nov. 5, 1864	*pow* Salisbury, N.C.
‡‡Center, William R.	C	Aug. 6, 1862	*dis* Helena, Ark.
Champney, Lewis C.	A	June 20, 1864	*mw* Petersburg
Chase, John A.	B	Jan. 20, 1863	*mw* Fredericksburg
**Chase, Seth C.	I	Apr. 3, 1865	*pow* Nantucket, Mass.
Childs, Cpl. George W.	F	Dec. 13, 1863	*k* Fredericksburg
Clark, James L., Jr.	E	May 21, 1864	*mw* Laurel Hill
Colby, Sgt. Hezekiah	K	Aug. 30, 1862	*k* 2nd Bull Run

**After transfer to Thirty-ninth Massachusetts Infantry
‡‡After transfer to United States Navy

Name	Company	Date of Death	Manner/Place of Death
Conroy, James	C	Oct. 30, 1863	*pow* Annapolis, Md.
**Conway, Patrick	K	Jan. 5, 1865	*pow* Salisbury, N.C.
Coolidge, Cpl. Francis E.	C	Aug. 30, 1862	*k* 2nd Bull Run
**Cowdry, Charles	E	Mar. 31, 1865	*pow* sinking of *Gen Lyon*
Crouse, Cpl. James T.	K	Dec. 15, 1862	*mw* Antietam
Curtis, Benjamin	G	Sept. 17, 1862	*k* Antietam
Cushing, Cpl. Charles E.	H	June 12, 1864	*pow* Andersonville, Ga.
Cushing, 1st Lt. Lysander F.	G	Sept. 17, 1862	*k* Antietam
Cushing, Thomas J.	B	Sept. 17, 1862	*k* Antietam
Darling, Cpl. Harvey A.	I	Sept. 17, 1862	*k* Antietam
Darrow, Sgt. John N.	A	May 6, 1864	*k* Wilderness
Davis, Walter R.	G	Dec. 26, 1862	*mw* Fredericksburg
**Day, John	K	Oct. 28, 1864	*pow* Annapolis, Md.
Dean, Warren F.	I	Dec. 27, 1863	*pow* Richmond, Va.
Decoty, William	E	Oct. 18, 1862	*mw* 2nd Bull Run
Dehon, 1st Lt. Arthur	F	Dec. 13, 1862	*k* Fredericksburg
Deshon, Sgt. Jason L.	H	May 6, 1864	*k* Wilderness
Desmond, Bartholomew	B	Sept. 17, 1862	*k* Antietam
Dhalberg, F. Malcomb	F	Dec. 18, 1863	*dis* Washington, D.C.
Donovan, Cpl. Daniel	B	July 2, 1862	*dis* Manassas, Va.
Donovan, Patrick	B	Sept. 17, 1862	*k* Antietam
Drew, Horace	F	May 12, 1864	*k* Spotsylvania
Dulick, Chandick	H	May 6, 1864	*m* Wilderness
Dunn, Samuel C.	A	May 12, 1864	*k* Spotsylvania
Duran, Alonzo G.	B	Sept. 17, 1862	*k* Antietam
Dyer, Cpl. Nathaniel H.	A	Sept. 17, 1862	*k* Antietam
Edson, Sgt. Galen	F	Feb. 20, 1864	*dis* Cedar Mountain, Va.
Elliott, John	E	July 1, 1863	*m* Gettysburg
Emerson, William F.	D	Apr. 7, 1864	*pow* Andersonville, Ga.
Emmons, Sgt. Charles	G	July 2, 1863	*mw* Gettysburg
Evans, Sgt. Horace B.	E	May 6, 1864	*mw* Wilderness
Evans, John	A	June 7, 1864	*mw* Wilderness
Ewell, George A.	I	Aug. 30, 1862	*k* 2nd Bull Run

**After transfer to Thirty-ninth Massachusetts Infantry

Name	Company	Date of Death	Manner/Place of Death
Fernald, Robert	B	Sept. 17, 1862	*k* Antietam
Fisk, Charles H.	E	Sept. 17, 1862	*k* Antietam
Fitts, James	G	Nov. 6, 1862	*mw* Antietam
Foley, Maurice	G	Sept. 17, 1862	*k* Antietam
Foster, 1st Sgt. Solomon	G	Sept. 4, 1862	*mw* 2nd Bull Run
**Freeman, John C.	F	Feb. 18, 1865	*pow* Florence, S.C.
French, Samuel L.	H	Jan. 24, 1864	*dis* Culpeper, Va.
**Frisbie, Albert	G	Sept. 8, 1864	*pow* Andersonville, Ga.
Frost, Aaron B.	F	Aug. 30, 1862	*k* 2nd Bull Run
Frost, Andrew J.	F	Aug. 9, 1862	*dis* Alexandria, Va.
Gale, Josiah B.	E	Sept. 17, 1862	*k* Antietam
**Gammon, Randall T.	G	Nov. 17, 1864	*pow* Salisbury, N.C.
GilMartin, Luke	K	Oct. 11, 1862	*dis* Westfield, Mass.
Gittins, Thomas	A	Jan. 1, 1863	*mw* Fredericksburg
Glasure, Cpl. James L.	G	Dec. 24, 1863	*dis* Culpeper, Va.
Godfrey, Franklin M.	F	Jan. 23, 1864	*pow* Richmond, Va.
Gould, Reuben	I	Feb. 2, 1864	*pow* Richmond, Va.
Goulding, Cpl. John	I	Sept. 20, 1862	*mw* 2nd Bull Run
Grant, Rufus H.	D	Feb. 28, 1862	*acc k* loc. unknown
**Green, John F.	A	Dec. 15, 1864	*pow* Salisbury, N.C.
Grover, Cpl. Hazel L.	E	Sept. 25, 1862	*mw* Antietam
Haley, Alonzo	B	Aug. 9, 1862	*dis* Culpeper, Va.
*Hamilton, John S.	F	Jan. 7, 1862	*dis* Georgetown, D.C.
Hand, Patrick	C	Oct. 26, 1863	*dis* loc. unknown
Hanson, Hans C.	I	Apr.il 15, 1864	*pow* Andersonville, Ga.
Hanson, Robert M.	G	May 6, 1864	*k* Wilderness
Hardy, George B.	C	May 5, 1864	*k* Wilderness
Hartnett, Sgt. Garrett	I	June 18, 1864	*k* Petersburg
**Harrington, Thomas J.	H	July 24, 1864	*pow* Andersonville, Ga.
Harris, Edward	I	May 6, 1864	*k* Wilderness
Harvey, John B.	D	May 18, 1864	*mw* Wilderness
Haskell, Cpl. Charles	D	Mar. 10, 1864	*dis* Salem, Mass.
Haskell, Sgt. William B.	K	Sept. 19, 1863	*dis* Washington, D.C.

*After transfer to Fifth United States Cavalry
**After transfer to Thirty-ninth Massachusetts Infantry

Name	Company	Date of Death	Manner/Place of Death
Hayward, James S.	I	Sept. 17, 1862	k Antietam
Hazeltine, Cpl. Moses	C	Oct. 16, 1862	mw Antietam
Hazeltine, Nathaniel	C	Aug. 30, 1862	m 2nd Bull Run
Healey, Cornelius	A	Dec. 13, 1862	k Fredericksburg
Heath, George E.	I	Sept. 12, 1863	dis Gettysburg, Pa.
**Hemmenway, Elbert O.	H	Jan. 1, 1865	pow Salisbury, N.C.
Henry, George P.	I	Nov. 17, 1862	mw Smoketown, Md.
Hockley, Edward J.	B	Dec. 13, 1862	k Fredericksburg
Hodge, Jerome K.	F	Dec. 13, 1862	k Fredericksburg
Holbrook, Randall J.	I	Sept. 17, 1862	k Antietam
**Holmes, 1st Sgt. Leonard	I	Aug. 5, 1864	pow Andersonville, Va.
Horrigan, Patrick	A	May 6, 1864	k Wilderness
Horne, John H.	B	Jan. 5, 1864	dis Culpeper, Va.
Hough, Palmer W.	B	Sept. 3, 1863	pow Annapolis, Md.
†Howard, Charles W.	G	Oct. 16, 1862	dis New York, N.Y.
Howard, Linus P.	F	Aug. 30, 1862	k 2nd Bull Run
Hoyt, William C.	E	Sept. 17, 1862	k Antietam
Hunnewell, John A.	G	Dec. 13, 1862	k Fredericksburg
Hurd, Hiram A.	F	Sept. 17, 1862	k Antietam
Ingersoll, Amos M.	K	Sept. 18, 1862	mw Antietam
Ingram, Samuel	D	July 20, 1863	dis Washington, D.C.
Isaac, Alexander	B	Sept. 17, 1862	k Antietam
Jacobs, William F.	G	Sept. 17, 1862	k Antietam
Jenks, John B.	C	Oct. 6, 1862	mw 2nd Bull Run
Johannes, Charles	C	June 10, 1864	mw Bethesda Church
Johnson, Sgt. Charles E.	I	Sept. 17, 1862	k Antietam
Jones, Frederick O.	A	May 10, 1864	dis New York, N.Y.
Jordan, James	F	May 12, 1864	k Spotsylvania
Judson, Isaac D.	E	Sept. 17, 1862	k Antietam
Kahle, William F.	C	Mar. 6, 1864	dis Culpeper, Va.
Kain, Isaac	C	May 10, 1864	mw Spotsylvania
**Keep, William J.	H	Mar. 16, 1865	pow Annapolis, Md.
Keith, 1st Sgt. Thaddeus	F	May 6, 1864	k Wilderness

**After transfer to Thirty-ninth Massachusetts Infantry
†After transfer to Second United States Artillery

Name	Company	Date of Death	Manner/Place of Death
Kendall, Asst. Surg. Albert	F&S	Sept. 17, 1862	*k* Antietam
Kennedy, Kelah H.	G	Aug. 30, 1862	*k* 2nd Bull Run
Kidder, 2nd Lt. Edward J.	F	May 10, 1864	*k* Spotsylvania
Kimball, Asa H.	I	Mar. 25, 1864	*pow* Richmond, Va.
Kimball, Charles H.	I	Oct. 3, 1862	*mw* Antietam
Kimball, Capt. Richard H.	A	Aug. 30, 1862	*k* 2nd Bull Run
Kirvan, Sgt. Henry	D	May 17, 1864	*mw* Wilderness
Kittredge, Paul C.	H	Feb. 28, 1864	*dis* Culpeper, Va.
Kohlman, William	C	Dec. 17, 1863	*dis* Kelly's Ford, Va.
Kummer, Henry W.	A	Sept. 17, 1862	*k* Antietam
**Ladd, Sgt. Edward	F	Apr. 23, 1865	*dr'd* Potomac River, Va.
Lajoy, Joseph	E	Sept. 17, 1862	*k* Antietam
Lane, John	A	Aug. 30, 1862	*m* 2nd Bull Run
Lane, John D.	G	May 17, 1864	*mw* Spotsylvania
**Lane, Sanford P.	I	Aug. 24, 1864	*pow* Andersonville, Ga.
Lathrop, Hiram G.	B	Aug. 30, 1862	*k* 2nd Bull Run
Lewis, George F.	H	July 1, 1863	*k* Gettysburg
Lively, Lawrence L.	K	Dec. 15, 1862	*mw* Fredericksburg
Lucas, Henry	H	Dec. 13, 1862	*k* Fredericksburg
Lufkin, Fitz O.	K	Feb. 8, 1864	*dis* Gloucester, Mass.
McCarthy, Thomas F.	A	Sept. 17, 1862	*k* Antietam
**McGee, James	C	Mar. 21, 1865	*pow* Annapolis, Md.
**McGowan, William A.	A	Aug. 10, 1864	*pow* Andersonville, Ga.
McGrath, William	K	Dec. 13, 1862	*k* Fredericksburg
McGuire, Francis	A	July 1, 1863	*k* Gettysburg
McKenna, Timothy	D	Aug. 30, 1862	*k* 2nd Bull Run
McMahon, Edward	E	Oct. 25, 1861	*dis* Budd's Ferry, Md.
Madden, John J.	D	May 5, 1864	*k* Wilderness
Maguire, John	E	Sept. 17, 1862	*k* Antietam
Mahar, Matthew	A	Dec. 13, 1862	*k* Fredericksburg
Mahoney, Patrick J.	D	Sept. 8, 1863	*pow* Richmond, Va.
Manley, John	B	Dec. 13, 1862	*k* Fredericksburg

**After transfer to Thirty-ninth Massachusetts Infantry

Name	Company	Date of Death	Manner/Place of Death
Mann, Charles	C	Aug. 2, 1862	*dis* Washington, D.C.
Maroni, Cpl. Charles N.	F	Aug. 30, 1862	*k* 2nd Bull Run
**Marsden, Joseph	A	Aug. 24, 1864	*mw* Petersburg
Maxwell, Charles L.	K	Sept. 17, 1862	*k* Antietam
Means, James H.	D	Feb. 19, 1862	*dis* Frederick, Md.
Merrill, James D.	B	Dec. 13, 1862	*k* Fredericksburg
Merrow, John	D	May 25, 1864	*mw* Laurel Hill
**Messinger, Charles	K	Sept. 20, 1864	*dis* Alexandria, Va.
Miller, Lewis L.	E	Oct. 3, 1862	*mw* 2nd Bull Run
**Millett, John H.	K	Dec. 1, 1864	*pow* Salisbury, N.C.
Mitchell, Sgt. Albert E.	A	Aug. 30, 1862	*m* 2nd Bull Run
Morey, Cpl. James N.	K	Sept. 17, 1862	*k* Antietam
Morse, Herbert C.	F	Mar. 13, 1864	*pow* Richmond, Va.
Mundell, John	H	May 7, 1864	*mw* Wilderness
Murphy, Edward	K	Jan. 13, 1863	*mw* Fredericksburg
Murphy, James B.	E	Oct. 25, 1862	*mw* Antietam
Murphy, Michael L.	K	June 6, 1864	*pow* Andersonville, Ga.
Murray, Hardy P.	K	July 6, 1863	*mw* Gettysburg
Murray, Cpl. Robert	B	Sept. 17, 1862	*k* Antietam
**Murphy, Thomas	H	Dec. 21, 1864	*pow* Salisbury, N.C.
Newhall, George H.	C	Jan. 10, 1863	*mw* Fredericksburg
Norwood, James W.	A	Sept. 17, 1862	*k* Antietam
**O'Brien, Cornelius	I	Feb. 22, 1865	*pow* Salisbury, N.C.
O'Brien, James	A	Sept. 17, 1862	*k* Antietam
O'Donnell, Michael	A	Sept. 17, 1862	*k* Antietam
Oliver, James H.	E	July 8, 1863	*k* Funkstown, Md.
Orcutt, George O.	H	Nov. 25, 1863	*dis* Rappahannock Station, Va.
Orne, 2nd Lt. George W.	A	Sept. 17, 1862	*k* Antietam
Packard, Richard	F	Dec. 13, 1862	*k* Fredericksburg
Palmer, John D.	A	Jan. 17, 1864	*dis* Washington, D.C.
Parker, Austin G.	G	Nov. 6, 1862	*mw* 2nd Bull Run
Parker, Clark	E	Sept. 14, 1862	*k* South Mountain
Parrott, Charles A.	C	Dec. 13, 1862	*k* Fredericksburg
Patterson Cpl. Calvin	K	Dec. 13, 1862	*k* Fredericksburg

**After transfer to Thirty-ninth Massachusetts Infantry

Name	Company	Date of Death	Manner/Place of Death
Peck, Rufus A.	I	Sept. 23, 1861	*acc k* Darnestown, Md.
Perkins, George A.	F	Sept. 17, 1862	*k* Antietam
**Phillips, Albert W.	F	Dec. 3, 1864	*pow* Salisbury, N.C.
Pierce, Sidney C.	D	Sept. 17, 1862	*k* Antietam
Pool, Elbridge G.	G	Oct. 14, 1862	*mw* Antietam
Pope, 1st Sgt. Charles A.	H	Nov. 30, 1863	*dis* Braintree, Mass.
Porter, George W.	B	Sept. 17, 1862	*k* Antietam
Porter, Richard	G	Sept. 17, 1862	*k* Antietam
Porter, Wesley K.	G	Oct. 24, 1863	*dis* Washington, D.C.
Potter, Francis B.	D	June 5, 1864	*mw* Wilderness
Puffer, Charles H.	E	Feb. 5, 1863	*mw* Fredericksburg
Purdy, William H.	B	July 1, 1863	*k* Gettysburg
Ramsdell, Seth	G	June 18, 1864	*k* Petersburg
**Rand, William L.	C	Mar. 31, 1865	*k* Petersburg
Raymond, Jasper S.	B	Aug. 30, 1862	*k* 2nd Bull Run
Reed, Charles E.	F	Aug. 9, 1862	*pow* Lynchburg, Va.
Rice, Cpl. Sylvester H.	E	Sept. 17, 1862	*k* Antietam
Richardson, Sylvester B.	C	Sept. 17, 1862	*k* Antietam
Rickards, Alden	I	Sept. 17, 1862	*k* Antietam
Ripley, Capt. John	I	Dec. 20, 1862	*mw* Fredericksburg
Robinson, 1st Lt. William	C	May 14, 1864	*mw* Spotsylvania
**Rogers, Daniel	H	Mar. 22, 1865	*pow* Annapolis, Md.
Rogers, Joshua	B	Feb. 22, 1863	*mw* Fredericksburg
Rogers, Nathan A.	B	Nov. 13, 1862	*mw* Antietam
Rollins, Andrew J.	D	Sept. 17, 1862	*k* Antietam
Russell, 1st Lt. Charles C.	D	July 1, 1863	*k* Gettysburg
Sanborn, William H.	A	June 10, 1864	*dis* Chester, Pa.
Sanford, Francis A.	F	Aug. 30, 1862	*k* 2nd Bull Run
Savage, Cpl. Miner W.	B	Sept. 17, 1862	*k* Antietam
Scott, John F.	A	May 10, 1864	*k* Laurel Hill
**Seavey, William H.	A	Sept. 3, 1864	*pow* Andersonville, Ga.
Sherman, Henry C. R.	I	Sept. 17, 1862	*k* Antietam
Shurtleff, Capt. Nathaniel B.	D	Aug. 9, 1862	*k* Cedar Mountain

**After transfer to Thirty-ninth Massachusetts Infantry

Name	Company	Date of Death	Manner/Place of Death
Simonds, Timothy	C	Sept. 18, 1862	*mw* Antietam
Slattery, John G.	H	Aug. 28, 1862	*k* Thoroughfare Gap
Smith, Dexter	G	Apr. 1, 1864	*pow* Andersonville, Ga.
Smith, Granville H.	B	Oct. 20, 1862	*dis* Sharpsburg, Md.
Smith, Henry A. F.	E	June 18, 1864	*k* Petersburg
**Smith, Henry R.	H	Nov. 6, 1864	*pow* Salisbury, N.C.
Smith 1st Sgt. James G.	G	June 6, 1864	*mw* Wilderness
Smith, Samuel C.	H	June 21, 1864	*k* Petersburg
**Smith, Stratton V.	H	Nov. 16, 1864	*pow* Salisbury, N.C.
Smith, Warren	F	Mar. 5, 1864	*pow* Andersonville, Ga.
Smith, William H.	B	Mar. 23, 1864	*pow* Andersonville, Ga.
**Smith, William S.	I	Nov. 8, 1864	*pow* Salisbury, N.C.
Spear, Irwin L.	C	July 1, 1863	*k* Gettysburg
Spencer, Samuel	E	June 25, 1864	*mw* North Anna
Spofford, Aaron	E	Aug. 30, 1862	*k* 2nd Bull Run
Staten, Henry	K	Sept. 17, 1862	*k* Antietam
**Start, Thomas	I	Dec. 4, 1864	*pow* Salisbury, N.C.
Stewart, James H.	I	Nov. 9, 1863	*pow* Annapolis, Md.
Stoddard, Sgt. Frank M.	F	May 10, 1864	*k* Laurel Hill
Stoddard, Capt. John S.	F	May 10, 1864	*k* Laurel Hill
Stone, Cpl. George W.	A	Feb. 23, 1863	*mw* Fredericksburg
Stone, Samuel A.	F	Jan. 11, 1864	*dis* Culpeper, Va.
Strong, Pratt V.	G	May 5, 1864	*k* Wilderness
*Swallow, Vinton F.	I	July 27, 1862	*k* Manassas, Va.
**Swan, Charles	I	Feb. 1, 1865	*pow* Salisbury, N.C.
Swears, Henry	H	Dec. 13, 1862	*k* Fredericksburg
Tannant, Sgt. James S.	F	July 13, 1862	*dis* Manassas, Va.
Taylor, John G.	G	Dec. 30, 1862	*mw* Fredericksburg
**Thayer, Noah W.	H	Nov. 4, 1864	*pow* Salisbury, N.C.
Thomas, 1st Lt. Francis	A	July 1, 1863	*k* Gettysburg
Thompson, Josiah	H	May 8, 1864	*k* Laurel Hill
‡Thompson, Samuel D.	G	June 8, 1864	*dis* Charlestown, Mass.

*After transfer to Fifth United States Cavalry
**After transfer to Thirty-nine Massachusetts Infantry
‡After transfer to Veteran Reserve Corps

Name	Company	Date of Death	Manner/Place of Death
Thompson, Weston	D	Aug. 31, 1862	*mw* 2nd Bull Run
Thorndike, Jeremiah F.	C	Nov. 15, 1863	*dis* Alexandria, Va.
Thorne, Benjamin F.	E	Sept. 17, 1862	*k* Antietam
Tibbetts, Harrison	A	Oct. 19, 1862	*dis* Alexandria, Va.
Tinkham, 1st Sgt. Cornelius	A	Sept. 30, 1862	*mw* Antietam
Todd, Joseph D.	A	Dec. 13, 1862	*k* Fredericksburg
Tolman, John A.	G	May 17, 1864	*mw* Laurel Hill
Torey, Lorenzo	H	Apr. 6, 1864	*pow* Andersonville, Ga.
Tracy, Charles	K	Sept. 17, 1862	*k* Antietam
Turner, Thomas	C	June 16, 1862	*dis* Washington, D.C.
Turner, Warren C.	D	Sept. 17, 1862	*k* Antietam
**Uhlich, Charles	H	Jan. 9, 1865	*pow* Salisbury, N.C.
**Van Cleef, John S.	F	Feb. 1, 1865	*pow* Salisbury, N.C.
**Vickery, John F.	F	Aug. 12, 1864	*mw* Petersburg
Vining, Cpl. George W.	H	July 1, 1863	*k* Gettysburg
Wadleigh, Rufus S.	K	Jan. 2, 1864	*dis* Culpeper, Va.
**Wadsworth, Charles	H	Nov. 10, 1864	*pow* Salisbury, N.C.
Walker, George B.	F	Sept. 24, 1862	*mw* 2nd Bull Run
Webster, Col. Fletcher	F&S	Aug. 30, 1862	*mw* 2nd Bull Run
Welch, Charles	F	Mar. 27, 1864	*dis* Worcester, Mass.
Welch, James	F	Dec. 8, 1863	*pow* Richmond, Va.
White, Sgt. Seth	I	Aug. 30, 1862	*k* 2nd Bull Run
White, 1st Lt. William G.	A	Sept. 17, 1862	*mw* Antietam
Whitmarsh, John Q.	C	Sept. 18, 1862	*mw* Antietam
Whitney, Edmund S.	A	Sept. 17, 1862	*k* Antietam
Whitney, George H.	I	July 1, 1863	*k* Gettysburg
Williamson, Franklin S.	G	Sept. 17, 1862	*k* Antietam
Willis, Dennison S.	E	Oct. 18, 1863	*dis* Alexandria, Va.
Wilton, Florence	D	Aug. 30, 1862	*m* 2nd Bull Run
Winter, Henry L.	F	May 5, 1864	*k* Wilderness
Young, Charles O.	A	Sept. 8, 1863	*dis* Rappahannock Station, Va.
Young, Cpl. Sumner B.	A	Feb. 27, 1864	*pow* Richmond, Va.
Younger, Oliver	K	Oct. 7, 1861	*dis* Darnestown, Md.

**After transfer to Thirty-ninth Massachusetts Infantry

APPENDIX B

Colonel Fletcher Webster's Last Hours

Colonel Gilman Marston,[1] commanding the Second New Hampshire, shared a recollection of Fletcher Webster just hours before his death:

On the morning of the thirtieth of August, 1862, before sunrise, I was lying under a fence rolled up in a blanket on the Bull Run battlefield. It was the second day of the Bull Run battle. My own regiment, the Second New Hampshire Volunteers, had been in the fight the day before and had lost one-third of the entire regiment in killed and wounded.

While so lying by the fence someone shook me and said, "Get up here." In answer I said, without throwing the blanket from over my head, "Who in thunder are you?" The answer was made, "Get up here and see the colonel of the Massachusetts Twelfth."

The speaker then partly pulled the blanket off my head and I saw that it was Colonel Fletcher Webster, whereupon I arose, and we sat down together and I sent my orderly for coffee.

We sat there drinking the coffee and talking about his father, Daniel Webster, and he told me about his father going up to Franklin every year and always using the same expression about going. He would say, "Fletcher, my son, let us go up to Franklin tomorrow; let us have a good time and leave the old lady at home. Let us have a good old New Hampshire dinner—fried apples and onions

1. Gilman Marston graduated from Dartmouth College in 1837 and Harvard Law School in 1840 and became a prominent attorney and politician in New Hampshire. His service as congressman overlapped his military service as colonel of the Second New Hampshire, which began on June 10, 1861. Promoted to brigadier general on November 29, 1862, Marston had an unspectacular career prior to his resignation on April 20, 1865. He died at Exeter, New Hampshire, on July 3, 1890. Warner, *Generals in Blue*, 312; Heitman, *Historical Register*, 1:691.

291

and pork." At about that time the adjutant of Colonel Webster's regiment came along and told him that the general commanding his brigade wanted to see him. Colonel Webster replied that he would be there shortly.

As he sat there on the blanket with me, he took hold of his left leg just below the knee with both hands and said, "There, I will agree to have my leg taken off right there for my share of the casualties of this day." I replied, "I would as soon be killed as lose a leg and the chances are a hundred to one that you won't be hit at all." "Well," said he as he gave me his hand, "I hope to see you again, good-bye." I never saw him again. He was killed that day. His extreme sadness, his depression, was perhaps indicative of a conviction or presentiment of some impending misfortune.[2]

Colonel Samuel H. Leonard,[3] Thirteenth Massachusetts, recalled another premonition shared by his friend Fletcher early on August thirtieth:

Colonel Samuel Leonard states that in the early part of the day, before the engagement began, he visited the camp of Webster and found him standing before a tree, on which was fastened a small looking glass, busily engaged in shaving himself. "It appears to me," remarked Leonard, "that you are slicking up a little." "Yes," replied Webster, "I expect to be killed this afternoon and I wish to make a clean-looking corpse!"[4]

As cannon fire sounded in the distance later that morning, Fletcher Webster sat down and wrote his last letter, describing the fight at Thoroughfare Gap two days earlier:

2. *New Hampshire Sentinel,* May 6, 1885.

3. Samuel H. Leonard joined the Massachusetts militia in 1846 and steadily rose to the rank of brigadier general by November 1860. He subsequently became major of the Fourth Battalion and was commissioned colonel of the Thirteenth Massachusetts on July 16, 1861. Wounded at Gettysburg, Leonard was mustered out on August 1, 1864. He joined the Ancient and Honorable Artillery Company in 1868 and remained active in veteran organizations until his death in West Newton, Massachusetts, on December 27, 1902. *Massachusetts Soldiers,* 2:71; *Two Hundred and Sixty-fourth Annual Record,* 114–15.

4. *Saratoga Springs (N.Y.) Saratogian,* May 22, 1884.

Head Qwts. 12th Light
Bull Run, Aug. 30/62

Dear Wife:

Since I wrote you last, we marched to Thoroughfare Gap, where
the enemy was expected to try and pass through. We got there
after a hard march Wednesday about 3 P.M. our Brigade in
advance. On getting near the Gap our Brigade was sent forward
skirmishing & as supports to Matthews battery. The coast was
reported clear.

On each side the Gap, which is just wide enough for a carriage
road, rise high, steep, thickly wooded hills. Just at the mouth of
the Gap, on the eastern side there is a small space for buildings
and there are some stone houses and a large stone mill. We
approached the Gap from the East to these buildings there on
our right. Coulter with the 11th Pa. supported by the N.Y. 9th
had the right, the Twelfth and Thirteenth the left of the advance.
No sooner had we got within a short distance, than the enemy
concealed in the woods & the stone buildings opened—

On the right Coulter had a sharp fight; the buildings were
too strong for him; he fought like a hero but was obliged to fall
back & with the 9th retreat up the road to the rear. He lost two
officers and 60 men. We sent out our skirmishers into the woods
in front of us & and for a time cleared them but shortly they were
reinforced—I drew up "Ours" well under cover and listened to
the balls as they whizzed over our heads. We saw the other Regts.
retiring; the battery on our side retired and I felt uncomfortable;
at last an order came for us to retire which we did across a plain
& when the enemy saw us crossing they opened pretty well. It
was a nasty business but the 12th marched as if on parade. Capt.
Kimball marched as if all the girls in Boston were looking at him.
Haviland the brave, rode smoking a cigarette, the major was
glorious; Arthur a young hero. I thought he was hit; a ball passed
between us & I saw him throw up his hand but it was nothing.
Officers and men were all good. Bryan was sick, and not in the
action at all.

We got here last night—to-day a great and decisive battle is
expected—Forrester Devereaux[5] has just called & here sits by me,

5. Forrester Devereaux, whose first name was John, had graduated from
Harvard in 1856 and served in the Salem Zouave company of the Eighth Mas-
sachusetts, a three-month regiment. Commissioned captain of Co. I, Eleventh
Massachusetts, on December 21, 1861, he was dismissed September 14, 1863.
Commissioned captain of the Sixth United States Colored Troops, Devereaux
was cashiered from that position on November 23, 1865, and died in Red Oak,

on the grass under a tree while I write. He was again in action the day before yesterday & has lost nearly all his company. He is unhurt. If a fight comes off, it will be to-day or to-morrow & will be a most dreadful & decisive one. Both sides are preparing, some three hundred thousand men are on the eve of conflict & Washington depends upon the issue. This may be my last letter, dear love; for I shall not spare myself—God bless and protect you & the dear, darling children. We are all under his protection. Love to 'Don' & Charlie. I have not means to write more. You must show this letter to *the girls* with my love.

Good bye, my own dear wife, darling Carry. Love to Bertie & dear Kori. I hope to have many a good gallop with them on nice horses. Bye bye dearest.

Yours
Fletcher[6]

Corporal Luther E. Alden,[7] Company F, Twelfth Massachusetts, described the regiment's movements as Colonel Webster led it forward on that fateful morning:

We fell in quite early, as I remember, and, after a short march to the right, halted. We were following a short train of ammunition wagons. As early as ten o'clock A.M. we could see the rebs forming their lines, or the dust where they were. We were changing positions from right to left without any particular object that I could see, until about 1 P.M., when we were started double-quick to the right and then back to the left. I should think we made four or five miles in this way. They said they were using us as a reserve.

Iowa, April 4, 1883. *Massachusetts Soldiers,* 1:803; 7:295; *Class of 1856, Harvard,* 14; *Harvard Crimson,* April 16, 1883; Headstones Provided for Deceased Civil War Veterans, 1879–1903, RG 92, NA.

6. "Webster's Only Son," 27–28.

7. Luther E. Alden enlisted as a private in Co. F, Twelfth Massachusetts, on June 25, 1861, and was promoted to corporal. Wounded at Second Bull Run, he was transferred to the Second Battalion, Veteran Reserve Corps, and discharged June 25, 1864. He enlisted again in Co. K, Fourth Massachusetts Heavy Artillery, on August 18, 1864, and was mustered out on June 17, 1865. Alden died on November 25, 1907, in Corona, California. *Massachusetts Soldiers,* 2:35; 6:50; *Riverside (Calif.) Daily Press,* November 26, 1907.

About 2:30 P.M. the 12th brought up to a piece of woods and were ordered to leave their knapsacks there. At this time occasionally a shell reached the woods from the reb batteries. After leaving the woods we could see the action coming on and started toward the left of our lines—in fact, very near the left. At this time, when the fight was on, there was a break in our lines further to the right and the 12th was ordered to fill it. The brigade should have been under Col. Stiles, 9th N.Y., but when we came to go into the fight we found we were under Gen. Tower. I never knew where he belonged, but he was a brave man.

As we went into the fight we found the 5th and 10th N.Y. coming out. Their uniforms were dark blue with red stripes on the jackets and pants, and, with the dust and blood, it looked as if not many of them had escaped. They were bringing out their wounded. They said: "You won't stay there long; too hot a place." We found it so. The 12th lost heavily. . . .

We were ordered to fire by volleys at first. At first we could not see the rebs, but from where they were shot and shell were coming thick. At this time every man was for himself. I worked to the left and think I may have been the left man in the regiment.

In the line near was one section of battery of two pieces. The first rebs I saw to shoot at were charging on these guns. They were coming in fours, as on the march. I think the horses and the men had been driven off or skedaddled from the piece nearest, as I saw only two men. They kept loading and firing until the rebs were very near, but probably never got any credit for what they did.

I kept busy after the rebs came in sight and my rifle began to grow hot. The rebs came to a halt just as they got to the guns. At this time I think I was within 40 yards of them. I could see they had Belgian rifles, by the brass mounts. About the second volley they fired, one took me in the upper right thigh, slivering the bone some and passing around out of the large cord under the leg and I went down all in a heap.[8]

---

8. *National Tribune,* May 7, 1903.

Private Charles H. Cobb,[9] *Company G, Twelfth Massachusetts, described how Colonel Webster fell:*

About 4 P.M. our brigade was sent in to save a battery which was retreating. Colonel Stiles put his regiment into the woods and the other three, under Colonel Webster, on the hill. After about half an hour an order came from Colonel Stiles, which said, "Colonel Stiles' compliments. We are flanked and must retreat."

Colonel Webster said, "Damned if I will change front. Forward!" That brought us to face the woods where Stiles had been driven out. After the movement had been completed, Colonel Webster jumped for the colors, lifted his sword and yelled: "Forward, Twelfth!" Those were his last words and it became our slogan and tradition.

I was the fifth man from him and as the colors passed him I saw his sword fall and hang by the knot from his wrist. I looked over my shoulder and he was lying in Adjutant Haviland's arms.[10]

Adjutant Thomas P. Haviland continued the Webster narrative:

I happened to be beside Webster when he fell and with two men started with him to the rear: had gone not more than twenty paces when one of the men was shot and the other seeing the regiment retire and the enemy close upon us, took to his legs. Col. Webster was perfectly helpless and unable to move and I, from my horse having fallen backward onto me at Cedar Mountain, had only strength enough to get him under a bush, in a little hollow, and there stayed with him, managing to remain unseen by two or three parties of rebel troops that passed on our right. When any of our (not of the 12th) soldiers passed, I used every effort in my power

9. Charles H. Cobb enlisted as a private in Co. G, Twelfth Massachusetts, on April 29, 1861, was wounded at Antietam, and was discharged for disability on March 17, 1863. He enlisted a second time in the United States Engineers on March 17, 1864, and was discharged on April 5, 1867. Cobb died in Flathead County, Montana, on February 22, 1926. *Massachusetts Soldiers*, 2:43; 7:50; Montana Death Index, 1868–2011, Department of Public Health and Human Services, Office of Vital Statistics, Helena.

10. *Boston Daily Globe*, August 14, 1924.

to induce them to carry him from the field, but to no purpose—
they were crazy for blood and went on with a yell. One or two,
slightly wounded, however, I sent in search of a surgeon, but none
came before I left. In the meantime we were exposed to both fires
and the colonel was getting worse. He wanted me to leave him,
but I was determined to save him if possible—at any rate not to
desert him. At last, bullets striking my hat, caused me to look up,
when I saw that we were discovered and a dozen rifles pointed at
us, not twenty yards distant. Seeing now that we must be prisoners,
any way, and not caring about being dead ones, I motioned them
not to fire; and now comes the worst—they would not carry the
colonel away. I begged them to let me stay with him and only left
by being driven at the point of the bayonet—not, however, until
an officer in command had promised faithfully to send an ambulance for him and have him removed from the field.[11]

William H. Blackford[12] *of the Eleventh Virginia came upon the scene as
Adjutant Haviland attempted to save Colonel Webster:*

It is out of my power to furnish you with any accurate information
as to his death, as I was only with him for a short time just after he
was wounded; and he was still alive when I left him, although in a
dying condition. This was about four o'clock in the afternoon and
some time before the fighting ceased. He was probably wounded
when the battery his brigade supported was taken, as I found him
lying on the ground within a short distance of the captured guns;
and supposed, therefore, from his position, that he fell when our
troops made the final assault upon your lines.

He was suffering great pain and had but little to say; but I remember that he asked me for some water; and, when I took off

11. *Springfield Republican*, September 20, 1862.
12. A member of the famous Blackford clan from Lynchburg, Virginia, William joined Co. G, Eleventh Virginia, on April 23, 1861, rose to the rank of
lieutenant, and served throughout the war. He became a prominent insurance
executive in Baltimore and died in that city on October 17, 1910. Blackford,
Annals of the Lynchburg Guards, 141; *Richmond Times Dispatch*, March 11, 1903;
Baltimore Sun, October 18, 1910.

my canteen and held it to his lips, he drank all the water it contained and asked for more. I also remember that the officer who remained with him behaved with great manliness and did everything he possibly could, under the circumstances, for the comfort and relief of Col. Webster, regardless of his own personal safety. I have never known his name until your letter was received informing me that he was T. P. Haviland, adjutant of your regiment. I did not take him prisoner, as stated in your letter, or in any way prevent his attentions to the wounded man. When I left him, an officer and three or four men from some other regiment came up; but whether he was taken to the rear by them I cannot state.

On the night of the 30th, Private Brough of Company G, Eleventh Virginia Regiment, came into camp with a haversack found on the field, which evidently belonged to Col. Webster, as some letters and other personal effects were found in it. I requested him to give me the letters, as I desired to return them to Mrs. Webster with his field-glass, which I had. Unfortunately, however, these letters were captured two days afterwards in my valise at Leesburg; and the glass was stolen from a gentleman to whom I had sent it for safe keeping until it could be returned, otherwise I should have sent it to Mrs. Webster at the first opportunity.[13]

Before the war, Robert Toombs,[14] a prominent Georgia politician, was good friends with Daniel Webster. U. R. Brooks related the following encounter between the Confederate general and the Yankee colonel:

General Toombs's brigade was driving the enemy from the field. A wounded Yankee colonel shouted, "Bob, don't you know me?" "Good God," exclaimed the general, "it is Fletcher Webster, Daniel Webster's son!" In an instant Toombs was leaning by the colonel's

13. Cook, *History of the Twelfth Massachusetts,* 160.
14. A graduate of Union College in New York, Robert Toombs became a powerhouse in Georgia politics, serving multiple terms as congressman and senator. He served as the first Confederate secretary of state until commissioned brigadier general on July 19, 1861. Wounded at Antietam, Toombs resigned on March 4, 1863. Known for his witty remark that the epitaph for the Confederacy should read, "Died of West Point," Toombs died in Washington, Georgia, on December 15, 1885. Warner, *Generals in Gray,* 306–307.

side. "And so we meet as enemies," said Webster. "Never," replied Toombs, "Daniel's son must always be my friend." "My wound is mortal," said Webster sadly. "God bless you, old friend, for your kindness. War is a bad thing." Weaker grew the dying man's pulse. He whispered a message for his loved ones and said, "Tell Bob I love him! God bless him!"[15]

———————

Charles F. Russell,[16] Seventh Virginia Cavalry, chanced upon the fallen colonel after Adjutant Haviland had been taken away as a prisoner:

We were charging and driving the enemy right along until we drove them from our front and we were very much scattered after the charge. I was riding along to join the command when I was attracted to a man lying upon the ground over which I was passing. He motioned to me. I at once dismounted and went to him. He asked for water, which I gave him. I at once noticed he was a ranking officer and then asked his name. He said, "I am Col. Fletcher Webster, of the 12th Massachusetts Volunteer Infantry." I saw he was dying and tried to find a surgeon. I had the good fortune to soon get one, who took charge of him. The surgeon took him in hand and said he would live only a short time.[17]

———————

Captain W. B. Prichard,[18] Thirty-eighth Virginia, told his mother about finding Colonel Webster after the battle, and she later recalled:

15. *Springfield Republican,* August 4, 1907.
16. Charles F. Russell was a student at the University of Maryland medical school until April 18, 1861, when he turned in his schoolbooks for a musket and enlisted in Co. G, Seventh Virginia Cavalry. He was wounded four times, captured three times, escaping twice and being exchanged once. Russell completed his medical studies after the war and died in Herndon, Virginia, on July 16, 1931. Moore, "Dr. Charles F. Russell," 366–67.
17. Ibid.
18. William B. Prichard was a student at the Virginia Military Institute when he left to train Virginia volunteers. Commissioned first lieutenant of Co. B, Thirty-eighth Virginia, on July 7, 1861, he was wounded at Seven Pines and promoted to captain the following December. He was wounded again at Chester Station in 1864. After the war Prichard became a civil engineer and moved to

Kneeling over his enemy, he asked if he could be of any service and received the reply, "Water! Water!" Captain Prichard brought him a canteen of water and asked if he could be of further service. Webster replied, "I am dying!" Captain Prichard assured him that he would see his body delivered to his friends. Webster handed Captain Prichard his eyeglasses and a ring, which Prichard restored to Webster's wife in Boston after the close of the war.[19]

News that Webster had fallen flashed to Massachusetts in a telegram from Surgeon Jedediah H. Baxter, who received his information directly from Captain Alpheus K. Harmon,[20] Company F, Twelfth Massachusetts, who had himself been wounded.

> Washington, Aug, 31.
> Peter Butler, Esq., Boston.

Captain Harmon of North Bridgewater has arrived, wounded. Saw Col. Webster shot, and says he is dead.

> J. H. Baxter, M.D.[21]

California. He designed San Francisco's Golden Gate Park and died in that city on November 16, 1913. "Capt. William B. Prichard," 9.

19. "Mrs. Mary G. Prichard," 460.

20. Alpheus K. Harmon was commissioned first lieutenant of Co. F, Twelfth Massachusetts, on June 26, 1861. Promoted to captain on May 10, 1862, he was wounded at Cedar Mountain and Second Bull Run. Mustered out on July 8, 1864, Harmon served as sheriff of Plymouth County for twenty-five years prior to his death in Plymouth, Massachusetts, on July 9, 1904. He was said to have been "one of the best known men in Massachusetts." *Massachusetts Soldiers,* 2:37; *Boston Journal,* July 10, 1904; *Thirty-ninth Annual Encampment,* 88.

21. Jedediah H. Baxter was commissioned surgeon of the Twelfth Massachusetts on June 26, 1861, and elevated to surgeon, U.S. Volunteers, on April 4, 1862. In charge of Campbell General Hospital until January 1864, Baxter then worked on compiling medical statistics for the provost marshal's office. Advancing through the medical purveyor's department, Baxter was appointed surgeon general with the rank of brigadier general on August 16, 1890. He died in Washington, D.C., on December 4, 1890. *Massachusetts Soldiers,* 2:3; 6:756; *Boston Herald,* December 5, 1890. Baxter's telegram appeared in the *Boston Traveler* on September 1, 1862.

Surgeon Jedediah H.
Baxter. Courtesy of the
U.S. Army Heritage and
Education Center

Private Maurice W. Collins,[22] *Company C, Twelfth Massachusetts, had
served as Fletcher Webster's orderly and wrote of how he and Lieutenant
Arthur Dehon searched for the colonel's body:*

The Union army retreated to Centreville and laid over there Sunday and Monday. On the 1st of September a flag of truce was sent back to the battlefield from General Pope's headquarters and in

22. Maurice Collins enlisted as a private in Co. C, Twelfth Massachusetts, on June 26, 1861, was wounded at Spotsylvania, and was mustered out on July 8, 1864. On June 15, 1875, he enlisted in Co. A, Second United States Cavalry and served until his discharge on June 14, 1880. He died on February 1, 1907, in the Los Angeles Soldiers Home. *Massachusetts Soldiers,* 2:18; U.S. Army Register of Enlistments, 1798–1914, RG 94, NA; National Homes for Disabled Volunteer Soldiers, 1866–1938, RG 15, NA.

charge of Dr. McFarland,[23] the medical director of General Pope's army. Lieutenant Arthur Dehon and myself were also in the party, the object of our return being to search for the body of Colonel Webster. When we arrived at the scene of the battle we rode up to the Henry house, which the rebels were using as a hospital. There a Confederate officer, dressed in the stolen uniform of one of our officers, stood on the porch and asked what we wanted. We told him we had come for the body of Colonel Webster, as we wanted to bury him. He then showed us where he had been buried already. Lieutenant Dehon and myself then dug up the body with our hands and then wrapped it in a sheet. It had been stripped of everything. Vest, pants, boots, saber belt, hat, gold watch and chain, some money in gold and greenbacks—over one hundred dollars—had all been taken. After wrapping the body in a rubber blanket, I took four straps from my saddle and tied them about the legs and body and then lifted it onto a saddle. Lieutenant Dehon led the two horses and I got between them to hold the body in place until we got in the main pike road, where we found an ambulance, into which it was transferred and sent to Alexandria, where it was embalmed and forwarded to Boston.[24]

Members of Boston's Board of Aldermen met on September 8 and passed the following resolutions honoring the deceased officer:

Resolved, That we have heard, with emotions of deepest sorrow, the intelligence of the death, in battle, of Colonel Fletcher Webster, of the Twelfth Regiment Massachusetts Volunteers.

Resolved, That we recall with satisfaction and pride the alacrity with which Colonel Webster, first among the foremost, sprang to

23. This was actually Thomas A. McParlin, who had received a medical degree from the University of Maryland and a commission as assistant surgeon on March 3, 1849. Promoted to surgeon with the rank of major on May 21, 1861, he became medical director of the Army of the Potomac under Grant. McParlin remained in the army and retired on July 10, 1889, as a colonel and brevet brigadier general. He died at Annapolis on January 28, 1897. Heitman, *Historical Register*, 1:680–81; Parlin, *Parlin Genealogy*, 255–56; *Boston Journal*, January 29, 1897.

24. *Oak Park (Ill.) Reporter*, December 4, 1896.

the defence of that Union which his lamented father so much loved and did so much to preserve; and we have observed with pleasure the devotion to duty which enabled his talents to overcome the difficulties incident to a want of previous military training, and placed him at an early day in the front rank of our trustworthy commanders.

Resolved, That we find new cause of admiration for his character in the stern courage and the calm unflinching resolution with which he led forward his brave regiment to the deadly encounter, which added his valuable life to the catalogue of noble sacrifices offered by the American people upon the altar of their beloved country.

Resolved, That as a mark of our great respect for Colonel Webster, as a citizen and an officer, the City Council will attend his funeral in a body.

Resolved, That a copy of these resolutions be transmitted to the family of Colonel Webster.[25]

The Boston Daily Advertiser *described the scene as Colonel Fletcher Webster's body lay in state in Faneuil Hall:*

The body of the late Col. Fletcher Webster, which, since its arrival in this city has been in charge of Messrs. Franklin Smith & Sons,[26] undertakers, was conveyed to Faneuil Hall at half past one o'clock yesterday afternoon, where it was received by a guard of honor, consisting of twenty men detailed from the Independent Corps of Cadets and commanded by Lieut. G. J. Fisher.[27] As the corpse was

25. *Boston Daily Advertiser*, September 9, 1862.

26. Martin Smith had been appointed "burier of the town of Boston" in 1816, and his son Franklin, followed in his footsteps, as did his grandson Benjamin F. Smith. Franklin Smith established his undertaking establishment at 251 Tremont Street on May 23, 1853, and buried many of Boston's citizens prior to his own death in Jaffrey, New Hampshire, on April 17, 1869. *Boston Daily Advertiser*, March 19, 1900; Roberts, *Ancient and Honorable*, 4:39; *Cornell's Lives*, 2:384.

27. George J. Fisher joined the Independent Corps of Cadets on August 16, 1858, and was a first lieutenant at Fort Warren in September 1862. The Boston press noted the part played by Fisher's men: "All night long the bayonets of a detachment of the Boston Independent Cadets, commanded by Lieut. George J.

borne into the hall the Boston Brigade Band which was stationed in the gallery played a solemn dirge.

The body is arrayed in a full military suit and lies in a handsome rosewood casket richly ornamented with silver. In the days of the American Revolution, at the battle of Bennington, Col. Eben Webster, the grandfather of Fletcher, commanded a regiment. The flag borne in that fight has been transmitted to posterity and its folds are now over the coffin of the grandson. The equipments worn by the deceased in battle are also placed on the casket which is adorned with choice flowers.

The inscription on the casket reads thus:

COL. FLETCHER WEBSTER
12 Mass. Vol.
Born in Portsmouth, N.H., 23d July, 1813
Fell at the head of his Regiment in
the Battle of Bull Run, Va.,
30th August, 1862

As there was no wasting sickness, there has been but slight change in the features of the deceased. In this sleep of death there is a closer resemblance to the father than was ever noticeable while the son was living. The massive forehead and heavy eyebrows are wanting to complete the likeness.

The interior of Faneuil Hall is appropriately decorated with the white and sable emblems of mourning, blended with the national flag. The hall was besieged at an early hour by numbers of people anxious to look for the last time on the son of the great statesman and the hall was filled throughout the afternoon.[28]

Fisher, gleamed in the hall in guard of State." Fisher's fifty-man detachment led the military portion of Fletcher Webster's funeral procession. Fisher resigned from the Cadets in November 1864. He died on October 28, 1907, in Boston. Gore, *Independent Corps of Cadets*, 25, 71; *Boston American Traveler*, September 13, 1862; *Boston Daily Advertiser*, November 14, 1864; Massachusetts Death Records, 1840–1915, MVR.

28. *Boston Daily Advertiser*, September 9, 1862.

Poor Fletcher Webster! Even on the day of his burial in the family plot at Marshfield, his memorial services were eclipsed by morbidly curious family friends who decided to dig up Daniel Webster's casket and take one last peek at the statesman's remains:

The funeral of Col. Fletcher Webster took place at his residence in Marshfield on Wednesday, Sept. 10. The body was brought down from Boston in a richly caparisoned hearse with four horses, by way of Hingham and South Shore. Several coaches conveyed his Boston friends from the Kingston Depot, while a large assemblage gathered from the neighboring towns. Rev. Mr. Alden,[29] the village pastor, conducted the services; the body resting on his father's writing table in the library, according to his dying request. A large procession followed his body to the tomb, where the coffin was deposited with the family whom a nation mourns.

By request of Peter Harvey, Esq.[30] and others, the oaken box containing the great statesman's coffin was opened and the metallic cover of the glass removed. How were the feelings of those personal friends stirred within them to find those lineaments and features, which no man ever looked upon to forget, retaining the same color and impress—natural as when ten years ago they gave him up to the grave.

The eyes were more sunken, but the heavy shadows beneath the brows were always there in life. Even in death and for a decade the captive of the grave, that kingly presence inspired the same deep reverence and speechless awe as when in the living temple of his matchless mind. Said one who looked upon his face again, "I forgot all else and cannot tell you anything of the tomb

29. Ebenezer Alden, an eighth-generation descendant of John Alden of the *Mayflower*, was installed at South Marshfield on October 30, 1850, and two years later gave a sermon at the funeral of Daniel Webster. He repeated that solemn task for Fletcher Webster and remained a minister until his death at Marshfield on January 3, 1899. *Boston Recorder*, November 28, 1850; *Boston Journal*, September 30, 1882; *Boston Daily Advertiser*, January 6, 1899.

30. A close personal friend of Daniel Webster, Harvey was a founder of the "Marshfield Club," an organization "formed with a view of doing honor to the memory of Mr. Webster." When important historical relics were pawned by the family after it fell on hard times, Harvey redeemed them and donated the priceless pieces to the Boston Public Library and the Massachusetts Historical Society. A banker and hardware executive, Harvey was also a minor political figure until his death in Boston on June 27, 1877. *Boston Journal*, June 27, 1877.

or surrounding objects." The velvet pall, with its rich embroidery, was in perfect preservation, though deprived of its primitive gloss.

In silence the lid was dropped and the box re-closed. Farewell, thou great departed! Earth's communion with thee is o'er. No more shall human eye behold that face over which thought and feeling once flashed the light and shade of that "imperial mind." Rest, noble statesman, with thy patriot sons. Thy memory "still lives" enshrined in a nation's admiration and gratitude.[31]

31. *Boston American Traveler*, September 27, 1862.

Appendix C

Memorial Day

In the hearts of thoughtful people who appreciate the sacrifices that were made for the supremacy of the Union, how tender are the memories awakened by each recurring Memorial Day.[1] How gently does its beautiful and impressive observance carry them back into the seeming presence of those stirring scenes that gave it birth. How that great love that they bear for the noble men who went forth to the battle but who never returned is quickened and intensified as they gaze upon the pathetic scenes now so generally enacted upon Memorial Day—that one blessed day of all the 365 when we may give ourselves up unreservedly to our tenderest emotions. Of Heaven must be its spirit, since it so sweetly teaches us lessons of human love and how to be brave and true.

Upon Memorial Day, while all over our broad land the thousands of little processions are marching to the silent resting places of the dead, with their solemn music and beautiful flowers, and are there engaging in the touching ceremony of decorating the humble mounds of those who died in the service of their country and of mankind, the saddest thought to me is how the now aged mother's heart must be wrung. How vividly must she then recall her noble boy, how plainly must she see him again, just as he looked that day when in all his youthful pride and strength he stood in the familiar doorway and bade her an affectionate *adieu.* How cheerful he seemed—even though he was leaving behind him at the call of country and at the mandate of honor everything

---

1. Kimball's Memorial Day musings were often plagiarized, one of the latest accounts being that published in the *Cambridge (Mass.) Tribune* on June 4, 1904.

that men hold dear. When I ponder upon this effect of Memorial Day I am half persuaded that it would be better not to observe it—that it is cruel to thus awaken in the mother's heart her half-buried grief—but I am reassured when I remember how grand and generous and blessed it is to honor and recall the memory of noble men who die that their country may live.

Memorial Day is the most appropriate occasion of the year in which to recall the memory of our loved ones in our quiet home circles, as well as in the public assemblies and in the "silent cities of the dead." How useful are the lessons that may be taught to the children by repeating to them the story of the great conflict as we remember it. Tell them how nobly the men whose memory is being honored fought and died for the preservation of the institutions under which we live and which they are to protect after we are gone. Bring out the faded photograph, the soiled uniform, the rusty sword, the bullet-scarred canteen and all the other relics of the march and the battle—they speak a language more eloquent than any that can be uttered by human lips. Read to them that now-faded letter, written upon the eve of the fight, wherein the brave defender of the flag commits his fate to the Father who notes even the sparrow's fall and in which he tells those who were the dearest idols of his heart how he shall try to do his duty when the crash of battle comes. It will strengthen our love of country as well as theirs; it will lift us above the trivial things of this busy world into the clearer and sweeter atmosphere of unselfish devotion to the interests of others.

A quarter of a century has now passed since the rude alarm of war aroused the young men of the North. Most of those who came back already plainly show the marks of Time's heavy hand. They are no longer young men—no longer to be called upon the nation's defence. They have been elbowed aside in the great march of the human race and now a new and mighty throng have taken the places they held when the summons to arms came to them. They have lost their distinctive character as soldiers, except on occasions like Memorial Day. But they are neither overlooked nor forgotten. The remembrances of their tender regard for their fallen comrades will bear fruit in patriotic devotion and in admiration for heroic deeds as long as the Republic shall last.

Those who, while the great contest was going on, did not feel that electric touch of elbow even now so well-remembered by the veteran—did not know the devoted men whose memory the Grand Army of the Republic honors upon Memorial Day as their comrades knew them—can have little idea of the peculiar place they hold in their hearts and memories. The citizen remembers them as they were last seen in their homes or in the streets and workshops of their native places or perchance they appear to him as they looked amid the hurry and excitement of departure for the war. But to their comrades, when recalled, they always stand forth as soldiers, fully armed and equipped for the deadly fray. They come to us in no other form but this. We see them amid the roar of battle, their faces lighted by the supreme excitement of the hour; we see them as they fell at our sides, torn and bleeding; we hear again their last wild cry as the fatal bullet did its cruel work; we remember how eagerly they pressed forward to overcome the foe. To the veteran, how peculiarly sad yet how grandly heroic are the memories of Memorial Day.

The custom of annually decorating the graves of deceased soldiers and sailors of the Union army and navy is not only a touching and beautiful ceremony, but one of great importance, indicating as it does useful lessons in human love, loyalty and patriotism. In the Third National Convention of the Grand Army of the Republic, held at Cincinnati in 1869, Comrade N. P. Chipman,[2] then adjutant general, thus spoke of its importance in his annual report: "If this feature alone was the result of the organization, I think the establishment of a national Memorial Day a sufficient reward to our comrades for all they have done and this alone would be motive sufficient to perpetuate our order."

In thus honoring the memory of their patriot dead, the living comrades of the Grand Army speak not only to the present

2. A graduate of Cincinnati Law School in 1859, Norton P. Chipman was commissioned major of the Second Iowa on September 23, 1861. Promoted to colonel on April 17, 1862, he served on the staff of General Samuel R. Curtis and acted as the judge advocate in the war crimes trial of Henry Wirz. Mustered out on November 30, 1865, Chipman finished the war as a brevet brigadier general. He died in San Francisco on February 1, 1924. Heitman, *Historical Register*, 1:299; Hunt, *Brevet Brigadier Generals in Blue*, 108.

generation but to the people of all time, for history cannot be silent upon the subject and literature is already permeated by it. The press and the pulpit of this and of other lands have spoken and will continue to speak in their commendation, while an impression is being made upon the mind and heart of the child of today which in time to come will bear fruit in a larger share of love of country, of material and political prosperity and of social culture and happiness than the generations of the past have been permitted to enjoy.

Education of feeling and sentiment is as important as education of intellect. Every veteran of the Civil War remembers how in the trying ordeal of battle the memories of the gallant deeds of former wars came flooding in upon him, how the recollection of some heroic act or instance of devotion to country and to mankind, of which he had read in schoolboy days, nerved him on to do his duty. Such remembrance made the fires of patriotism burn with a brighter glow and strengthened his courage a hundred fold.

The thought of Sergeant Jasper[3] leaping over the parapet of Fort Moultrie, picking up the flag that had been shot away, mounting it upon a sponge-staff, walking back with it through the storm of iron hail which was poured upon him from the British fleet and then restoring it to its place amid the cheers of his comrades, doubtless tightened the grip of many a color-bearer upon his flag-staff nearly a hundred years after in the war for the nation's life. On the weary march or around the bivouac fires, cold and hunger were made easier to bear when we thought of the greater sufferings of our forefathers at Valley Forge. And who shall say that the heroes under Admiral David Farragut[4] were not inspired and

3. Sergeant William Jasper of the Second South Carolina was present during an attack by the British fleet on Sullivan's Island in South Carolina on June 28, 1776. When the South Carolina flag was shot down, he improvised a flagstaff and held the flag aloft under cannon fire until a new staff could be procured. Jasper died during an attack on the British lines at Savannah, Georgia, in 1779. Goodrich, *Biography of Eminent Men*, 2:106–109.

4. David G. Farragut was appointed a midshipman in the United States Navy on December 17, 1810, at the age of nine. Promoted to lieutenant in 1825 and captain thirty years later, he was commissioned rear admiral following his successful operations on the Mississippi River at New Orleans in 1862. Following the victory at Mobile Bay—where he famously cried, "Damn the torpedoes!"— Farragut was promoted to vice admiral on December 23, 1864, and admiral on July 26, 1866. He died on August 14, 1870, in Portsmouth, New Hampshire. *Dictionary of American Biography*, 6:286–91.

encouraged by their recollection of John Paul Jones[5] and other heroic spirits aboard the *Bon Homme Richard* in their gallant fight with the *Serapis?*

Truly, good impressions upon the minds and hearts of the young are never lost. God grant that our beloved country may never again be called upon to pass through such a bitter experience as that of the Civil War of 1861. But if she does, if traitorous hands are ever again raised against our glorious Union or if a foreign foe ever seeks to destroy us, the lesson taught by the loyalty and devotion of the soldier and sailor of the Union and the honor paid their memory by their surviving comrades in these memorial services will surely bear fruit in equal devotion and similar deeds of valor. The history of the past is potent in shaping the course of the future.

Naturally enough, in thinking of the importance of Memorial Day, we wonder where and when and how this beautiful ceremony originated. The practice of laying tributes upon the graves of departed friends is, of course, as old as humanity itself. Where and when and by whom the graves of the Union soldiers first began to be decorated are unknown. Doubtless very early in the war many of the graves of those who fell were thus honored by friends and relatives, but just when these attentions became broadened so as to include the graves of others, not personally known to them, is uncertain.

There are many who claim to have been first to perform this service. Sarah Nichols Evans,[6] of Des Moines, Iowa, always claimed

5. John Paul Jones was an unemployed sailor when the Revolutionary War started, but was commissioned lieutenant on December 7, 1775. Promoted to captain in 1776, Jones "soon established a reputation for professional success that was second to none." Jones is best remembered for the confrontation between his own ship, *Bonhomme Richard*, and the larger British vessel *Serapis*. Jones outmaneuvered the heavier-gunned *Serapis* and forced the British ship to strike her colors. Jones was the only naval officer of the Revolution to receive a gold medal from Congress. His later career was not so lustrous, however, and he died in Paris on July 18, 1792. *Dictionary of American Biography*, 10:183–88.

6. Sarah J. Nichols married George H. Evans and, when he enlisted in Co. B, Second Michigan, she followed him to serve as a nurse. Her efforts to mark Union graves with flowers were officially recognized by Crocker Post No. 12, G.A.R., in Des Moines, Iowa, in its meeting of February 1873. Sarah Nichols Evans died on February 1, 1884, in Des Moines. She was accompanied on her humanitarian mission by Marcia Stafford May, who died May 8, 1876, and her children Josephine, who died April 11, 1872, and Ella. Josephine's diary contains

that she, with the wife and two daughters of Chaplain Franklin May[7] of the Second Michigan Infantry, inaugurated the ceremony of Memorial Day. On the 13th of April, 1862, these four ladies decorated the graves of many Union soldiers upon Arlington Heights. In May of the following year they repeated their work of love at the same place. In May of 1864, they visited Fredericksburg and decorated Union graves in that vicinity. There may have been many others and doubtless were, in different parts of the country, who thus honored the graves of Union dead before the work was taken up by the Grand Army of the Republic.

It is impossible to say who were the real originators of Memorial Day, but one thing is sure. We did not "borrow" it from our former foes, as has sometimes been claimed. They may have decorated the graves of their dead before there was any organized movement to decorate ours by the Grand Army, but the early members of that organization did not copy from them. We learned the lesson from loyal teachers.

The first general order emanating from the Grand Army of the Republic for the observance of Memorial Day was issued by Commander-in-Chief John A. Logan[8] in 1868 and in the spring of that year the day was quite generally observed. Every May 30th

the following notations: "Camp near Alexandria, Va., April 13, 1862. We have been to take a walk, mother, Mrs. Evans, sister Ella and myself. While wandering in the woods we found a poor soldier's grave. He belonged to the Second Michigan, Company D. We made up our minds to come up the next day (Monday), make a fence and fix it up. April 14th—Visited the soldier's grave and covered it with flowers." *Des Moines Daily Iowa Capital,* May 25, 1900; *Kalamazoo (Mich.) Gazette,* May 12, 1876, and May 29, 1903; *Ludington (Mich.) Daily News,* May 31, 1935; *New York Times,* May 25, 1902.

7. Franklin W. May was commissioned chaplain of the Second Michigan on May 25, 1861, and served until being mustered out on July 22, 1864. He continued in the ministry until forced to retire shortly before his death on September 145, 1880, in Kalamazoo, Michigan. *History of Kalamazoo County, Kalamazoo Gazette,* September 17, 1880.

8. Logan served in the Mexican-American War as a lieutenant in the First Illinois and was a congressman when the war broke out. After serving as a volunteer aide at Bull Run, he raised the Thirty-first Illinois and became its colonel on September 18, 1861. Promoted to brigadier general on March 21, 1862, he was elevated to brigade, division, and corps command by the time he resigned on August 17, 1865. Wounded several times, he also won a Medal of Honor. As a civilian he represented Illinois in both houses of Congress until his death on December 26, 1886, in Washington, D.C., Warner, *Generals in Blue,* 281–83; Heitman, *Historical Register,* 1:638.

since that time, the day has been religiously kept and its importance has increased with the growth of our loyal order.

On the 30th of this month, our comrades of the Grand Army throughout the country will again engage in this beautiful service. Every cemetery will be visited. On every known grave in which sleeps the form of a soldier of the Union will be laid our emblems. The flag that he loved will again wave above him. The tap of the drum, once sufficient to call him to his place in the ranks, will reverberate in the "silent cities of the dead." Orators and poets will do him honor. Comrades will repeat the story of his heroism and loyalty. They have not forgotten how bravely he fought, how nobly he died, for the flight of decades, with all of life's changes, has only intensified our recollection of his virtues. The memory of our fallen comrades will remain enshrined in our hearts.

> As long as men shall stand
> For home and native land,
> And while our starry flag flies o'er the true and free;
> Honor, and love, and truth,
> Shall give immortal youth,
> And we'll remember them upon the land and sea.
>
> Then say, oh singing birds,
> Echo these tender words:
> While bosoms nobly throb, and woman's eyes are wet,
> While roses bud and blow,
> While stars at evening glow,
> While daylight breaks for us, we never will forget.

The graves of the fallen are many, for the losses by death in our Civil War were frightful. The Quartermaster General of the Army reports that at least 300,000 of those buried in National Cemeteries were Union soldiers. This number does not include those who died during the war and were buried at home or those whose burial places have not yet been discovered. We shall probably never know the exact number of deaths that occurred while the war was in progress. Thousands are still borne upon the rolls as missing and even as having deserted, who were without doubt killed in battle, murdered by guerrillas or who died while they were prisoners and were buried in unknown and unfrequented places. A careful statistician has said that out of every nine men enrolled, one died. Thousands have died since the war from causes directly traceable to it. These losses by death do not represent all it cost to preserve the Union, although it is the largest item. What it cost in a pecuniary way can never be computed. Neither can the human mind form anything like an adequate idea of the suffering that has resulted to individuals because of impaired health, nor to the 280,000 men who were wounded in battle. Truly we have abundant reason to hold in perpetual esteem our re-established Union—now free, now great. What a price is that which has been paid to make it so!

We know not how many generations after ours will observe Memorial Day—at any rate as we observe it—but judging from the ever-growing sentiment of respect for the patriots of the Revolution, we may safely believe that the preservers of the Union will not suffer in the estimation of future Americans when compared with its founders.

The memory of those who die for their country has ever been honored by all peoples. Their blood, like dragons' teeth, planted in the soil for which they fought, has ever sprung up in other defenders in after times of peril. Let us therefore honor the men who died that the Union might be saved and teach our children to honor them. We will thus cultivate a sentiment which will surely defeat any possible attempt that may be made in the future to repeat the mistake of twenty-five years ago.

While we lay our offerings upon the graves of those who sleep in the burial places of their native cities and towns and villages, let us not forget those who lie in national cemeteries and in graves throughout the South. The one thought that will sadden our hearts as we gather about the graves of those who lie buried near their homes will be of the brave boys who went down in the whirl of battle and were left where they fell, with no slips of paper or rudely inscribed boards to reveal their names. These men rest in unknown places—in trackless forest, in dreaded prison pen, beneath the waters of river and sea, in loathsome trenches upon the battlefield—above whose forms no flower is ever dropped save by God's hand, which alone is able to seek them out.

APPENDIX D

Address at the Dedication of the Monument of the Twelfth (Webster) Regiment, Gettysburg, October 8, 1885

Comrades and Friends: All the way along the rugged pathway of human progress and development, from the very infancy of the race, are sharp turning points—great epochs—fraught with mighty consequences to empires and peoples. Seen afterward upon the page of history, they sometimes seem like simple accidents, brought about by the forethought of no particular leader of thought or action and occasioned by no fortuitous combinations of circumstances. And yet, when we view the great and benign results which always follow—the spread of civilization, the growth of human liberty, the advancement of the moral and material welfare—we can readily detect the finger of Him who fashions and directs all things that are for the permanent good and well being of the children of His care.

One of these turning points was the great battle we have met today to commemorate. This little town has been aptly termed "the high water mark" of the Southern rebellion. Here, in all its majesty and power, the outraged sentiment of the loyal North, stung to that point where it could no longer trifle or dally with the foes of human progress and speaking through its brave defenders, uttered, with no uncertain voice, that stern decree, "thus far and no farther" and from that moment the great conspiracy began to totter to its fall.

Fancy for a moment what would have been the result had Lee triumphed here. With Baltimore within a two days' march; with Harrisburg and Philadelphia and even Washington at his mercy; with New York and even Boston, teeming with rioters, conspiring for the overthrow of all constituted authority and ready to break out in open resistance to the draft; with the disloyal elements in the so-called loyal states plotting to overthrow the Government; with France and England waiting only for a pretext to recognize the Confederacy and to break the blockade; with the tremendous impetus that would have given the armed forces of the South as the effect of such a victory; what, I ask, with all these possibilities, would have been the result had the brave old Army of the Potomac, so often baffled and beaten, not risen to the fullest requirements of the hour, had it not stood here like a wall of adamant against the farther advance of the foe? It is one of the noblest gifts of mankind, that when great occasions arise, when a good cause is at stake and there is need of supreme strength and supreme devotion, it is always manifested God then somehow seems to whisper to the heart of man that the time has come for him to do his best.

The battle of Gettysburg, in the number killed and wounded, was the third largest of the 2,261 engagements of all kinds that occurred in the four years, one month and thirteen days of our Civil War. It was exceeded in loss upon the Union side only by the three days' battle in the Wilderness and the ten days' fighting about Spotsylvania Court House. In intensity, it exceeded every other contest that took place during that eventful period in our country's history. It would need the power to speak "as never man spake" to give those of you who were not here at that time even the faintest idea of the surging, seething, roaring conflict that raged upon these hills and in these fields and valleys on the first three days of July, 1863. The scene is beyond the power of words to describe or brush to paint and can be but partially recalled even in the memories of the survivors themselves.

Without attempting to comment upon the movements of the various corps of the Army of the Potomac during the campaign that preceded it and the battle itself, I shall confine myself in what I shall say within the limits of that to which our regiment was attached—the First Corps, under the gallant and lamented Reynolds. No corps of the army, I believe, marched harder on that long journey from the Rappahannock and no body of troops fought more desperately during the two days that followed than did the First Corps on that memorable 1st of July. This was due in large measure, I believe, to the great soldier who rode at our head. Reynolds was an ideal leader. We loved him and relied upon him implicitly. We were content to follow whither he led; we felt and knew that the headquarters flag of the corps would always be in the van.

The morning of the 1st of July found us at Marsh Creek, four miles from here. We had two days before marched twenty-three miles, in mud and rain, to Emmitsburg, and were well-nigh worn out by the hardships of the campaign. Nevertheless, the enemy was near and this served to give us strength for the struggle we knew was approaching. Buford's guns were ringing out on the morning air as we left our bivouac and we could plainly hear them. The roar of artillery nerved us on.

Wadsworth's first division took the lead and, on their arrival, went immediately into action, Cutler's[1] brigade in advance. Reynolds himself had been here forty minutes, watching the movements of the enemy, when the head of Cutler's column came upon the ground and, while forming Meredith's Iron Brigade[2] for a charge upon Archer's[3] men, a rebel sharpshooter succeeded

1. A businessman at the outbreak of the war, Lysander Cutler was commissioned colonel of the Sixth Wisconsin on July 16, 1861, and brigadier general on November 29, 1862. He commanded a brigade until the Wilderness when he assumed command of Wadsworth's division. Removed from active campaigning at his own request, Cutler resigned on June 30, 1865, and died in Milwaukee, Wisconsin, on July 30, 1866. Warner, *Generals in Blue*, 110–11; Heitman, *Historical Register*, 1:349.

2. Solomon Meredith was a prominent Hoosier politician when he received a commission as colonel of the Nineteenth Indiana on July 29, 1861. Wounded during Pope's campaign, Meredith was advanced to brigadier general on October 6, 1862. He was wounded again at Gettysburg while leading the Iron Brigade, the only brigade in the Army of the Potomac composed entirely of western regiments. Removed from combat duty because of his health, Meredith was mustered out May 22, 1865, and died at Cambridge City, Indiana, on October 2, 1875. Warner, *Generals in Blue*, 319–20; Heitman, *Historical Register*, 1:704.

3. A graduate of Princeton, James J. Archer served with distinction in the Mexican-American War and resigned his position as captain in the Ninth United States to accept a commission as colonel of the Fifth Texas. Advanced to brigadier general on June 3, 1863, Archer was a solid brigade commander until he was captured at Gettysburg. Confined in Johnson's Island Prison, he was exchanged after about a year and returned to duty, but died soon after on October 24, 1864, in Richmond, Virginia. Warner, *Generals in Gray*, 11; Heitman, *Historical Register*, 1:168.

in giving him a mortal wound. They carried him to the rear in company with the prisoners the gallant men of Wisconsin had captured.

Doubleday, with the third division, followed closely after Wadsworth and behind him came our own division, the second, under our brave and trusted leader, Major General John C. Robinson. Who that marched that day beneath our flag can ever forget how swiftly the men pressed forward, how wildly they cheered as they turned into the field from Cordori's house over yonder, on the Emmitsburg Road, and came down to the Seminary on the double-quick? We had never witnessed anything like it before in all the hard-fought battles that had preceded this. Such eagerness to meet the foe! Why was it? It was the same enemy we had met many times before; it was the same cause we were battling for. Somehow, every soldier knew that the time had come for him to strike an effective blow and to strike it at the expense of his life if need be. "We have got them upon free soil this time!" shouted a sergeant in my company. We breathed the air of freedom that morning and drank deep of the sentiment that nerved our fathers to heroic deeds. It was another "glorious morning for America."

It was my lot to be one of a detail from the various regiments of the brigade that marched in the rear of the division. We had been guarding the wagon train. We came upon the field while our regiment was in line at the foot of this hill and while Captain Hazel with Company K was driving back the enemy's skirmish line. The officer in charge of the detail, Captain Edward P. Reed of our own regiment, halted us a short distance in the rear, although in plain sight of the line of battle. The men became uneasy. They asked what they were being kept there for. The uneasiness increased. They cried, "Let us go to our regiments!" The officer himself, unable to quell the tumult, went forward to consult with General Baxter. The general rode back with him. "What is all this row about?" "We want to go to our regiments if there's to be fighting," exclaimed a score of voices. "You do?" replied the general. "Well, if that is the case, go to your regiments. You are just the men I want there." And every man of that detail ran gladly to his place in the ranks. I mention this to show the spirit that animated the men.

It was everywhere the same. The best traits of the volunteer soldier manifested themselves here.

The first and third divisions were now heavily engaged on our left and the Eleventh Corps, under General Howard, was hurrying forward to help us. They came in and took position on our right. Word comes that the enemy in front of the position where we now stand are making a demonstration. We make a half wheel to the left and advance to the brow of this hill. Eight of our companies place themselves behind this stone wall. The enemy are down there within easy range and we pour a deadly crossfire upon them. It is more than they can stand and they lift their muskets over their heads and display tokens of surrender. Our men clamor to be led "forward," so eager are they to rush upon the foe. Adjutant Wehrum leaps over the wall and cries, "Forward, Twelfth!" We rush down, the enemy surrenders and we drive large numbers of them back before us. Simultaneous with our advance, other regiments of the brigade rush upon the foe in their front and the Fifth, Twentieth and Twenty-third North Carolina regiments are captured entire. Captain Cook, with Company E, takes charge of the prisoners and conducts them to the rear.

All this time the other two companies are battling with the foe over there beyond the Mummasburg Road. The enemy now brings heavy reinforcements forward and another change of front is necessary. The Twelfth and the Ninetieth Pennsylvania meet this new danger and the enemy is still held in check. Ammunition is now exhausted and Paul's brigade comes to our relief. We are ordered to the rear, yet are kept there but a short time, for a new danger has arisen. The enemy is now crowding forward in a desperate attempt to secure this vantage ground. Something must be done or all is lost, so the regiment is again placed in the front line of battle, a little to the left of where we now stand. The men have no cartridges, but they fix their bayonets and resolve that they will hold their position with that weapon alone. They stand there like statues for more than an hour, fired at, but without the power of returning a shot. The open and empty cartridge-box, cut upon the base of our monument, typifies this fact, and will tell the inspiring story as long as the granite shall last. Nothing more heroic was seen in all those three days of battle than that grim and silent defiance of the foe.

Our brave comrades on our left were fighting gallantly and had the men of the Eleventh Corps on our right been able to have kept the enemy from our rear, the day would have been ours and the disastrous retreat to Cemetery Hill would not have occurred. But the right was forced to give way. We were outflanked and retreat was necessary. Without hurry, without the slightest semblance of panic, the movement began. General Robinson reported that the division "held the ground after all other troops had retired and fell back fighting with the enemy, not only in front, but on both flanks." Out of 2,500 men taken into action, the division numbered but 833 when it arrived upon Cemetery Hill. The corps entered the fight with 8,200 men and came out with 2,450. General Robinson says, "No troops ever fought better." Colonel Dick Coulter says, "Not a single case of faltering came under my notice." It is said on competent authority that the enemy in the first day's battle numbered 27,000.

Of the 200 men our regiment carried into the fight, 9 were killed and 44 wounded. Those killed were Lieutenant Francis Thomas, Lieutenant Charles G. Russell, Sergeant Charles L. Emmons,[4] Corporal George W. Vining,[5] Privates Irwin L. Spear,[6] Hardy P. Murray,[7] George F. Lewis,[8] J. S. Taylor[9] and William H.

4. Charles L. Emmons enlisted as a private in Co. G, Twelfth Massachusetts, on April 29, 1861, and was promoted to corporal and sergeant. He was wounded at Second Bull Run and died of wounds at Gettysburg on July 2, 1863. *Massachusetts Soldiers*, 2:43.

5. George W. Vining enlisted as a private on June 26, 1861, in Co. H, Twelfth Massachusetts, attained the rank of corporal and was killed at Gettysburg on July 1, 1863. *Massachusetts Soldiers*, 2:54.

6. Irwin L. Spear enlisted as a private in Co. C, Twelfth Massachusetts, on June 26, 1861, and was killed at Gettysburg on July 1, 1863. *Massachusetts Soldiers*, 2:22.

7. Hardy P. Murray enlisted as a private in Co. K, Twelfth Massachusetts, on September 26, 1861, and died on July 6, 1863, of wounds received at Gettysburg. *Massachusetts Soldiers*, 2:65.

8. George F. Lewis enlisted as a private in Co. H, Twelfth Massachusetts, on June 26, 1861, and was killed at Gettysburg on July 1, 1863. *Massachusetts Soldiers*, 2:51.

9. There was no one by this name in the Twelfth Massachusetts who was killed at Gettysburg. Kimball may have meant John G. Taylor of Co. G, but he died December 30, 1862, of wounds received at Fredericksburg.

Purdy.[10] Sergeant William Carr died from wounds a few days after the battle. The officers wounded were Colonel James L. Bates, Captain Edwin Hazel, Captain J. Otis Williams, Captain Erastus L. Clark, Adjutant Charles C. Wehrum, First Lieutenant George H. French and Second Lieutenant Cornelius Batchelder. In addition to this heavy loss, 61 men belonging to our regiment were captured by the enemy on the retreat to Cemetery Hill. But they were taken in every case with muskets in their hands and a number of them afterward escaped.

One incident of the battle I wish to mention because of its historic importance. It is not often among any people that citizens join with organized troops in opposing a common foe. The battle of Gettysburg has hitherto publicly presented but one case—that of John L. Burns. Happily the Twelfth Massachusetts is able now to give the world another. Some of you will remember a young man—not more than sixteen years old—who joined Company A on the road from Emmitsburg to this place, because, as he said, he "wanted to fight the rebels." He could not be enlisted or mustered in because the company books were in the wagon, but he was given a gun and went into action with us, behaving with the steadiness of a veteran. You will also remember that he was severely wounded here. From that day until recently his name has been unknown among us, but at last, after many inquiries, I have been informed by Lieutenant George E. Whitman of Company A, who had kept a record of it, that our young hero's name was J. W. Weakley and that he was admitted to the hospital at Carlisle after the battle. I thereupon wrote to the Surgeon General of the army for a verification and for further facts, giving this information, and briefly telling the story of the boy's heroism. In reply I have received a letter stating that "the records of the Post Hospital at Carlisle are not on file at this office. It appears, however, from records of General Field Hospital, First Army Corps, Gettysburg, Pa., that *C. F. Weakley*, private, Company A, Twelfth Mass., was admitted to that hospital," etc., "wounded in two places." No further record of him can be found by the Surgeon General and it is not

10. William H. Purdy enlisted as a private in Co. B, Twelfth Massachusetts, on June 26, 1861, and was killed at Gettysburg on July 1, 1863. *Massachusetts Soldiers*, 2:15.

known, of course, what became of him finally, but it is cause for congratulations that we now know at least our young hero's name.

The duty which fell to the lot of the regiment on the second and third day was hazardous and wearisome, though not attended with heavy loss. While the fearful cannonade was going on on the afternoon of July 3d, the regiment lay upon Cemetery Hill and later, with the rest of the division, was ordered to aid in repulsing Pickett's charge.

We do well, comrades, to commemorate, as we do today, these heroic services. They were rendered in a glorious cause, as we have since seen. The Union we so much loved has proved itself worthy of the sacrifices made in its behalf. It has rid itself of the blot of human slavery; it has risen to heights of justice and power scarcely dreamed of by the Fathers, until it has the esteem even of its old-time foes and is respected throughout the world. Fifty-five millions of loyal American citizens now live beneath its sway, with millions yet to come. To all of these, and for all time, let this monument speak. Let it say to every American: Love the Union of the States as the men of the Twelfth Massachusetts loved it; defend it, if it is ever assailed, as bravely as they did. In no spirit of exultation over the people of the South do we place it here; neither do we raise it as a memorial of the passions that ruled men's hearts in those trying years. Let it stand forever as a silent monitor, warning the people of all sections of our country never to repeat the mistake of twenty-five years ago.

We do well to thus honor our native state. Massachusetts has ever been foremost in every good work and she is worthy of our warmest love. We owe her more gratitude than ever now that she had aided us so nobly in commemorating the services of our regiment upon this historic spot.

In the design of our monument, in the medallion of the great Defender of the Constitution upon its face, in the motto from his lips which we have chosen, we have linked ourselves with an immortal name, as the fact of our being called into service and organized by Webster's gallant and patriotic son gave us the right to do. In this, too, we have acted wisely, for Webster's great work in the Senate of the United States made the consolidation of the North in defense of the Union possible.

The flag which has this day been placed upon our monument speaks of the great uprising of the North in a language which we best understand and appreciate. While we look upon it, our minds go back to Boston Common, as it looked to us on the 18th of July, 1861, with its great concourse of people and with our long line of eager men, for that was before shot and shell had made such deep inroads upon our number. The Honorable Edward Everett, the colleague in the Senate of the father of our colonel and the most gifted orator of the time, steps forward again and in behalf of the ladies of Boston presents us with this beautiful banner. Again we hear him declare, "Dust and blood may stain it; the iron hail of battle may mar its beautiful blazonry; it may hang in honorable tatters from its staff; but loyalty and patriotism shall cling to its last shred; treachery shall blast it never." Again we hear Colonel Webster say and, in view of what happened a little more than a year later, it has a most pathetic meaning, "Some of us will bring it back, and it shall hang in our halls when

> Danger's troubled night is o'er,
> And the star of peace returns.

Yes, comrades, danger's troubled night *is* o'er and the star of peace *has* returned to stay, let us hope, forever. Nevermore may the red hand of war deluge our fair land, much less a fratricidal strife. One Gettysburg is enough.

We come here, comrades, few in number, it is true, but standing upon such well-nigh holy ground, who of us can doubt the presence of Webster and Bates, and Dave Allen and Major Burbank, and Doctor Kendall and Arthur Dehon, and Francis Thomas and Charles G. Russell and all the dear, brave boys who once marched and fought by our side, but who have long since joined the innumerable company; they who have been mustered out of service here by the greatest of all commanders, to enter upon a higher service in another and a better world. I believe they are here. And I hear them say, in a voice which reaches the soul through a surer channel than the human ear, "God bless you, boys. God bless you." It is most fitting that we now place this memorial here, for soon, ah! how soon, will it be when the small minority who yet linger here will have joined the fuller ranks on the other side and the Webster Regiment be heard of no more except in history.[11]

11. The Twelfth Massachusetts monument stands along Doubleday Avenue, northwest of Gettysburg on Oak Ridge. This granite column is almost eleven feet high and depicts a flag draped over an image of Daniel Webster. In memory of the regiment's stand after expending its ammunition, the base of the monument depicts a bayonet, scabbard, and empty cartridge box.

Bibliography

Manuscripts

California Death Index, 1905–39. California Department of Health and Welfare, Vital Records. Sacramento.

Maine Death Records, 1617–1922. Maine State Archives. Augusta.

Massachusetts Vital Records, 1840–1915. New England Historic Genealogical Society. Boston.

Montana Death Index, 1868–2011. Department of Public Health and Human Services, Office of Vital Statistics. Helena.

Pennsylvania Veterans Burial Cards, 1929–90. Pennsylvania Historical and Museum Commission, Bureau of Archives and History. Harrisburg.

South Carolina Death Records, 1821–1955. South Carolina Department of Archives and History. Columbia.

United States. Card Records of Headstones Provided for Deceased Union Civil War Veterans, 1879–1903. Records of the Office of the Quartermaster General, Record Group 92. National Archives, Washington, D.C.

———. Civil War and Later Pension Files. Department of Veterans Affairs, Record Group 15. National Archives, Washington, D.C.

———. Eighth Census of the United States, 1860. Records of the Bureau of the Census, Record Group 29. National Archives, Washington, D.C.

———. Historical Register of National Homes for Disabled Volunteer Soldiers, 1866–1938. Records of the Department of Veterans Affairs, Record Group 15. National Archives, Washington, D.C.

———. Register of Enlistments in the U.S. Army, 1798–1914. Records of the Adjutant General's Office, Record Group 94. National Archives, Washington, D.C.

———. Seventh Census of the United States, 1850. Records of the Bureau of the Census, Record Group 29. National Archives, Washington, D.C.

Books and Articles

Annual Report of the Adjutant General of the Commonwealth of Massachusetts for the Year Ending December 31, 1862. Boston: Wright and Potter, 1863.

*Annual Report of the Municipal Officers of the Town of Madison, for the Fiscal Year End-
ing February 24, 1894.* Madison, Me.: Madison Bulletin Steam Job Print,
1894.

Annual Report Presented by the Executive Committee of the Bible Society of Massachusetts.
Boston: T. R. Marvin & Son, 1862.

"Annual Reunion of Pegram Battalion Association in the Hall of House of Delegates, Richmond, Va., May 21st, 1886." *Southern Historical Society Papers* 14
(1886): 5–34.

The Appomattox Roster. New York: Antiquarian Press, 1962.

Avary, Myrta L. *Dixie after the War.* New York: Doubleday, Page, 1906.

Bates, Samuel P. *History of Pennsylvania Volunteers, 1861–65.* 5 vols. Harrisburg,
Penn.: B. Singerly, 1869.

———. *Martial Deeds of Pennsylvania.* Philadelphia: T. H. Davis, 1876.

Battles and Leaders of the Civil War. 4 vols. New York: Century Co., 1887.

"The Beggar Student—a Recollection." *Irish Playgoer* 1 (January 1900): 371–76.

Binney, Lewis E. *Dalhousie Lodge F. & A. M.: Newton, Massachusetts, Fiftieth Anniversary, 1860–1910.* Newtonville, Mass.: Dalhousie Lodge, 1910.

*Biographical Review Containing Life Sketches of Leading Citizens of Plymouth County,
Massachusetts.* Boston: Biographical Review Publishing Co., 1897.

Blackford, Charles M. *Annals of the Lynchburg Guards.* Lynchburg, Va.: J. W. Rohr,
1891.

The Boston Directory. Boston: Adams, Sampson & Co., 1861.

The Boston Directory. Boston: Adams, Sampson & Co., 1862.

The Boston Directory. Boston: Sampson & Murdock, 1904.

Bowen, James L. *Massachusetts in the War, 1861–1865.* Springfield, Mass.: Clark W.
Bryan & Co., 1889.

Brockett, L. P. *Woman's Work in the Civil War.* Boston: Zeigler, McCurdy & Co.,
1867.

Brown, Francis H. *Harvard University in the War of 1861–1865.* Boston: Cupples,
Upham and Co., 1886.

Brown, J. Willard. *The Signal Corps, U.S.A. in the War of the Rebellion.* Boston: U.S.
Veteran Signal Corps Association, 1896.

Burr, Fearing, and George Lincoln. *The Town of Hingham in the Late Civil War.*
Boston: By the Town, 1876.

Butterfield, H. Q. *A Delegate's Story.* Philadelphia: U.S. Christian Commission,
1863.

"Capt. William B. Prichard." *Confederate Veteran* 24 (January 1916): 9.

Catalogue of Library of Lieutenant Colonel John Page Nicholson. Philadelphia: J. T.
Palmer Co., 1914.

Century War Book: Battles and Leaders of the Civil War, People's Pictorial Edition. New
York: Century Co., 1894.

Coffin, Charles C. *Marching to Victory.* New York: Harper & Bros., 1899.

Cook, Benjamin F. *History of the Twelfth Massachusetts Volunteers (Webster Regiment).*
Boston: Twelfth (Webster) Regiment Association, 1882.

Cook, Louis A. *History of Norfolk County, Massachusetts 1622–1918.* 2 vols. New
York: S. J. Clarke Publishing Co., 1918.

Cornell's Lives of Clergymen, Physicians and Eminent Business Men of the Nineteenth Century. 3 vols. Boston: H. Gannett, 1881.

Curtis, George T. *Life of Daniel Webster.* 2 vols. New York: D. Appleton and Co., 1870.

Dadmun, John W. *The Melodeon.* Boston: J. P. Magee, 1860.

Davis, Charles E., Jr. *Three Years in the Army.* Boston: Estes and Lauriat, 1894.

DeForest, Heman P., and Edward C. Bates. *The History of Westborough, Massachusetts.* Westborough, Mass.: By the Town, 1891.

Dictionary of American Biography. 21 vols. New York: Charles Scribner's Sons, 1928–37.

Dimmock, William R. "Nathaniel B. Shurtleff, Jr." In *Harvard Memorial Biographies,* vol. 2, 44–54. Cambridge: Sever and Francis, 1866.

Dornbusch, C. E. *Regimental Publications and Personal Narratives of the Civil War.* 3 vols. New York: New York Public Library, 1961.

Eliot, Samuel A. *Biographical History of Massachusetts.* 10 vols. Boston: Massachusetts Biographical Society, 1911–19.

Evans, G. F. "The Early History of the Pierian Sodality." *Harvard Graduates Magazine* 16 (March 1908): 423–32.

Exercises at the Presentation to the Commonwealth of Massachusetts of a Bronze Relief of General Thomas G. Stevenson, December 7, 1905. Boston: The Memorial Association, 1906.

Goldsmith, Oliver. *The Deserted Village: A Poem.* London: J. Rivington and Sons, 1779.

Goodrich, Samuel G. *Biography of Eminent Men, Statesmen, Heroes, Authors, Artists, and Men of Science, of Europe and America.* 2 vols. New York: Nafis and Cornish, 1840.

Gore, H. W. *The Independent Corps of Cadets of Boston, Mass. at Fort Warren, Boston Harbor in 1862.* Boston: Rockwell and Churchill, 1888.

Grinspan, Jon. "Young Men for War: The Wide Awakes and Lincoln's 1860 Presidential Campaign." *Journal of American History* 96 (September 2009): 357–78.

Harrington, Thomas F. *The Harvard Medical School.* 3 vols. New York: Lewis Publishing Co., 1905.

Harvard Memorial Biographies. Cambridge, Mass.: Sever and Francis, 1866.

Hebert, Walter H. *Fighting Joe Hooker.* Indianapolis: Bobbs, Merrill Co., 1944.

Heitman, Francis B. *Historical Register and Dictionary of the United States Army.* 2 vols. Washington: Government Printing Office, 1903.

Hepworth, George H. *The Whip, Hoe and Sword.* Boston: Walker, Wise and Co., 1864.

Higginson, Thomas W. *Massachusetts in the Army and Navy during the War of 1861–65.* 2 vols. Boston: Wright and Potter, 1895–96.

Higginson, Waldo. *Memorials of the Class of 1833 of Harvard College.* Cambridge, Mass.: J. Wilson and Son, 1883.

Hillard, G. S. *The Franklin Fifth Reader.* New York: Taintor Brothers, Merrill and Co., 1878.

Hillman, Joseph. *The Revivalist.* Troy, N.Y.: By the Author, 1872.

328   BIBLIOGRAPHY

History of Cumberland and Adams Counties, Pennsylvania. 3 vols. Chicago: Warner, Beers & Co., 1886.
History of Kalamazoo County, Michigan. Philadelphia: Everts & Abbott, 1880.
History of the 13th Regiment, N.G. S.N.Y. New York: George W. Rodgers, 1894.
A History of the Town of Freetown, Massachusetts. Fall River, Mass.: J. H. Franklin & Co., 1902.
History of the Town of Hingham, Massachusetts. 3 vols. Hingham, Mass.: By the Town, 1893.
History of the Twenty-third Pennsylvania Volunteer Infantry. Philadelphia, 1904.
Hunt, Roger D., and Jack R. Brown. *Brevet Brigadier Generals in Blue.* Gaithersburg, Md.: Olde Soldier Books, 1997.
Jordan, Ervin L., Jr., and Herbert A. Thomas, Jr. *19th Virginia Infantry.* Lynchburg, Va.: H. E. Howard, 1987.
Journal of the Thirty-first Annual Encampment, Department of Massachusetts, Grand Army of the Republic. Boston: E. B. Stillings & Co., 1897.
Journal of the Thirty-ninth Annual Encampment, Department of Massachusetts, Grand Army of the Republic. Boston: Griffith, Stillings Press, 1905.
Kelly, Howard A., and Walter L. Burrage. *American Medical Biographies.* Baltimore: Norman, Remington Co., 1920.
Kingman, Bradford. *History of North Bridgewater, Plymouth County, Massachusetts.* Boston: By the Author, 1866.
Krick, Robert K. *Lee's Colonels.* Dayton, Ohio: Morningside, 1979.
Lathrop, John. *Massachusetts Reports, 137.* Boston: Little, Brown, 1885.
Lawrence, Abbott. *T. Bigelow Lawrence.* Boston, 1869.
A List of the Soldiers, Sailors, and Marines of the Civil War Surviving and Resident in Massachusetts on April 1, 1915. Boston: Wright and Potter Printing Co., 1916.
Massachusetts Soldiers, Sailors, and Marines in the Civil War. 8 vols. Norwood, Mass.: Norwood Press, 1931.
McKenna, Charles F., ed. *Under the Maltese Cross.* Pittsburgh: The 155th Regimental Association, 1910.
"Medical Director of Lee's Army." *Confederate Veteran* 31 (December 1923): 447.
"In Memoriam." *New England Historical and Genealogical Register* 17 (April 1863): 192–93.
Moore, R. Walton. "Dr. Charles F. Russell, of Virginia." *Confederate Veteran* 39 (September 1931): 366–67.
"Mrs. Mary G. Prichard." *Confederate Veteran* 20 (October 1912): 460.
Nason, George W. *History and Complete Roster of the Massachusetts Regiments, Minute Men of '61.* Boston: Smith & McCance, 1910.
"The Origin of the John Brown Song." *New England Magazine,* new ser., vol. 1 (December 1889): 371–76.
Our War Songs North and South. Cleveland: S. Brainards' Sons, 1887.
Palmer, Joseph. *Necrology of Alumni of Harvard College, 1851–52 to 1862–63.* Boston: John Wilson and Son, 1864.
"From Paper by Dr. B. F. Ward, Vaider, Miss." *Confederate Veteran* 21 (November 1913): 537–38.

Parlin, Frank E. *The Parlin Genealogy: The Descendants of Nicholas Parlin of Cambridge, Mass.* Cambridge, Mass.: T. R. Marvin & Sons, 1913.

Pratt, George W. *The Forty-third Regiment Mass. Volunteer Militia.* Stoughton, Mass.: The Sentinel Print, 1914.

Pringle, James R. *History of the Town and City of Gloucester, Cape Ann, Massachusetts.* Gloucester, Mass.: By the Author, 1892.

Rand, John C. *One of a Thousand.* Boston: First National Publishing Co., 1890.

Record of the Massachusetts Volunteers, 1861–1865. 2 vols. Boston: Wright and Potter, 1868, 1870.

The Report of the Secretary of the Class of 1856, Harvard. Boston: Geo. C. Rand & Avery, 1865.

Reports and Resolutions of the General Assembly of the State of South Carolina. Columbia, S.C.: Charles A. Calvo, Jr., 1896.

Roberts, Oliver A. *History of the Military Company of Massachusetts Now Called the Ancient and Honorable Artillery Company of Massachusetts.* 4 vols. Boston: A. Mudge, 1895–1901.

Roster of Wisconsin Volunteers, War of the Rebellion, 1861–1865. 2 vols. Madison, Wisc.: Democrat Printing Co., 1880.

Schroeder-Lein, Glenna R. *The Encyclopedia of Civil War Medicine.* Armonk, N.Y.: M. E. Sharpe, 2012.

Simon, John Y., ed. *The Papers of Ulysses S. Grant.* 26 vols. Carbondale: Southern Illinois University Press, 1967–2003.

Small, A. R. *The Sixteenth Maine Regiment in the War of the Rebellion 1861–1865.* Portland, Me.: B. Thurston & Co., 1886.

Smith, S. F. *History of Newton, Massachusetts.* Boston: American Logotype Co., 1880.

Stine, J. H. *History of the Army of the Potomac.* Philadelphia: J. B. Rodgers Printing Co., 1892.

Thompson, Waldo. *Swampscott: Historical Sketches of the Town.* Lynn, Mass.: T. P. Nichols, 1885.

The Two Hundred and Sixty-fourth Annual Record of the Ancient and Honorable Artillery Company of Massachusetts. Boston: Alfred Mudge & Son, 1902.

Underwood, Lucien M. *The Underwood Families of America.* 2 vols. Lancaster, Penn.: New Era Printing Co., 1913.

United States Christian Commission for the Army and Navy. Philadelphia: By the Commission, 1866.

Warner, Ezra J. *Generals in Blue.* Baton Rouge: Louisiana State University Press, 1964.

———. *Generals in Gray.* Baton Rouge: Louisiana State University Press, 1959.

The War of the Rebellion: A Compilation of the Official Records of the Union and Confederate Armies. 128 vols. Washington: Government Printing Office, 1880–1901.

Webster, Fletcher, ed. *Private Correspondence of Daniel Webster.* 2 vols. Boston: Little, Brown, 1857.

"Webster's Only Son." *Dartmouth College Library Bulletin* 5 (December 1949): 26–29.

White, Richard G. *Poetry Lyrical, Narrative, and Satirical of the Civil War.* New York: The American News Co., 1866.

"A Young Hero of Gettysburg." *Century Magazine* 33 (November 1886): 133–34.

Newspapers

(Gettysburg, Penn.) Adams County Sentinel and General Advertiser
(Boston) American Traveler
Baltimore Sun
Barre (Mass.) Gazette
Boston Daily Advertiser
Boston Daily Globe
Boston Evening Transcript
Boston Herald
Boston Journal
Boston Liberator
Boston Post
Boston Recorder
Boston Traveler
Cambridge (Mass.) Tribune
Cape Ann Light and Gloucester (Mass.) Telegraph
(Boston) Congregationalist
(Washington, D.C.) Critic-Record
(Boston) Daily Atlas
(Des Moines) Daily Iowa Capital
Dallas Morning News
(Washington, D.C.) Evening Star
Frank Leslie's Illustrated Newspaper
Gettysburg Compiler
Gettysburg Star and Sentinel
Gettysburg Times
Harrisburg Patriot
Harvard Crimson
Irish American Weekly
Kalamazoo (Mich.) Gazette
Lowell (Mass.) Daily Citizen and News
Ludington (Mich.) Daily News
(Worcester, Mass.) National Aegis
The National Tribune
New Hampshire Sentinel
New York Herald
New York Times
New York Tribune
Oak Park (Ill.) Reporter
Philadelphia Inquirer

Pittsfield (Mass.) Sun
Portland (Me.) Daily Advertiser
Richmond Times Dispatch
Riverside (Calif.) Daily Press
Salem (Mass.) Observer
Salem (Mass.) Register
(Saratoga Springs, N.Y.) Saratogian
Springfield (Mass.) Republican
Trenton (N.J.) State Gazette
(Troy, N.Y.) Times
Watertown (N.Y.) Daily Times
Worcester (Mass.) Daily Spy

Websites

Ancestry.com. http://www.Ancestry.com
FamilySearch. http://familysearch.org
Fold3. Historical Military Records. http://www.Fold3.com

Index

333

White, Richard Grant, 27 & n
White, William Greenough, 172 & n,
173–74; death of, 176–83
White Oak Swamp, Battle of, 34n, 274
White Plains, Va., 119
Whitman, George A., 212 & n, 321
Whitman, Walt, 256n
Whitney, Allston W., 18 & n
Whiton, John C., 19 & n, 22
Wilderness, Battle of, 23n, 85, 101 &
n, 110, 137n, 204 & n, 214n, 217n,
256, 257, 259–63, 264n, 266, 274,
316, 317

Wilderness, Va., 247
Williams, Alpheus S., 128 & n
Williams, Joseph Otis, 228 & n, 321
Wilson, Henry, 34 & n
Winchester, Va., 54, 89
Winslow, Charles P., 278 & n
Wisconsin, Infantry: Third, 57; Sixth,
317n; Twenty-first, 25n
Woodbury, Moses, 86 & n, 87–88
Worcester, Mass., 14n, 18n, 241
Worth, Benjamin F., 196 & n

Young Men's Christian Association, 28

www.ingramcontent.com/pod-product-compliance
Lightning Source LLC
Chambersburg PA
CBHW020446100426
42812CB00036B/3465/J